# Constructing Meanings and Identities in Child Protection Practice

# Constructing Meanings and Identities in Child Protection Practice

Heather D'Cruz

TERTIARY PRESS

First published 2004

**Tertiary Press**
**12–50 Norton Road**
**Croydon, Victoria 3136**

Tertiary Press is the registered business name of the publishing unit of Swinburne University of Technology.

National Library of Australia
Cataloguing-in-Publication data

D'Cruz, Heather.
 Constructing meanings and identities in child protection practice.

 Bibliography.
 Includes index.
 For TAFE students.
 ISBN 0 86458 335 4.

 1. Abused children - Services for - Textbooks. 2. Child welfare - Textbooks. 3. Child abuse - Prevention - Textbooks. I. Title.

362.76

© Tertiary Press 2004

This book is copyright. Apart from any fair dealing for the purposes of private study, research, criticism or review as permitted under the *Copyright Act* 1968, no part may be reproduced by any process without written permission. Enquiries should be made to the Manager, Tertiary Press, 12–50 Norton Road, Croydon, Victoria 3136.

*Copying for educational purposes*

The Australian *Copyright Act* 1968 ('Act') allows a maximum of one chapter or 10 per cent of this book, whichever is the greater, to be copied by an educational institution for educational purposes provided that the educational institution (or the body that administers it) has given a remuneration notice to Copyright Agency Limited ('CAL') under the Act.

Details of the CAL licence for educational institutions are available from CAL, 19/157 Liverpool Street, Sydney, NSW 2000, telephone: (02) 9394 7600, facsimile: (02) 9394 7601, email: info@copyright.com.au

The information contained in this book is to the best of the author's and publisher's knowledge true and correct. Every effort has been made to ensure its accuracy, but the author and publisher do not accept responsibility for any loss, injury or damage arising from such information.

Acquisitions editor: Elizabeth Vella.
Editor: Tudor Day.
Indexer: Michael Ramsden.
Printed and bound by: Brown Prior Anderson, Burwood, Victoria.

Brand and product names used in this book are trademarks or registered trademarks of their respective companies.

This book is printed on paper sourced from plantation timber.

# Contents

|   | List of tables | vii |
|---|---|---|
|   | Preface | viii |
|   | Acknowledgments | x |
|   | Publisher's acknowledgments | xi |
| 1 | Introduction | 1 |
|   | *Social constructionism and child protection practice* | |
|   | *Social constructionism and the social organisation of child protection* | |
| 2 | Methodology – Addressing a complex practice reality | 12 |
|   | *A complex practice reality – 'a fractured lens'* | |
|   | *Constructing my fractured lens: some important pieces* | |
|   | *Social constructionism and relativism* | |
|   | *Social work research as knowledge/power in practice* | |
|   | *Conclusion* | |
| 3 | Protecting children within discourses of the normal child and family | 42 |
|   | *Child protection as a discursive formation* | |
|   | *Intersecting discourses of 'the family', 'the child' and 'the parent'* | |
|   | *Constructing meanings and identities in child protection* | |
|   | *Constructing maltreatment* | |
|   | *Constructing identities of responsibility* | |
|   | *Child protection practice* | |
|   | *Conclusion* | |
| 4 | Policy as discourse | 75 |
|   | *A genealogy of child protection in Western Australia* | |
|   | *Protection of non-Aboriginal children in Western Australia: 1829–1972* | |
|   | *Protection of Aboriginal Children in Western Australia: 1829–1972* | |
|   | *Protection of non-Aboriginal and Aboriginal children in Western Australia from 1972* | |
|   | *Conclusion* | |
| 5 | Sites of practice | 106 |
|   | *Child protection in practice: policy contexts* | |
|   | *Child protection in practice: prescribing practice* | |
|   | *Urbania: 1995* | |
|   | *Urbania as a linguistic community in 1995* | |
|   | *Suburbia: 1995* | |
|   | *Suburbia as a linguistic community in 1995* | |
|   | *Urbania and Suburbia: linguistic communities in 1995* | |
|   | *Conclusion* | |

6 'Something happened': Constructing maltreatment 131
*Stages of child protection intervention*
*Re-presenting the cases*
*Categorisation: 'sexual abuse substantiated'*
*Categorisation: 'sexual abuse unsubstantiated'*
*Categorisation: 'physical abuse unsubstantiated – at risk'*
*Categorisation: a 'hierarchy of maltreatment'*
*Categorisation: 'sexual abuse substantiated'*
*Categorisation: 'sexual abuse substantiated'*
*Conclusion*

7 Identities of responsibility 162
*Re-presenting the cases*
*'Dangerousness' and the identity of the 'person believed responsible'*
*Identity as contextual, partial and multiple*
*Responsible mothers, invisible men: both parents are reported, father officially 'disappears'*
*Responsible mothers, invisible men: father is reported, he officially 'disappears'*
*Responsible mothers, invisible men: 'the unprotective mother' and 'the dangerous man'*
*Responsible mothers, invisible men: patriarchal mothering and disabling practices*
*Responsible mothers, invisible men: father is reported, mother is suspected, both 'responsible'*
*Responsibility for emotional abuse: the cultural idealisation of motherhood*
*Constructing versions of maternal responsibility to meet case objectives*
*Conclusion*

8 Who is a child? Who is a parent? 194
*Re-presenting the cases*
*The gendering of victimisation and dangerousness, and the identity of the 'child'*
*The child as a body of evidence: constructing 'physical abuse' – protecting children or regulating mothers?*
*'Child protection': differentiating 'normal families' from 'welfare families'?*
*'Home Alone' – constructing 'the normal child', 'the good mother' and 'happy families'*
*The child as a body of evidence: constructing 'neglect' – legitimating surveillance of mothers?*
*Normal and abnormal mothers – foster mother and biological mother*
*'The intergenerational transmission of sexual abuse' – a concept and its practical meaning*
*Girls: born mothers; boys: more than a father*
*Child protection – ethnocentric meanings of 'the family'*
*Conclusion*

9 Constructing meanings and identities in child protection practice 238
*Constructing meanings and identities: the social organisation of child protection*
*Constructing meanings in child protection practice*
*Constructing identities in child protection practice*
*Reflexive and reflective critiques: looking through a fractured lens*
*Reconnecting the 'sociological' to the 'social'*
*Conclusion*

References 262

Index 295

# List of tables

2.1 Cases by type of maltreatment (sites and years)
2.2 Practitioners by sex (sites and years)
2.3 Practitioners by occupational group (sites and years)
5.1 Priority Responses (New Directions and Child Protection: A Guide to Practice)
8.1 Mapping bodily abnormalities – 'physical abuse'
8.2 'She wasn't at all what we expected' – Constructing the 'heterosexual welfare mother' in a 'child protection family'
9.1 Combining concepts about professional knowledge for practice
9.2 Professional skills: Interviewing and case file recording
9.3 Expanded professional roles: legislators and interpreters

# Preface

This book explores how official knowledge about social problems is generated through professional practice. It does this through an examination of a contemporary and contentious social problem, child maltreatment; and the policy and practice response to it, child protection. The primary focus is on how reports that 'something happened' to a child are transformed through child protection intervention into categories of maltreatment and associated identities of responsibility. The book also explores the legal and cultural assumptions influencing child protection practice, about children and how their welfare may be protected.

Children's protection organisations have a legal and social obligation to protect children as defined by policy or statute. Organisational policies are usually formulated in general and abstract ways. Practitioners are expected to implement organisational policies in ways that are relevant and appropriate to the particular circumstances of individuals, families and communities. The task of making general and abstract policies relevant to particular and specific people and their lives is known in professional literature as discretion or autonomy. However, within contemporary child protection practice, professional discretion is strictly regulated to prevent children's deaths and serious injuries, seen as consequences of "idiosyncratic decision making" (Jones 1993: 251), failures of individual discretion (Howe 1992) and deficient knowledge (Walton 1993).

An overall aim of this book is to show how and why it is important to validate rather than suppress professional discretion as essential to effective policy implementation. It offers a way of improving child protection practice by challenging taken-for-granted assumptions underpinning knowledge, policy and practice. The book also challenges perceptions of benign neutrality associated with professional discretion. The apparently well-meaning and knowledgeable child protection professional is also a representative of state power and authority. Thus the book also shows how practitioners exercise a great deal of power through their professional knowledge, in the service of the state. Professional knowledge/power (Foucault 1972, 1980) may be used oppressively or productively. That is, the protection of children may be achieved in ways that either maintain an adversarial and "policing" role (Donzelot 1980; Parton 1991) or facilitate improved ways of caring for and protecting children (Ferguson 1997; Howe et al. 1999).

This book challenges the assumptions of the dominant medico-scientific (Parton 1985) and risk paradigms (Parton, Thorpe & Wattam 1997) that inform approaches that seek to regulate practice. These paradigms are critically analysed from a social constructionist perspective, showing how child protection knowledge, policy and practice are not unproblematic and absolute truths, but outcomes of institutional and social relations in which power is pervasive and knowledge is an 'accomplishment', rather than 'fact'.

The analysis relies on reviews of files and policy documents, participant observation and interviews with practitioners. To protect the anonymity of individuals I have changed all names and other identifying details. However, to make it familiar to readers who are likely to be practitioners, I have renamed the children, parents and practitioners using randomly selected names. (If some of the families' surnames seem familiar, it is because I have given them the surnames of famous painters.)

You will notice that two forms of inverted commas have been used in this book. Double inverted commas are used when material from published sources is cited. Single quotation marks indicate that I am either creating a phrase of my own as part of the analysis or challenging the taken-for-granted nature of a word or phrase, showing that it is open to critique.

# Acknowledgments

I am grateful to the Department for Family and Children's Services (now Community Development), Western Australia, for allowing me to conduct this research and for facilitating my access to staff and files. I would like to thank the managers and staff at the two practice sites for their willingness to support and participate in my research. My thanks are also due to John Booth, Gary Bowler, Jane Brazier, Marian Maughan and John Priestley for sharing their experiences as former employees of the Native Welfare and Child Welfare Departments; and to all those children and families, some of whose stories appear in this book as 'cases', as well as the many other people who have taught me much as a social worker.

I am also grateful to the staff at the Department of Applied Social Science, Lancaster University, for their generosity when I was doing the research for the PhD on which this book is based. In particular, my thanks to David Thorpe, David Smith, Veronica Holmes, and Keith Soothill. Special thanks go to Sue Wise, who supervised my PhD and whose ongoing encouragement and collegiality have been invaluable.

Finally I would like to thank Tudor Day for editing this book, and Elizabeth Vella, Cathy Grundy and Kellie Hughes of Tertiary Press for their helpfulness and encouragement during the publishing process.

Heather D'Cruz
July 2003

# Publisher's acknowledgments

For all copyrighted material reproduced in part or in whole, the publishers would like to acknowledge that permission has been granted as below.

Berliner, L, 'The problem with neglect', *Journal of Interpersonal Violence*, volume 9, issue 4, page 556, © 1994 by Sage Publications Inc. Reprinted by permission of Sage Publications Inc.

Biskup, P, *Not Slaves, Not Citizens: The Aboriginal Problem in Western Australia 1898–1954* © University of Queensland Press, 1973. Reproduced with permission.

*Child Abuse and Neglect*, volume 19, no 5, Smith, D W & Saunders, B E, 'Personality Characteristics of Father/Perpetrators and Nonoffending Mothers in Incest Families: Individual and Dyadic Analyses', pages 607–618 © 1995, with permission from Elsevier.

*Child Abuse and Neglect*, volume 20, no 12, Haskett et al, 'Absence of Males in Maltreatment Research: A Survey of Recent Literature', pages 1175–1182 © 1996, with permission from Elsevier.

Cousins, M & Hussein, A, *Michel Foucault*, 1984, Macmillan London, reproduced with permission of Palgrave Macmillan.

Denzin, N & Lincoln, Y, *Handbook of Qualitative Research*, page 262–272, © 1994 by Sage Publications Inc. Reprinted by permission of Sage Publications Inc.

English, D, 'The Extent and Consequences of Child Maltreatment', *The Future of Children: Preventing Children from Abuse and Neglect*, volume 8, number 1, © The David and Lucile Packard Foundation, 1998. Reprinted with the permission of the David and Lucile Packard Foundation.

Finkelhor, D, 'The Victimization of Children: A Developmental Perspective', *American Journal of Orthopsychiatry*, volume 65, no 2, © by the American Orthopsychiatric Association, Inc, 1995. Reproduced with permission.

Foucault, M, *The History of Sexuality, Volume 1, An Introduction*, © Penguin, 1979. Reprinted with permission.

Haebich, A, *For Their Own Good: Aborigines and Government in the South West of Western Australia, 1900–1940*, © University of Western Australia Press, 1992. Reprinted with permission.

Jenks, N, *Childhood*, © Routledge, London, 1996. Reproduced with permission.

Matthews, R et al, *New Directions Evaluation Report*, © Family and Children's Services, 1995. Reproduced with permission.

Rose, N, *Governing the Soul: The Shaping of the Private Self*, © Routledge, London, 1989. Reproduced with permission by Free Association Press.

Scott, D & Swain S, *Confronting Cruelty: Historical Perspectives on Child Protection in Australia*, © Melbourne University Press, 2002. Reproduced with permission.

Smokowski, P R & Wodarksi, J S, 'Effectiveness of Child Welfare Services for Poor, Neglected Children: A Review of the Empirical Evidence', *Research on Social Work Practice*, volume 6, issue 4, page 504–523, © 1996 by Sage Publications Inc. Reprinted by permission of Sage Publications Inc.

Taylor, D, Critical Social Policy: A Reader: Social Policy and Social Relations © David Taylor, 1996. Reprinted with permission.

Material taken from Western Australia Parliamentary Debates, *Hansard 1947 volume 119* © 1947. Reprinted with permission.

# 1

# Introduction

This chapter establishes a case for an approach like social constructionism in understanding how child maltreatment becomes a social problem. It illustrates why this book is an important resource for child protection practitioners, and also validates practice discretion in a complex area like children's protection. However, it also explains why practice discretion must require accountability to parents and children. This is a particularly important issue because the exercise of discretion is not a neutral and benign process, but one that encapsulates professional knowledge and power exercised within private contexts and lives.

These issues are addressed by analysing social constructionism as it is practised in particular cases, which is the main focus of this book. Chapters 6 to 8 show how meanings and identities known as official and abstract categories are outcomes of social relations in specific case contexts. However, child protection practice must be understood in terms of how it is organised institutionally, organisationally and in situated contexts. The social organisation of practice has implications for how knowledge is understood and implemented in practice, and this is addressed in chapters 3 to 5. These two main features – social constructionism in child protection practice and the social organisation of child protection practice – are set out below, explaining the relevance of each feature to the other and to the overall aims of the book. The conceptual, theoretical and ethical assumptions informing the analysis and arguments presented are set out in chapter 2.

## SOCIAL CONSTRUCTIONISM AND CHILD PROTECTION PRACTICE

This book challenges the dominant perspective of contemporary children's protection practice by taking a perspective of social constructionism. Through an original methodology that primarily focuses on language as a rhetorical device of power and strategy, the book shows how practice is "accomplished" in social relations (Dingwall 1976, 1983; Rueschmeyer 1983; Pithouse 1987; Scott 1989). The 'accomplishment' of practice is a complex concept. This perspective assumes that the regulation of practitioners in their daily work through "technocratization" (Dominelli & Hoogveldt 1996), "bureaucratisation" and "proceduralisation" (Howe 1992) is both counterproductive and unrealistic. Instead, it is assumed that the processes of practice are unpredictable because of the dynamic and complex social relationships that must be negotiated to achieve a conclusion. The worker is not the sole participant, although he or she is often in a central position in a network of social relationships that comprise other professionals, as well as children, parents and other significant parties.

Participation in these processes becomes even more complex if one takes into account the ideas of "positioning" or "subjectivity" (Riessman 1994). These concepts offer a different view of practice, that who we are (identity) and our beliefs, affiliations and values (positioning) influence how we perceive the world and our experiences. Therefore, no amount of organisational regulation can entirely suppress the interpretation by practitioners of what is prescribed in policies and procedures, and how these may be implemented with children and parents.

Beyond the exercise of each practitioner's subjectivity, however constrained, it is necessary to interpret policies and procedures because every case is different. And, if the practitioner interprets policies and procedures within the specific context of the family, as an exercise of his or her subjectivity, then it is also the case that any other participants in the process called 'child protection practice' will also exercise their subjectivity. From this perspective of practice as an 'accomplishment', "[v]ariation is the norm and quality control is unlikely" (Walton 1993: 151).

However, a strong case is also made for professional accountability that requires ongoing reflection on and critique of practice. This book shows how and why there needs to be a reintroduction and revalidation of a version of professional accountability that is substantive (focused on values inherent in what is done in practice) and client-centred. This would complement accountability to the organisation, and balance the contemporary emphasis on instrumental accountability that is procedurally driven and that minimises the exercise of, and reflection on, values intrinsic to policies in, and as, practice. A critical awareness of values in policies and practices like child protection that are inherently regulatory would minimise the "dangers" (Ferguson 1997) of oppressive and unproductive deployment of professional knowledge and power in families on behalf of children, and would instead enhance "opportunities" (Ferguson 1997) for productive engagement.

Significant studies that have explored child protection practice show in different ways how it is accomplished through social relations and the implications for professional accountability. Dingwall et al. (1983) validated practice discretion by showing how practitioners in a British local authority were able to achieve a balance between protecting children and respecting family privacy. Through a culture of practice that was encapsulated in the "rule of optimism"

(Dingwall et al. 1983: 81–2), workers were neither "deficient" nor "rapacious" in implementing their statutory responsibilities. They achieved such practice without excessive organisational regulation. In fact, Dingwall et al. (1983: 218) were moved to remark that they found no evidence to support the "pessimistic vision" of writers like Foucault and Donzelot, of the "panoptic state" and "family policing" as its consequence.

However, this optimistic view of child protection practice was destroyed through several public inquiries in the UK into the deaths of Jasmine Beckford, Tyra Henry and Kimberley Carlile (Parton 1991). The dominance of the medico-scientific model and a *legalistic* response (Dingwall 1986) to these tragic deaths sought individual scapegoats – namely, practitioners and their supervisors. The public and political discrediting in Britain of practice discretion associated with deficient knowledge, loss of objectivity and distorted judgments of practitioners (Parton 1991) led to more prescriptive legislation, policy and procedures as the best ways of minimising such tragedies. Within a political ideology of the New Right, the adequacy of organisational resources, the complexity of child protection practice and the implicit assumptions of the medico-scientific model were not considered (Parton 1991; Dingwall 1986).

In addition to validating practice discretion, a social constructionist perspective also allows for a critical analysis of social assumptions, processes and practices that usually are taken for granted as 'normal', but which may instead replicate and maintain institutionalised oppression. For example, Thorpe (1994), in an Australian study, commented on the influence of assumptions about 'normal' children, parents and families on practice processes and outcomes. Such assumptions tended to maintain oppression and inequality through the over-representation of individuals and groups that were considered to breach cultural assumptions of 'normality'. For example, sole mothers living in poverty and Aboriginal mothers were over-represented in reports and as 'persons believed responsible', and their children were more likely to enter care. In general, the limited categories to which practitioners were expected to allocate instances of child maltreatment also did violence to the diversity of family circumstances and problems, and of children's experiences of oppression and disadvantage.

Janko (1994), in a US study, also commented on the potential for oppressive child protection practice, of already "vulnerable children, vulnerable families". Her critique of practice related to the increasingly narrow focus of contemporary child protection knowledge, policy and social organisation on "specific, harmful acts, rather than the contexts of child maltreatment" (Janko 1994: 120). Child protection intervention was primarily a policing activity that did not address socioeconomic disadvantages associated with problematic parenting.

Social constructionism also shows how knowledge that is assumed to be neutral and objective may become an instrument of discriminatory practice, with unequal (and apparently predetermined) outcomes for some groups. Parton, Thorpe & Wattam (1997), for example, explored child protection practice as a part of their critique of the risk paradigm and the bureaucratisation of practice. They showed how risk is identified in case files as records of socially constructed practice. They also challenged the taken-for-granted official categories of "risk" and "sexual abuse", by analysing how these are outcomes of practical social constructions. Similarly, they show how "ordinary children" make a "transition" in the files to the officially taken-for-granted identity, "child of concern" (1997: 102). Their analysis explicates how official meanings given to children's experiences in their families and key identities are influenced by cultural assumptions of normality, rather than being 'objectively real' as assumed in the medico-scientific model.

Similarly, in two US studies, Margolin (1990, 1992) discusses how official and seemingly indisputable identities of responsibility are outcomes of social constructionist practices. In his 1990 study, Margolin explored how practitioners identified "caretakers" as 'persons believed responsible' (or not) by focusing on cases of "fatal child abuse" that from a contemporary child protection perspective would be assumed to pose no doubt at all of 'responsibility'. Instead, he showed how practitioners, *in interaction* with caretakers as "accounters or deceivers", "managed or neutralized the appearance of guilt" (1990: 375). The importance of caretakers' language as a strategic device through "vocabularies of motive" influenced how social workers attributed responsibility for family violence and children's deaths. Caretakers' identities that intersected with parenting, such as disability, further influenced how workers perceived their explanations. Some caretakers were "excused" whilst others were categorised as "responsible", showing that parents were active participants in the process and outcome of the case.

Margolin (1992) also showed how the contentious and assumed to be taken-for-granted identity of "sexual abuse perpetrator" is not automatically shared by participants with an interest in the case and its outcomes: for example, victims or agencies. Instead, a professional and organisational image of sexual danger and risk and a presupposition of "guilt" influenced the final case outcome. Participants who had different views were considered to be wrong. Nor was the accused person interviewed, an exclusionary practice that Smith (1990a) says is common when individuals are categorised as abnormals or deviants.

This book extends these explorations of child protection practice outcomes as accomplishments, by showing through case studies, *how* official (and public) knowledge of child maltreatment emerges through interactions between individuals in relation to events in a particular child's life. The analysis of each case as a separate contextual entity, in which the particular meanings of maltreatment and identities of responsibility emerge through the social relations of *that* case, strengthens claims that child protection knowledge is accomplished, rather than absolute. The most important feature of the case analysis in this book is how language operates as a device for representing knowledge, and as a strategy of power by which knowledge claims can be made and contested, legitimated and de-legitimated. The child protection practitioner at a child welfare organisation is positioned as a coordinator of the social relations of importance to the case. Different participants with an interest in the case and its outcomes are engaged by the practitioner and with each other. Each participant (including the practitioner) has an explanation of the events that are under investigation. Often multiple and conflicting versions may be offered, from which the practitioner must decide on the legitimacy of different versions, in relation to his or her own and to what is organisationally mandated in policies and procedures.

Chapters 6 to 8 explore in detail these processes and their outcomes that were represented as case statistics including type of maltreatment, 'person believed responsible' and the profiles of children as victims and their families of origin. These chapters show how language as a device of power operates to make some versions of knowledge legitimate (and 'factual') and others not. These chapters also show how constructions of the normality or abnormality of identities of participants in the process of meaning construction influence how the legitimacy of knowledge is constructed. These chapters are the main focus of the book, showing how professional and organisational knowledge emerges through practice.

Chapter 6, 'Something happened': Constructing maltreatment, shows how reports made to child welfare/protection organisations about particular children's experiences are transformed into official categories of maltreatment. It focuses on how categorisation as a discursive resource and linguistic strategy (Potter 1996; Smith 1990a) operates in child protection interventions as sociolinguistic practices. Through selected cases I show how categorisation has structured child protection 'investigations', and contributed to reproducing and maintaining a "hierarchy of maltreatment" (Berliner 1994; Dubowitz 1994; Doyle 1996), and how official categories may also be reinterpreted so that particular case outcomes are produced. The chapter is significant for two main reasons. Firstly, it shows how official categories of knowledge such as types of maltreatment and their definitions are associated with particular ways of knowing and establishing the truth status of what happened to a child. The exploration of categorisation as a practice, in which language is deployed as a strategy of power, shows how an official category establishes the rules for knowing and validating the category, precluding other ways of knowing or other possible explanations of the events. Thus there is a circularity of process and outcome, one reinforcing the other. Secondly, and fortunately, practitioners are not entirely rule-governed but can and do exercise their discretion by interpreting the meaning of the categories in each case. Thus individuals can both maintain and transform official knowledge through their engagement with and divergence from what is prescribed.

Chapter 7 looks at Identities of responsibility. It explores how the official identity category of 'person believed responsible' is an outcome of linguistic strategies by which the abnormality (and normality) of an individual may be constructed (Potter 1996). This process of constructing official identities in practice is structured within dominant discourses of 'the dangerous individual' from whom children and the community must be protected. The chapter shows how the identities of individuals are not fixed but are instead contextually meaningful, depending on the relationship with other significant persons in a child protection case network as to whether and how 'responsibility' is constructed. An interesting feature of the practical construction of identities of responsibility is that the positioning of participants within the case network and their relationships with the person identified as 'responsible' may limit each participant's ability to 'see' alternative or complementary identities that may also be plausible. The responsibility attributed to women/mothers and the official invisibility of men is another significant feature (Milner 1993; Stark & Flitcraft 1988). The selected cases show how these overwhelmingly gendered patterns discussed in the literature are consequences of sociolinguistic practices. The analysis of sociolinguistic strategies is informed by concepts of "patriarchal mothering" and the heterosexual family as a site of power relations structured by gender and generation (Stark & Flitcraft 1988; Featherstone 1996, 1997; Frost & Stein 1989).

Chapter 8, Who is a child? Who is a parent? shows how discursive assumptions about 'normal' children, parents and families influence child protection practice. Selected cases illustrate how in practice the social construction of 'the child' is accomplished, along with related identities of 'parent' and 'adult'. Assumptions about 'normal' familial identities, roles and relationships named in particular ways may preclude engagement with arrangements that do not fit these assumptions: for example, different cultural practices. The cases also demonstrate how the protection of children operates as an official strategy of surveillance and regulation of women as mothers. Images of 'normal' mothers, for example as foster carers, are contrasted with images of 'abnormal' mothers, whose children are the subjects of child protection intervention.

Together, these three chapters strengthen the critiques of "bureaucratisation" and "proceduralisation" (Howe 1992) of contemporary child protection practice. In particular the reliance on statistics as official knowledge of incidents of maltreatment, profiles of 'persons believed responsible', children as victims and their families of origin, cannot be accepted unproblematically, as an absolute truth. Instead the cases show that statistics are outcomes of complex social interactions and that they represent the outcomes of such processes rather than reflecting an objective reality.

## SOCIAL CONSTRUCTIONISM AND THE SOCIAL ORGANISATION OF CHILD PROTECTION

The main focus of this book is on the analysis of particular cases to show how language as a device of power is implicated in the interactions between participants in child protection case processes and outcomes. However, each individual's practices must be understood within the institutional and organisational contexts in which they emerge. For example, Scott (1998), Hood (1997) and D'Cruz (1993) explored the influences of organisational contexts on individual's practices of "meaning construction" (Scott 1989).

Practitioners' interpretations of child protection and their practices in relation to children and families were significantly influenced by organisational mandates (Hood 1997; Scott 1998). Thus, aggregated patterns of practice – for example, case statistics – are not just outcomes of individual discretion or meaning construction, but have a particular organisational profile. Scott (1998), who compared hospital social workers and child protection workers' practices in child maltreatment cases, commented that "[a]ny comparison of [the] . . . workers' assessments and models of practice must take into account the fundamental differences in their organizational mandates" (Scott 1998: 83). This included differences in terminology to describe case processes – for example, "assessment" and "investigation" – and different practices conditional on the authority vested in particular organisational roles. Therefore, child protection workers with greater statutory authority could conduct investigations in the family home, which was outside the mandate of hospital social workers.

A study that I conducted in 1993 for a child protection organisation showed how practice discretion may also be influenced by another level of social organisation: the offices in local communities from which practitioners work. This study was part of an organisational review of perceived 'practice inconsistency' across five practice sites, whose child protection statistics showed different patterns. The study explored how intake practices may be influenced by situated cultures (D'Cruz 1993). A documentary review showed that each site of practice operated under particular cultural rules that influenced individuals' practices. For example, some rules were 'when in doubt, check it out', 'see the referral as family support, as a case category or type of service if categorised as child maltreatment', and 'less intrusive intervention wherever possible'. This study showed that practice sites as collectives interpret organisational policies and construct their own versions of how to practise that nonetheless remain connected to the organisationally prescribed version. These examples of the social organisation of child protection practice show how practitioners' discretion is rarely completely idiosyncratic, but influenced by organisational and situated constructions of child protection knowledge, policy and practice.

This book locates the micro-practices as socially constructed knowledge in particular cases, re-presented in chapters 6 to 8 within various layers of social organisation and associated versions of knowledge. These are institutionally legitimated knowledge represented as literature (chapter 3); organisational knowledge represented as policy (chapter 4) and the situated versions associated with each site of practice (chapter 5). An original methodology provides an analytical approach that recognises these multiple levels of social organisation, and the knowledge associated with each level (as literature, policy, situated and case) as a socially constructed version. Each version of knowledge contextualises other versions, and yet each version does not have a one-to-one correspondence with other versions because of contextual differences between each. This methodology is explained and justified in chapter 2, Methodology – Addressing a complex practice reality, which sets out different yet connected theories about the role of language in social constructionism, showing how it informs the research design and the overall analytical approach.

Foucault's concept of "discourse" (Foucault 1978b; Cousins & Hussain 1984), which he developed primarily through an analysis of institutional documents and texts, informs the reading and analysis of the literature set out in chapter 3. A concept related to discourse, "genealogy" (Foucault 1971, 1978b, 1980), provides an analytical approach to contemporary policy, set out in chapter 4. However, Foucault did not explore how knowledge, language and power operate as actual practices in particular social contexts (Dreyfus & Rabinow 1982). Bourdieu's (1991) concept of "linguistic communities", developed through anthropology, offers a way of understanding how language operates as situated cultural rules in collectives, in the case of this book at two practice sites where practitioners were located. This is discussed in chapter 5. The limitations of both Foucault and Bourdieu in exploring the micro-practices of knowledge, language and power in each case are explained in chapters 6 to 8 and the relevance of Potter's (1996) compilation of rhetorical devices for case analysis justified. The connections between and contributions of the three primary theoreticians and the limitations of the methodology are also discussed in chapter 2. An *ethical* position of "dualism" (Heap 1995), which recognises the potential for an analytical approach like social constructionism to appear to trivialise the legal and moral imperatives of child protection practice, is also explained. A dualist position recognises the material reality of children's experiences of oppression and disadvantage, whilst exploring the politics of different meanings and explanations given to that reality through social constructionism.

Chapter 3, Protecting children within discourses of the normal child and family, sets out the literature that organises an international knowledge network (Smith 1990c) through the dissemination of texts across national boundaries. For example, the international journal *Child Abuse and Neglect* has included contributions about "a developing country" (Farinatti et al. 1990); Australia (Goddard et al. 1990); Korea

(Kwang-iel Kim & Bokja Ko 1990); South Africa (Haffejee 1991); Nigeria (Mejiuni 1991); India (Segal 1992); New Zealand (Kotch et al. 1993); Norway (Bendixen et al. 1994); Malaysia (Kasim et al. 1994); Finland (Sariola & Uutela 1994); and Bangladesh (Khan & Lynch 1997). Thus, the concepts and problems they describe, written in one context and read in another, appear to transcend jurisdictional boundaries, and are assumed to be directly applicable regardless of context. Such literature defines what legitimate child protection knowledge is, including the meanings of maltreatment, identities of responsibility and children as victims, and protective practices. Chapter 3 discusses this literature as socially constructed, as a discourse representing dominant Western concepts of the normal child, family, parenting and child-rearing practices that have now colonised the developing world (Boyden 1990).

Chapter 3 presents child protection knowledge as a set of assumptions about normal children, parents and families, and discusses how child protection policy and practice relies on discourses of normality in order to ascertain abnormality and, therefore, risk (DePanfilis & Scannapieco 1994; Murphy-Berman 1994). Within the dominant medico-scientific paradigm, the body of the child becomes an object of knowledge. The positivist paradigm that informs the model and conceptions of risk not only assumes that there is a materially real object called 'child maltreatment', but also that this can be directly observed through the senses through "risk assessment". The child's body as a physically real entity is central to identifying maltreatment, as a 'body of evidence' that can be seen, measured and recorded through body maps and "colour atlases" of bodily abnormality (Coulter 1997). Bodily abnormalities such as bruising or fractures, as "clinical evidence" (Dingwall et al. 1983: 31), come to represent the direct effects of 'dangerous' parenting practices as causes of maltreatment. This is combined with "social evidence" (Dingwall et al. 1983: 31), such as features of the child's environment, including the material circumstances and parental conduct, to produce a syndrome called 'child maltreatment', in keeping with the medico-scientific model (Thorpe 1994; Parton et al. 1997). Furthermore, the body as a site of knowledge ('evidence') is directly implicated in what is known as the "hierarchy of maltreatment" (Berliner, 1994; Dubowitz, 1994; Doyle, 1996). This concept means that certain 'types of maltreatment' are given greater 'priority' than others: for example, 'abuse' over 'neglect', and 'sexual abuse' over 'physical abuse'. To achieve this hierarchy, the body of the child is partitioned, in discourse that defines the 'types of maltreatment' as related to, or manifested in, 'body parts'.

Chapter 3 also explores the shifting boundary between the state and family in regard to the care and protection of children. Different ideological positions about children and their rights and family autonomy, underpinned by patriarchy, are identified (Fox Harding 1991; Rose 1989), and also a child liberation perspective that offers a more political construction of 'the child' (Freeman 1983; Franklin

1986). A social constructionist perspective of childhood and family life shows how concepts of 'normality' mask difference and power relations. The chapter shows how 'responsibility in the dominant discourse focuses on "dangerous individuals" (Hearn 1990), and the gendering of 'responsibility' more generally, by which women as mothers are held responsible for harm done to children by male associates. From a feminist perspective, a social constructionist analysis shows how contemporary child protection discourse regulates women-as-mothers through a focus on child care as a mothering responsibility. Children's bodies represent the normality of mothering and levels of risk. Feminist discourses argue that the dominant discourse maintains patriarchy by overwhelmingly constructing women-as-mothers as "responsible" for maltreatment, while men who may be directly responsible become "invisible" (Milner 1993; Stark & Flitcraft 1988). Feminist discourses show how the dominant discourse maintains "patriarchal mothering" (Stark & Flitcraft 1988; Featherstone 1996), particularly through benign constructions of the heterosexual family as an idealised entity, rather than power relations between gender and generation (Stark & Flitcraft 1988; Frost & Stein 1989).

Chapter 4, Policy as discourse, shows that concepts and practices of child protection and risk management are shared across jurisdictional boundaries, as suggested by an international literature. However, their *emergence* in each context and their implications must be understood within particular political and social institutions at particular times (Hacking 1991; Hendrick 1990; Gordon 1985, 1986; Scott & Swain 2002). Thus, the example of contemporary Western Australian child protection policy and practice is analysed drawing on Foucault's (1971, 1980) concept of genealogy. The analysis shows how particular meanings of 'protection' in relation to 'children' differed over time, for example in the transition from a colony through to self-government, as part of the Australian federation and into contemporary times. This is an example of how 'policy' may be understood as socially constructed through *institutional* knowledge relations, in a particular legal jurisdiction at a particular time. The features of the analysis show how in the Western Australian context, 'race' (as 'Aboriginality') primarily defined how 'protection' of 'children' was understood and practised has different meanings over time. Contemporary policy is but one of many versions employed by the state at different times in its response to children and their protection. The shifting meanings of 'protection' articulating with 'race' are shown as dimensions of 'difference': as exclusionary practices from colonisation up to the 1970s, and then by claims of equality through the erasure of 'racial difference'. The chapter also shows how globally shared concepts and practices can have particular local meanings and consequences; in this case, for race relations as manifested in the protection and care of children. Thus generalised analyses of the over-representation of children and families from racial and ethnic minorities in statutory services (Dutt & Phillips 1996; Thorpe 1994) can only chip away at surface patterns. An in-depth exploration of social history, as written in official documents and experienced, must be understood within the particular institutional context in which oppressive and discriminatory practices emerged. This would allow for the construction of contextually relevant solutions that take account of lived experiences within legal, cultural and social institutions at different times, and in different places.

Cultural rules define each site as a "linguistic community" (Bourdieu 1991). Chapter 5, Sites of practice, shows how local office cultures as linguistic communities may differ from each other and yet provide a version of a protective service that conforms to what is organisationally mandated. The cultural rules expressed in a collectively shared language about children, parents and families at two practice sites are explored. Different rules generated different meanings of problems presented at each. These different meanings as policy interpretations also influenced preferred practices and precluded others. The local cultures shaped individual practice by providing justifications through rules but did not necessarily restrict individual discretion. Instead, depending on the local culture, individual deviations from situated rules were incorporated in various ways into the linguistic community.

The final chapter, Constructing meanings and identities in child protection practice, summarises the claims made for the role of professional practice in generating official knowledge. Official and professional knowledge, policy and practice are shown to be contextually constructed entities. Furthermore, these three dimensions are dynamically interrelated, rather than being a simplistic linearity and hierarchy between knowledge, policy and practice. The contributions and limitations for professional practice of social constructionism with a focus on language as a device of knowledge and power are also discussed. An alternative approach, which incorporates principles of social constructionism within the ethical position espoused, is explored. Through a discussion of sociological concepts and their potential relevance for child protection practice, the approach taken addresses the tendency to restrict practice by a focus on "dichotomous thinking" (Berlin 1990). Instead, it explores the potential for seeing apparent conceptual polarities as two ends of a continuum in which the concepts may be combined in multiple ways across the continuum, offering a range of practice options, rather than choices between just two options.

# 2

# Methodology – Addressing a complex practice reality

I started the research that is the subject of this book in January 1993. At the time I was employed as a research officer in a public sector child welfare organisation, where I had begun work in January 1979 as a newly graduated social worker. After nearly 18 years working in various roles in that organisation, I had witnessed and participated in many changes in relation to the delivery of services to children and families. I had begun my practice in 1979 in a mining community a long way from the city. In 1981 I moved to the city where I worked until 1983 from an office located in a suburban community.

During these years, child abuse was narrowly defined as one of many problems associated with children and family life confronting us as generic social workers (Kamerman & Kahn 1993). Most of the services that were offered may be described as 'child welfare' in which parents and families were assisted wherever possible to care for their children, through in-home and community-based services and, where these failed, through wardship and alternative care in foster homes and institutions. Child protection was at that time a part of, but not entirely, child welfare.

It was not until 1985 that 'child protection' became the new approach to child welfare following the recommendation of the Welfare and Community Services Review. This change in the concept of the state's role in relation to children and families radically altered the approach taken: from public and community responsibility and resources to more individualistic, normative and legalistic interventions.

By this time I was working in a policy and research role in the centrally based head office. In 1987 I moved to an urban, regional setting as a consultant to community-based practitioners and their managers/supervisors, who wanted to enhance their practice through research and program development. Although I was no longer a casework practitioner my role in relation to practitioners, supervisors and policy makers offered me particular insights into the values, processes and outcomes of practice in relation to children and families. I was often troubled by what I perceived to be unnecessary and hasty categorisations of cases as 'child maltreatment'. Categorisations as child maltreatment seemed to offer very limited assessments that did not allow for alternatives that took account of contexts in which problematic parenting occurred. Furthermore, I wondered if a less punitive approach could inform a more collaborative and empathic response to the problems of parenting and family life, without losing sight of the children involved. In my perception, the dominance of a particular network of child protection experts severely limited the influence of those who challenged such practices, who were seen as uninformed or ignorant. There were some of us who feared to disagree too strongly because we would be dismissed as uncaring of children – and I certainly did not want those accusations levelled at me. However, I was increasingly troubled by what appeared to be an oppressive response whilst ostensibly aiming to represent relatively vulnerable and voiceless children.

These concerns continued even after I had returned to head office in 1991 as a research officer. As a participant in this organisation, I felt culpable even though I was not at this stage developing policies or implementing them through practice. At the same time, having completed my MSW in 1989, I also felt the need to undertake some more postgraduate study. The knowledge I had gained through my MSW now seemed too limited and my professional development seemed stultified. Perhaps a PhD would be the direction to take? I had a general topic in mind, which related to an alternative approach to child protection. As it happened, Dr David Thorpe, a researcher in child protection/child welfare and academic from Lancaster University, UK, visited Australia so I discussed my ideas with him, along with the possibility of doing a PhD. By January 1993 I had been accepted to do a PhD at the Department of Applied Social Science at Lancaster.

The research topic that developed from my professional history set out above has now become the subject of this book. The organisation in which I was employed is the context in which the research was conducted. I began my research in 1993 when I was employed as a research officer in the child protection organisation, but I finished it in 1999 as an 'academic'. My professional and intellectual journey as a professional public servant and later as a social work academic has been recounted as part of a process of 'seeing differently', indeed through a "fractured lens" (D'Cruz 2001). Hence, informed by my experience in social work policy and practice and, since 1996, as an academic, I have sought through this research to bridge a gap between 'practice' and 'academia', to offer what may be both critical yet familiar to practitioners and policy makers in child and family welfare.

The main aim of this research is to explore how official meanings and identities are constructed in child protection practice, rather than being outcomes representing an objective 'truth' that can be ascertained by the rigorous application of risk assessment criteria. Specific questions may be expressed as to how practitioners construct meaning for 'child maltreatment' of particular 'types', and the identity of the 'person believed responsible'. Additionally, there are questions about how assumptions about 'children', 'parents' and 'family life' influence constructions of 'maltreatment' and identities of 'responsibility'. These questions about the constructions of meanings and identities in child protection practice are addressed in chapters 6 to 8. However, subsidiary questions that are nonetheless important relate to the contexts within which practitioners work and that structure practice in various ways. These subsidiary questions may be expressed as what is the social organisation of practice and how is it constructed? How does the social organisation of practice relate to the social construction of meanings and identities by practitioners in specific cases? These subsidiary questions are addressed in chapters 3 to 5. In particular, these chapters set out the social construction of legitimate professional knowledge (chapter 3) and its expression in a particular legal jurisdiction and mandated organisation(s) as policy (chapter 4). Furthermore, each office in communities where practitioners are located may represent a particular version of organisational policy consistent with the local practice culture yet still conform to organisationally prescribed policies (chapter 5). Thus, practitioners who construct meanings and identities in particular cases work in a complex reality that must be understood to adequately address the main aim of this book.

## A COMPLEX PRACTICE REALITY – 'A FRACTURED LENS'

The methodology for addressing the questions set out above may be described by the metaphor of a "fractured lens" (D'Cruz 1999, 2001). Given the complex practice reality within which practitioners construct meanings and identities in each case that is referred to them, it is necessary to select appropriate ways of engaging with that complexity. Because each layer comprising the social organisation of practice has different features that may be known in different ways, it has been necessary to construct a fractured methodological lens by which to engage with those layers. For example, professional knowledge conveyed in literature, and organisational policies and procedures are usually in the form of texts or documents; while policies implemented by practitioners in different community-based offices are known through interactions as practices and talk between workers and clients. Furthermore, practices in particular cases are influenced by the participants involved in each case and known through case files, statistics and talk between workers, supervisors, children and parents. Thus each layer of practice reality is represented differently and therefore must be engaged with by drawing on appropriate analytical resources.

The metaphor of a fractured lens encapsulates two important features in the research process. Firstly, the idea of a lens represents ways of seeing literally and figuratively (Haraway 1991). In research that claims to explore how professional knowledge is generated through processes of social constructionism, it is important to acknowledge that the researcher also generates and constructs knowledge. The researcher is a "positioned investigator" (Riessman 1994: 133–8) whose ways of engaging with the research, its aims and conceptual and analytical approach are influenced by particular ways of knowing as a theoretical and ethical position (Stanley & Wise 1993). Secondly, the description that the lens is fractured conveys that the reality that I have engaged with and have represented here in this book is not seamless and tidy but extremely messy and complex.

The fractured lens for this research relies on three main theoretical perspectives: those of Foucault, Bourdieu and Potter. It is possible to criticise as incompatible the methodological articulation of Foucault, Bourdieu and Potter, because each may be regarded as epistemologically different from the others (D'Cruz 2001: 22). However, as an applied social researcher and social work academic, to me such critiques seem less important than a search for ways to understand complex social conditions and problems. In my view, the conceptual, epistemological and methodological fractures represent the social world and the multiplicity of ways in which we understand and engage with or in it. I have commented that:

> a fractured lens has put my methodology in perspective by showing why and how multiple ways of seeing were and are necessary . . . A fractured lens allows for multiple, if somewhat disjointed, ways of seeing a fractured reality which can be known in different ways, yet which can be connected, if somewhat tenuously at times. (D'Cruz 2001: 26)

This is particularly important if the aims of this book are to be achieved in ways that make an ethical and practical contribution to social work knowledge and practice, particularly within a contentious specialism called 'child protection'. However, having acknowledged that my methodological lens is fractured, I have constructed connections between each major 'piece' of the lens; namely, between the writings of Foucault, Bourdieu and Potter.

The main concepts that influence this research are discourse and its relationships to power/knowledge, to the body, to identity and to genealogy (Foucault 1971, 1972, 1977, 1978a, 1978b, 1980); symbolic capital and power, and linguistic communities (Bourdieu 1977, 1990, 1991; Jenkins 1992); and rhetorical devices (Potter 1996). Whilst each of these theories and approaches to knowledge and power has been developed in different ways (different epistemologies), they are nonetheless connected by the idea of language and its place in giving meaning to 'reality' as knowledge and its place as a device of power. In the sections following, I will discuss these concepts and show how they have contributed to the overall approach and to the analysis.

## CONSTRUCTING MY FRACTURED LENS: SOME IMPORTANT PIECES

Reading and writing through Foucault: discourse, power/knowledge, the body, identity, and genealogy

### Discourse and power/knowledge

"Discourse" is a key concept in understanding and analysing how professional knowledge and professional power intersect and are expressed in policies and practices. The integral relationship between knowledge and power is expressed by Foucault (1972, 1977, 1980; Rabinow 1984) as "power/knowledge".

Foucault (1978b: 9) defines a "discursive formation" as a "similar set of rules" that exist:

> if the statements in it refer to one and the same object . . . if there is a regular 'style' to the existence of statements . . . if there is a constancy of concepts employed . . . if the statements all support a common 'theme', a strategy, a common institutional, administrative or political . . . pattern. (Cousins & Hussain 1984: 84–5)

This definition links language (vocabulary and ways of expression) to legitimate knowledge that prescribes particular and shared strategies, purposes and outcomes. Therefore it is argued here that child protection can be understood as a discourse. There is an identifiable language and associated meanings that prescribe particular practices as appropriate responses, excluding others. Professionals who are considered to be knowledgeable communicate through commonly understood language and it is possible for lay people and members of the public also to be engaged by this common language and purpose (Ferguson 1997).

Discourses may be expressed through texts such as images, policy documents and published professional literature about theory and research (Fairclough 1992; Foucault 1972, 1978a, 1978b; Bacchi 1998). Discourses as legitimate versions of knowledge rely on networks of individuals or groups who are seen as experts. Experts are placed in a hierarchical relationship with those seen as less (or not) knowledgeable, and may include parents, children and even other professionals. Knowledge constituted as discourse only becomes legitimate through power struggles between various interest groups, and some versions may be discredited as wrong, lies or subversive (Devaux 1994; LeCercle 1990).

### Discourse and the body

In addition to documents and images, the body of the individual also may be regarded as a text. The body becomes a text about identities that are constructed through multiple discourses: for example, about gender, race, disability, age and sexuality and what it means to be 'normal' in the culture and society (Roseneil & Seymour 1999; Weedon 1999; Foucault 1977, 1978a, 1980; Young 1990; Hewitt 1991). The body of the individual becomes a body of knowledge and a site of power (Hewitt 1991) in professional practice. Expertise is closely related to technologies – for example, medical technologies, risk assessment criteria or forms of profiling (Joffe 1999; Kemshall 2002; Lupton 1999a, 1999b) – that allow for legitimate knowledge to be generated and accumulated. The various techniques by which knowledge may be generated allow for identification and classification of individuals (Hacking 1990; Rose 1989): for example, children as victims, or 'persons believed responsible'. Classifications allow for individual profiles according to 'normality' in comparison to others in the population (Hewitt 1991; Hacking 1990; Rose 1989). These comparisons are generated through "dividing practices", by which "abnormals" – for example, 'dangerous persons' – are separated from "normals" and categorised in an 'either/or', 'positive/negative' relationship, known as a binary relation (Foucault 1977, 1980). You cannot belong to both categories at once, and one category is 'better' than the other (Fraser 1997).

Professionals come to 'know' individuals as "cases" and develop profiles of knowledge about groups of such individuals represented by "statistics" (Hacking 1990; Australian Institute of Health and Welfare 2003). Individuals who are seen as abnormal or deviant may be placed under professional surveillance and offered interventions by which to 'become normal' (Rose 1989, 1998, 1999). The discipline of individuals is known as "bio-power" and the discipline of groups or populations as "bio-politics" (Foucault 1977, 1980; Hacking 1990; Hewitt 1991).

The centrality of the body in child protection is discussed in chapter 3 as it relates to abstract knowledge and concepts about 'types of maltreatment' or 'persons believed responsible' and risk assessment. The case analysis in chapters 6 to 8 looks at how the idea of the body operates in child protection practice to construct meanings of maltreatment and identities of responsibility, as well as who may be children, parents and adults.

**Discourse and identity**

Identity, for example, gender, race, class, disability, sexuality and age, is usually taken to be a fixed 'way of being' that is the same for all individuals who may be categorised in particular ways (Weedon 1999; Roseneil & Seymour 1999). Similarly, identities of the child and parent (and adult) are assumed to be the same for all individuals so categorised. In this book, identity is understood as related to context, and as relational. Identities are defined through discourses that represent particular cultural ways of being. Identities are constructed in particular contextual interactions and can only be meaningful if in relationship with a complementary identity. For example, 'woman' is only meaningful if understood in relation to 'man' because the definition of each identity is placed in a binary relationship with the other (Weedon 1999; Fraser 1997; Young 1990). Being one identity precludes being the other and at the same time each identity defines itself in relation to the other in particular contexts. Similarly, 'child' is only meaningfully defined explicitly and implicitly in relation to 'adult' and 'parent' identities, and has particular contextual meanings (Jenks 1996; Prout & James 1990; Gittins 1998). Furthermore, some identities may be 'better' than others. For example, feminists argue that in most cultures and in discourses being a 'man' is considered superior to being a 'woman' (Fraser 1997; Weedon 1999; Young 1990). 'White' people are considered as superior to 'black' people in many cultures (Brah 1992; Young 1990) and often associated with colonisation as a political process with particular consequences for 'white'/'black' relations (Said 1978; Tuhiwai Smith 1999). Identity is also understood as multiple rather than singular (Weedon 1999; Brah 1992). This means that many identities intersect or articulate in the embodied individual, and may contribute to an intensification of the experience of oppressive practices that Yeatman (1995) refers to as "interlocking oppressions": for example, a black woman with a disability. In child protection, a 'parent' may be a mother on a low income and of a particular ethnic group. A 'child' may be boy or girl of a particular age, ethnicity, disability and social class and this has consequences for their lived experiences and how 'protection' may or may not be extended to them. The intersections of multiple identities in time and place may give particular meanings to the identities of 'mother' and 'child'. Although identities may be multiple, all aspects of identity are not necessarily apparent in an interaction or context. Only those aspects of identity that are 'relevant' to the interaction or issue may be engaged in the interaction. For example, gender and sexuality may be 'relevant' in discussions about parenting in a child sexual abuse case in terms of 'responsibility' as culpability and protective function (Stark & Flitcraft 1988; D'Cruz 2002a), whereas social class or ethnicity may not. These aspects of identity in practice are explored further in the cases set out in chapters 6 to 8, as well as in chapter 3, where abstract concepts of identity are discussed in relation to the 'child', 'parent' and 'person believed responsible'.

**Discourse and genealogy**

Foucault's (1971, 1978b, 1980) "genealogical method" as a "history of the present" analysed knowledge as shifting meanings and identities, embedded in power relations, and contingent in time, place and related sociopolitical and cultural institutions. Knowledge at any one time is not a consequence of progressive and evolutionary processes. It emerges, depending on the context and the relations of power that generate particular versions of knowledge, some of which are seen as legitimate and others not. Language represents meanings and identities as knowledge, not as a one-to-one correspondence with 'reality', but as a particular, legitimated image (Foucault 1983). Identity is not a single, fixed way of being that is replicated in different contexts. Instead, identity is multiple and fluid and related to the contexts of knowledge in which particular identities have relevance and meaning. Furthermore, identities are constructed through discourses, whereby knowledge about who is 'normal' and who is 'abnormal' positions individuals and groups in relation to each other in particular ways. For example, Hendrick (1990) and Scott & Swain (2002) have shown how policies in relation to children have changed as a feature of social and political constructions of 'the child' rather than being 'progressive' developments over time.

The genealogy of contemporary child protection discourse in chapter 4 shows how the concept of 'protection' was associated with the identity of 'child' in a particular place (Western Australia) over time, from colonisation to 'the present', and was differentiated by 'race-as-Aboriginality'. To show these how these differences and connections between the meanings of 'child', 'protection' and 'Aboriginality' have operated to influence different legislation, policies, practices and outcomes, chapter 4 is organised according to time and Aboriginality.

## The limitations of Foucault

Foucault's Theory of Knowledge, especially as outlined in *The Archaeology of Knowledge* (1972), conceptualises institutional processes and discursive practices in the construction of knowledge, and problematises ontology (the nature of 'reality' and social problems) and epistemology (how we know about 'reality' and social problems and respond to them). Foucault's concept of discourse (and its related aspects) and genealogy represent patterns of legitimate knowledge relations between social institutions or group identities such as social workers, doctors and police officers. Statistical categories and related texts represent official knowledge at different times. Although Foucault argues that discourses are power relations *in practice* and must be understood as an "*ascending* analysis of power" (Foucault 1980: 99) (original emphasis), he does not provide conceptual tools for understanding these micro-practices of power/knowledge. The genealogical method does not show how these macro-patterns and categories are "accomplished" (Dingwall 1976) as 'outcomes' of particular ("invisible") practices (Pithouse 1987; Scott 1989) between social workers and other professionals in interaction with 'family' members.

Instead, Foucault's main focus was on a macro-analysis of discourses as structures and rules for social practice (Dreyfus & Rabinow 1982: viii; Jupp & Norris 1993: 39). He relied on official texts as data by which to generate his Theory of Knowledge: for example, in relation to madness (1965), prisons (1977) and sexuality (1978a). However, he did not investigate the interpersonal processes by which these identities were constructed (Dreyfus & Rabinow 1982: viii), which is the primary aim of this book. Therefore, I now turn to Bourdieu to provide another piece of my methodological lens, through his concepts of capital and symbolic power, and linguistic communities.

## Reading and writing through Bourdieu: Capital and symbolic power, and linguistic communities

### Capital and symbolic power

Bourdieu's anthropologically generated Theory of Practice addresses human interactions within broader cultural contexts, social rules and power relations (Bourdieu 1990; 1991; Jenkins 1992). Language is both social practice and a currency of power within relationships. Participants engaged in linguistic exchanges are given status and legitimacy according to the symbolic value given to the "capital" that each brings to the transaction, thus also constituting each participant's "symbolic power" (Bourdieu 1990, 1991; Jenkins 1992).

To make a somewhat tenuous theoretical connection between Foucault and Bourdieu, I have read Bourdieu's concept of "capital and symbolic power" as equivalent to Foucault's concept of "discourse", where knowledge and power are integrally related. Capital is a composite of cultural, economic, social, linguistic and symbolic attributes, whereby an individual or group's status may depend on combinations of the various forms of capital. For example, someone with a lot of economic capital (wealth) may also accumulate greater social, linguistic and symbolic capital (as the power to be heard, to be influential and to be validated). Bourdieu & Passeron (1990) give the example of differences in capital and symbolic power in relation to education, and the inequalities in participation and outcomes in relation to class and ethnicity. Hence, participants in an interaction about an allegation of child maltreatment may be positioned differently in relation to perceptions of capital and symbolic power, with potential consequences for the case processes and outcomes. For example, a parent's challenge to a professional's allegations that a child has been maltreated by the parent may not be given credence if the parent is seen as less knowledgeable, if he or she is on a low income or is poorly educated (limited economic and social capital). These differences may be intensified if the parent is from a minority ethnic group or has a disability. Child protection practitioners may also be familiar with the opposite scenario where parents who are wealthy and have access to good lawyers (greater economic and social capital) may be able to challenge successfully professionals' cultural and symbolic capital in relation to their parenting practices.

### Linguistic communities

Bourdieu contributes to an understanding of social groups as "linguistic communities" (1991: 45), and the relationship between language as representation (knowledge about 'reality') and formulation of cultural rules, identities and social practices. For example, Bourdieu described how men and women in Kabyle society were associated with different parts of houses and times of day, these daily practices structuring gender relations materially and symbolically (Bourdieu 1977,

1990; Jenkins 1992: 30–5). A very useful illustrative example was the ways in which the doors to and spaces in people's homes had particular names and were associated with times of day. More importantly, these apparently neutral physical structures called 'doors' and 'spaces' also structured (made rules about) gender relationships in the community and within families. The concept of linguistic communities has informed the analysis in chapter 5. This chapter shows how organisational policies and procedures structured practice at each office but cultural rules in each context represented the purpose of child protection practice differently with consequences for case outcomes and the children, parents and families who received services.

**The limitations of Bourdieu**

Bourdieu's theories were generated through anthropological observation and his immersion in cultures. He theorised social practices as power relations, expressed in language and interactions between individuals and groups. However, he does not discuss *how* particular discursive capital (knowledge) is produced through language: that is, how language itself operates as both a device of knowledge and a device of power in interactions between people. For this, I turn to Potter's (1996) compilation of linguistic resources known as "rhetorical devices" by which people "represent reality".

### Reading and writing through Potter: a compilation of rhetorical devices

Language is the way in which knowledge about social 'reality' is represented, through naming and giving meaning to human experiences and the material world. However, this linguistic process of meaning making or "representing reality" (Potter 1996) is also associated with social relations of power, through rhetorical devices. Potter has compiled a range of rhetorical devices giving "an overview of the main traditions of fact construction: the sociology of scientific knowledge [Knorr Cetina], ... ethnomethodology and conversation analysis [Sacks, Smith], and the 'structural tradition' of semiology, post-structuralism and postmodernism" (Potter 1996: 1). Potter discusses how rhetorical devices, as devices of power and persuasion and expressions of "practical epistemology", are deployed by participants in different contexts to construct and legitimate particular meanings and identities, simultaneously destroying other versions (Potter 1996: 112–13). Through discourse analysis of talk and texts, it is possible to extend ethnographic understandings to how accounts are "established as literal and objective, and what it is being used to do" (Potter 1996: 105–6). The main rhetorical devices that have been relevant to the analyses of case practices (chapters 6 to 8), represented in interview transcripts with practitioners and case files, are set out below.

## Some rhetorical devices and their applications

Consistent with the previous discussions about knowledge/power and identity (Foucault), and capital and symbolic power (Bourdieu), the speaker's identity constitutes a personal and group "stake and interest" (Potter 1996: 122–32) and "category entitlements [to knowledge]" (Potter 1996: 132–42). *Stake and interest* linked to identity – for example, 'person believed responsible' – may be deployed to destruct a version, as 'self-interested', not 'independent'. *Category entitlement* also associated with identity – for example, 'mother', 'child as victim', 'doctor'– allows for particular knowledge claims to be made from socially or institutionally legitimated positions. These devices construct the participant as a particular identity in the context of the case (Potter 1996: 115), and influence how participants may validate each other, and each other's knowledge and expertise, as capital (Potter 1996: 114).

Other persuasive devices rely on representations of events or participants through "categorization", "extrematization" and "minimization", and "normalization" and "abnormalization" (Potter 1996: 176–201). *Categorisation*, which names events or identities in particular ways, may ". . . hav[e] various implications and consequences" (Potter 1996: 177) by setting in train particular processes that build up the version as 'truth' and thereby preclude or exclude other versions. For example, Smith (1990a) in "K is mentally ill" shows how the opening categorisation of 'K *as* mentally ill' is then constructed into a version that 'K *is* mentally ill'.

"Extrematization" or "extreme-cases" (Potter 1996: 187–92), as persuasive devices, justify, accuse or argue for particular conclusions as being the only possible outcomes. *Extreme-cases* can be constructed by using extreme descriptions and "modalizing terms" (Potter 1996: 188): for example, "everybody", "never", "always", "quantification" (numbers, statistics).

Individuals' identities may be made acceptable (legitimated) or not through "*normalization*" and "*abnormalization*" (Potter 1996: 194–9): how "individuals and groups . . . [present] their own and others' actions as normal and natural, or as unwarranted, deviant or problematic" (Potter 1996: 177). Descriptive devices that achieve these identity constructions include "contrast structures" (Smith 1990a; Potter 1996: 194–5) and "three-part lists" (Potter 1996: 195–7).

*Contrast structures* construct abnormality by showing how the participant's behaviour is contextually anomalous by breaching the rules of 'normal' behaviour. Smith (1990a: 32) generalises these rules as "do such and such" and its logical but equally normative opposite, "do not do such and such". *Three-part lists* appear to be conventional devices used "to summarize some general class of things" (Potter 1996: 196), as representing either normality or abnormality of identity and knowledge claims by generating a list of three apparently related items as typical of the category.

Another strategy by which some versions of knowledge may be made more plausible (and others destroyed) is through "externalizing devices" (Potter 1996: 150–74), which aim to separate the 'fact' from the 'observer' as a means of achieving 'objectivity'. Examples of *externalizing devices* are "empiricist discourse", "corroboration and consensus" and "detail and narrative". These three techniques give the impression of "objectivity" and therefore "truth", rather than "subjectivity", influenced by participant's "stake and interest".

*Empiricist discourse* deploys technical language that achieves "fact agency" (Potter 1996: 158): colloquially, the 'facts speak for themselves' – for example, scientific knowledge or medical reports that suggest that the participants are dispassionate observers of 'truth' rather than implicated in constructing 'truth' from what is observed.

*Corroboration and consensus* rely on cumulative witnessing to strengthen the version being constructed, especially if witnesses are perceived as "independent", ("objective", with minimal "stake and interest"), rather than "collusive" (for example, a mother and her male partner who may be accused of maltreating their children).

*Narrative complexity and detail* that gives "access to the scene" (Potter 1996: 165) operates to build the authoritative version. Faller's (1988b) "criteria for judging the credibility of children's statements about sexual abuse" is a specific and formalised example of this device.

### The limitations of Potter

Whilst rhetorical devices operate as devices of power and persuasion about 'truth', Potter represents them as techniques available to, and deployed by, participants equally: for example, how a husband and wife represent their versions of the wife's behaviour in a pub. Potter does not represent rhetorical devices as resources that also reflect the potential or actual inequalities between participants related to different capital and symbolic power.

I argue that rhetorical techniques are devices of power, connecting particular and situated practices to 'structure', represented as "discourse" (Foucault 1972) or "capital" (Bourdieu 1990, 1991):

> [D]iscourses are not "unlocated universes of meaning" (Rodger, 1991: 68). Instead, the deployment of rhetorical devices in the practical construction of meanings and identities must be located within cultural, structural and discursive contexts of identity. For example, a mother's practices in relation to her child are embedded and understood within the cultural idealization of mothering (Rose, 1989), not solely as a specific and situated incident. Capital associated with particular identities as "sites of power" (Barrett, 1987) is differentially allocated (Bourdieu, 1990, 1991), along with the distribution of opportunities to deploy rhetorical devices: for example, the processes of exclusion of "abnormals" or

"deviants" from construction of legitimate accounts (Smith, 1990a). The privileging of particular constructions over others is also not just a feature of rhetorical techniques (as power neutral), but contingent on the relations of power by which different versions are validated or not, depending on the identities and positionings of participants (Barrett, 1987). (D'Cruz 2001: 25)

Rhetorical devices are understood as the linguistic resources that people use in everyday and more formal interactions as ways of 'representing reality' rather than 'reality' being an objective fact, separated from social and linguistic interactions. Knowledge about linguistic resources in 'constructing reality' has been generated through studies of taped and transcribed conversations in various settings (Sacks 1992; Silverman 1998; Potter & Wetherell 1987; Hutchby & Wooffitt 1998). However, an unresolved question for me is how people 'know' to use linguistic devices to achieve the outcomes in which knowledge and power are linked at a level of everyday interactions. We do not formally learn "how to do things with words" (Austin 1975), so how do we know? If it is 'just something we know' akin to Chomksy's "deep structure" in language development (Potter 1996: 169), then is this a deterministic way of understanding the connections between subject and object, structure and agency? However, within these methodological puzzles, which have been debated at length (Potter 1996; Hutchby & Wooffitt 1998), the case analysis in chapters 6 to 8 has support from similar analyses (Potter 1996; Potter & Wetherell 1987; Taylor & White 2000; Silverman 1998; Sacks 1992; Smith 1990a; Hutchby & Wooffitt 1998).

## My fractured lens: Foucault, Bourdieu, Potter (and others)

In this section I have summarised the construction of my 'fractured methodological lens' from three primary sources: Foucault, Bourdieu and Potter, linking key concepts from each: for example, versions of knowledge intersecting with power, as "discourse" (Foucault 1972, 1978a, 1978b, 1980), "capital" (Bourdieu 1990, 1991) and "rhetorical devices" (Potter 1996). Language structures discursive/ social relations, and represents and legitimates some knowledge claims, de-legitimating others (Foucault 1972, 1980; Bourdieu 1991). Potter connects both Foucault and Bourdieu by his focus on language as a device of power/knowledge to construct meanings and identities in social practices. Holstein & Gubrium (1994: 262–72) discuss similar approaches to research – for example, Gubrium (1986), Miller (1991), Loeske (1992) – that link "micro and macro level concerns" within organisational and "collective representations", drawing on "new analytic resources":

> New analytic resources are being mobilized... for example... Foucauldian insights into overarching collective representations and discourse structures are linked to local interpretive procedures... linkages between ostensibly micro- and macro-level

concerns ... to explicate more fully the roles of discourse, conversational structure, and the content and context of interactional exchanges. (Holstein & Gubrium 1994: 269–70)

Whilst Foucault, Bourdieu and Potter comprise the primary pieces of my fractured lens, I have filled in the fractures with slivers and fragments from other writers, particularly identity and power as positioned subjectivities (for example, Barrett 1987; Stanley & Wise 1993; Brah 1992; Weedon 1999) to construct an incomplete version of 'reality'.

## SOCIAL CONSTRUCTIONISM AND RELATIVISM

Social constructionism is criticised for its "epistemological and ethical relativism" (Smart 1993: 103), whereby all knowledge and ways of knowing are seen as relative. There is no absolute truth (a statement that in itself is contradictory in its absolutism!). Nonetheless, it is possible to use social constructionism as a fascinating intellectual exercise and puzzle about social processes and their outcomes. However, as a former social work practitioner and now a social work academic, I could not justify a purely relativist position in relation to ontology (the nature of reality and social problems) and epistemology (how we know about reality and social problems). I wanted to critique the policies and practices as necessary to professional accountability, but not in a way that ignored the role of child protection practitioners in responding to the legal, moral and ethical imperatives associated with child maltreatment.

The approach that seemed to best address these intellectual and moral questions was to juxtapose normally polarised concepts of "realism" and "relativism" (Edwards, Ashmore & Potter 1995) through "dualism" (Heap 1995). Usually, realism (best associated with current child protection knowledge as objective and absolute) and relativism (best associated with social constructionism) are seen as mutually exclusive. A dualist position acknowledges that there is a material reality but that meaning that is given and negotiated between participants may incorporate the relativist aspects of knowledge and power. A "monist" position (Heap 1995), on the other hand, would see all 'reality' as 'relative' constructions. A dualist position recognises children's lived experiences, manifested as bodily abnormalities and even death, whilst simultaneously recognising that the child protection process involves engagement with multiple, relative and potentially equally plausible meanings, with particular meanings accepted as legitimate and valid while others are not. This research has explored this process of constructing meanings and identities as legitimate professional knowledge.

## SOCIAL WORK RESEARCH AS KNOWLEDGE/POWER IN PRACTICE

This research, which explores how meanings and identities are constructed as micro-practices in particular cases, centralises language in regard to how 'reality' is represented as knowledge, as the currency of social practices, and as devices of power. This section summarises the methods of inquiry by which the aims of the research were achieved. However, it is essential to point out that the research process and its outcomes are not neutral procedures and techniques of inquiry, but instead political processes of knowledge construction. I have written about these processes through a reflective and reflexive analysis of "social work research as knowledge/power in practice" (D'Cruz 2000). Research as knowledge/power in practice shows how research processes and outcomes cannot and do not represent objective facts and truths, partly because the researcher is positioned in particular ways, as I have discussed above (Stanley & Wise 1993; Riessman 1994; Marcus 1994: 571–2). These 'positionings' have influenced how the research has been conceptualised, designed, analysed and reported (Guba & Lincoln 1982: 248; Stanley & Wise 1993: 186–233; Marcus 1994: 568–73; Kincheloe & McLaren 1994: 152). Additionally, identities that have explicitly and implicitly positioned me in relation to the research and in my engagement with key informants and gatekeepers may initially be expressed as a "formulaic incantation" (Marcus 1994: 572). I am a non-white, visibly ethnic, heterosexual, forty something, relatively able-bodied woman, and an immigrant to Australia. My identities and those of stakeholders (gatekeepers and informants) have been engaged in complex relations of power by which knowledge has been constructed (Burgess 1984; Smart 1988, in Everitt et al. 1992: 87; Humphries & Martin 2000; Byrne-Armstrong 2001). Thus, procedures such as sampling, interviewing and gaining access, which are normally represented as neutral techniques, are instead discussed below as expressions of knowledge/power between myself as the researcher and various participants and stakeholders in the research process (D'Cruz 2000). As 'knowledge/power in practice', research is also influenced by concepts of representation, the de-centred subject, *'différance'*, and "writing" (Hassard 1993).

The concept of *representation* understands knowledge as symbolic and relativist, rather than actual and realist, as understood in child protection. All knowledge claims are positioned, political and partial, not objective or absolute truths. "Our knowledge of the world is constructed as a problem of 'representation' rather than one of factual accuracy." (Hassard 1993: 12). This concept informs my engagement with the literature, policies, case files and key informants – as representing different versions of knowledge, and is expressed through acknowledgment of my positioning as discussed above. It is also practised through "active interviews" (Holstein & Gubrium 1995) and recognition that documents are "socially constructed realities" (Smith 1974), as further discussed below.

Through *de-centring the subject*, words cease to be linked to the authority of speakers and assumptions of single, privileged meanings. Instead, meaning becomes more open and fluid, allowing relative positions (Hassard 1993: 15). *Différance* is a deferral of meaning (no fixed version) that accounts for difference (as relative meanings). Both assumptions are espoused in this research and the claims made. This concept allows for continual questioning of what is normally represented through mutually exclusive categories expressed as binaries (pairs), where one of the pair is 'better' than the other (Fraser 1997; Hassard 1993: 10–11): for example, 'maltreatment'–'not maltreatment', 'person believed responsible'–'not responsible'. These binary categories may not be so distinct in practice. The boundaries between them may seem blurred and shifting and therefore represent potential confusion *and* opportunities for discretion. The construction of meanings and identities in practice depends on the positioning of participants in negotiating the categories and the shifting boundaries between them.

## Methods of inquiry

The aims of exploring how meanings and identities were constructed in child protection practice relied on a range of triangulation strategies to achieve theoretical generalisability (Bryman 1988: 131–4; Mason 1994: 104). The design combined "multiple observers, theoretical perspectives, sources of data and methodologies" (Denzin 1970, in Bryman 1988: 131), similar to Corby (1987); Dingwall, Eekelaar & Murray (1983); and Rojiani (1994). The aim of understanding how meanings and identities are constructed in practice was achieved through reading sampled case files, interviewing practitioners who were the case managers at the time of the interview and transcribing the taped interviews. A discourse analysis of these data, drawing primarily on rhetorical devices (Potter 1996), is re-presented in chapters 6 to 8.

Subsidiary questions relating to the social organisation of child protection practice and the construction of knowledge as organisational layers are addressed through discourse analysis (Foucault 1972, 1977, 1978a; Fairclough 1992) of literature (chapter 3) and a genealogy of policy as discourse (Foucault 1978b) (chapter 4). The genealogy relies on published texts by historians and anthropologists; official documents available on public record (for example, Western Australian Parliamentary Debates, annual reports and policies); and organisational archives (for example, memoranda by long-serving staff, minutes of meetings). Additionally, the analysis of policy changes from 1972 to 'the present' is informed partially by my own observations and participation as an employee of the organisation from 1979 to 1996.

Through participant observation at two community-based offices (re-named as Urbania and Suburbia), cultural constructions of organisational policies and procedures are re-presented as ethnographies of "linguistic communities" (Bourdieu 1990, 1991) (chapter 5). Participant observation included access to informal interactions in the 'staff common areas' such as staff rooms, photocopying rooms and waiting rooms; and formal interactions such as case conferences and pre-trial conferences. In this way I was able to observe the usually "invisible" worker–client interactions, which I could not otherwise have done (Burgess 1984). I also observed interviews between practitioners and clients who came to the office without appointments or on matters unrelated to active cases. This process was known as "doing duty". Additionally, I interviewed managers, senior casework supervisors, team leaders and practitioners who would not otherwise be interviewed because their cases had not been selected for the case sample. I also attended training programs and other professional activities, which gave me insights into connections between situated practice and policy prescriptions.

It is recognised that an analysis of practices in a particular child welfare/child protection organisation cannot be exactly compared to, or generalised across, other similar organisations, or even within the same organisation at a different time. This is because the context (time and place) may change some substantive details: for example, legislation or policies. However, at the same time, it is recognised that it is possible to make generalisable claims related to theoretical propositions and contextual transferability (Guba & Lincoln 1982: 247; Schofield 1993: 203–21). The concepts, processes and outcomes are generalisable, offering insights into professional knowledge and power, and organisational policies and practices in relation to a controversial field of social policy and social work practice: child protection. The analysis also offers lessons for practice from each case, even though every case is, of course, different. It is also important to recognise that I did not directly observe and record verbatim the interactions between workers and clients in the sampled cases, but had to rely on records of past and sometimes current events and on how these were reconstructed to me by practitioners in the interviews. However, a study in which I as researcher could sit in and observe the direct interactions in a child protection case posed many serious ethical and legal problems. Ethically it seemed quite intrusive for me to be only an observer of a process that is normally quite distressing for parents and children. Also there were legal implications, including whether or not my field notes or audio-tapes for research purposes could be subpoenaed if court action was taken, either to prosecute the parents or to place the child under state guardianship. Hence, the approach taken seemed to be a reasonable compromise.

### Personal positioning and negotiating, maintaining and terminating access

Negotiating, maintaining and terminating access to sites, documents and informants is part of the ethical process of research (Burgess 1984). The researcher seeks particular outcomes, such as informed consent of participants, and establishes the limits of access to informants, sites and privileged documents (Hall & Hall 1996: 17; Burgess 1984: 38–40; Lindlof 1995: 106–10 in Hall & Hall, 1996: 17). However, through the process of 'access', the researcher is positioned as a participant/observer, whereby negotiations with gatekeepers and key informants and their outcomes become 'data'. These data must be accounted for as part of the validation of the research process, because 'access' is not a neutral concept but is only permitted to researchers under particular conditions that reflect the exercise of power by gatekeepers (Arber 1993). Hence, the data generated are entirely related to the degree of access permitted and this has consequences for the analysis and outcomes.

### Accessing 'professionals' – achieving participation and consent

My professional experiences (Burgess 1984: 89) and "occupational identity" (Chandler 1990: 128) gave me some advantages in conducting research in my employing organisation. For example, I could access a "familiar system" (Burgess 1984: 47) and colleagues who might be cooperative to the extent of giving me unrestricted access to 'reliable, valid and credible knowledge'. In return, I gave a commitment that the organisation would not be exploited and would benefit from the research (Hall & Hall 1996: 18). I also minimised potential pressure to conform to an agency agenda (Burgess 1984: 47–8) by undertaking the research in unpaid time outside work, except for a few days granted for data collection. I hoped that this independence would minimise colleagues' anxieties and suspicions (Burgess 1984: 47–8) but, for some gatekeepers and informants, I was a "spy" (Burgess 1984: 50; Bhopal 2000: 73) on behalf of the organisation.

When negotiating access to Suburbia in 1993, my role as the organisational research officer added a complication. I was researching child protection intake practices at the request of a regional director who was responsible for Suburbia and four other community-based offices in his region. My role in this research enhanced my expertise for this director, but simultaneously created anxiety for workers at Suburbia who had been the focus of a coroner's inquiry into a child's death.

Thus, maintaining independence for 'my' research meant I had to undertake most of the negotiation process without powerful sponsors negotiating on my behalf. In seeking access to the two practice sites, practitioners at those sites and related documents such as case files, I engaged in a protracted process through a "hierarchy of consent" (Burgess 1984: 195). In addition to gaining formal permission from organisational gatekeepers, I had to negotiate "multiple access points" (Burgess 1984: 48) to sites (Burgess 1982: 120–1), and to different informants (Hall & Hall 1996: 18; Chandler 1990: 125).

The particular cultures at Urbania and Suburbia and perceptions about me influenced the collective 'willingness' to grant access. Both rounds of data generation (1993 and 1995) involved similar processes of negotiation (D'Cruz 2000: paragraphs 5.1–6.6) throughout the hierarchy of consent (Burgess 1984: 195). Negotiating access included written summaries of the research supported by letters of consent from gatekeepers higher up in the hierarchy, phone discussions with gatekeepers at practice sites and attendance at staff meetings to explain the research, protection of anonymity and voluntary participation (Burgess 1984; Chandler 1990) and to answer questions. However, in 1993 I confined my request for access solely to practitioners and case files/local policy documents to minimise concerns about disruption and intrusiveness. In 1995 I hoped that ten days of participant observation at each site would also be acceptable, in addition to accessing files and workers.

During the participant observation process, I provided weekly feedback sheets to minimise "potential hostility" (Fuller & Petch 1995: 49), promote basic "honesty and openness" and keep people "informed about progress" (Fuller & Petch 1995: 49). The feedback sheets summarised, in two to three handwritten pages, my completed and proposed activities and observations. My observations were contextualised as those of an outsider to local knowledge, and I invited clarification by informants. In general, these feedback sheets significantly eased tensions and anxieties about my presence. Additional strategies that aimed to ease anxieties and maintain relationships with informants (D'Cruz 2000: paragraphs 7.8, 7.11) have also been discussed by Bryman (1988); Oakley (1981, in Hall & Hall 1996: 177) and Burgess (1984: 49).

### Accessing clients – issues of participation and consent

During the negotiation of access I considered whether clients' consent should be sought, as I would have access to their files. While clients' identities would be concealed in the analysis, my concern related to whether they would be treated as objects in the research process and an extension of oppressive power/knowledge in practice.

My proposals that practitioners could seek clients' consent for access to their files on my behalf were rejected by senior departmental managers and experts on ethics from the Australian Association of Social Workers. They cited the potential for distress to clients in 'closed' cases, the blurring of 'coercion' and 'consent' in 'active' cases, and increased workload for staff. Furthermore, they argued that as a departmental employee I automatically had access to clients' files (D'Cruz 2000: paragraphs 4.4 – 4.5). There was no legal requirement to seek clients' consent as, for example, in British legislation (Broad 1994). Hence, I was obliged to accept gatekeepers' views that seeking clients' consent to access their files would create more problems than it would solve.

### Sampling

The practice sites, cases and workers were selected through non-probability sampling to meet the aims of theoretical generalisability (Arber 1993). The two practice sites, renamed here as Urbania and Suburbia, were selected opportunistically/judgmentally (Burgess 1984: 55; Honigman 1982: 80), based on personal

Methodology – Addressing a complex practice reality | 31

knowledge as a long-term employee of the organisation about particular aspects such as population and community features, and staff characteristics.

The sampling process was related to gatekeepers' perceptions of the research and to situated cultural differences at different times, thus influencing access in particular ways. The sample of cases and practitioners is summarised in table 2.1, Cases by type of maltreatment; table 2.2, Practitioners by sex; and table 2.3, Practitioners by occupational group.

| Type of maltreatment | Urbania 1993 | Suburbia 1993 |
|---|---|---|
| Sexual abuse | 4 (Allston, Blake, Constable, Eakins) | 0 |
| Physical abuse | 2 (Davis, Francis) | 1 (Gilman) |
| Emotional abuse | 0 | 1 (Hamilton) |
| Neglect | | |
| Subtotal | 6 | 2 |
| Type of maltreatment | Urbania 1995 | Suburbia 1995 |
| Sexual abuse | 3 (Jones, Lewis, Martini) | 1 (Underwood) |
| Physical abuse | 1 (Ibsen) | 2 (O'Keefe, Riley) |
| Emotional abuse | 0 | 0 |
| Neglect | 2 (Kelly, Nicholson) | 1 (Park) |
| At risk | | 2 (Quinn, Turner) |
| Subtotal | 6 | 6 |
| Total | 12 | 8 |

Table 2.1: Cases by type of maltreatment (sites and years) – anonymised family names in brackets

| Practitioners' sex | Urbania 1993 | Suburbia 1993 |
|---|---|---|
| female | 1 | 2 (a) |
| male | 1 | 0 |
| **Subtotal** | **2** | **2** |
| **Practitioners' sex** | **Urbania 1995** | **Suburbia 1995** |
| female | 3 | 4 (a) (b) |
| male | 3 | 1 |
| **Subtotal** | **6** | **5** |
| **Total** | **8** | **7 (a)** |

Table 2.2: Practitioners by sex (sites and years)

*Note:* *(a) one worker was interviewed in 1993 re the Gilman family and in 1995 re the Riley family*
*(b) one worker identified as Aboriginal*

| Practitioners' occupational group | Urbania 1993 | Suburbia 1993 |
|---|---|---|
| Senior Social Worker | 0 | 2 (a) |
| Social Worker | 1 | 0 |
| Family Welfare Officer | 1 | 0 |
| **Subtotal** | **2** | **2 (a)** |
| **Practitioners' occupational group** | **Urbania 1995** | **Suburbia 1995** |
| Senior Social Worker | 2 (a, b) | 1 (a) |
| Social Worker | 3 | 3 |
| Family Welfare Officer | 1 | 1 |
| **Subtotal** | **5** | **5** |
| **Total** | **8 (a, b)** | **7 (a)** |

Table 2.3: Practitioners by occupational group (sites and years)

*Note:* *(a) usually Senior Social Worker (Child Protection)*
*(b) One worker was known as Senior Social Worker ('generic') (that is she was not a Child Protection worker)*

In 1993 selection of four cases and two caseworkers each from Urbania and Suburbia depended partly on what/who was accessible although I was given access to a list of cases and case managers. The remaining 12 cases and 11 practitioners were selected by different sampling processes at each site in 1995 that seemed to represent cultural differences. At Urbania, I selected cases by systematic theoretical sampling (Mason 1994; Bryman 1988) from a list of all cases classified as 'maltreatment' over a three-month intake period. At Suburbia, after I had explained the theoretical sampling approach, the manager and acting senior casework supervisor selected the cases (and workers) for me as 'typical' of the work at that site: 'dangerous' and 'contentious'. These observations of the relationship between practices by gatekeepers and research processes such as sampling are political processes in how knowledge is constructed in research (D'Cruz 2000: paragraphs 6.3–6.4).

## Data generation/analysis: engagement with key informants, sites and documents

### Participant observation: engaging within the practice sites as linguistic communities

A researcher who is a participant observer at locations where she is not usually located may occupy a range of identities that encapsulate the transition from "the outsider" or "stranger" to "the insider" (Atkinson 1990). These identities are categorised by Jones (1961, in Burgess 1984: 84) as "newcomer", "provisional acceptance", "categorical acceptance", "personal acceptance" and "imminent immigrant". The cultures at Urbania and Suburbia influenced how I was perceived and relationships that developed between participants at each office and myself. At both sites I was more an "observer-as-participant" rather than "participant-as-observer" (Gold 1958, in Burgess 1984: 80–2), because I was perceived as not sufficiently competent to engage as a 'participant' in the primary work. For example, my offers to undertake social work practice through 'doing duty', similar to Burgess's (1984: 40) participation as a teacher, were declined. I was told it would create more work because I would have to be supervised closely. However, like Burgess (1984: 85–6), I achieved a measure of competence at Urbania as 'social work researcher', whilst at Suburbia, I remained a 'visitor'.

At Urbania my identity changed from "newcomer" to "provisional acceptance" (Jones 1961, in Burgess 1984: 84) by the majority, as illustrated when my notes from observing an interview were used for casework in the absence of other information. My "categorical acceptance" (Jones 1961, in Burgess 1984: 84) was shown by achieving a measure of competence, like Burgess (1984: 85–6), as a 'knowledgeable researcher'. I was also told case information voluntarily (Cole 1991: 162); and some practitioners took the opportunity to discuss their social work experiences with someone who was both insider and outsider.

At Suburbia my identities remained at the initial "phases" of "newcomer" and "provisional acceptance". The emphasis was on my 'ignorance' rather than my social work identity, disrupting my apparently more powerful identity as 'researcher'. Examples of these experiences as they relate to age (Burgess 1984: 89–90; Chandler 1990: 128) and ethnic identity as "colour of skin" (Burgess 1984: 91–2) have been discussed in D'Cruz (2000: paragraphs 7.4, 7.6). These experiences of insider and outsider identity operated as signposts in developing an understanding of each site as a linguistic community (Bourdieu 1990, 1991). They offered insights into how each culture perceived differences in identity, especially in relation to those who were 'outsiders' as I was, and presumably clients would be.

As a "foreign presence" (Stanley & Wise 1993: 158–9) at both sites, I was self-conscious about 'sitting in' on various activities while listening but saying very little to avoid appearing judgmental, unlike Cole (1991: 159–64). I had to carefully time when I asked questions of clarification. This contrasted with my ongoing presence at my usual work location or at conferences or seminars, where I was both participant and observer, the latter being covert to participants. As organisational research officer, my observations of policy, research and evaluation issues in relation to child protection provided broader organisational insights into localised practice issues.

### Interviewing child protection practitioners/case managers

The interviews were understood as "active" processes (Holstein & Gubrium 1995) or "guided conversations" (Fielding 1993: 136). The assumption that the researcher and the informant are in an "asymmetrical" relationship (Chandler 1990: 129), because the former asks the questions and the latter answers them, is held in tension with the possibility that the informant can also exercise power in the relationship. The most basic exercise of power by informants is in how each shares the "special knowledge" (Chandler 1990: 129) that is sought by the researcher through the questions that are asked. Informants may withhold their knowledge in various ways, including refusal to answer questions, making partial or misleading responses, and so on (Smart 1988: 42–3, in Everitt et al. 1992: 87). For example, one worker, consented to be interviewed, but refused to provide details about her country of birth and ethnicity, or permission to tape-record the interview.

Interviews with practitioners about the sampled cases began and ended with discussions of protection of anonymity and "reassurance" (Chandler 1990; Fuller & Petch 1995: 49), informed consent, including audio-taping (Burgess 1984: 40; Hall & Hall 1996: 161–4) with handwritten notes also taken. The right of refusal was also offered but, as Burgess (1984: 197) comments, this is "seldom taken up".

My shared identities (Burgess 1984: 41) as former social work practitioner, employee and colleague helped in engaging with interview participants/ practitioners. I was able to discuss the organisation, policies and practices in a knowledgeable way (Burgess 1984: 41, 89; Chandler 1990: 128). Simultaneously, differences between the practitioners and myself related to the different contexts of our experiences in the organisation. Firstly, I had been a casework practitioner between 1979 and 1983 with a different policy context, and the practitioners/informants were practising in the 1990s. Their practice and mine was demarcated by the 1985 Welfare and Community Services Review, whose recommendations for 'child protection' to replace 'child welfare' significantly altered the policy context. Secondly, during the interviews my role in the organisation was as a policy researcher, not a practitioner. Therefore I needed the practitioners' "special knowledge" (Chandler 1990: 129) about their practice. Thus, I was able to present myself as not totally ignorant of the contemporary context, and could ask legitimate but possibly naive questions: an "acceptable incompetent" (Lofland 1971, in Pithouse 1987: 125), or "ignorant" inquirer (Chandler 1990: 127).

Interviews with workers were structured by three themes. The *first theme*, 'talk about yourself', sought information on how the worker's gender, age, ethnicity, culture, religion and qualifications might influence how they practised as a child protection worker (Truman & Humphries 1994). I deliberately but unwillingly did not enquire about workers' disability and sexuality. I did not want these topics to provide excuses for refusing me access to the sites and workers, especially as asking about religion received an angry response from Suburbia when I was negotiating access in 1993. This had been seen as intrusive. However, I knew from lesbian colleagues' stories and managers' reluctance to employ people with disabilities that both homosexuality and disability were marginal identities for employees and possibly also for clients. Nonetheless, the implicit assumptions that 'heterosexuality' and 'ability' are normative identities have emerged in how practitioners constructed meanings and identities at their local offices, and in case practices discussed in chapters 5 to 8.

In addition to my occupational identities discussed above, I also engaged with practitioners/informants in relation to gender – theirs and mine (Burgess 1984: 90; Smart 1988: 42–3, in Everitt et al. 1992: 87). As a woman interviewing women practitioners, I shared with the interviewees a gendered identity that was also differentiated because we did not share ethnicity or cultural identities (Bhopal 2000: 71–3). Thus, knowledge generation in the interviews could be both points of connection and difference that could be actively explored (Holstein & Gubrium 1995; Phellas 2000: 52–64). Gender differences facilitated discussions with men, when I expressed my interest in how those differences gave different knowledge. Most of the workers discussed at length how their identities as men and women connected to their discursive understandings and practices in relation to men, women and children as clients.

Ethnic differences between researchers and informants is discussed by Burgess (1984: 91–2) as "linguistic problems" between "black and white", and "colour of skin" separating "insiders" and "outsiders". The advice that is given in addressing these differences assumes that the researcher is 'white, English speaking' and the informants are 'black, non-English speaking'. In my case this was partially reversed, because although I am not white I speak fluent English, my only language. These complexities in ethnic difference generated some interesting insights. Most informants became anxious when asked about their ethnic and cultural identities. White, Anglo-Saxon/Celtic informants (the majority of respondents) perceived ethnicity as 'other', that they personally 'did not have an ethnic identity' or that it was an irrelevant question for them (hooks 1981; Frankenberg 1993). However, the few workers who were white, western European immigrants had little trouble with this question. After I explained how ethnicity/culture might be relevant to practice, using my practice experiences as an example, most workers gave considered responses, some in extensive detail. Unfortunately, in one case, a white woman interpreted my example as meaning that I had difficulties working with people of other ethnic backgrounds, which she did not, prompting her to dismiss the question about her ethnicity as irrelevant.

Most workers reconstructed the question about the influence of their age on their practice as 'life experience' or 'qualifications'. 'Qualifications' as part of the first interview theme were understood by informants as a social work identity. For example, a practitioner who was not a social worker, claimed he was not (seen as) 'qualified' by the organisation until encouraged to think beyond social work to qualifications he considered relevant. Some practitioners justified their 'non-social worker' identity as temporary. One practitioner esponded that a social work qualification was unimportant at Suburbia, as the "only real question [she] was asked [at the job interview] was how did [she] feel about taking children away from their parents". Five social workers equated their qualifications to years of experience since graduation. They spoke of their varied experiences as social workers, especially as child protection workers. Others included prior employment and social work identity as qualifications. All these versions of knowledgeable identities of self (and by implication, others) required different strategies by me to encourage, reassure and validate informants' contributions.

The *second theme* was an open-ended question about informants' perceptions of their roles in child protection as a variation of the structured questions on "role orientation" in research on how pathologists responded to sudden infant death cases (Ballenden, Laster & Lawrence 1993). This caused a great deal of anxiety, many seeing it as a trick or trap. Most answered with concrete descriptions, such as 'hard', 'difficult' or 'challenging'.

The *third theme*, 'talking about the case' was based on some prepared questions to begin the discussion about all the cases, enhanced by additional questions related to issues emerging from my reading of the case files prior to the interviews. This particular section of the interviews was a process fraught with problems. I represented a pseudo-supervisor asking for details of practice, which normally would only be given to superiors within a carefully preserved identity of competence (Pithouse 1987). I also asked awkward questions which the worker(s) had either not thought about previously or preferred not to discuss: for example, in the

Gilman case how it came about that, although both biological parents were reported for physical abuse, only the mother was interviewed (D'Cruz 2002a: paragraphs 8.12–8.13). Or why it was that in a clearly violent family context, such as the Underwood family, the worker had never interviewed the mother on her own? I had to disguise the intent and tone of the questions, including posing as ignorant and naive, to avoid offence or judgment (not always possible), while still pursuing clearly important theoretical issues for the research. My identity as social worker precluded responses that were implausible, yet workers could and did avoid responding. My being 'less knowledgeable' in relation to them as child protection workers complicated the relationship, some workers communicating their perceptions of my 'ignorance' by their patronising and exasperated tones.

However, the benefits of the interviews for at least some workers – for example, as opportunities to "reflect-on-action", particularly by their "stimulation by surprise" (Schon 1988: 68) – disrupted the assumption of total asymmetry and exploitation. This was possible through our shared social worker/practitioner identities intersecting with our differences as researcher/not researcher. I was able to ask questions, which allowed critiques of the taken-for-granted assumptions structuring practice (Cole 1991).

As a way of equalising relationships between researcher and participants, researchers are often advised to ask the participants to read transcripts and "check evidence" (Burgess 1984: 206). However, such a strategy is at odds with a social constructionist perspective because it assumes there is only one 'truth', and that is the informant's. There is also potential for censorship, particularly if checking occurs after the analysis is completed. Informants had the opportunity for censorship during interviews by making off-the-record comments, which were respected. While I offered to send participants a copy of their interview transcript and related handwritten notes, I did not treat this as checking. Instead, I invited additional comments as clarification. On completion of the research, offers to conduct staff seminars were not taken up.

**Data organisation**

All the data were eventually represented as documents with all identifying details deleted (Jupp & Norris 1993). Documents from case files included intake forms, case notes, case discussions and conferences, statistical collection forms and court reports. The audio-tapes of the interviews were transcribed to include computer-generated line numbering. Transcripts were kept with handwritten notes and related case documents, organised in folders identified by case number(s) and corresponding practitioner/informant(s).

Index cards (13 cm × 25 cm) were used to group chunks of text from case documents and transcripts, with appropriate dates, line and page numbers. The text was grouped according to reporting, investigation and outcome, mirroring the key practice stages, and included statistical categories that represent profiles of practice processes and outcomes. Thus, the reporting stage covered the reporter's identity, reporting context (including case history) and content of report (nature of allegation [category], description and interpretation), receiver of report, and interpretation informing action (including status of case [category]). The investigation stage covered participants (including family members and professionals involved), their contributions to the processes, and categories related to the result of the investigation: action responsible for the injury, resulting injury/harm, substantiation/at risk category, persons believed responsible, child being investigated, caregiver's family structure and decision following investigation.

The participant observation was recorded in separate field diaries for each site. Each diary entry on numbered pages included the date, participants' first names or initials (later anonymised), their organisational positions/roles in the recorded events, and a detailed description of the context of the event (Bogdewic 1992; van Maanen 1988). Policy documents and other artefacts from each site, such as pamphlets and posters, were pasted into the diaries and annotated with the date/page numbers. Journals were used to document emerging analytical and theoretical questions related to the various data and the connections and disparities between them (Guba & Lincoln 1982; Huberman & Miles 1994).

**Epistemological issues**

Data generated in various forms do not represent objective facts about the sites (Linstead 1993; Atkinson & Hammersley 1994) as linguistic communities (Bourdieu 1990, 1991), or about child protection practices and the children, families and life events that are the focus of such practices. Instead, data generated are constructions in the research process by active participants – myself, as the researcher, and key informants (Linstead 1993).

Case files are "social constructions of documentary reality" (Smith 1974), constructed by practitioners who interpret organisationally determined categories (Garfinkel 1974: 115–18) and "managed [organisational] language" (Cicourel 1974: 95), writing versions of people's lives that are perceived to be "authentic", "credible" and "representative" (MacDonald & Tipton 1993: 187–200). Furthermore, child protection files are organisationally managed (Pithouse 1987; Zimmerman 1974) biographies/histories, in which collections of disparate events, often recorded by different individuals, are linked together in linear chronology to represent a coherent whole (Stanley 1992). However, because files exist as physical objects, they represent objectivity and "plain facts" (Zimmerman 1974). Furthermore, the potential for different readings of the case files (mine, as researcher; the practitioners, as case managers) introduced complexity in understanding the files as "documentary realities" (Smith 1974) and discussing them in interviews.

Practitioners who were interviewed were not necessarily the sole writers of the files. Different practitioners had written in the files at different times throughout the life of the case or in the same time-frame as co-workers. Furthermore, my particular positioning as discussed above influenced how I read the files prior to the interviews with practitioners. How practitioners read the files related to some extent to "shared, practical and entitled understanding" as organisational employees (Garfinkel 1974: 121). Practitioners' responses to my questions did not necessarily encapsulate a single "intended" meaning of the file text (Potter 1996: 82–5), but may have changed through the reworking of the text as multiple readings and in the talk (Potter 1996). Concerns about informants "telling the truth" (Dean & Whyte 1978) are meaningless, because it ". . . presuppose[s] that the analyst has access to some unproblematic truth against which the truth of participants' utterances can be tested" (Potter 1996: 656).

An important methodological issue for the genealogical analysis relates to disputes about 'historical facts', known as "historiography"; namely, that 'historical fact' is only what particular people document for particular reasons and in particular contexts, and does not necessarily constitute 'the entire truth' (Tuchman 1994). Historiography means "historical methods" that include "philosophy of method and narrative" as well as the "nuts and bolts" of methods (Tuchman 1994: 315). History is a "text" (documents, practices and oral accounts) that may be interpreted in many ways, and the "historian's account" is also "assembled" or constructed from primary and secondary sources rather than being a presentation of objective fact and truth (Tuchman 1994: 315–16).

## Data analysis

Organisational policy documents and professional literature were analysed through critical discourse analysis (Bryman 2001; Fairclough 1992), and case files and interview transcripts through "talk and texts in interaction" (Potter 1996; Silverman 1998). In practice the case analysis meant repetitive reading of files and interview materials, which for me was exceedingly difficult because I was so immersed in the shared organisational culture and language of child protection despite my concerns about it. This problem was especially apparent in direct interactions with workers, or when reading the files; when I was speaking or reading in the familiar, shared language of child protection, whilst simultaneously having access to an alternative theoretical language. I chose to participate with some difficulty in the research process through the shared language, to minimise perceptions of my "foreign presence" (Stanley & Wise 1993), and to maximise my connectedness, although the theoretical and unshared language was always invisibly present. As I discussed elsewhere:

> [I] was viewing that world [of the public service] through a pair of lenses: one of which was my fractured constructionism, and the other, the clear, unitary lens of

the "bureau-professional" (Dingwall et al. 1983). This made the daily view of my work somewhat uncomfortable, but I adapted to its disorienting effects. (D'Cruz 2001: 22)

Ongoing reflexivity helped, but posed its own contradictions, especially related to methodological and ethical considerations of 'subjectivity' and 'objectivity'. For example, files and transcripts were read several times, each reading requiring reflexive critique of my taken-for-granted assumptions in how I read what I read, and how I interpreted it, including the meaning of my critical responses: cognitive, emotional and ethical. From the initial reading, which produced major panic because 'there was nothing there' (which I attributed to my occupational identity and inculcation), to each subsequent reading in which reflexivity paradoxically produced a version of objectification/objectivity, I 'saw more things'. This also coincided with my increasing distancing from the organisation and my subsequent identity change from organisational researcher to social work academic.

Additionally the analytical process seemed to me to be linked in a circular way to formal and emergent theories and my connection to both (D'Cruz 2002a: paragraphs 4.1–4.3). Therefore, analysis that appears in subsequent chapters gives the reader access to the data and as much as possible to my own positioning in relation to the data and analysis.

At a more practical level, I have used a particular convention in the discourse analysis of text extracts. Each extract that I have selected to illustrate particular analytical/theoretical points is indented within the analysis. Words, phrases, clauses and other features of the extracts of text that illustrate analytical points are identified using figures and/or lower case letters enclosed in square brackets. The numbers break up the text into different features, while the lower case letters represent connections between features that share the same number. My analysis of the text refers to these features, using the number/letter convention to link the analysis to the text. This analysis is mainly used in exploring the cases in chapters 6 to 8 but, where required, has also been used in chapters 3 and 5.

## Writing research

I have not sought particularly to "disguise the name of the firm" (Burgess 1984: 205) as I have engaged with a single, easily identifiable, public organisation (Cole 1991: 164). However, Thorpe (1994; 1997), Parton et al. (1997) and Scott & Swain (2002) have set precedents whereby their research has identified and focused on particular organisations. Additionally, the case analysis in Thorpe (1994; 1997) and Parton et al. (1997) refers to the same organisation that I have written about here. Furthermore, the identity of the organisation has only been relevant to conceptualise the policies and practices that I analysed. The analysis is not intended to single out this organisation for criticism but to offer the analytical issues as broader considerations for all child protection organisations, policy makers and practitioners, as a point from which they can critically engage with their own contexts. The reliance on individual cases to explore practical constructions of meanings and identities has necessitated anonymising all client details and altering or omitting details that do not affect the analysis (Burgess 1984: 205–6). Names that have been given to children, parents and practitioners are entirely ficitious and are only used to make the text more acessible to readers. Finally, the writing process is my representation as a "positioned investigator" (Riessman 1994: 133–8) of case practices, professional knowledge, policies and organisational contexts as a particular time in a particular place. The writing "holds still" (Cooper 1991) what are in actually dynamic processes and thus needs to be read as such.

## CONCLUSION

In this chapter I have discussed the conceptual, epistemological and methodological issues for this research. These have been connected to ethics/politics associated with exploring social problems from sociological perspectives, particularly social constructionism; and to the research process itself as knowledge/power in practice. The next chapters re-present my reading of the literature, policy as discourse, analysis of sites as linguistic communities, and cases, all informed by the concepts and methods outlined above, in relation to how official meanings and identities are constructed in practice, within institutional knowledge/power relations.

# 3
# Protecting children within discourses of the normal child and family

Professional knowledge conveyed in published literature presents research about the extent and dimensions of child maltreatment as a social problem, theories about its causes, and evaluative research about protective responses through laws, policies and practices. This chapter presents a particular reading of the literature through a Foucauldian lens (D'Cruz 2001: 20–1), arguing that child protection is a discourse whose primary focus is on the care of children in and by their families. The focus on families persists despite increasing professional and public awareness of allegations that people in positions of authority have sexually and physically abused children. However, while allegations made against clergy (Coldrey 1993: 344–403), school teachers (Phaneuf 1994, cited in Baker 2001: 141) and care professionals (Phaneuf 1994, cited in Baker 2001: 141) are included under definitions of child maltreatment, direct mistreatment of children by government policies and practices is not. Take, for example, the extended mandatory detention of asylum seekers and refugees, many of whom are children (Mares 2001; Manne 2001a: 136–9; MacCallum 2002). 'Protective' intervention as a discourse of risk involves a comparison of actual children, parents and families with images of 'normality' to ascertain the level of risk to children and whether or not maltreatment has occurred. The body of the child is a central feature in this discourse. The boundaries between what is normal and what is not are continuously disputed, as are the roles and responsibilities of the state and families in relation to the care and protection of children.

    The critical perspective of the literature taken in this chapter is not intended to devalue the importance of child protection in addressing the lived realities of many children throughout the world, including extreme poverty, disadvantage, exploitation and even death. However, it is insufficient to be comforted by the apparently ethical and legal importance of child protection work and its expression through legislation policies and professional knowledge. Instead, the ethical, moral and legal agendas underpinning child protection knowledge, policy and practice must be placed under scrutiny, because they are not neutral but inextricably intertwined with professional power in the service of 'the state'.

## CHILD PROTECTION AS A DISCURSIVE FORMATION

Child protection may be understood as a "discursive formation" (Cousins & Hussain 1984: 84–5), whereby particular knowledge is represented as the sole legitimate version of what maltreatment is, how to know or distinguish 'maltreatment' from 'not maltreatment', and how to protect children. A particular body of knowledge is represented by a shared vocabulary and ways of speaking or writing about the problem (Foucault 1972, Cousins & Hussain 1984), in this case, 'child maltreatment', and policy and practice responses, 'child protection'. Familiar language and concepts include categories of 'types of maltreatment', and identification as 'persons believed responsible' or 'perpetrators' of maltreatment. Furthermore, the identity of the 'child' is taken for granted as a legal category and is assumed to be the same in every case and in every context.

This chapter draws from texts predominantly from the late 1980s to the late 1990s. The texts do not represent a neutral position in relation to knowledge. Instead, they operate as devices of knowledge and of power to demarcate what is legitimate knowledge and what is not. Smith (1990c) argues that professional texts are "active" in coordinating knowledge and practice across place and time: for example, the international journals *Child Abuse and Neglect*, and *Journal of Child Sexual Abuse*, which are written in one jurisdiction and read in another. Readers in one context are connected by/to writers from another, in relation to increasingly globalised meanings of 'child' and 'protection' and the relationships between 'child' and 'protection' as policy and practice concepts.

Additionally, professional knowledge is disseminated across professions and disciplines, such as psychology, social work, medicine and law. Examples of multidisciplinary networks are the International Society for the Prevention of Child Abuse and Neglect (ISPCAN), the National Association for the Prevention of Child Abuse and Neglect (NAPCAN, Australia) and the National Society for the Prevention of Cruelty to Children (NSPCC, UK). Multidisciplinary knowledge networks coordinate what is considered as legitimate child protection knowledge (Gallmeier & Bonner 1992; Fargason et al. 1994; Thorpe 1994; Humphreys 1995; Palusci & McHugh 1995). Through coordination, networks of professionals and related professional bodies and organisations "seek consensus" on policies about "intervention" and "prevention" (Lamb 1994; Lytle 1994; Krugman 1995; Agathonos-Georgopoulou 1998). Similarly, practice coordination involves "collaboration of child welfare, mental health and judicial systems" (Butler et al. 1995), a complex yet crucial alliance in balancing "continued danger to the child" against "family integrity and parental liberty".

Dominant versions of knowledge about child maltreatment and child protection also become known outside professional groups: for example, members of the public engaged through media stories. Media may be used by child protection interest groups to further particular aims (Krugman 1995; Thorpe 1994; Wise 1991; Nelson 1984; Ferguson 1997): for example, lobbying to address reports of paedophilia by school teachers or clergy. Media also report the deaths and injuries of children, especially those seen as "practice mistakes" (Jones 1993) by practitioners as "wimps" or "bullies" (Franklin & Parton 1991; Franklin 1989). Public debates conducted through the media around usually extreme or sensationalised incidents or claims of a "system out of control" (Scott & Swain 2002) centralise questions about professional knowledge and power and the responsibilities of the state and family in relation to children. The increasing access by lay people to what is normally considered to be professional expertise may encourage women and children in particular to report experiences of "current and past abuse" (Ferguson 1997: 230) that may otherwise remain hidden. Examples of the consequences of such knowledge are the willingness of individuals and groups, many now adults, in the USA, the UK and Australia, to make claims of maltreatment by clergy and school staff that are reported almost daily in mass media.

Whilst this book draws on policies and practices in Western Australia in the 1990s as data in understanding how child protection operates as a discourse, it is important to contextualise these policies and practices within the internationally shared literature that operates as legitimate professional knowledge. The Western Australian version of knowledge represented as policies and practices connects sufficiently to internationally recognised concepts, meanings and practices. However, as chapter 4 will show, the meanings of the concepts 'child' and 'protection' and the relationships between the two concepts had a particular history in Western Australia with particular consequences for how child protection operated.

## INTERSECTING DISCOURSES OF 'THE FAMILY', 'THE CHILD' AND 'THE PARENT'

The family is the main focus of child protection practice, with many problems experienced by children as consequences of the 'extrafamilial' excluded. For example, children's experiences of war, as refugees, and of political violence and community change are included in an issue of the *Journal of Child Abuse and Neglect*. However, these experiences are presented separately, in a "special section on children and war" (Garbarino 1993; Magwaza et al. 1993; Elbedour et al. 1993; Rosenfeld 1993; Ajdukovic & Ajdukovic 1993). Furthermore, the "effects" of these "special experiences" are understood solely as individual pathology or "adjustment problems" (Rose 1989) expressed as psychological well-being (Qouta et al. 1995; Goldson

1996), "post traumatic stress" (Almqvist & Brandell-Forsberg 1997), "mental health" (Walton et al. 1997) or "moral reasoning" (Elbedour et al. 1997).

The role of the state in relation to the family in promoting the care and protection of children within/by the family relies on two dimensions. These are how 'the family' is understood within a particular political and cultural context that shapes relations between 'the family' and 'the state', and how intrafamilial relations are understood.

## 'The family' as a social institution

Feminism, gay pride and multiculturalism have challenged entrenched cultural, political and social assumptions about 'the normal family' but have not necessarily influenced social policy in a consistent way in Western liberal democracies such as the UK, Australia and the USA or in Europe (Deacon 2002; Agathonos-Georgopoulou 1998). Apart from domestic politics and their outcomes for social policy – for example, in setting priorities – there has also been an emergence throughout the world of New Right ideologies and religious fundamentalism (Charles 2000: 187–93). Despite social and cultural changes that have generated significant changes in family arrangements (Baker 2001: 69–89), the 'normal family' in child protection policy and practice continues to be implicitly understood as two heterosexual adults who are the parents of the children in the household. This definition of 'the family' in child protection policy and practice has complex consequences for how same-sex parenting and partnering (and maltreatment) are theorised because most critiques of child protection assume heterosexual relations (Renzetti 1992).

Legitimate identities, roles and relationships between "family members" are constituted through subtle social and cultural processes that regulate what is a 'normal family' (Rose 1989: 129) through processes of "familialization" (Rose 1989: 126):

> The representations of motherhood, fatherhood, family life, and parental conduct generated by expertise were to infuse and shape the personal investments of individuals, the ways in which they formed, regulated and evaluated their lives, their actions, and their goals [. . .] but this was to be done not through coercive enforcement . . . but through the production of mothers who would want hygienic homes and healthy children. (Rose 1989: 129–30)

Discourses of sexuality regulate bodies, particularly the sexual organs, kinship relations and interpersonal relations (Foucault 1978a; Foucault 1980: 210). Marriage has traditionally implied both heterosexual monogamy and reproduction (Foucault 1978a: 38–9), although increasingly in Western societies there is concern that "procreative behaviour" (Foucault 1978a: 104–5) has been separated from marriage as evidenced through the falling birth rate (Land 1999; Baker 2001: 126–7). This concern has generated political and medical strategies to encourage reproduction amongst some groups and restrict it amongst others. For example, IVF programs (Baker 2001: 129–35), apart from the ethical issues they engender, tend to be most accessible to those with an ability to pay (Baker 2001: 131). Political strategies include financial incentives to heterosexual couples to have children, particularly targeting women in the paid workforce (Jackman et al. 2003; Mellish 2003; Rector 2003).

The implicit definition of 'parent' conflates biological and social parenting identities and restricts same-sex couples from being parents (Foucault 1980: 220–1), at least where a degree of state regulation is possible. For example, the federal government in Australia sought to prevent lesbians from accessing IVF programs on the grounds that this service was only for heterosexual couples (Lumby 2003; Cumming 2002). In Britain, homosexual couples may adopt or foster children (LegalDay, accessed 21 July 2003), although Hicks (1996) argues that these couples are often a choice of "last resort".

In particular, women's bodies and their relationship to the social body, are regulated through medical technologies of reproduction and the "cultural idealization of motherhood" (Rose 1989: 125; Lupton 1999b: 62–3). Women's roles in reproduction are extended through daily responsibility for child care (Foucault 1978a: 104; Charles 2000), although this role is increasingly under challenge as more women enter the paid workforce (Saunders 2002; Baker 2001). Additionally, despite the "sexual revolution" and available contraception that has allowed women choices in regard to motherhood, "single" or "unwed mothers" continue to disrupt the "carefully calibrated norms of motherhood" (Smart 1996: 47). For example, in Australia the federal government has sought to prevent single women from accessing the IVF program on the grounds of "social infertility" because it is argued that children "need to have fathers" (Lumby 2003; Cumming 2002). Similarly in the USA, strategies to deter women welfare recipients from 'dependency' on state welfare, include explicit policies and programs that promote marriage, and childbirth within marriage (Rector 2003).

These complex political and cultural constructions show how personal and political objectives intersect in 'the family'. "The modern [heterosexual?] family is both a legal institution, the target of various health, education and welfare practices, *and* a product of voluntary association" (Hirst 1981: 71) (original emphasis).

Pervasive images of "domesticity" and "familialization" (Rose 1989: 126) regulate normal conduct with minimal state coercion, in which individuals participate in self-regulation and the regulation of others. 'Family autonomy' and privacy, legally and politically validated, are preserved as long as 'competence' is demonstrated:

> The autonomy of the family comes to depend not on law or proprietorial right but on *competence*. It enjoys a loosely supervised freedom to the extent that it meets

social norms. Control from above is coupled with the active commitment of the majority of families to 'social promotion', the economic and cultural betterment of their members. Supervision falls lightly on those families who succeed in this commitment. (Hirst 1981: 73–4) (original emphasis)

### 'The family' and 'the state': the care and protection of children

As discussed above, the state "governs families" (Parton 1991) by pervasive cultural images of 'normal' family life, childhood and parenting. Additionally medical, psychosocial and legal professionals provide knowledge to achieve these images of normality. Family members govern themselves by an acceptance of cultural norms and through displays of "competence" (Donzelot 1980; Hirst 1981). It is only when there is sufficient deviation from what is considered as normal – that is, when there are "failures and deficiencies" (Donzelot 1980, in Hirst 1981: 73) – that the state intervenes in family life: for example, to regulate violence or sexual conduct. However, the state cannot intervene in the family without legal justification because to do so would breach the norms of family "privacy" and "autonomy". Legal justification is achieved by the state being given access in a limited way through what is defined as the "social" space.

### The social space

The social space is constituted as a compromise between the separation of public (state) and private (family) spheres, where the liberal, democratic state's guarantee of liberty, privacy and autonomy of individuals and families at various times must be negotiated to achieve the objective of justice (Donzelot 1980; Hirst 1981; Rose 1998). However, the grounds for negotiation are not fixed and are therefore often contentious in relation to the rights of the state to regulate private conduct (Donzelot 1980; Hirst 1981). These controversies are usually associated with the regulation of adult sexuality, interpersonal violence; and the care, protection and discipline of children (Rose 1989). Professionals such as social workers are legally permitted in certain circumstances to enter the 'private' space of 'the family' to implement 'public' and political objectives predicated on images of normal families (Rose 1989).

The social space operates as a sort of vestibule to 'the family' by the limits placed on the extent of access to family life, justified legally and within time limits. Access to the social space does not give access to the entire life of the family, and some family members may strenuously dispute or deny access.

### Conceptualising 'family'–'state' relations

Fox Harding (1991), conceptualised the relations between '(heterosexual) family' and 'state' in relation to the care, protection and regulation of children as "patriarchal", "paternalistic" and "pro-birth family". The "*pro-birth family*" perspective is primarily associated with the welfare state (Fox Harding 1991). 'The family' is legitimated as a public institution. 'Family support' and 'prevention' discourses are incorporated within public policy objectives, whilst validating family privacy/autonomy. *"Paternalist"* perspectives are associated with child protection discourses (Fox Harding 1991). The state's role is to rescue the child from "inadequate", "damaged" or "dangerous" parents (Fox Harding 1991), who are powerful in relation to the child. Family privacy/autonomy is given less priority to achieve "the best interests of the child" (Fox Harding 1991).

It is possible to argue that the third perspective, *"patriarchy"* (Fox Harding 1991), intersects with these two perspectives, rather than being differentiated from them:

> ...however potent is the legal ideology of family privacy, in decisions as to the best interests and welfare of children [for example] in cases concerning care and custody ... *legal functionaries operate according to ideological and patriarchal beliefs as to morality, responsibility and family life and what is best for children.* (Rose 1989: 125) (emphasis added)

Pro-birth family and paternalistic perspectives of state–family relations about the care and protection of children intertwined with patriarchy were anchored within versions of the liberal democratic welfare state in Western societies such as Australia, the UK and the USA up to the 1980s (Baker 2001: 210–2). Since the 1980s and the advent of economic neo-liberalism (Saunders 2002), the main tenets of child and family policy, primarily represented as child protection, include privatisation, individualism, self-governance and self-help. Thus, with the state taking a minimalist role in many aspects of public and social policy, the care of children has become primarily the private responsibility of 'the family', and particularly women as a consequence of economic objectives of minimal public responsibility for private relations (Charles 2000). Fox Harding (1996) characterises this approach as "public and private patriarchy", practised as "patriarchal mothering" (Stark & Flitcraft 1988), which constructs mothers as primarily or solely responsible for the care of children. Assumptions of normative gender roles in "family" contexts (Gatens 1998) underpin the "breadwinner" approach to economic and social relations of the family (Sainsbury 1996; Mitchell 1998; Charles 2000). Women are seen as economic dependants of male breadwinners or, in their absence, of the state: for example, through particular forms of income support (Fox Harding 1996; Charles 2000; Baker 2001). The breadwinner/dependants model of 'the family' is increasingly contested as more women enter the paid workforce, especially as this challenges the gendered division of labour associated with "production" and "reproduction" (Baker 2001).

Fox Harding (1991) along with other child rights proponents (Freeman 1983; Franklin 1986) advocated a fourth perspective for child and family policy, *"children's rights and liberation"*. This perspective, discussed in detail in the

'Constructions of the child' section below, explains children's experiences of oppression and domination in the family as an extension of children's overall socio-cultural and political inequality associated with an arbitrarily defined age of majority and rule by adults ("senocracy") (Hearn 1988).

**Private and public patriarchy**

Donzelot (1980), discussed by Hirst (1981: 69), argues that women's "domestic power" has been "strengthened" by their "selection . . . as the partner and collaborator of various forms of disciplinary, medical and educative intervention . . . as agent of socialisation and moralisation of her family [including] over men". Feminist writers argue that claims of women's greater power in regulating the domestic sphere prescribe "patriarchal mothering" (Stark & Flitcraft 1988), in which women are cast as completely responsible for intrafamilial relations (Baker 2001; Charles 2000; Farmer & Boushel 1999). Women/mothers/wives become the focus of public surveillance of intrafamilial relations, constructing them as responsible for not regulating transgressions by children (for example as "delinquents" (Rose 1989) and male adults/partners (for example, as "perpetrators of violence" (Stark & Flitcraft 1988)). Milner (1993) describes this process as a "[male] disappearing act", in which mothers are constructed as "responsible" and men become "invisible".

Rose (1989) locates state–family relations associated with the care of children within a broader political agenda; namely the governance of childhood, and the shaping of "the young citizen". The development of future citizens is achieved primarily through the family, with both subtle and explicit interventions by public institutions, such as "the medical apparatus of public health", "the juvenile court" and "the child guidance clinic", known as "technologies of government" (Rose 1989: 128–9):

> These technologies of government, which Donzelot terms the 'tutelary complex', enabled the difficulties posed by working-class families and children to be acted upon with a degree of force, universality, and certainty but without disabling the family mechanism. . . . Through the ministrations of expertise in the service of health, hygiene, and normality, the family would be returned to its social obligations without compromising its autonomy and responsibility for its own members and destiny. (Rose 1989: 129)

**Intrafamilial relations**

Ways of conceptualising 'the family' include "the political economy", as a "system", and from "feminist" or "postmodern" approaches (Baker 2001: 69–89). This analysis takes two perspectives that resonate best with contemporary child protection: a "haven in a heartless world" or "the politics of gender and generation" (Frost & Stein 1989).

## A haven in a heartless world

The dominant view of a "haven in a heartless world" (Frost & Stein 1989) intersects with political and legal ideologies of family privacy/autonomy (Charles 2000; Baker 2001). In this view, the heterosexual family is a place of safety and security, an escape from the world outside in which intimate relations between parents/partners and between parents and children are normally egalitarian and benign. The family is represented as an entity in its own right. This may be strategic to avoid the debate about "what is a family", and instead references to 'the family' operate as "short-hand expressions . . . often express[ing] cultural norms about what 'the family' is and does, and they mask intrafamily differences and conflicts of interest" (Gordon 1986: 471). Adults/parents are assumed to have the same interests as children, and are therefore entitled to make decisions on their behalf (Fox Harding 1991). This perspective is taken for granted in paternalist, patriarchal or pro-birth family perspectives of state–family relations (Fox Harding 1991). Child rescue agendas that underpin contemporary child protection policy and practice do not challenge the fundamental assumption of the family as a haven. Instead, families that breach the norm of the 'family as a haven', seen as pathological or deviant, are policed and regulated to ensure that they may achieve these norms. Thus, a limited understanding of power relations and inequality in 'the family' significantly influences policy objectives and how they are implemented in practice.

## The politics of gender and generation

An alternative construction of family relations is the "politics of gender and generation" (Frost & Stein 1989; Stark & Flitcraft 1988). This perspective positions men and women within unequal gender relations, and 'child' and 'parent'/'adult' as unequal due to age (generation). The intersection of gender and generation produces particular family politics of oppression, sometimes expressed as overt and covert violence by adults as parents (mothers and fathers) to children; and between male adults/partners/fathers towards female adults/partners/mothers, sons and daughters. Identities, roles and relationships are not fixed, but instead are contextual relations of "inconsistencies and complex allegiances" (Doane & Hodges, 1992: 79, in Featherstone 1996: 185). Rose (1989) locates the "politics of the (heterosexual) family" (Stark & Flitcraft 1988) within the politics of patriarchal state–family relations:

> On the one hand, the state representing dominant male interests chooses the nature and objectives of public regulation; on the other, a domain is constituted outside legal regulation and designated 'private' where welfare agencies enforce the ideology of motherhood, and where male power is not even subject to the limited protections of the rule of law. (Rose 1989: 125–6)

Relations of inequality and power within the family expressed as violence may be exacerbated by inequalities focused on material resources and physical strength: of children in relation to adults/parents (Prout & James 1990; Gittins 1998) and between men and women (Farmer & Boushel 1999; Charles 2000: 135–55). Relations between same-sex partners and the care of children are under-theorised or ignored in most literature on family violence (Stark & Flitcraft 1988; Milner 1993; Farmer & Boushel 1999; Charles 2000), except where such families are regarded as deviant and as posing risks to children (Carabine 1996; Baker 2001; Cameron & Cameron 1998; Hicks 1996).

## Constructions of the child

In child protection, the 'child' is defined legally as an individual aged under 18 years. This legal boundary differentiating 'child' from 'adult' is associated with particular assumptions about the relationship between the identities of the 'child' and the 'adult'. The 'child' is an "undeveloped (or evolving) adult" (Jenks 1996). The 'child' is a "savage" (Scott & Swain 2002), or "community threat" (Eeklaar et al. 1982) to be "civilized" as the "future [adult] citizen" (Rose 1989). The 'child' is a "waif" (Scott & Swain 2002) and a "vulnerable victim" (Eekelaar et al. 1982) in relation to 'parents' and 'adults'.

The 'child' as a universal identity with common childhood experiences is differentiated from the 'adult' on the basis of four "intrinsic" characteristics informed by developmental psychology:

> (i) that the child is set apart temporally as different, through the calculation of age; (ii) that the child is deemed to have a special nature, determined by Nature; (iii) that the child is innocent; and (iv) therefore is vulnerably dependent. (Hockey & James, 1993, quoted in Jenks 1996: 123)

The 'child' is characterised as inferior to the 'adult', justifying paternalistic policies in which 'adults' may legitimately speak for and act for 'children' (Fox Harding 1991).

There are two perspectives that challenge this construction of 'the child'. The first perspective, social constructionism, argues that the identity of 'child' and 'childhood' is not a single, fixed experience across all contexts (Kessen 1983; Prout & James 1990; Hendrick 1990; Gittins 1998). Whilst there are clearly commonalities of 'being a child', children's own experiences show pluralities of childhoods, both within and across cultures (Aries 1962; Kessen 1983; Hendrick 1990; Boyden 1990; Scott & Swain 2002; Agathonos-Georgopoulou 1998):

> ... the experience of childhood is fragmented and stratified by class, age, gender and ethnicity, by urban or rural locations and by particularized identities cast for children through disability or ill health. (Jenks 1996: 122)

Furthermore, definitions of 'the child' and 'childhood' in policy and in particular experiences of childhood are related to place and time (Aries 1962; Hendrick 1990; Scott & Swain 2002). Hendrick (1990), for example, shows how changing policy objectives in Britain transformed and constrained the 'lived' meaning of childhood. Hendrick (1990) identified nine different discourses of "the child", including the "delinquent", the "welfare", the "psychological" and the "family" (as "private" child). Scott & Swain (2002) have discussed the "natural history of child abuse" (Parton 1979) in Australia, where constructions of cruelty have included different definitions of children as "waifs" and "savages" with corresponding policy and practice responses.

Whilst social constructionist perspectives help in understanding the differences within the identity of 'child', Prout & James (1990: 26) argue that the child must be recognised as "*both* biological and social" (original emphasis). Generational inequality as dependency and vulnerability is at least partially related to physical size and muscular strength (Gittins 1998) – and cognitive and linguistic capacities, which often marginalise children's participation in decisions about themselves (Davies 1991).

The second perspective that challenges paternalistic constructions of the child is "children's rights and liberation" (Fox Harding 1991), which extends the analysis of generational oppression beyond the family. Children are constructed as "subjects" with rights, possibly equal to adult rights (Fox Harding 1991; Freeman 1983; Franklin 1986). This perspective argues that children's treatment generally in the society is characterised by inequality and oppression associated with age. It is a controversial position that enters the socio-legal domain of civil rights and citizenship as an individual's connection to the state:

> The rights basis of citizenship, which must of necessity fix and abstract human actions into a set of legislative entitlements, should be tied to a dynamic concept of needs, as a set of conditions necessary for the individual and social fulfilment of human development. (Taylor 1996: 166)

Contemporary child protection is influenced by a version of children's rights, as paternalism and child rescue. However, paternalistic approaches to children's rights, and therefore protection, construct the child as a fixed identity, as an object of official concern. The actual child may become polarised against his/her parent and even against his/her social and cultural community (Boyden 1990: 208). As an approach to child liberation expressed as citizenship, Wexler (1990: 173) suggests that the identity of 'the child' may be reconstructed legally and politically through "shared individual life histories", similar to the women's movement. This approach may offer insights into how 'being a child' may be reconceptualised for policy purposes. However, at the very least, this approach does not account for how children who are unable to contribute their 'individual life histories' – if, for example, they are pre-verbal or have disabilities – may be heard without some form of adult representation.

## Policy and practice consequences of constructions of the child

Constructions of the child and childhood informed by developmental psychology influence professional knowledge, producing a "forced commonality of an ideological discourse of childhood" (Jenks 1996: 122). This 'common ideological discourse' has consequences for policy and practice that include the regulation of 'children's' lives, assumptions about 'children's' sexuality, and the child's place in risk assessment.

In regard to the regulation of children's daily lives, Jenks comments that:

> [r]outinely, children find their daily lives shaped by statutes regulating the pacing and placing of their experience. Compulsory schooling . . . restricts their access to social space and gerontocratic prohibitions limit their political involvement, sexual activity, entertainment and consumption . . . implicit socializing rules . . . set controls on behaviour and limits on the expression of unique intent, [and] also by customary practices . . . articulate the rights and duties associated with 'being a child' [. . .] [as lacking responsibility, having rights to protection and training but not to autonomy]. (Jenks 1996: 122)

Sexuality, as an adult practice, is prohibited to children, as a "crime against childhood" (Kitzinger 1990: 158–60), because of its "corrupting" effects, especially the "loss of innocence", which "disqualifies children from childhood" (Gittins 1998: 9). Discourses of sexuality centralise the regulation of reproductive bodies, within which children's sexuality is normalised through "pedagogization" (Foucault 1978a: 104):

> . . . a double assertion that practically all children indulge or are prone to indulge in sexual activity; and that, being unwarranted, at the same time 'natural' and 'contrary to nature', this sexual activity posed physical and moral, individual and collective dangers; children were defined as 'preliminary' sexual beings, on this side of sex, yet within it, astride a dangerous dividing line. (Foucault 1978a: 104)

In an extensive cross-cultural study, Goldman & Goldman (1982) took a broader construction of children's sexuality, as "sexual thinking"; a developmental process understood as psychosexual (Freud), cognitive (Piaget) and moral (Kohlberg). They defined "sexual thinking" within these developmental perspectives as:

> 'thinking about' mothers and fathers, differences between men and women, their own identity as boys or girls and the sexual role of other persons whom they encounter in the long process of socialisation within the family and in society. (Goldman & Goldman 1982: 5)

Goldman & Goldman (1982) assume hetrosexulaity as a dominant cultural principle underpinning "sexual development". They also do not consider that children may engage in practices with each other that may be seen as 'sexual' and that are seen as problematic in contemporary child protection discources due to the ambiguity and blurring between "play" and "abuse" (Lamb & Coakley 1993).

**Children and risk assessment**

Risk assessment may be characterised as the use of "grids of codeability" (Rose 1989), which arrange children as a population according to age and stage of development, representing the 'normal' evolution of the child into a socialised adult citizen (Gittins 1998). The actual child can be identified, compared and normalised in relation to the population of children of similar age. Children who are reported as victims of maltreatment become the focus for judging the "competence" of families/parenting (Donzelot 1980; Hirst 1981) through risk assessment.

Child protection policy and practice aim to minimise or prevent the consequences of maltreatment on the child as 'present victim' and 'future citizen'. Assumptions that all children's experiences are exactly the same do not allow an understanding of how children as 'victims of maltreatment' may differ according to gender, age, race and ethnicity, disability and social class, in terms of experiences and outcomes of maltreatment and child protection intervention. Instead, identity differences are presented solely as categories of risk associated with 'types of maltreatment':

- "sexual abuse in the developmentally disabled" (Elvik et al. 1990)
- "risk factors for behavioral dysfunction: the relative impact of maltreatment, SES, physical health problems, cognitive ability" (Herrenkohl et al. 1995)
- "deaf and hearing children" (Porter et al. 1995)
- "gender differences in abused children with and without disabilities" (Sobsey et al. 1997)
- "sexual abuse and exploitation of children and adults with mental retardation and other handicaps" (Tharinger et al. 1990)
- "the maltreatment of intellectually handicapped children and adolescents" (Verdugo et al. 1995).

Children's sexual identities are represented by absence: as asexuality; that is, only represented as "sexual victim" (Kitzinger 1990).

Whilst it is clearly important to consider differences between children as more than 'risk factors', it is also important to take into account children's vulnerabilities (Prout & James 1990; Gittins 1998) that might exacerbate generational inequalities of age and stage (Frost & Stein 1989). "*Developmental victimology*" (Finkelhor 1995: 178), "the study of victimization across the changing phases of childhood and adolescence" constructs "childhood [as] a period of enormous change in size, strength, cognitive capacities, gender differentiation, relationships, and social environments – all of which affect the potential for victimization". These "developmental aspects of risk", associated with "children's characteristics" and those of their environments, affect their "suitability as targets" and "ability to protect themselves". The risk of victimisation of children may also be influenced by an imbalance between "motivated offenders" and "capable guardians". However:

> the picture is not a simple one of children becoming more vulnerable to more victimization as they move into less supervised environments, but a complex pattern of change in type of victimization as children change environments. When children are in the home, the 'motivated' offenders may be parents, relatives and siblings, and the 'capable guardians' may be nonfamily members, such as neighbours or community professionals. (Finkelhor 1995: 180)

Children's autonomy of choice of environments is central to understanding their victimisation, including the "ability to regulate contact with motivated offenders and capable guardians" (Finkelhor 1995: 180).

The construction of the 'child as victim' has consequences for the identity of the child as "future citizen" (Rose 1989). This approach is influenced by developmental psychology, which assumes a continuous link between 'past', 'present' and 'future', between 'child' and 'adult' identities, and related biographies (Stanley 1992). "[P]atterns originating in the past exert a major influence... in the present." (Dale et al. 1986: 16) The 'child' is a 'victim' at the time of the incident, which may be reported at a different time and place, even when socio-legally an 'adult' (Finkelhor et al. 1990; Femina et al. 1990; Martin & Elmer 1992; Moeller et al. 1993).

Maltreatment as a 'child' is assumed to determine 'adult' identity and behaviour in various ways that construct the adult as posing risks to the self:

- "functioning/adjustment" (Greenwald et al. 1990; Fox & Gilbert 1994; Varia et al. 1996; Jumper 1995)
- "academic achievement" (Himelin 1995; Kendall-Tackett & Eckenrode 1996; Perez & Widom 1994)
- "avoidance and fear of sexual and physical intimacy", "thoughts about sex", "role of sex in relationships" and "attraction/interest in sexuality" (Matorin & Lynn 1998)
- "sexual dysfunction" (Kinzl et al. 1996; Sarwer et al. 1997; Sarwer & Durlak 1996)
- "homosexuality" and "bisexuality" amongst men (Delgado 1992; Doll et al. 1992)
- "suicidality" (Peters & Range 1995)
- "trauma" (Rowan et al. 1994; Rodriguez et al. 1996)

and to others:
- "public health" risks, for example HIV (Cunningham et al. 1994; Carballo-Dieguez & Dolezal 1995)
- "criminality" (Widom & Ames 1994)
- "parenting adequacy" (Cole et al. 1992; Casanova et al. 1994; Banyard 1997);
- "abusiveness" (Bagley et al. 1994; Briggs and Hawkins. 1996).

The *intergenerational cycle of maltreatment* is an assumption that expresses the link between maltreatment as a child and its eventual effects as "cumulative risk" and a "chain of experiences" (Rutter 1989: p 323, cited by Zuravin et al. 1996: 316) when the child becomes an adult/parent. This concept influences how responsibility for maltreatment is constructed because maltreatment as a child is assumed to determine parenting competence, including maltreatment of children:

> Research on the effects of abuse and neglect shows that abused/neglected children exhibit low self-esteem, depression, withdrawal, anxiety, poor social skills, and developmental deficits (Howing et al. 1992). These effects further exacerbate the concerns plaguing the multiproblem family. *They also engender possible risk factors for intergenerational transmission of abuse* (Kaufman & Zigler, 1989 in Smokowski & Wodarski 1996: 509). (emphasis added)

The *intergenerational transmission of maltreatment* is a concept that particularly influences constructions of women as "protective mothers" (Stark & Flitcraft 1988). Women's experiences of maltreatment as children are perceived to influence their ability to protect their own children from 'dangerous men' (Kreklewetz & Piotrowski 1998). However, not all adults who have been maltreated as children maltreat their own children (Egeland, Jacobvitz & Sroufe 1988, in Smokowski & Wodarski 1996: 505–6; Gilgun 1991; Wurtele & Miller-Perrin 1992). "[T]he pathway to abusive parenting is far from inevitable or direct" (Kaufman & Zigler 1989, in Smokowski & Wodarski 1996: 506).

## CONSTRUCTING MEANINGS AND IDENTITIES IN CHILD PROTECTION

Child protection policy and practice aim to give meaning to children's experiences that are reported as maltreatment and to identify who is responsible. The identity of 'the child' and the place of the child in 'the society' and 'the family' are contentious issues in the relationship between 'the state' and 'the family' and in child and family policy. Contemporary child protection policy and practice rely on risk assessment that represents particular images of 'normal' children, parents and families, against which actual children, parents and families are compared and judged. The body of the child becomes the main focus of risk assessment – as a 'body of evidence' of a 'type' (or 'types') of 'maltreatment' from which the child must be protected, and as a commentary on the "competence, failures and deficiencies" (Donzelot 1980; Hirst 1981) of parents or caregivers.

### Technologies of the body in the risk society

The "risk society" is a paradigm for how problems of everyday life are constituted in contemporary Western societies as prediction, management and minimisation of conceptions of danger (Beck 1992; Ferguson 1997; Lupton 1999a; Kemshall 2002). The strategies and language of risk have been incorporated into child protection discourse by which prediction, management and minimisation of extreme danger to children, represented as death and sexuality, are the purpose of intervention (Ferguson 1997; Parton et al. 1997, Parton 1998, 1999). Risk management includes surveillance and monitoring of children, parents/adults and families who are assessed as posing risk to children.

Some commentators (Parton et al. 1997; Parton 1998, 1999; Thorpe 1994; Howe 1992; Walton 1993) criticise the potential for total control and intrusive surveillance of families by the state. Ferguson (1997) acknowledges that "child protection and the risk society" present the "dangers" of excessive bureaucratisation and control over professional work and child rearing practices. He sees "risk management" as attempts to "colonize the future" (Ferguson 1997: 228), in which death and sexuality in particular are approached as "ultimately manageable and predictable" (1997: 231). However, he critiques this analysis as "one-dimensional" (Ferguson 1997: 222), instead suggesting that institutionalised risk assessment presents "opportunities" through "advanced capacities of professional systems to keep children alive" (1997: 229), and exposure of the "darkest secrets" of the traditional family to state intervention (Ferguson 1997: 230).

### Risk assessment

"Risk assessment instruments 'are formalised methods that provide a uniform structure and criteria for determining risk' (Keller, Cicchinelli & Gardner, 1988, p. 2)" (cited in Doueck 1995: 191). They are templates of legitimate knowledge and detectors of 'truth': for example, of "sexual abuse" (Faller 1988a, 1988b) or "physical abuse" (Milner 1994). Risk assessment aims to assist practitioners to "accurately define", "detect" and "differentiate" the abnormal (as "high risk" or "dangerous") from the normal ("low risk") groups (Doueck 1995: 192; Doueck et al. 1993; Murphy-Berman 1994). Additionally, risk assessment aims to predict potentially abnormal identities and practices "across family types" (Burrell et al. 1994; Mandel et al. 1994), as a "general assessment of risk and dangerousness" (Murphy-Berman 1994: 194). As grids of specification (Foucault 1980; Cousins & Hussain 1984), risk assessment allows practitioners to continually compare individual children and families as 'cases', with abstract and generalised 'normal' children and families represented in the checklists.

Risk assessment aims to balance "family [autonomy] preservation" and "child protection" (DePanfilis & Scannapieco 1994): for example, "by weeding out of false or inappropriate reports and assessing levels of risk to establish priorities of response"

(Downing et al. 1990: 358). Risk assessment assists in evaluating the "effectiveness" of normalising strategies, as "changes in risk status can be measured" (DePanfilis & Scannapieco 1994: 234), rather than solely "policing [families]" and "substantiating" allegations (DePanfilis & Scannapieco 1994: 229–30).

Risk assessment techniques differ across knowledge domains, with inter-agency and multidisciplinary coordination being important for enhancing risk management. Psychosocial professionals rely on "risk assessment checklists" (DePanfilis & Scannapieco 1994; Murphy-Berman 1994; Fanshel et al. 1994), "screening devices/procedures" (Caliso & Milner 1992; Downing et al. 1990; Hutchison 1989), "context free discourse techniques" (Fairclough 1992) such as "interviewing" and "anatomically correct dolls" (Kendall-Tackett 1992a, 1992b). Medical professionals rely on technologies of the body to differentiate normal from abnormal bodies: for example, through colposcopy (Sinal et al. 1997), anal dilatation (Hobbs 1995), cranial scans, magnetic resonance and radiography (Doueck 1995; Feldman et al. 1995; Dubowitz 1994). Legal knowledge relies on claims about the "competence" (Hirst 1981) of the particular family/parent(s), which can be contested within a positivist binary of "separating fact from fiction" (Daro 1991) to establish what happened to the child and identities of responsibility (as "cause/culpability"). Protection of the child is a contest between the state and the particular family's claims to "privacy/autonomy" and "parental rights" (Jones 1993).

The methodological, ethical and practical challenges inherent in developing a valid classificatory and predictive system have been acknowledged: for example, Doueck (1995), DePanfilis & Scannapieco (1994), Doueck et al. (1993). Nevertheless, risk assessment checklists are privileged as techniques of examination of the child's body and intrafamilial roles, relationships and practices (Hewitt 1991).

There is an expectation that through risk assessment, "discrete and objective data" will yield a true "determination [of] an individual's proneness to child abuse and neglect . . . by assessing his/her standing on some empirically derived scales . . ." (Murphy-Berman 1994: 193). Concerns about "underprediction" and "overprediction" (Murphy-Berman 1994: 196) underline assumptions about accuracy of assessments. However, 'dangerousness' is not easily predicted if taking account of the complexity of behaviour in daily life; "infrequently occurring [violent] behavior"; "individuals who have not yet clearly behaviorally demonstrated harmful acts"; and "passive acts" such as "neglect" (Murphy-Berman 1994: 194). Furthermore, as DePanfilis & Scannapieco (1994) found when they compared ten decision making/risk assessment models used in the USA, "*[t]here is no apparent consensus on what to consider the most important maltreatment related criteria. The most frequently cited were 'abuse of the child' and 'inadequate parental supervision.'* [. . .]" (DePanfilis & Scannapieco 1994: 235–9) (emphasis added).

## CONSTRUCTING MALTREATMENT

Child protection as a discourse is knowledge that has a particular linguistic structure: vocabulary and syntax (how words are expressed in sentences and relationships between words) (Huddleston 1988: 1). The definitions of 'types of maltreatment' illustrate three features. Firstly, the common 'syntax' of child protection takes the generic form, 'someone did something to a child' as the basic structure of definitions. Secondly, the structure of cause and effect associates 'cause' with 'doing something' (or 'not doing something') with intent, and 'effects' on the child. Thirdly, the centrality of the body of the child has particular consequences for how 'body' is defined and associated with different 'types of maltreatment' and 'priorities' for professional intervention. These three features are integral to risk assessment by which maltreatment may be identified by comparing actual children, parents and families with images of who and what are considered 'normal' and represented by risk assessment criteria.

### 'Intentional' or 'accidental'? 'Normal' or 'abnormal'?

In dominant child protection discourse, maltreatment (abuse/neglect) is represented as an objective reality, as something that can be seen on or beneath bodily surfaces by experts, from which a particular categorisation of bodily abnormality called 'maltreatment' may be made. Bodily abnormality categorised as maltreatment differentiates 'normal cause(s)' – for example, "accidents" (Cohen et al. 1997), or "congenital" (Wardinsky 1995) – from 'abnormal cause(s)' (for example, "non accidental" or "inflicted") (Ewing-Cobbs et al. 1998; Boyce et al. 1996).

The association of 'intent' with bodily abnormalities as 'effects' links particular practices of identifiable person(s) as 'causes', which I have constituted as a generalised rule: 'someone did something to a child'. The task of child protection is to make the general rule specific, by naming the 'something' as a category of maltreatment, and the identity of person believed responsible for 'doing something to' a particular child (Barnum 1997). Technologies of the body facilitate how it is seen, measured, grasped and categorised as 'abnormal/normal' – as an intersection of medical, legal and social knowledge (Hewitt 1991).

### Types of maltreatment – partitioning the body

Each type of maltreatment is associated with different partitionings of the physical body, as surfaces and interiors, as an intersection of medical and social knowledge that ultimately must meet legal tests of 'truth' (Daro 1991; Kerns 1998: 459).

**Sexual abuse**

Sexual abuse is defined according to specific body parts and practices that are culturally constructed as 'sexual', and enforced by legal, medical and social knowledge. For example, most jurisdictions prohibit "sexual contact" between individuals who are socially and legally defined according to age ("adults" and "children"), between anyone in relationships in which there are particular biological and social relations ("incest"), and between heterosexual individuals regardless of age where there is coercive "sexual contact". Some jurisdictions prohibit all "homosexual practices", and in others such practices may be legitimate, depending on the legal "age of consent" (Foucault 1978a; Jenks 1996; Gittins 1998).

A narrow definition of sexual abuse requires three aspects at a minimum. First, identification of body parts, for example, "genitals", "perineal", "rectal" (Bond et al. 1995); second, an association with practices culturally defined as 'sexual', for example, "oral sex", "anal and genital penetration" (Parra et al. 1997; Faller 1988a: 123–4), "fondling, mutual masturbation, frottage" (Faller 1988a: 123–4); and third, involving a 'child' and usually (but not always) an 'adult male', for example, "adolescent caregivers" (Margolin & Craft 1990).

Broader definitions may refer to "non-sexual, sexual abuse" (Conte 1991: 8) equated with "less sexual", particularly "non genital" (Kaufman et al. 1994) practices such as "fondling" and "kissing" (Faller 1988a). "Least intrusive" forms of sexual abuse do not involve "contact", and include "inappropriate sexual statements to the child" or occasions when body parts deemed to be 'private' and 'sexual' of one or other of "participants" are made visible and public to the other, for example, by "exposure" or "voyeurism". "Extensiveness" as a context includes duration, frequency, coercive practices, numbers of victims and other participants, whether intrafamilial and/or extrafamilial (Faller 1988a).

The centrality of the child's body in constructing sexual abuse relies on medical technologies. Body parts defined as 'sexual' or likely to be associated with 'sexual practices' are examined for "physical signs of abuse [such as "penetration" (Parra et al. 1997)] and sexually transmitted diseases" (Siegfried et al. 1998; Ingram et al. 1992; Ingram et al. 1997; Bays & Chadwick 1993; Horowitz & Chadwick 1990; Kadish et al. 1998). Standard examinations of genitals (vaginal, penile and rectal) and the throat assume that abnormalities in the 'normal child' must be "caused by sexual abuse" (Adams & Wells 1993), although abnormalities from non-sexual causes are differentiated: for example, "unintentional perineal injury" (Bond et al 1995).

However, some medical techniques for diagnosing sexual abuse have been controversial (Kerns 1998) – for example, the anal dilatation test (Parton 1991; Hobbs 1995) – and others do not necessarily offer an unequivocal conclusion. For example, colposcopic photographs of genitalia that apparently show the "physical findings in child sexual abuse" may be negated by the child's "clinical history" (Sinal et al. 1997). And "sometimes physical findings *including normality* are consistent with abuse" (Adams et al. 1994; Hobbs et al. 1995: 465) (emphasis added).

Thus, even medical technologies must often be corroborated by a detailed narrative of practices, contexts, identities and effects within the heterosexually parented/partnered family (Faller 1988a, 1988b). The concept of "disclosures" (Lamb & Edgar-Smith 1994; Roesler & Wind 1994), primarily associated with sexual abuse, emphasises the "secrecy" and "suspicion" of incidents (Kaufman et al. 1994) that often cannot be "substantiated", because the "child denies it" and there is "no physical evidence" (Morison & Greene 1992).

'Truth' as an objective and legal "fact" (Morison & Greene 1992; Myers 1993) does not allow contradictions or ambiguity (Kerns 1998). Hence, to prepare children appropriately to participate in legal proceedings (Saywitz & Camparo 1998) special techniques include "facilitated communication" (Jones 1994a; Botash et al. 1994) and "explaining conversational rules to children ... to facilitate accurate responses" (Mulder & Vrij 1996). Other techniques aim to enhance "credibility of disclosure" (Wood et al. 1996; Gordon & Follmer 1994): for example, by modifying the structure of the interview, including the effects of "peer support and misleading questions" (Greenstock & Pipe 1996). The usefulness of "anatomically correct dolls" as "reliable" techniques to ascertain 'what happened' through a re-enactment of events (Bays 1990; Kendall-Tackett 1992a; Realmuto & Wescoe 1992; Everson & Boat 1994; Boat & Everson 1994; Lamb et al. 1996; Levy et al. 1995) is debated (Heiman et al. 1998: 300).

The construction of sexual abuse as a policy concept and in practice is based on the imbalance of power between children and adults, and the related concepts of "consent" and "coercion" (Bell 1993). These concepts are informed by psychological and legal discourses related to 'consent'. A psychological perspective associated with 'developmental age and stage' and the capacity to consent "refuse[s] the very possibility of consensual sexual relations between an adult and a child" (Bell 1993: 151). Adult–child sexual relations are "extremely questionable" (Foucault 1988, in Bell 1993: 152), with "children constructed as a 'high risk', vulnerable segment of the population" (Bell 1993: 152), and an associated parallel "construction of the 'dangerous individual' [. . .] or 'pervert'" (Bell 1993: 152). From a legal perspective of contract theory and consent (Bell 1993: 158), child sexual abuse is a breach of an implicit "contract of relationship" (Bell 1993). Feminist approaches to child sexual abuse that analyse the inequalities of power associated with gender and generation (Bell 1993: 158) rely implicitly or explicitly on these perspectives of "informed consent" and/or "coercion" that are implicated in adult/child sexual relations.

However, consent and coercion are not unproblematic concepts, even in adult to adult sexual relationships often assumed to be equal and mutual (Bell 1993: 158). In practice, consent in any sexual relationships is fraught with complexities of "who can consent" (Bell 1993: 160), and what 'consent' might mean.

Notions of 'consent' and 'coercion' become even more complicated in relationships between children, including differentiating between "sexual play" and "abuse" (Heiman et al. 1998). Lamb & Coakley (1993) reported on a study of female undergraduates who responded to a survey on "childhood game experiences", of which just under half described cross-gender play that included "persuasion, manipulation or coercion" seen to have "a strong relationship with abuse". Lamb & Coakley (1993) concluded that ". . . the amount of bullying that occurs in 'normal' sexual play and games may make that distinction [between abuse and play] more difficult to make than we thought" (Lamb & Coakley 1993: 524–5).

**Physical abuse**

Much of what is known publicly and professionally as 'physical abuse' is informed by discourses of 'dangerous families' featured in child death inquiries in Australia (Armytage & Reeves 1992; Scott & Swain 2002), the UK (Parton 1985, 1991) and the USA (Johnson 1990). In all these cases, young children died through violence, systematic cruelty and deprivation of food and material care. It is these "worst case scenarios" (Jones 1993) that dominate in professional and public awareness and symbolise 'physical abuse' as images of "immediate danger", giving a "sense of urgency" (Jones 1993: 247). Examples of extreme practices are "infanticide", "cruel treatment" associated with child labour, and the "battered baby syndrome" (Oates 1982: 1–2). However, the difficulty arises in relation to expectations that parents should "discipline" or "control" their children as part of their socialisation as "future citizens" (Rose 1989). Parental discipline is described as "child rearing violence" (Hemenway et al. 1994), socially and culturally "acceptable punishment" (Oates 1982: 4), "physical punishment" (Graham 1981; Wolfner & Gelles 1993; Kaufman et al. 1994; Gough & Reavey 1997), and "spanking" (English 1998). However, parental discipline and its consequences for children tend to be over-represented in child-abuse statistics (Baumrind 1994); and are often difficult to separate from "abuse" (Oates 1982: 4; Straus et al. 1998). In attempting to differentiate 'normal' from 'abnormal' "disciplinary action" (English 1998), the definitions also highlight the ambiguous acceptance of some forms of physical discipline of children. "Physical punishment" becomes "physical abuse" as extreme actions: "hitting with objects", "hair pulling" and "shaking" (Kaufman et al. 1994), or extreme consequences: "death", "bruises", "injuries", "burns or fractures", "requiring medical care" or "hospitalization" (Kaufman et al. 1994; English 1998: 41). "Abusive violence" would be considered a criminal act if the victim were a stranger (Wolfner & Gelles 1993: 200–1).

The ambiguities between "physical punishment" and "physical abuse" are not just confined to professionals. Graham's (1981) study of "anger and aggression" by "ostensibly non-violent" (1981: 39) mothers towards their babies who were not receiving child welfare/protection services found that the mothers differentiated their "aggression" according to "verbal and physical"; "spontaneous and premeditated"; and "mild and severe". They also considered that their behaviour was "acceptable" and different from that of "baby batterers" (Graham 1981: 47–8).

In assessing risk of physical abuse, the child's body is partitioned into non-sexual body parts as surfaces and interiors, accessible by medical technologies (Nimkin & Kleinman 1997). The body itself may be represented as a map of abnormalities representing physical abuse: "a colour atlas" (Coulter 1997). Medical technologies can access the body beneath the visible surface: for example, through cranial scans, magnetic resonance and radiography (Doueck 1995; Feldman et al. 1995; Ewing-Cobbs et al. 1998; Ito et al. 1998; Rooks et al. 1998). These technologies may reveal invisible physical abnormalities that may be differentiated as "inflicted" and "non-accidental" injuries; or "non-inflicted" and "accidental" injuries (Ewing-Cobbs et al. 1998; Boyce et al. 1996). Some bodily abnormalities may have 'normal' explanations/causes, yet may "mimic" (Look & Look 1997) or be "mistaken" (Cohen et al. 1997) for physical abuse. For example, "poor weight gain, bone fractures or skin lesions" associated with "genetic or congenital defects" (Cohen et al. 1997), "resuscitation" practices causing rib fractures (Betz et al. 1994), or cultural practices like "skin scraping or cupping" (Wardinsky 1995; Look & Look 1997). However, medical technologies may also "uncover" "unusual" or "unsuspected" cases of "non-accidental injury", for example, "penetrating pencil injury" (Lee et al. 1998) or "cervical spine injury" (Rooks et al. 1998).

Whilst physical abuse is primarily manifested in the child's body, the psyche or emotions are treated as physical entities on which the consequences of physical abuse may be seen. Examples are "negative mental health sequelae" (Frosh & Lewandowski 1998), or "post traumatic stress disorder and other psychiatric diagnoses" (Ackerman et al. 1998).

**Emotional abuse**

"Emotional (or psychological) abuse" (Hansen et al. 1997; Brassard et al. 1993) is defined as:

> an act of commission or omission that includes rejecting, isolating, terrorizing, ignoring, or corrupting a child . . . An important component of emotional or psychological abuse is that it must be sustained or repetitive. (English 1998: 41)

The psyche is treated as a physical entity on which the consequences of emotional and psychological traumas may be manifested. As Oates (1982: 3) comments: "emotional abuse" – "*the scars are less obvious* and it is probably more common than the combined total of child physical and sexual abuse" (emphasis added). This connection between emotional abuse and the materialisation of the psyche was made on an NSPCC billboard that I saw in Liverpool, UK, in 1995. Underneath a picture of a forearm and hand with three parallel scars on the wrist was a caption: "I was emotionally abused and I have the scars to prove it".

The psyche of the child is linked to the "emotional economy of the family" (Rose 1989: 151–77), with "effects" categorised as "adjustment/maladjustment" (Rose 1989: 155), "damag[ing] immediately or ultimately the behavioral, cognitive, affective, or physical functioning of the child" (Hart, Germain & Brassard 1987, p. 6 in Seaberg 1993: 22):

> The processes of emotional development of the child within its family were reconstrued as delicate and fragile, liable to distortions in so many directions that would produce pathologies in the child, ranging from naughtiness through criminality to frank insanity. (Rose 1989: 156)

More importantly, the mother is primarily responsible for the child's "emotional adjustment" (Brassard et al. 1993; Sanders & Becker-Lausen 1995; Back & Lips 1998), where "the mundane tasks of mothering came to be rewritten as emanations of a natural and essential state of love" (Rose 1989: 156–7).

Although emotional abuse is accepted by psychosocial professionals, it is difficult for practitioners to identify (O'Hagan 1995) and validate within legal requirements of "fact" because of "its high level of abstraction" (Seaberg 1993: 22) and no bodily evidence. Legal validation techniques include medical knowledge of the psyche, particularly through psychiatry, and instruments to "reliably" identify, quantify and predict "emotional abuse" as psychic trauma, such as psychological maltreatment rating scales (Sanders & Becker-Lausen 1995; Brassard et al. 1993) and Child Abuse and Trauma Scales (Kent & Waller 1988). However, protective action is rarely taken solely for emotional abuse (Doyle 1996; Levesque 1998).

## Neglect

"Neglect" is:

> an act of omission by a parent or caregiver that involves refusal or delay in providing health care; failure to provide basic needs such as food, clothing, shelter, affection, and attention; inadequate supervision; or abandonment. This failure to act holds true for both physical and emotional neglect. (English 1998: 41)

Neglect, defined as "acts of omission" (what has not been done), generates an interesting problem of how to judge causality where causal events are absent but are nonetheless judged to have particular effects on the child. Naming the 'omission' transforms inaction into an action that is intended to cause harm.

An alternative view of neglect is that the narrow focus on parents as "negligent" and "holding low income families accountable for their circumstances" (Dubowitz 1994: 558) does not address poverty and impoverished environments (Dubowitz 1994; Drake & Pandey 1996). It also does not solve children's problems/needs, which may include "poorer psychological development" and "greater risks of injury and death" (Minty & Pattinson 1994: 733).

Categorisations of neglect that predominate amongst ethnic minorities, for example, Aboriginal children, are represented as outcomes of ethnocentric and racist practices (Human Rights and Equal Opportunity Commission 1997;

Thorpe 1994), and of greater socioeconomic inequality amongst these groups (Thorpe 1994; Saunders et al. 1993). The response to prevent such outcomes has been "reverse discrimination", an intersection of "racism, cultural relativism and child protection" whereby ethnic minorities receive minimal services when problematic parenting practices towards children are seen as "culturally relative" (Channer & Parton 1990). The most extreme consequences of these assumptions in the UK have been the deaths of children, who became the subjects of public inquiries (Parton 1991).

## Types of maltreatment – hierarchies and priorities

The four main "types of maltreatment" are defined as apparently discrete entities (McCurdy & Daro 1994; English 1998). However, some researchers claim that the types are not easily differentiated in practice and indeed often occur together (Berliner 1994; Dubowitz 1994; Ney et al. 1994). "An environment of violence does not distinguish between cases of sexual and physical abuse" (Goddard & Hiller 1993: 20). There is criticism of a tendency to create a "hierarchy of maltreatment" (Berliner 1994; Dubowitz 1994), prioritising types of maltreatment that attract greater resources and professional and public concern. Thus "sexual abuse" and "physical abuse" are given priority over "emotional (psychological) abuse" and "(physical/emotional) neglect" (Dubowitz 1994; Berliner 1994). "Sexual abuse" incites "outrage" that "physical abuse" despite "physical evidence" does not (Jones 1993). "Physical neglect remains on the sidelines, [and] emotional abuse, as the major or sole form [of abuse], merits barely a mention" (Doyle 1996).

The differentiation between sexual abuse/physical abuse and emotional abuse/neglect is explained as a set of distinctive characteristics. The characteristics of "abuse" [1] in contrast with "neglect" [2] evoke, incite and repress (Foucault 1978a) dramatic "horror and interest" (Berliner 1994) within cultural discourses of "sex and violence":

> There is something about abuse [1]; that it is acts [1] not omissions [2], that it is intentional [1] not inadvertent [2], that it is discrete [1] not diffuse [2], that it is brutal [1] not insidious [2], that makes it more evocative not only for the professionals but society at large [1]. [. . .] is it part of a peculiar . . . fascination with sex and violence, with individuals not context? (Berliner 1994: 556)

These differences are reinforced in law. "Responses tend to consider emotional maltreatment as subordinate and secondary to some *legally prohibited* sexual and physical assaults" (Levesque 1998) (emphasis added). There is currently no legal right to protection from emotional maltreatment.

"The neglect of neglect" (Wolock & Horowitz 1984; Dubowitz 1994) may be understood as an outcome of particular discursive practices that legitimate particular forms of knowledge and ways of knowing, which Hacking (1991) refers to as "the making and molding of child abuse". For example, research funding, conference topics and publications submitted (Dubowitz 1994; Kerns 1998), cited and nominated as "influential" (Oates & Donnelly 1997) privilege physical and sexual abuse over neglect and emotional abuse. The priority given to sexual abuse, for example, through "a medical research agenda" (Kerns 1998) and improved medical diagnostic technologies (Dubowitz 1994) is not matched by an equivalent professional interest in "neglect".

Practitioners screen out reports of neglect "unless [they are] extremely severe or life-threatening" (Dubowitz 1994: 556–7; Parton 1995). "Home alone" cases (Lewis 2003; Sweeney 2002; Collins 2002; McDonald 2003; McCarthy 2003) are the exception, representing "drama" in "neglect" cases (Dubowitz 1994: 558). The complexity of defining neglect in terms of its causes, particularly poverty (Dubowitz 1994: 557; Drake & Pandey 1996), and the immensity and pervasiveness of the problems associated with 'neglect' generate a sense of futility in achieving change "either on a voluntary or statutory basis" (Minty & Pattinson 1994: 734). "Professionals", often "middle- and upper-class" and parents themselves, may be uncomfortable in judging "neglectful parents" whose practices may mirror their own (Dubowitz 1994; Portwood 1998: 449), and may "distance [them]selves from those judged neglectful" (Dubowitz 1994: 559) or be more "lenient" (Portwood 1998).

The greater emphasis on easy categorisation of problems, individual responsibility and quick interventions at a time of ever-decreasing resources tends to favour physical or sexual abuse, which are more easily categorised within shorter time frames (Minty & Pattinson 1994). "We 'escape from the debate' and abandon the search for social justice and equity to the small successes that result from our discrete professional interventions (Edgar, 1991, p. 10)" (Janko 1994: 120–1).

## CONSTRUCTING IDENTITIES OF RESPONSIBILITY

A 'person believed responsible' is part of the general definition of maltreatment that 'someone did something to a child'. 'Responsibility' for maltreatment is usually attributed to particular individuals, identified as "dangerous" (Hearn 1990; Bell 1993). This view of individual dangerousness, pathology and abnormality is central to child protection discourse that aims to differentiate such individuals from 'normal people/parents' in the community. An alternative understanding of 'responsibility' considers the relations of power and inequality, particularly those of children in the society, as the "politics of gender and generation" (Frost & Stein 1989) and "hegemonic masculinity" (Bell 1993; Leahy 1992). Children's general powerlessness in the society through lack of citizenship, and through paternalistic responses to their welfare, tend to create the conditions that allow what is narrowly defined as 'child maltreatment' to flourish (Baker 2001; Agathonos-Georgopoulou 1998). In constructing responsibility for maltreatment, gender is a significant feature, differentiated by 'types of maltreatment', 'direct' and 'indirect' responsibility, and identities of 'dangerousness' and 'risk'. Additionally, feminist critics of child protection argue that an overwhelming feature is the attribution of responsibility to women even when men are actually culpable (Stark & Flitcraft 1988; Milner 1993; Korbin 1989).

## Persons believed responsible for types of maltreatment

Women are overwhelmingly identified in statistics as persons believed responsible for neglect or emotional abuse, being judged on how they undertake "the mundane tasks of mothering" (Rose 1989: 156–7). Men are rarely represented as responsible for neglect or emotional abuse. Poverty, sole parenthood and racism may complicate women's competence as mothers (Janko 1994; Thorpe 1994; Minty & Pattinson 1994, Swift 1995; Gordon 1985, 1986).

However, in regard to 'responsibility for (cause of) sexual abuse', statistics show that men are over-represented and women under-represented (Forbes 1993; Goddard & Hiller 1993; Hearn 1990; Hetherton & Beardsall 1998; Hetherton 1999). The identification of individual men as 'dangerous' contributes to a profile of 'dangerous men' or 'predators'. For example, different profiles are suggested for "intrafamilial" and "extrafamilial" sexual abuse, the former associated with "incest" by stepfathers and fathers, and the latter with "non incest" and "paedophiles" (Conte 1991: 6). However, these distinctions are less clear in practice. Children and adult women within and outside families can be "victims" (Conte 1991). Fischer & McDonald (1998) comment that "there is little difference in level of intrusion perpetrated by intrafamilial and extrafamilial offenders, both are highly intrusive". "Hegemonic masculinity", as dominant heterosexual masculinity that is culturally accepted (Bell 1993; Leahy 1992), allows the expression of male power in oppressive ways in family relations, including sexual abuse towards children. A study of step and biological fathers' meanings of "incest" (Phelan 1995) found that expressions of men's "control, power and anger" and assumptions of "family sanctity" and "patriarchal prerogatives" (Phelan 1995: 20) were supported by *"ordinary, routine, patterned family interactions..."* (Phelan 1995: 21) (emphasis added).

There is considerable debate about the under-representation of women as 'persons believed responsible' in sexual abuse cases. Under-representation is viewed by some as a consequence of social or methodological biases: "overlooked" (Kaufman et al. 1995) or "underreported" (Lawson 1993). Those who consider that women's responsibility for sexual abuse is "underreported" (Lawson 1993) explain this as cultural resistance to asking about "maternal sexual abuse and neglect" in research studies. Elliott (1993) argues that this resistance is "the ultimate taboo" because of fear of accusations of being "anti-female" or "get[ting] male abusers off the hook" (Elliott 1993: 1–2). Although women's responsibility for sexual abuse is "sizeable" in statistics of prevalence (Kaufman et al. 1995), women are "overlooked" in policies and protective interventions (Hetherton & Beardsall 1998). Hetherton (1999) explains the "minimization" by professionals of women's responsibility for sexual abuse as a consequence of the "idealization of women", related to cultural myths and theoretical justifications, including those by feminists for political reasons.

As with sexual abuse, women's and men's responsibility for physical abuse is also a topic of debate. If statistics alone are compared, it could be argued that there is equivalence in men's and women's representation as 'responsible for physical abuse' (Haskett et al. 1996; Creighton 1987, in Hearn 1990: 65). However, if the relatively small amount of time spent by men caring for children is taken into account, men may be regarded as over-represented in responsibility for physical abuse (Carlson 1992; Hearn 1990).

### Direct and indirect responsibility

*Direct* responsibility refers to causing particular injuries or harm to the child as a consequence of particular, intentional ('non-accidental') actions (Thorpe 1994; Parton et al. 1997). This category of responsibility links a particular 'person believed responsible' to a 'child'. *Indirect* responsibility refers to failure to protect children from harm or injury, and is overwhelmingly attributed to mothers whose male associates may be directly culpable for harm caused to the children (Stark & Flitcraft 1988; Campion 1995: 33).

Indirect responsibility is also associated with "the intergenerational transmission of abuse" (Rutter 1989: 323, in Zuravin et al. 1996: 316; Smokowski & Wodarski 1996), where victimisation as children is considered to determine parenting competence and protective behaviour. Women are typically constructed as indirectly responsible due to their childhood experiences of maltreatment. Women's 'choice' of physically and sexually abusive male partners and/or their 'collusion' with them through a "cycle of 'learned helplessness" (Bagley 1991: 20) may contribute to their indirect responsibility for harm to their children. In their "helpless or powerless adult state . . . women ['unprotective mothers'] are unable to protect their own children . . ." (Bagley 1991: 18). Women's indirect responsibility features in sexual abuse, being attributed to their socioeconomic "dependency" (Faller 1988a, 1988b), or their failure to "fulfil [the] role as wife" through "sexual frigidity" (Herman 1981, in Breckenridge & Berreen 1992: 101).

Women as mothers are also:

> weak, subtly hostile toward their victimized daughters, immature, and irresponsible [. . .] overtly or covertly 'collud[ing]' with father/perpetrators . . . or . . . permit[ting] or . . . promot[ing] their children's abuse [. . .] (Smith & Saunders 1995: 608)

## Persons believed responsible as identities of dangerousness and risk

Child protection intervention aims to identify individuals as 'persons believed responsible' as "dangerous" individuals (Hearn 1990) from whom children and the community must be protected. Individuals become part of a collective profile as professional knowledge. The individual and collective profile is central to the "politics of 'dangerousness' . . . as individual, localized, and particular", represented by the "particular case" (Hearn 1990: 64). Through professional knowledge of dangerous individuals, the protection of children may be achieved through professional power, exercised through surveillance, normalisation through therapies and legally sanctioned punishment of those 'responsible'.

Identities that may be considered to be 'ways of being', circumstantial or chance, become categories of risk in child protection. These identities of risk include parental (usually maternal) physical disabilities and mental illness (Hugman & Phillips 1992/1993; McMahon et al. 1996; Fleming et al. 1997), women in lower socioeconomic groups and/or on social security (Janko 1994; Thorpe 1994; Thorpe 1996), black or ethnic women (Thorpe 1994, Thorpe 1996). Homosexuality is a further category of risk: lesbians are seen as bad mothers (Carabine 1996) and gay men as paedophiles (Cameron & Cameron 1998; Hicks 1996). Predominantly, these identities of risk share a common feature, that of being associated primarily with *women* as carers of children.

## Responsible mothers, invisible men

Feminist researchers have acknowledged that women are directly responsible for physical and sexual maltreatment of children (Graham 1981; Ong 1985; Wise 1985; Featherstone 1996, 1997). However, debates around gender and responsibility for child maltreatment encapsulate the "politics of gender and generation" within the family (Stark & Flitcraft 1988; Frost & Stein 1989) and more contemporary challenges to feminist theories and cultural myths that "idealize women" (Hetherton & Beardsall 1998; Hetherton 1999).

Claims of "statistical equivalence" (Stark & Flitcraft 1988; Carlson 1992; Forbes 1993; Featherstone 1996, 1997) between men's and women's responsibility for physical and sexual maltreatment are disputed by feminists as an "anti-woman" (Forbes 1993) political strategy to deflect attention from men's over-representation in violence to children and to women. Other feminist critics argue that even when men are identified as culpable for violence, women are held responsible "in law, social service practice and psychological theory" (Stark & Flitcraft 1988: 98, 101). This is known as "patriarchal mothering" (Stark & Flitcraft 1988). In relation to sexual abuse, women who are seen as "co-offenders" and "accomplices of men", "allowing exploitation by others" (Kaufman et al. 1995: 330), may be violently coerced into such practices (Stark & Flitcraft 1988; Forbes 1993), and thus may be both "victims" and "villains" (Featherstone 1996).

Hetherton (1999) disputes explanations that portray women as victims of men, as contributing to the cultural myths and theories that "minimize" women's responsibility. In addition to being 'directly responsible', women are overwhelmingly held indirectly responsible, being seen as failing in their "protective function" towards their children (Stark & Flitcraft 1988).

Men who are identified as 'responsible', may nonetheless "disappear" (Milner 1993) from public scrutiny, redirecting interest onto the woman's 'responsibility' as an unprotective mother. Thus the woman may be held partially, equally or fully responsible for practices of male associates (Stark & Flitcraft 1988; Korbin 1989; Milner 1993; D'Cruz 1998). For example, Hetherton (1999: 167) cites White (1992) in arguing that women's responsibility for sexual abuse must not be "minimized": "The effects of female sexual abuse are particularly devastating. If you are abused by your father you feel your mother has let you down, but when it's your mother, it's a double betrayal". In Korbin's (1989) study of "fatal maltreatment by mothers", "[e]ven if the father, stepfather or mother's boyfriend inflicted the fatal injuries, these women were charged and convicted with the rationale that [their] non-protectiveness reflected complicity in the crime" (Korbin 1989: 483).

Knowledge about child maltreatment generated by research tends to maintain the gender relation, 'responsible mothers, invisible men':

> [D]espite the fact that fathers or father figures are identified as the abusers in one-half of all physical abuse cases, the database on which theoretical models of abuse are grounded and on which prevention and intervention approaches are designed is based almost exclusively on research using abusive mothers. (Haskett et al. 1996: 1175)

To demonstrate their competence and "protective function" (Stark & Flitcraft 1988), women are expected to choose between male partners and their children. This expectation does not address potential ambivalence, the "inconsistencies and complex allegiances" (Doane & Hodges 1992: 79, in Featherstone 1996: 185) of family relationships. The women may abhor the violence to themselves and/or their children, whilst simultaneously valuing an intimate relationship with the man. Women's apparent unprotectiveness may also be associated with fear of the man (Gary 1991; Forbes 1993). Additionally, acknowledging the violence may precipitate the loss of their children into care (Stark & Flitcraft 1988: 110–11).

Gender and responsibility for child maltreatment is complex, and requires a more fluid understanding of power within and outside the family. It is important not to cast women as eternal victims, but as active agents (Pengelly 1991, Wise 1985; Featherstone 1996, 1997) and at the same time acknowledge the unequal relationship between women and the children in their care (Wise 1985; Hetherton & Beardsall 1998; Hetherton 1999). Furthermore, violence in same-sex relationships, in which children may be living (Renzetti 1992), remains under-theorised.

## CHILD PROTECTION PRACTICE

Practice refers to implementing child protection policies in direct work with actual children, parents and families, in what is known as the "social space" (Parton 1991; Hewitt 1991; Bacchi 1998). Key stages of practice are "reporting/intake", "investigation" and "substantiation" (or not) of reports or "allegations" (Murphy-Berman 1994; Kalichman et al. 1990; Zellman 1990; Eckenrode et al. 1988). Child protection legislation and policies recognise that practice is a political activity, balancing objectives of "liberty" (family autonomy/privacy) and "justice" (protection of the child) in the "private domain" of "the family" (Donzelot 1988; Fox Harding 1991). The difficulties for practitioners to achieve a balance between these objectives is encapsulated by their identification in media as "wimps and bullies" (Franklin & Parton 1991; Franklin 1989). These organisational, professional and political issues have generated two competing perspectives of 'practice': as a technical activity and as a negotiated process.

### Child protection practice as a technical activity

Contemporary approaches to child protection are increasingly emphasising practice as a technical activity (Walton 1993; Howe 1992; Dominelli & Hoogveldt 1996). Practice is a means to an end that is defined according to "practice consistency" (Jones 1993: 251), represented by statistics that record the "outputs" of interventions (Walton 1993). Outputs are statistical categories that record a profile of practice in each case that is then aggregated into a profile of all cases. Statistics that are assumed to represent a one-to-one correspondence with maltreatment as an objective fact (McGee et al. 1995) are read as true measures of practitioners' competence and expertise and of practice quality. Case statistics are judged against measures – for example, epidemiological data (Wissow & Wilson 1992) – that claim to represent the true extent of child maltreatment. Additionally, professionals are compared within their discipline or across disciplines to judge the patterns of variability/variation and agreement between them (Zellman 1990; Hibbard & Zollinger 1990; Davey & Hill 1995; Realmuto & Wescoe 1992; Reidy & Hochstadt 1993; Adams & Wells 1993). Statistics that deviate from an expected number represent 'practice inconsistency', as "problems of overreporting and underreporting" (Deisz et al. 1996: 275–6). The preoccupation with 'output' measures and consistency of practice profiles does not necessarily attend to "outcomes" ("effectiveness") of intervention (Walton 1993).

The emphasis on practice consistency has emerged as a political, professional and organisational response to media publicity about children's deaths and injuries and through coronial inquiries (Walton 1993; Howe 1992; Parton 1991; Scott & Swain 2002; Armytage & Reeves 1992). These publicly known tragedies have been represented as "practice mistakes", as the outcomes of inconsistent practice due to deficient knowledge (Walton 1993), "idiosyncratic decision making" (Jones 1993: 251), failures of discretion (Howe 1992), and practitioners as "wimps" (Franklin & Parton 1991; Franklin 1989).

To avoid "practice mistakes" and to achieve "practice quality" defined as "consistency" (DePanfilis & Scannapieco 1994; Murphy-Berman 1994), professional discretion regarded as "idiosyncratic" and "subjective" (Jones 1993: 251) is increasingly restricted. Instead, "practice" is regulated by increased "governance" (Walton 1993), through "legalistic and bureaucratic solutions" (Howe 1992: 491), "technological procedures", "the collection, classification and storage of information [statistics and registers]" (Walton 1993), and "predictive techniques of dangerousness" (Howe 1992: 499–500): for example, "risk assessment" (Murphy-Berman 1994). Coordination and collective decision making through "common indicators and procedures" and "team decision making" is strengthened by increased "supervision" (Jones 1993: 251) and training (Deisz et al. 1996; Reiniger et al. 1995; Zellman 1990; Kalichman et al. 1990; Winefield & Castell-McGregor 1987). Definitions may also be changed (narrowed or broadened) (Kinard 1998; English 1998) to minimise over-reporting and under-reporting.

### Child protection practice as an accomplishment

A different perspective of practice is that it is negotiated, mediated and "accomplished" in social relations (Dingwall 1976, 1983; Gelles 1987b; Rueschmeyer 1983; Davies 1983; Pithouse 1987; Scott 1989). The primary focus is on processes that validate professional discretion in regard to how "outcomes" in cases are "accomplished" (Dingwall 1976). This approach accepts that "[v]ariation is the norm and quality control is unlikely" (Walton 1993: 151). Even official inquiries in Britain into "child abuse fatalities and cases of extreme concern" (Sanders et al. 1999: 263, 266) concluded that the deaths were unpredictable, although other practice issues were identified as problematic.

Several studies have explored how child protection practitioners 'accomplish' their practice (Dingwall et al. 1983; Corby 1987; Margolin 1990, 1992; Hood 1997; Thorpe 1994; Parton et al. 1997; D'Cruz 1993). These studies recognised the social processes that involve professionals in constructing problems in particular ways in and through their daily practice and the complex relationships between legislation, policies and practices. These studies did not deny that child maltreatment is a social problem. However, they raise critical questions about professional knowledge, practice and participation in how lived experiences become social problems of different types and thus constitute professional and organisational formal knowledge, theories and policies.

The recognition that professional discretion is a valuable feature of practice because lived experiences of children and families do not fit easily into predetermined procedures and fixed policy categories has generated new approaches to social work practice. For example, critical reflection (Fook 1996,

1999) and reflexivity (Taylor & White 2000; Sheppard et al. 2000) are promoted as important practice approaches to raise awareness of the relationship between practice knowledge and formal theories, and to enhance professional accountability. "Constructive social work" (Parton & O'Byrne 2000) includes reflection on, and in, practice as well as dialogue with children and parents. These approaches, which rely on critiques of both language and practice, feature in Gough & Reavey's (1997) innovative approach to working with parents who physically punish their children. Their analysis of "parental accounts regarding the physical punishment of children" as "discourses of dis/empowerment" identified "various oppositional discourses ... of justifications and consequences". These discourses that parents generated were: "for the good of children AND parents"; "our parents' methods (a) disapproved AND reproduced"; "our parents' methods (b) admirable AND misguided"; "not (illegitimate) aggression"; and "parents in- and out-of-control". Parental justifications omit "children's rights" and see themselves as "supreme and sovereign" (Gough & Reavey 1997: 428). Working with parents who justify physical punishment of children "... could challenge orthodox, singular perspectives ... held by some professionals (and ... many parents)" (Gough & Reavey 1997: 428). Engagement with the language of justification may "disrupt their linguistic supports for [physical punishment of children]" (Gough & Reavey 1997: 428–9).

## CONCLUSION

This chapter has represented child protection as a discourse of abnormality, within discourses of normality: of families, children and parent(s) (mothers and fathers). Particular political objectives are achieved as normative practices and identities within families, and between families and the state, particularly through unobtrusive, yet pervasive regulatory strategies. Normative practices and identities are achieved through self-regulation, and through participation in the technologies of government that form a web of surveillance and normalisation of bodies.

Identities of 'child' and 'parent', and associated practices judged to be abnormal by the self or private or professional others, begin the processes of child protection. The 'child' as embodied evidence of familial practices then directs the gaze to other identities. Child protection facilitates regulation of the intrafamilial space by the state.

Child protection practices are regulated in contemporary contexts to minimise 'practice inconsistencies' associated with 'professional discretion'. Alternative perspectives normalise inconsistencies, as "disorderly practice" (Walton 1993: 151), involving negotiation with parent(s) and children in decisions about the meanings of reported events, and the identities associated with them.

Subsequent chapters explore how professional knowledge contained in texts/literature is represented in particular organisational contexts as policies, practice cultures and in individual cases. The next chapter presents a "genealogy" (Foucault 1980; Dreyfus & Rabinow 1982) of (child) protection policy as discourse, showing how state/family relations regarding children were constituted in different macro institutional and sociopolitical contexts in Western Australia during different times.

# 4

# Policy as discourse

Practitioners working in child protection organisations are expected to implement policies and procedures that represent preferred practices for responding to problems called 'child maltreatment'. Policies and procedures are presented as up-to-date and rational responses that have been developed through the lessons of past policy 'failures'; sometimes, tragically, the deaths or serious injuries of children (Walton 1993). Policies and procedures and new legislation often emerge following public and coronial inquiries into the deaths of children. Examples are Maria Colwell, Jasmine Beckford and Tyra Henry in the UK (Parton 1991), Paul Montcalm (Lawrence Report 1982 cited in Armytage & Reeves 1992) and Daniel Valerio (Scott & Swain 2002) in Australia. These children's deaths were seen as consequences of practitioners favouring parents/caregivers through unwarranted "optimism" or "cultural relativism" (Parton 1991) or for being "wimps" by not being sufficiently assertive when investigating allegations (Franklin & Parton 1991). Additionally, the adequacy of their knowledge or accountability was criticised as "subjective" (Walton 1993; Jones 1993; Parton 1991). Sometimes, for example with the Cleveland Inquiry in the UK (1987), workers may be blamed for being "bullies" (Franklin & Parton 1991), for overzealous practice (Parton 1991; Campbell 1988). These instances of 'policy failures' and 'practice mistakes' illustrate organisational struggles to balance family privacy with the equal, public expectation of protecting children who may be victims of maltreatment at the hands of their families.

Thus child protection policies aim to manage the boundary between the state and parents in implementing different versions of child welfare and child protection, with continual renegotiation of the boundaries between public (state) and private (family) responsibilities. This chapter extends these analyses of child protection policies as discourses, showing how policies in the 'present' are not linear and progressive developments or evolving and enlightened approaches built on 'failures' and 'mistakes' of the past.

The analysis of policy as discourse in this chapter draws on Foucault's (1971, 1978b, 1980) concept of "genealogy" as a "history of the present" (Dreyfus & Rabinow 1982). A "genealogical analysis" (Foucault 1971, 1978b, 1980) shows how categories and concepts – for example, 'child', 'protection', and 'maltreatment' of various 'types' – are part of particular discourses. Furthermore, categories and concepts that are taken for granted by professionals and even enter the language of lay people through mass media (Ferguson 1997) do not necessarily have the same meaning between groups or even individuals, and may also differ depending on time and place. For example, the social, cultural and legal meaning of 'child' has changed related to time, place and context (Aries 1962; Hendrick 1990; Jenks 1996; Prout & James 1990; Boyden 1990; Scott & Swain 2002). The identity of 'child' as an abstract policy concept may mask different definitions of 'child' that may be applied, and how and why different definitions influence policy responses in relation to 'children'.

The meaning of 'protection' associated with 'children' has also changed over time, place and context, and the association of 'child' with 'protection' is relatively recent (Hacking 1991). Other policy concepts have been associated with 'child', such as 'cruelty' (Dingwall & Eekelaar 1988; Scott & Swain 2002; Gordon 1985, 1986), 'welfare' (Hendrick 1990), and 'family support' (Gilbert 1997; Hellinckx et al. 1997) with associated policy objectives. These concepts have been displaced by or have an uneasy relationship with the concept of 'protection' associated with 'children' (Spratt 2001; Jack 1997; Kamerman & Kahn 1993).

## A GENEALOGY OF CHILD PROTECTION IN WESTERN AUSTRALIA

Using child protection policies in Western Australia as an example, this chapter constructs a 'history of the present', looking at how current policies have emerged over time as political responses in which the interactions between knowledge and power have generated a context-specific genealogical pathway. Whilst the policy content presented below is specific to a particular jurisdiction (Western Australia) and may seem irrelevant to practitioners and policy-makers outside that jurisdiction, the main aim of the chapter is to take a sociological perspective in relation to policy. A genealogical analysis offers insights into the politics of policy-making in relation to a contentious and controversial social problem called 'child maltreatment'. It offers an approach by which practitioners and policy-makers can critically engage within their own policy contexts.

This genealogy of child protection in Western Australia has two main features that cut across the separate meanings of 'child' and 'protection' and the relationships between these two concepts. These two features are 'time' and 'race-as-Aboriginality', summarised in figure 4.1 Genealogy of child protection discourse – place, time and Aboriginality.

| NON-ABORIGINAL | TIME | ABORIGINAL |
|---|---|---|
| Colonisation – assist "indigent" people, especially women and children | 1829 | Colonisation – equals before British law; ethnocentrism – 'smoothing the dying pillow' |
| Guardian of juveniles – assimilation, apprenticeships and misdemeanours | 1842 | |
| Industrial Schools Act – care and education of orphans, destitute and neglected children; reform offenders and delinquents | 1874 | |
| Poor Relief Department – accommodation for the vulnerable – elderly and children | 1882 | |
| | 1886 | Aborigines Protection Act |
| Responsible government | 1889 | Responsible government – Aborigines as 'rural pests', paternalism; ethnocentrism; Social Darwinism = 'white' superiority = 'protection' = control of 'black' bodies |
| Adoption of Children Act – regulate care of children outside 'natural family' | 1896 | |
| | 1897 | Aborigines Protection Act |

| NON-ABORIGINAL | TIME | ABORIGINAL |
|---|---|---|
| Health Act (Infant Life Protection clauses) – mandatory registration of paid female carers; children aged under two years; child mortality | 1898 | Aboriginal children's institutions excluded from Industrial Schools Act |
|  | 1905 | Aborigines Act – legal and social distinctions based on 'skin colour' – 'black'/'white'; 'paternalism'; police 'arrest' and 'protect'; 'segregation' |
| State Children's Act/Department – response to Alice Mitchell Baby Farm case (40 babies died); replaced Industrial Schools Act – 'protect, control, maintain and reform neglected and destitute children' | 1907 | State Children Act also intended to cover Aboriginal children |
|  | 1911 | Special national legislation to protect and restrict Aborigines |
| State Children Act Amending Act => Child Welfare Act/Department | 1927 | Wood Royal Commission – mistreatment of Aborigines |
|  | 1934 | Moseley Royal Commission – mistreatment of Aborigines – increasing segregation |
|  | 1936 | Native Administration Act – assimilation ('biological absorption') of 'mixed race'/'half-caste' children; segregation of 'full bloods' |

Policy as discourse | 79

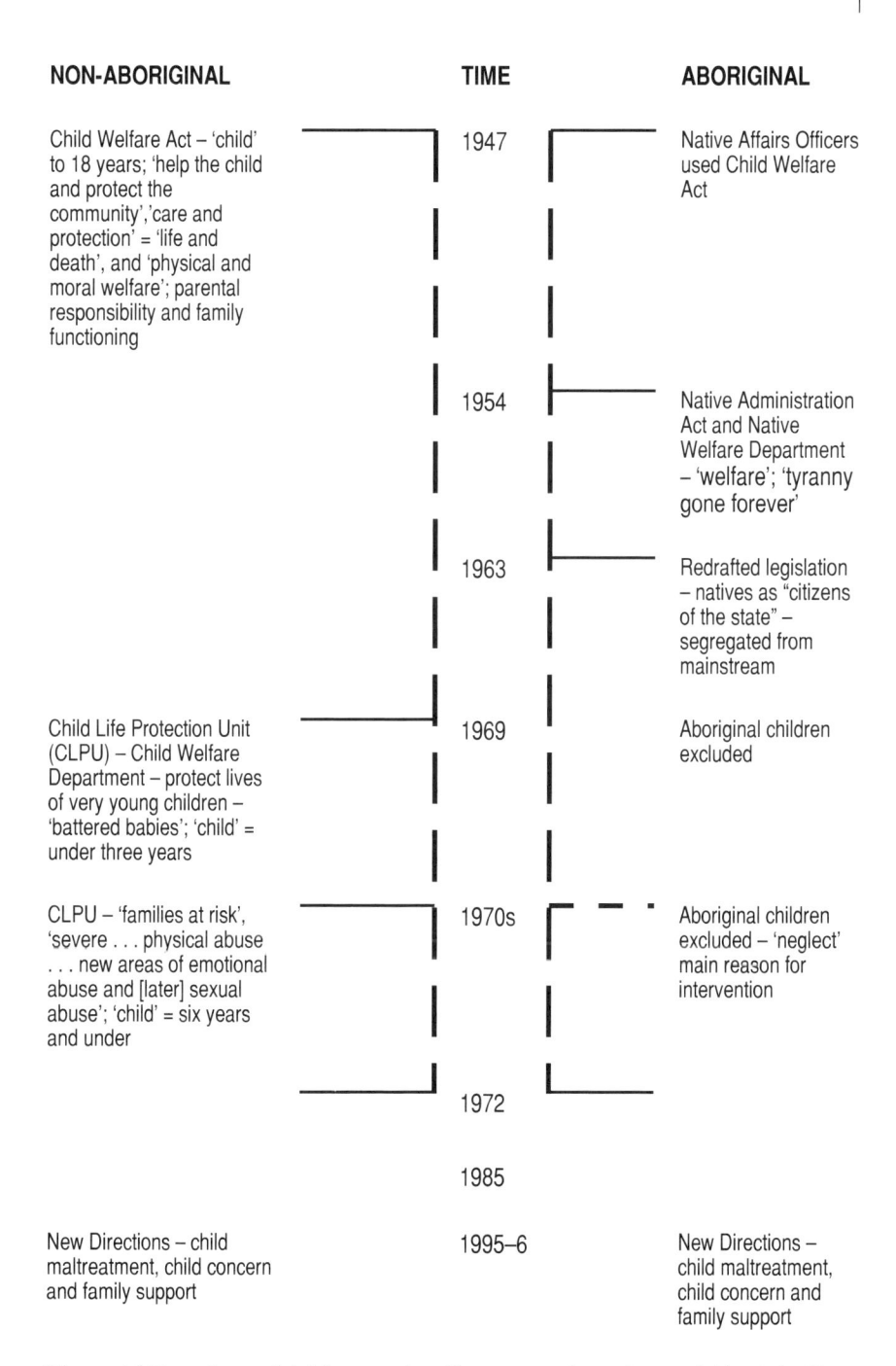

| NON-ABORIGINAL | TIME | ABORIGINAL |
|---|---|---|
| Child Welfare Act – 'child' to 18 years; 'help the child and protect the community','care and protection' = 'life and death', and 'physical and moral welfare'; parental responsibility and family functioning | 1947 | Native Affairs Officers used Child Welfare Act |
| | 1954 | Native Administration Act and Native Welfare Department – 'welfare'; 'tyranny gone forever' |
| | 1963 | Redrafted legislation – natives as "citizens of the state" – segregated from mainstream |
| Child Life Protection Unit (CLPU) – Child Welfare Department – protect lives of very young children – 'battered babies'; 'child' = under three years | 1969 | Aboriginal children excluded |
| CLPU – 'families at risk', 'severe ... physical abuse ... new areas of emotional abuse and [later] sexual abuse'; 'child' = six years and under | 1970s | Aboriginal children excluded – 'neglect' main reason for intervention |
| | 1972 | |
| | 1985 | |
| New Directions – child maltreatment, child concern and family support | 1995–6 | New Directions – child maltreatment, child concern and family support |

Figure 4.1 Genealogy of child protection discourse – place, time and Aboriginality

*The Human Rights and Equal Opportunity Commission Report (1997)* Bringing Them Home *(Appendix 5) shows "laws applying specifically to Aboriginal children" and "general child welfare laws/adoption laws" in Western Australia. Figure 4.1 extends this through the following analytical features. The two columns, headed 'Non-Aboriginal' and 'Aboriginal' are connected by a timeline. The timeline sets out key dates that relate to particular legislation and/or policies that had implications for non-Aboriginal children, Aboriginal children or both groups, shown by horizontal lines. Additionally, the vertical lines represent movement through time. Solid lines represent complete exclusion of one or other group of children from particular laws or policies of the time, dotted lines represent partial exclusion or inconsistent inclusion, and no lines represent the application of the laws and policies to all children.*

Inspection of figure 4.1 shows these analytical features. There are two columns, headed 'Non-Aboriginal' and 'Aboriginal' connected by a timeline. The timeline sets out key dates that relate to particular legislation and/or policies with implications for non-Aboriginal children, Aboriginal children or both groups, shown by horizontal lines. Additionally, the vertical lines represent movement through time. Solid lines represent complete exclusion of one or other group of children from particular laws or policies of the time, dotted lines represent partial exclusion or inconsistent inclusion, and the absence of lines represents the application of the laws and policies to all children.

## Policy changes over time

The genealogical analysis shows policy changes over time related to the shifting meanings of 'child' and 'protection' within a single place (sociopolitical context), Western Australia. Similar analyses by Hendrick (1990) and Scott & Swain (2002) have shown how policies in relation to children in Britain and in Victoria, Australia, respectively, had a particular "natural history" (Parton 1979). Hendrick (1990) identified various constructions and reconstructions of British childhood from 1800 to 'the present', including "the factory child", "the delinquent child" and "the welfare child". Each period that associated the child with a particular policy concept and a related agenda expressed a particular cultural, social and political place of the child in the society. Protection, expressed implicitly or explicitly, operated simultaneously as both care and regulation of children, as "victims" to be protected; and "threats" to be regulated (Eekelaar et al. 1982).

Similarly, Scott & Swain (2002) explored how "cruelty" to children has been "confronted" as part of a "history of child protection in Australia". Scott & Swain (2002) show how child abuse, as "cruelty" to children, has "passed through various stages . . . each . . . posing different questions" (Scott & Swain 2002: xii–xiii), as a "natural history of child abuse" (Parton 1979). Furthermore:

> the stages do not represent a simple, linear transition . . . from a *laissez-faire* philosophy to a modern welfare state in which children's rights are enshrined.

Different 'types' of abuse, such as physical abuse and sexual abuse, have different 'natural histories', the notions of children's rights remain contested and there is a growing discourse that attempts to deconstruct the reification of child abuse. (Scott & Swain 2002: xiii) (original emphasis).

By linking place and time in relation to a genealogical analysis of policy as discourse, this chapter also shows that it is not necessarily the case that the problems experienced in a place are exactly the same elsewhere at that time. For example, in the early days, first as a British colony and then as a newly emerging society, Western Australia experienced problems similar to those Britain had already addressed ten to twenty years before (Hendrick 1990; Eekelaar et al. 1982). For example, the British Reformatory and Industrial Schools legislation (1854 and 1857) was passed in Western Australia in 1874; and the British Infant Life Protection Act 1872, an act of the same name and purpose, was passed in Western Australia in 1898. A second example of the differences between places at the same time is in Scott & Swain's (2002) analysis of child protection in Australia, primarily its history in Victoria – a separate legal jurisdiction from Western Australia, although both are states in the Australian federation. Child protection in Victoria, unlike Western Australia, relied heavily until the mid-1990s on a non-government organisation, the Children's Protection Service (CPS). In Western Australia, the state government took primary responsibility for children's welfare from the start of the twentieth century and the non-government CPS lost prominence (Department for Community Welfare 1979: 13). These institutional differences suggest that in the same time-frame, even in the same country, there are context-specific influences on policy changes.

However, in contemporary times, due to technology and the speed of mass communications, problems in different places may appear to be replicated, thus encouraging the direct transplantation of policies from one context to another. This chapter aims to show why it is necessary to understand social problems called 'child maltreatment' and policy responses called 'child protection' within both local and global contexts. There are many lessons to be learned from a variety of sources in the international professional community, but such lessons need to be made relevant for local contexts.

## Policy changes and race-as-Aboriginality

This genealogical analysis of policies of protection in relation to children in Western Australia also explores how race-as-Aboriginality was associated with particular meanings of 'protection'. However, the meanings of 'child' and 'protection' and their relationship to Aboriginality changed over time. From colonisation in the mid-nineteenth century to the early 1970s, 'race' was the explicit organising principle in policies about 'protection' and about 'children'. From the 1970s, an acceptance of 'racial equality' was predicated on ethnocentric assumptions of 'normal parenting', and therefore produced a version of racial inequality related to outcomes. These outcomes of intervention meant that indigenous children have been over-represented in child welfare/protection and alternative care, particularly for neglect (Thorpe 1994, 1997; HREOC 1997; D'Souza 1993; SNAICC http://www.snaicc.asn.au/news/bp_abuse.html). These outcomes are judged according to the proportion of indigenous children in child protection/alternative care services and their proportion in the overall population (Human Rights and Equal Opportunity Commission 1997). To address what are perceived as implicit and ongoing colonialist practices, jurisdictions responsible for child welfare/protection have implemented Aboriginal Child Placement policies. These policies aim to ensure culturally appropriate practices that minimise unnecessary placement of children in care; and, if placement is necessary, to ensure that it is with culturally appropriate carers (D'Souza 1993; HREOC 1997: 439–60; Law Reform Commission (NSW) 1997). Since the beginning of the twenty-first century, there has been increasing criticism from indigenous people of state child protection services for failing to protect indigenous children from sexual abuse and physical abuse by adult members of their communities. As reported in print media (Albrechtsen 2003: 11; Toohey 2003: 11), the reasons cited include political correctness, fear of being seen as racist, and resistance from indigenous community members to welfare authorities. These criticisms have led to public inquiries and policy changes: for example, in Western Australia (Western Australian Parliamentary Debates (WAPD) 2002) following the tabling of the Gordon Report in Parliament, and in Queensland related to child abuse allegations on Palm Island (Toohey 2002: 11; Vernon 2002: 4). These emerging changes in child protection policy in relation to indigenous children have occurred after the research for this book was completed and so they will not be included in the analysis.

The foregrounding of 'race' as a feature of policies relating to 'children' and 'protection' in this chapter differs from other similar historiographical analyses of policies in relation to children (Scott & Swain 2002; Hendrick 1990). These analyses either generalise the policy aims and outcomes as common to all children (Hendrick 1990) or acknowledge that the analysis relates to the protection from "cruelty" of non-Aboriginal children only (Scott & Swain 2002). However, in addition to race, age and gender influenced the meanings of 'child' and 'protection' in Western Australia as they did in other contexts (van Krieken 1991; Scott & Swain 2002; Gordon 1985, 1986; Barn 1994; Prout & James 1990).

Finally, protection and associated practices in relation to children, parents and communities had/has potential to achieve positive and important outcomes for children, at the same time being oppressive and repressive of particular individuals and groups in the society (Thorpe 1994, 1997, Janko 1994; HREOC 1997). A policy question that ought to accompany debates about the role of the state in relation to the care and protection of children is how the tensions between constructive and destructive knowledge/power can be managed in protecting children.

**Aboriginality and identity**

In this genealogy, the category 'Aboriginal' is used as a general description of identity of indigenous Australians. Unlike the ways in which identity is understood in this book – for example, 'child', as fluid and dynamic and related to context – the category 'Aboriginal' is used in a way that appears to treat all indigenous Australians as the same. Furthermore, the category may well entrench racist stereotypes and colonialist practices (Tyler 1993: 326). However, in this chapter the category 'Aboriginal' is deliberately used to show how racialist assumptions of "classic colonialism" and, later, "welfare colonialism" (Tyler 1993: 324) that were applied to particular forms of 'protection' had, and continue to have, particular meaning for people categorised as 'Aboriginal'. 'Protection' had a different meaning for children categorised as 'non-Aboriginal'. In contemporary times and as part of indigenous politics, being "Aboriginal" has become a unifying identity as a "site of resistance" (Tyler 1993: 328). At the same time, there are conflicts in resolving claims of identity as 'Aboriginal' both within the Aboriginal community, and between Aboriginal and non-Aboriginal communities (Stokes 1997; Nicholls 2000; Fischer 2000; Tuhiwai Smith 1999: 72–4).

To structure the analysis in relation to Aboriginality and time, this genealogy is presented in three main sections:
1 Protection of non-Aboriginal children (1829–1972)
2 Protection of Aboriginal children (1829–1972)
3 Protection of children from 1972.

The first two sections are focused around time (1829–1972) but differentiated between non-Aboriginal and Aboriginal 'children', respectively. Within each section, the differences in how these two groups of 'children' were 'protected' over time are explored. The third section looks at another time period where all children were ostensibly treated as 'equal', erasing the differences associated with Aboriginal identity and all being subjected to the 'same' policies on 'protection'.

## PROTECTION OF NON-ABORIGINAL CHILDREN IN WESTERN AUSTRALIA: 1829–1972

In 1829 Western Australia began as a British colony. Protection at that time was associated primarily with building a viable community. Amongst threats to the community were non-Aboriginal children who were either abandoned by their families or orphaned, and who came to public attention because they relied on crime or begging to survive (van Krieken 1991). Community protection from "necessitous", "delinquent" or "indigent" children (Department for Community Welfare (DCW) 1979: 9–12; History of the Department for Community Welfare

1842–1972 (History) undated) was achieved by regulation through laws, severe punishment, and institutional care (WAPD 1907: 1917; Department of General Studies (DGS): Children's Courts, undated: 2; DGS: Child Welfare History 1965: 2). The protection of children as it is now understood was minimal at that time. Whilst certain categories of children were "victims" to be protected, other children were "threats" from which the community was to be protected (Eekelaar et al. 1982; van Krieken 1991: 45–79; Ramsland 1986). 'The family' was the main place for the care, protection and regulation of children. 'Normal families' were constructed as two-parent heterosexual, the adult male as breadwinner and adult female as dependent carer (Gordon 1985; Western Australian Parliamentary Debates (WAPD) 1927: 1121; WAPD 1947; WAPD 1907: 1908; DCW 1979: 9–12). The analysis shows an overarching theme of how the meanings of 'protection' have shifted according to the boundaries between state, family and community relations, with particular implications for women as mothers.

## Protection of non-Aboriginal children

Until the beginning of the twentieth century, small children (especially babies) were considered to be well cared for by their mothers – whether through adequate support by male breadwinners or through public assistance (DCW 1979: 16–17; WAPD 1907; Gordon 1985, 1986). However, state responsibility for the protection of children was minimal until 1888, with publicity given to the death of a baby who had been "farmed" (placed in the care of a child-minder) whilst its (unmarried) mother undertook paid work (DCW 1979: 10). The baby's death was reported in the *West Australian* newspaper of 9 January 1888 (DCW 1979: 10). Eight and ten years later, respectively, two laws were passed that aimed to protect infants in adoptive or foster care: the 1896 Adoption of Children Act, and the 1898 Health Act incorporating Infant Life Protection clauses (DCW 1979: 10–11). The legislation was similar to the Infant Life Protection Act (1872) in Britain about twenty years before (Dingwall & Eekelaar 1988). It was the earliest response by the government to regulate adoption and foster care that had previously been arranged privately between parents and carers (DCW 1979: 10–11). The legislation's main focus was the regulation of women as "fit and proper" carers of children (DCW 1979: 11). However, at this stage 'the natural family' remained outside the responsibility of the state. The aims of the legislation in relation to infants were similar to those in Britain: to prevent "cruelty" and promote the physical care and nurturance of infants (Hendrick 1990: 49), and to prevent "avoidable infant mortality" in public care as a public health issue. Parental "cruelty" to children was a separate matter (Dingwall & Eekelaar 1988; Gordon 1985, 1986).

Until the early twentieth century, state responsibility for non-Aboriginal children was expressed in various pieces of unrelated legislation (figure 4.1). There were different constructions of the child as both 'vulnerable victim' and 'dangerous threat'. However, a public scandal in 1907 known as the Alice Mitchell Baby Farm Case (Ball 1972) provided the impetus for formalising state responsibility for all children (WAPD 1907).

Alice Mitchell was charged with the deaths of about 40 infants, who had been placed in her care by their unmarried mothers who needed to obtain paid work. The deaths reported in 1907, occurred in spite of the 1898 legislation under which "responsible authorities" had been appointed to prevent infants' deaths by overseeing their care. The infants' deaths were condemned by a jury as "disgraceful neglect in the administration of the Infant Life Protection clauses of the [Health] Act". (DCW 1979: 12) The government responded by passing new legislation that same year. The State Children Act (1907) consolidated existing legislation relating to children up to 18 years (WAPD 1907: 1175) and established a State Children Department (WAPD 1907: 1176). The new legislation "repealed four Industrial and Reformatory Schools Acts from 1894 to 1893 and . . . that portion of the Health Act of 1898 which relate[d] to infant life protection" (WAPD 1907: 1174). It aimed "to protect, control, maintain, and reform neglected and destitute children" ("Halstead" 1938), regulate foster care (not adoption), regulate employment of children in public spaces, and control juvenile offenders (DCW 1979: 12–14; WAPD 1907). The new legislation was modelled on "the methods adopted in New South Wales, Victoria and South Australia" (WAPD 1907: 1173). There was recognition of the contribution by the Children's Protection Society to the "rescue and care" of children aged under three years who were neglected by their parents (WAPD 1907: 1909, 1911, 1912).

In 1927 the Western Australian government replaced the State Children Act (1907) with the Child Welfare Act (1927) principally "to change the title of the State Children and Public Charities Department to that of Child Welfare Department" (WAPD 1927: 1121). The change was partly related to similar changes in three other Australian states since 1913 (WAPD 1927: 1121) and also in other parts of the world (WAPD 1927: 1157). There was a "slight stigma" associated with children known as "State children" (WAPD 1927: 1121), an implication of "a measure of dependence and . . . some degree of pauperdom" (WAPD 1927: 1157). The renamed legislation and department might alleviate some of this stigma (WAPD 1927: 1121, 1157) and the children would now be known as "wards" (WAPD 1927: 1121). The legislation also acknowledged the importance of families and providing financial assistance to destitute women and children (WAPD 1927: 1121, 1157), although men as breadwinners who reneged on their financial responsibilities would be "made to pay" (WAPD 1927: 1122, 1160).

The Child Welfare Act (1927) maintained its primary focus on "delinquent" and "mischevious" [sic] children (DGS Courts, undated: 2). The public regulation of the family also emerged as a means of protecting children, particularly infants (WAPD 1927). Regulatory strategies included advice on baby care and "investigation of all complaints regarding neglected, destitute and ill treated children" (DGS Child Welfare Review undated: 4).

The expressed reason for the Child Welfare Act (1947) was to "consolidate and reprint [the Child Welfare ACT (1927) as amended]" (WAPD 1947: 497). The 1947 act gave "power to apprehend neglected or destitute or incorrigible or uncontrollable children" (WAPD 1947: 986). Neglected or destitute children were differentiated from uncontrollable children, the latter being offenders and "not necessarily innocent little children" (WAPD 1947: 1104). The state's role in child welfare was:

> the care of children and their correction . . . is one of the greatest things that we of this generation can attempt, because children are the coming citizens of our country and upon them will fall, when they reach adult years, the responsibility which we are now shouldering. (WAPD 1947: 498)

Children of "low-privilege" should "be given every opportunity to develop . . . in the same way as [children] . . . in more favoured circumstances" (WAPD 1947: 498). The act consolidated the powers of the Children's Courts and the Child Welfare Department (WAPD 1947). These two institutions would "work together . . . to help the child and *protect* the community" (DCW 1979: 16) (emphasis added). A child was defined as "neglected if his [sic] life, health, safety [and welfare] is endangered through employment in a circus or acrobatic entertainment"(WAPD 1947: 502). "Neglect" included abandonment or "not being properly looked after" (WAPD 1947: 513), or "destitute" (WAPD 1947: 514). Parents would be charged with neglect (WAPD 1947: 515). In keeping with "principles of British justice", "a man is responsible for supporting his own family" (WAPD 1947: 1107–8).

The 1947 act (as amended) prescribes the regulation of children's public conduct, and under Section 4, definition 'k', the legal grounds for declaring a child to be in need of "care and protection": from harm or injury, parental "immorality", or other abnormal circumstances which could "place a child in physical or moral jeopardy". This Child Welfare Act (with amendments) has provided the legal mandate for child welfare/protection in Western Australia well into the late 1990s, despite a legislative review recommending new legislation (Laws for People 1991). It is only since the start of the twenty-first century that new legislation is being drafted (Department for Community Development Corporate Affairs email, 21 February 2003).

Despite the clauses on the care and protection of children, the focus on uncontrolled or delinquent children dominated. Probation officers and welfare officers implemented dual public objectives of regulation and protection of children (WAPD 1947; DGS Child Welfare Review undated: 3; Tay 1976).

Whilst the rhetoric in parliamentary debates expressed the intentions of the Child Welfare Act, the treatment of children in practice did not appear to conform to these ideals. For example, from the 1930s, British children were accepted in Australia under the (now) controversial "child migration" scheme, sponsored by state and church institutions (DCW 1979; Coldrey 1993; Bean & Melville 1989). Despite legislation as far back as 1955 recognising that children, particularly girls, could be victims of adult offenders, including through sexual assaults (DCW 1979: 16), the 'protection' offered usually meant institutionalisation (van Krieken 1991). Temporary institutional care and assessment was also offered to "neglected and destitute children", and "emotionally disturbed children" under (public) guardianship (DCW 1979: 18).

Family support services in the late 1960s regulated maternal responsibility, through child care/minding for children of "married women in employment", to ensure the physical and mental growth of children, and their hygiene and safety (History undated).

The protection of children within the family, as opposed to their regulation, was further elevated with the establishment of the Child Life Protection Unit (CLPU) in 1969, as part of the Child Welfare Department. The unit's role was the management of "... cases involving the ill-treatment of babies and young children (commonly called 'battered babies')" (Williams 1982: 37), coinciding with the "discovery" of the "battered baby syndrome" by Kempe and associates in the USA during that time (Thorpe 1994). Local concerns for children aged under three years whose lives and physical well-being were seriously threatened, and who required medical attention, were partly informed by Kempe's 'discovery' and by the need for an appropriate health and welfare response to these children's experiences (Brazier & Carter 1969).

The professionalisation of child welfare through the emergence of social work provided new knowledge of "the social" sphere, the 'space' straddled by the state in relation to the family (Donzelot 1988; Parton 1991). Social work of the late 1960s and early 1970s was informed by developmental and ego psychology (Rojek et al. 1988). This allowed a professional partnership with clinical psychologists whose expertise on intra-psychic and intrafamilial dynamics informed social work theory and practice, especially in relation to child and family welfare.

The 'discovery of child abuse' by Kempe as a problem of deficient parenting brought together the combined expertise of psychosocial experts on intra-psychic, intrafamilial and social domains. The CLPU engaged social workers and psychologists, who were seen as organisationally and professionally superior to generic and mainstream child welfare workers (Williams 1982: 12–15).

The task of protecting children's lives was constructed as a "complex socio-medico-legal" problem, needing "long-term intensive rehabilitation" (Williams 1982: 37). All family dysfunction was considered to be potentially abusive. However, the problem was constructed primarily as a psychosocial problem of children's care within the family.

Responsibility for children in need of 'life protection' was now extended to children aged up to six years. There was an expanded responsibility for children presenting with "severe... physical abuse" to "new areas of emotional abuse and (later) sexual abuse" (Williams 1982: 3). Other children were assisted by mainstream departmental services or by community agencies.

The socio-medical discourse dominated the assessments and interventions, and parental 'normalisation' was the aim. The legal domain was engaged minimally, through occasional prosecutions through the criminal justice system, and transfers of guardianship from parent(s) to the state (Williams 1982).

A separate apparatus to respond to child abuse within mainstream child welfare was significant, as the protection of children was differentiated from and elevated above their other welfare needs, ideologically and organisationally. 'Protection' was given priority, being reconstructed as a 'life and death' issue, which offered a powerful policy agenda that would engage politicians, professionals and the public alike, especially in relation to the well-being of (vulnerable) pre-school-aged children.

Specialist knowledge was needed to protect particular groups of children, whilst non-specialists provided welfare services to other children and families. It is notable that the CLPU focused on protection of non-Aboriginal children, in keeping with the broader mandate of the Child Welfare Department.

Whilst the CLPU was establishing the 1970s discourse on child abuse, the Child Welfare Department, of which it was a significant part, amalgamated with the Native Welfare Department and was renamed the Department for Community Welfare.

I will now break with this particular segment of the genealogy of the protection of non-Aboriginal children (1829–1972) as, after this time, the care and protection of Aboriginal and non-Aboriginal children was governed by the same legislation and modes of organisation. However, before I present the transformed discourses from 1972 onwards, I examine the discourses of protection as they applied to Aboriginal children (1829–1972).

## PROTECTION OF ABORIGINAL CHILDREN IN WESTERN AUSTRALIA: 1829–1972

Two interconnected features were associated with the protection of Aboriginal children during this period. First, children and adults were undifferentiated, being constructed as 'eternal children' (Rintoul 1993; Mickler 1998). Secondly, 'protection' of/for Aboriginal children/adults/communities was associated with different meanings and institutional practices, compared with discourses associated with the protection of non-Aboriginal children. 'Protection' was a central feature of the discipline of all Aboriginal people in Western Australia.

This analytical position is embedded in an ongoing national controversy in which protagonists have been engaged since the Human Rights and Equal Opportunity Commission (1997) (HREOC) released its report into past laws and policies in relation to Aboriginal children, coining the term "the Stolen Generations". Prior to this in the 1980s, state jurisdictions with responsibility for child welfare/protection had implemented Aboriginal Child Placement policies to ensure culturally appropriate interventions including placement of Aboriginal children (D'Souza 1993; HREOC 1997; Law Reform Commission (NSW) 1997). The claims of the HREOC report of enforced removal of children and racist forms of protection encapsulated as 'the Stolen Generations' have involved participants from the Aboriginal community, politicians, members of the public, historians, and media (Markus 2001; Manne 2001b; 2001c, 2001d; Windschuttle 2002; Reynolds 2000). The controversy rages around the intent of the policies of removal, and the importance and significance of the treatment of the indigenous population in the overall history of colonisation in Australia. The controversy is captured in pithy phrases expressed by some factions as a 'black armband view of history' that accuses critics of being unnecessarily negative, and by others as a 'white blindfold view' that denies the profound consequences of these policies for indigenous people in Australia (Manne 2001a, 2001b; Horne 2001: 53–55, 56; Reynolds 2000; Blainey 2000). "The contemporary debate about historiography is an argument about both power *among* historians and power *in* history" (Scott 1989, in Tuchman 1994: 317) (original emphasis).

## The meaning of 'protection' of/for Aborigines

Clauses in the Aborigines Act (1905) and the Native Welfare Act (1954) refer to the welfare of Aboriginal children as being legitimately met by 'mainstream' child welfare legislation. However, in practice, they were excluded. 'Race' was the organising principle in legislation governing Aboriginal children and adults, rather than the identity of 'child' (Biskup 1973; Haebich 1992; Morgan 1987; Rowley 1970, 1971, 1972; HREOC 1997).

Colonisation provided the context for these disciplinary practices. The state's relationship with Aborigines was enshrined in 'protectionist' legislation generated by governing institutions and supported by the wider settler community. 'Protection' would "save" Aborigines from the worst aspects of physical and sexual violence by the settler community (Haebich 1992). The population as a collection of bodies described as the "political anatomy" (Foucault 1977: 221; Turner 1992: 58–62) would also be controlled, by minimising the numbers of "half castes" born of covert, involuntary and voluntary sexual contact between non-Aboriginal men and Aboriginal women (Haebich 1992: 116–17).

'Protection', which restricted the movement and activities of Aboriginal people, furthered economic interests by allowing settlers free reign in traditional lands and access to a source of cheap labour (Rowley 1971: 2–4).

'Protection' became a concept of division based on distinctions between Aboriginal and non-Aboriginal people, made according to "obvious cultural differences", represented by skin colour and physical appearance of the body of the Aborigine, and influenced by Social Darwinism and the "White Australia" policy (Haebich 1992: 128). Individuals as bodies who were included and excluded from these categories varied over time as did the meanings of who was 'black' and who was 'white', and the changing relations between the groups (Haebich 1992; Rowley 1970, 1971; Sackett 1993).

Aboriginality and 'blackness' represented 'abnormality' compared with 'white' people and the culture they represented as 'normal'. The position of 'non-Aboriginal' (or 'white') people as 'normal' also placed them in a dominant position over 'Aboriginal' (or 'black') people as 'abnormal' (Haebich 1992: 57; Young 1990). Skin colour, that is, physical bodies, came to symbolise particular identities, embodied characteristics and stereotypic images (Rowley 1972: 14, 45–6; Young 1990), and "unacceptable differences" (Henderson 1992: 6). The physical and symbolic visibility of Aborigines within the population meant that as individuals and a group they were always under public surveillance and control. 'Protection' would civilise, reform or rehabilitate the 'uncivilised natives', and ensure they created no obstacles or opposition to economic objectives of settlement (Rowley 1971: 2–4).

The earliest form of protectionist policy towards Aborigines, following achievement of responsible government, was represented by the 1897 Aborigines Act. Informed by Social Darwinism, the objective was "smoothing the dying pillow" (Haebich 1992: 54; Rowley 1970: 103), with basic assistance being provided until the 'inferior' Aborigines "died out".

At the start of the twentieth century, the 1905 Aborigines Act increased state intervention and:

> ... incorporated the policies of protection and rigid segregation of Aborigines: for their own physical protection and to check the decline of their numbers ... forcibly remov[ing them] from the wider community and [keeping them] indefinitely on segregated reserves.(Haebich 1992: 57–8)

Under the 1905 Act, the Chief Protector was given legal status with broad powers over Aborigines throughout the state. Local police were often appointed as honorary 'protectors'. The combination of a 'protective' role with existing police powers placed them virtually in total control of the Aborigines in their locality.

Each new law increased state powers over Aborigines, expressed as "protection" (Rowley 1970: 303). The 1936 Native Administration Act, which brought the "whole coloured population" under the act, "condemned them to live under rigid government control, segregated from the wider community in accordance with the whims of the government and the general public" (Haebich 1992: 348–9).

"Protection" placed together the "biological absorption" policy with segregation. "Full blood" Aborigines would be "protected" through segregation, and their "mixed race" relatives would be "assimilated" ("absorbed") into the "white" community through social engineering, training and state control (Haebich 1992: 348–51; Rowley 1970: 20, 66–7). Children were to be trained in "elementary principles of civilised life" (Haebich 1992: 339).

Following the second world war there was a "... greater emphasis on welfare ... [but] the [...] system was basically paternalistic, even though the tyranny of former days had gone forever" (Biskup 1973: 265). By 1963, dissenting voices and a greater recognition of the principle that "natives" were "citizens of the State" (Department of Native Welfare (DNW) undated circa 1964: 10) influenced institutional and legislative changes, including the National Referendum on Aboriginal Citizenship (HREOC 1997; Mickler 1998). The referendum was passed and gave the Australian federal government the right to legislate on behalf of the indigenous population, when previously it had been solely a state responsibility. This change to the Australian Constitution, at least in theory, offered potential for more positive policies and treatment of the indigenous population.

In Western Australia, redrafted legislation removed many restrictive clauses and added new sections to assist members of the Aboriginal community. However, despite the apparent softening in the rigid system of control over the indigenous population, the 'natives' continued to be segregated within the Western Australian community.

### 'Protecting' Aboriginal children

Throughout this time, child welfare (and related) legislation that applied to all children did not in practice include Aboriginal children. Institutions such as missions, where Aboriginal children were placed, were not accountable under the 1874 Industrial Schools Act, which theoretically governed all children's institutions. Instead, institutions caring for Aboriginal children were accountable under the Aborigines Act 1905. The act gave "the [Aborigines] Department greater power over the enforced assimilation of Aboriginal children and also served further to separate the institutional care of Aboriginal and white [sic] children" (Haebich 1992: 85).

Aboriginal children, their parents and communities were subjected to state 'protectionist' practices and their consequences, living in extreme poverty and squalor on state-controlled, but poor quality land such as rubbish tips allocated as reserves and settlements, or in camps (Rowley 1972: 144–5). Police, public health and education institutions of the late 1920s and 1930s refused to provide services for Aboriginal people (Haebich 1992: 260).

High morbidity and mortality rates, especially amongst children as consequences of poor living conditions, for humanitarian reasons led to state intervention on behalf of the children. "On the one hand, parental demoralisation often [made] it impossible for authorities to leave the children; on the other, old fears of such action help to produce despair and demoralisation" (Rowley 1972: 134). Many parents were seen as unfit to provide suitable care for their children, who were placed in state institutions:

> With the rapid breakdown of Aboriginal patterns of socialisation, the groups in contact would have shared the methods of child-rearing in the fringes and camps, producing a new generation likely to appear barbarous by the standards of either culture. (Rowley 1972: 17)

Several royal commissions and official investigations found that Aboriginal children (and women) were being exploited in employment, illegally employed or harshly treated (Rowley 1970; Haebich 1992; HREOC 1997). For example, the Roth Royal Commission (1905) found that the Aborigines Protection Act was contravened with "small children . . . being indentured, some for pearling: the Chief Protector of Western Australia thought that six years was a suitable age for indenturing a lad" (Rowley 1970: 193). Children of 14 to 16 years (suspects or witnesses in "cattle killing" offences) could be "brought in" by police using neck chains. A child of ten could be sentenced to six months' imprisonment for "cattle killing" (Rowley 1970).

More insidious, however, through the "Policy of Indirect Rule" (Rowley 1970: 92), was the use of children as instruments for "diluting" the Aboriginal population. As far back as the 1905 Aborigines Act, the Chief Protector had power to remove an Aboriginal child from the custody of its parents. If Aboriginal Welfare officers considered that children had "Aboriginal features" and dark skin, they could be placed in institutions for Aboriginal children. Children not fitting this description would be placed with non-Aboriginal children and be supervised by Child Welfare Departments (Rowley 1972: 159):

> [T]his provision was later applied with increasing ruthlessness, *in an attempt to suppress all individual and social characteristics different from those of the average Australian*, thereby ensuring the eventual disappearance of [A]borigines by a process of thin spreading of colour among the white population. (Biskup 1973: 264) (emphasis added)

'White' people, primarily supervisors of institutions and missions, were instrumental in 'breeding out' the characteristics of the 'black' individual and community, through care and training of Aboriginal children, especially those described as 'half caste'. 'Blackness' was more than skin colour: it symbolised a community and a culture which was devalued and thus to be obliterated by the superior white culture. Aboriginal children, as symbols of cultural continuity, were sites of struggle between 'white' and 'black':

> The fight for the minds of the children went back to the very beginning of Aboriginal administration and missionary effort in every state; and in this debate there were enough to defend the means as the only way to give children 'a chance' (Rowley 1972: 24). [. . .] [T]he mission schools competed with the adults for the minds of the children. (Rowley 1972: 63)

State 'protectionist' policy was justified as "for their own good" (Haebich 1992). In practice, rigid social hierarchies were enforced. "Blacks" occupied a "lowly place in the wider community" (Haebich 1992: 49) as "useful workers" . . . and "humble labourers" (Haebich 1992: 57). State intervention in Aboriginal lives, even in the 1900s, "contrasted markedly with the stated aims of the 1907 State Children Act to provide for needy children without undue interference in family relationships" (Haebich 1992: 111). Care and 'protection' provided by the state through settlements and other institutions can only be described from a contemporary perspective as prisons or slave labour camps (Haebich 1992: 188–94).

Moore River and Carrolup were the two most notorious settlements designed by Chief Protector Neville in the 1920s and 1930s to further his biological absorption policies. Both sites had "places of confinement" (Haebich 1992: 182), punishment sheds for children who ran away to join their parents or resisted the authoritarianism of staff (Haebich 1992: 175).

State 'protection' of Aboriginal children (and adults) at these sites is typified by Moore River settlement (Haebich 1992: 208–14; van den Berg 1994). The children had lives of "strict and dismal routine" (Haebich 1992: 208). Schooling was of poor standard and abilities of the children were grossly underestimated. They were not allowed to engage in play activities, and were generally treated poorly in terms of their basic care – clothing, hygiene and food.

"Vocational training" provided was related more to the economic survival of the settlement than skills that could be usefully offered to employers in the wider community (Haebich 1992). Those young people who were employed were exploited by low wages paid into a trust account, and risked assaults, and social and physical isolation (Ward 1987; Morgan 1987).

By the end of World War II, Aboriginal children assisted by the Native Welfare Department were also included under the child welfare legislation. They could be made wards under the Child Welfare Act, although services continued to be provided, primarily through the Native Welfare Department.

By the 1960s, the Aboriginal child became "a kind of hostage" (Rowley 1972: 273):

> Management often improperly used the child as a control over the parents; so Aboriginal parents also used their children in their institutionalised world to embarrass authority, for example to provide them with refuge and shelter. (Rowley 1972: 273)

I interviewed several former employees of the Native Welfare Department. They identified the contradictions and conflicts associated with working in an organisational and political context where 'native welfare' represented the control of Aborigines in all aspects of their lives. Care and control aspects of policies were influenced by colonialist and racist assumptions and were implemented in paternalistic or repressive ways that regulated even the most minor details of indigenous Australians' lives: for example, keeping dogs (Department of Native Welfare (DNW) Instruction Manual 1965).

The effects of poverty, destitution, poor health, poor education and limited employment opportunities were constructed as examples of individual/cultural abnormality. Resources were allocated to making Aboriginal people as much like white people as possible. Large numbers of children were made wards from birth to 18 years for 'neglect[1]', ostensibly for the children's welfare.

Aboriginal children were segregated from child welfare services available to other children in the community until 1972 when they were included under the new Community Welfare Act. The Native Welfare Act 1954 was repealed and replaced by the Aboriginal Affairs Planning Authority Act 1972 (DCW 1979: 18; WAPD 1971, 1972a, 1972b). The newly created Community Welfare Department implemented the Child Welfare Act 1947, and the legislative changes included Aboriginal children and families as part of the Western Australian community (WAPD 1972a: 683–6). However, despite the rhetoric of racial equality in law, the outcomes of protection of Aboriginal children were unequal, the children being over-represented in 'neglect' cases, and in placements in care away from their families and communities (McCotter & Oxnam 1981; D'Souza 1993; Thorpe 1994, 1997; HREOC 1997). These consequences of the well-intentioned principle of racial equality are attributed to ethnocentric assumptions (Channer & Parton 1990). Being Aboriginal continues to be a differentiating principle by default in contemporary policy and practice due to continuing ethnocentric assumptions.

---

[1] As a social work student in 1977, undertaking research as part of my summer employment at the (then) Department for Community Welfare, I came across numerous files in which Aboriginal children had been made wards from birth to 18 for 'neglect'. I was very puzzled by this because it seemed unnecessarily draconian. It was not until 1979 when I began working for the same department that I learnt about what passed for child welfare in relation to the indigenous population.

## PROTECTION OF NON-ABORIGINAL AND ABORIGINAL CHILDREN IN WESTERN AUSTRALIA FROM 1972

Since 1972, the protection of children has been associated mainly with conflicts and changes regarding what legitimate knowledge about child maltreatment is, and the state's role in implementing such knowledge as policies. The official construction of the 'child' has been broadened. It must be noted that the contemporary concept of child protection did not emerge until the mid-1980s.

Changes in the law in 1972 reflected an altered sociopolitical context. Priority was given to adequate community resources, rather than individual normalisation as official responses to social problems. International, national and local influences included the Seebohm Report in Britain (1968), and similar developments in Australia, nationally and in other state jurisdictions (Hon. Attorney-General 1972; WAPD 1972a: 685; King 1972).

The Native Welfare Act was repealed and the Community Welfare Act passed. The Department for Community Welfare amalgamated the functions of the Child Welfare Act with 'native welfare'. 'Community' was defined inclusively, characterised by 'racial equality' that erased 'difference' by promoting assimilation, in part as a way of redressing the destructive effects of colonisation as loss of land, "culture, health, pride and purpose in life" (WAPD 1972a: 683). The Community Welfare Act intended "to bring the Aboriginal population into the ambit of the welfare and assistance services provided by the State for all other members of the community" (WAPD 1971: 1183). "Individuals irrespective of colour" (WAPD 1972a: 686) would be assisted by the state. Although the Community Welfare Act established the Community Welfare Department, the Child Welfare Act continued to define child and family welfare policies and service provision (WAPD 1972b).

However, 'child' now included 'Aboriginal' children – and their parents/families. The 'child' continued to be legally and socially defined according to 'age and stage', as individuals aged under 18 years. In keeping with the intent of the Community Welfare Act, 'child (family and community) welfare' would be implemented primarily through and in the family, facilitated by state-provided financial, preventive and supportive services, and community resources. Service provision, predicated on 'equality', was mostly well intentioned, but did not question the implicit ethnocentric assumptions underpinning universality and 'equality'. Thus, Aboriginality became invisible within policy assumptions of equality and universality.

The state's role was defined primarily as 'child welfare', with 'protection' as a relatively small part of this role. Definitions of 'protection' continued to differentiate between 'child life protection' of the 'vulnerable child', and 'community protection' through child regulation/juvenile justice of the 'dangerous child'.

The CLP continued to coordinate 'child life protection' and was recognised as the legitimate educator about child abuse. The CLPU's "leadership", nationally and internationally, was emphasised (DCW Annual Reports 1973–84). Mainstream child welfare workers made referrals to the CLPU, consulted it on all concerns about small children's lives, and talked about "neglect" as a more widespread problem (DCW Annual Reports 1973–84). However, the vulnerable child in need of state 'protection' continued to be defined as non-Aboriginal, under six years old. State intervention, through the CLPU, was necessary only in extreme "life-threatening" instances, categorised as "physical abuse" and "emotional abuse" (Williams 1982: 3) and defined as problematic parent/child relationships.

Children over six years of age were outside the state's 'protective' mandate, but their 'welfare' was still a state responsibility. They were perceived as less vulnerable due to public visibility through their involvement in institutions such as schools. Public mainstream services could more easily protect their lives. Furthermore, life-threatening events such as poverty, infant morbidity and mortality that were primarily consequences of state policies were excluded from the definition of 'child protection'. Instead these problems were attributed to 'neglect', as a parental failing.

Aboriginal children predominated in official interventions for 'neglect', receiving a 'child welfare' service. Guardianship for an overwhelming number of these children was transferred from parents to the state (Morgan 1987; van den Berg 1994; McCotter & Oxnam 1981; HREOC 1997). Despite the rhetoric of racial equality, for all practical purposes the Native Welfare Act remained.

Community protection from older children, particularly adolescents, as "dangerous children" (Eekelaar et al. 1982), was achieved through their regulation and institutionalisation (van Krieken 1991). This group was further differentiated according to race/Aboriginality and gender. Teenage boys, as 'criminal' and 'dangerous', were subjected to "training, discipline and treatment" (DCW 1979: 16). Teenage girls who deviated from culturally prescribed norms of 'good women' through "running away" or "promiscuity" were subjected to appropriate education, regulation and 'protection' in institutions (History undated). 'Aboriginal' identity was over-represented in both groups (HREOC 1997), suggesting that racially 'equal' policies and practices that excluded 'difference' had oppressive effects (Dutt & Phillips 1996; Barn 1994). Yet these state practices were excluded as examples of child maltreatment.

Until the 1980s, the CLPU and the mainstream department focused on physical abuse and emotional abuse. In 'child life protection', 'neglect' was a by-product of physical abuse, rather than a separate entity. Emerging feminist movements, which challenged patriarchal power expressed through adult male sexual violence to females, identified child sexual abuse as a special example of this power (Bell 1993; Scott & Swain 2002). Child protection discourse was transformed by the addition of sexual abuse as a legitimate object for official concern. In this case, the 'child' was white and female, and the focus was on adult males' sexual practices in the family, as opposed to 'deficient parenting'.

However, where state intervention in saving children's lives was limited to pre-school-aged children who were less publicly visible, intervention in sexual abuse was extended to children up to 18 years (DCW Annual Reports 1980–4). This difference in age-related criteria associated with state protection suggests that the ongoing privacy of adult/child sexual practices justified an extended licence for public entry into the private space of the family. Public awareness alone of the child sexual abuse victim was insufficient to ensure protection, because the usual tension confronting child protection practitioners of the need to respect family privacy is exacerbated by the even more private and secretive nature of sexuality, especially if it involves children (Back & Lips 1998: 1240).

The Child Sexual Abuse Unit (CSAU) was established in the 1980s to respond to reports of child sexual abuse and to develop professional knowledge about child sexual abuse through practice. The CSAU and CLPU became the Children's Protection Service (CPS) (DCW Annual Reports 1980–4).

The protection of children in the 1980s was associated with different types of maltreatment, each with different theoretical perspectives and forms of intervention, and involving different professional domains. The CLPU with its primary focus on the normalisation ("rehabilitation") of parents/mothers was a socio-medical partnership (Williams 1982). Both physical and emotional abuse could be diagnosed by medical technologies, seen as sufficient to identify the non-accidental nature of harm and to justify (psycho) social intervention. Temporary transfers of guardianship were taken in relatively few cases (Williams 1982).

On the other hand, sexual abuse was defined by the Criminal Code as primarily a legal problem, but also situated in 'the family', justifying state intervention. The main theoretical approach was the family systems model borrowed from the west coast of the USA, which proposed that child sexual abuse was due to (heterosexual) family dysfunction (Faller 1988a, 1988b; Gary 1991: 19–32). Interventions were influenced by legal requirements and this was reflected in the language used.

The male parent/partner, usually reported as the 'perpetrator', was held criminally culpable. The mother was perceived as 'negligent', due to perceived complicity. Women's identities solely as 'mothers' prescribed that 'good mothers' would 'choose' their children (usually daughters) and 'reject' their male partners. Women's ambivalence or vacillation between polarised loyalties was constructed as "unprotective" (Wurtele & Miller-Perrin 1992: 38–40). Gender also overtly emerged as the primary organising principle that tended to implicitly influence all child protection practice (Stark & Flitcraft 1988; Milner 1993; D'Cruz 1998, 2002a).

In child sexual abuse cases, legal forms of protection were sought through prosecution of perpetrators, restraining orders or bail conditions; or through removal of children from the family through wardship and/or placement. Medical technologies were instrumental in transforming practices within the family deemed as 'sexual' into visible and public facts, concretised by measurements and descriptions of normal/abnormal bodies, and acceptable in legal contexts (Adams et al. 1994; Oberlander 1995).

At this stage, child abuse became a grab bag of objects called 'physical abuse', 'emotional abuse' and 'sexual abuse', loosely connected by their representation of 'intrafamilial' events and dysfunctional parenting practices. Differences between protective practices for different types of maltreatment were minimised, with the legal domain engaged increasingly, even in physical abuse cases, much to the consternation of reporting agencies such as hospitals, medical practitioners and family support agencies (Williams 1982).

The melding of the protective discourse was more at a level of institutional and professional practices than of abstract 'knowledge'. Protectionist practices brought together the social, medical and legal domains as partners in the state's response to 'physical abuse', 'emotional abuse' and 'sexual abuse'. Specific identities of 'perpetrator' and 'unprotective mother' that had primarily applied in sexual abuse interventions came to be generalised across all categories of 'abuse', along with the continuing heterosexual construction of parenting (Stark & Flitcraft 1988; Milner 1993; D'Cruz 2002a).

Expertise relating to child protection remained with the CPS although the service communicated its 'discoveries' and associated knowledge to mainstream child welfare practice. During this time, a small number of children (identified only by age) received 'child life protection' services, mainly from the CPS, and the remaining population of children (older than six years) received mainstream child welfare services. Statistics indicated that state protection of children was confined to a relatively small population (DCW Annual Reports 1973–84). Only in sexual abuse cases were children described statistically by both age and sex. Race remained invisible except in Child Placement statistics. The statistics would suggest a high probability that Aboriginal children did not receive 'life protection' services, instead being significantly over-represented as 'neglected' wards, "drifting" in Eurocentric foster and institutional care (McCotter & Oxnam 1981; D'Souza 1993; Thorpe 1994, 1997; HREOC 1997).

The official invisibility of race due to claims of 'universal' and 'equal' services did not necessarily place racist assumptions about problems or their outcomes under scrutiny. Instead, Aboriginal people's experiences of oppression were exacerbated due to the ethnocentric policies and practices that perceived different cultural and social practices as problematic (HREOC 1997; Morgan 1987). Furthermore, inadequate public provision of social and economic services prevented appropriate standards of parenting within already severely disadvantaged contexts, much of which was a consequence of colonisation. Additionally, ethnic differences in an increasingly multicultural society were also incorporated within assumptions of 'equality' (as 'equal treatment') (Patel 1995; Dutt & Phillips 1996; Barn 1994). The cultural norm remained 'white' and Anglo.

The contemporary child protection discourse emerged in 1985 following the Welfare and Community Services Review. Child protection was constructed as "the quintessence of a welfare service" (The Wellbeing of the People (Wellbeing) 1984: 103), transforming the focus on 'life protection' into a more generalised construction of protection, universalised throughout the organisation as 'child welfare'.

The new concept of child protection represented major transformations in the boundaries of legitimate knowledge and its objects, the reorganisation of child welfare as child protection, and associated institutional relations. Child protection had a more inclusive mandate. The 'child in need of protection' was anyone "under the age of 18 years who [is] at risk of physical, sexual, or psychological abuse or neglect" (Wellbeing 1984: 103). Child protection was now located within a legal discourse of children's rights (Wellbeing 1984 vol. 1: xvi), when previously it was a social (welfare) concern, and a version of (psycho) social need (Woodhead 1990).

The 'rights' discourse differentiated the child as an individual entity and a version of citizen, challenging the oppression of children due to arbitrary definitions of 'adulthood' and legal 'majority' (Frost & Stein 1989; Hearn 1988). However, the individual rights discourse also separated the child from the family and community context, and introduced potentially contested relations between child and family, child and community, and child and culture (Boyden 1990).

The public institutional network that normally worked to protect children was expanded, bringing together "relevant agencies, the media and the non government welfare sector", connected and coordinated by "a commitment to the principles of children's rights" (Wellbeing 1984: vol 1: xvi). The Advisory and Consultative Committee on Child Abuse (ACCCA) was expanded to include police (the legal/criminal domain) and health (medical domain), with "co-ordination" replacing its "consultative" function (Wellbeing 1984: 115–16). The breadth of the institutional network formalised the tripartite professional division of labour in protecting children by integrating social, medical and legal discourses.

The Welfare and Community Services Review criticised the state's treatment of children who were juvenile offenders, as contravening children's rights (Wellbeing 1984). Community-based alternatives to institutional regulation of children were proposed, so that community protection did not override concerns for the more broadly constructed protection of children. In particular, it condemned the institutionalisation of girls for perceived breaches of 'normal femininity'. However, the regulation of children continued to be separated from their protection in policy and practice, the former objective represented by 'juvenile justice'.

The expertise that had resided within the CPS was mainstreamed to ensure that "quality" child protection services were available throughout Western Australia (Wellbeing 1984: 110–11). The creation of positions called Senior Social Worker (Child Protection) elevated child protection as an organisational purpose and particular expertise.

Practice knowledge developed by the CPS was formalised as the Child Protection: Guide to Practice in 1987, following the relocation of CPS workers into community-based service providing offices throughout the organisation (A Review of Departmental Responses (A Review) 1995: 28). The Guide to Practice facilitated the dissemination of legitimate child protection knowledge, and education of non-experts. The Guide to Practice was challenged by members of the Aboriginal community and by some departmental workers as ethnocentric, and insensitive to the inadequacies of public provision for Aboriginal people, and was accordingly revised.

The revised Guide to Practice (Department for Community Services (DCS) 1992) interleaved "culturally sensitive" knowledge by Aboriginal workers (pp. 20–4), within dominant meanings and identities. 'Culturally sensitive' practice was confined to "traditional" (remote, rural) Aboriginal communities. Ways of working and alternatives to statutory action such as community resources were emphasised, particularly where large numbers of children were likely to be included in protectionist interventions for neglect (Thorpe 1994, 1997).

The renamed Department for Community Services developed computerised statistics, which recorded the general features of child protection cases. These statistics, as objective measures of the dimensions of child abuse and practice outcomes, became institutional knowledge. The distinction according to Aboriginality is maintained through the categories of 'Aboriginal', 'non-Aboriginal', (and 'Unknown') (DCS Annual Reports 1985–92; DCD Annual Reports 1993–5). This practice of categorisation treats Aboriginality as the 'Other', against the 'non-Aboriginal' norm. Furthermore, the 'Aboriginal' category treats all people so categorised as the same, therefore stereotyping them. Finally, the 'non-Aboriginal' category is over-inclusive and misrepresents multicultural and multi-ethnic diversity.

The child protection discourse of the late 1980s, formalised by practice guides, statistical collections and professional expertise, was implemented zealously. Child protection workers achieved considerable prominence organisationally and professionally. However, by the early 1990s, professional, political and organisational voices of dissension within and outside the department and child protection network expressed a variety of contradictory concerns.[2] Simultaneously, the election of a Coalition government in 1993 associated with the New Right elevated the privacy of the family, narrowing the boundaries of public responsibility for the protection of children.

Professional and organisational concerns were about net widening and the perceived opposite, gatekeeping. Concerns about net widening challenged the breadth of the definition and over-intrusiveness of public institutions into private life, presenting the "rapacity argument" (Dingwall et al. 1983). Concerns about gatekeeping legitimated the broad definition, offering scenarios about potentially life-threatening risks to children, and the role of the state in preventing these through the "policing of families" (Donzelot 1980). Both these perspectives were associated with the boundaries of legitimate child protection knowledge, in which the ontology and epistemology of child maltreatment were central.

Concerns about "over reporting" (net widening) and "under reporting" (gatekeeping) (Deisz et al. 1996) were linked by the notion of 'inconsistency', suggesting that individual practices were deviating from normalised practice, in which every event ought to be constructed against a standardised object called 'child maltreatment'. A related issue was the legitimate relationship between families and state in achieving the care and protection of children.

These debates raised specific concerns about the effects of net widening and gatekeeping for Aboriginal children and families. The former group urged caution in contemporary 'protection', being mindful of not revisiting the oppressive legacies of protectionist native welfare. This position was seen by its opponents as 'cultural relativism' in which Aboriginal children would receive a second-rate service. Anti-racist, culturally appropriate protectionist practices (Channer & Parton 1990; Dutt & Phillips 1996) were not seen as a viable possibility.

At the same time, in 1993, the historical division between vulnerable children (in need of protection) and dangerous children (in need of regulation) was formalised, when the latter became the responsibility of the adult criminal justice system. The renamed Department for Community Development now dealt only with the protection of (vulnerable) children.

An extensive debate over three years about child protection knowledge and state responsibility culminated in the New Directions (Family and Children's Services (FCS) 1996a), suggesting a radical transformation, rather than

---

2 These debates were not generally played out in the public arena nor formally documented. I have recorded these debates as a participant observer (an employee) of the organisation and theorised about them.

reformulation of 'old directions'. This transformation was informed by extensive research (D'Cruz 1993; Cant & Downie 1994; A Review 1995).

An exploration of intake decision-making at different practice sites showed different cultures which mediated organisational policies and procedures (D'Cruz 1993), generating different statistical profiles and documented practices. 'Child centredness' reconstructed the problems of other family members (for example, assaults on mothers) as 'child protection', simultaneously minimising the plight of the women themselves. Cultural differences were often seen as child abuse, although in some cases, alternative versions were considered. Practice focused on complying with the requirement to achieve accurate and consistent categorisations of reported events ("nominalization") (Hodge & Kress 1993), in preference to problem-solving action.

This research reconstructed the organisational problem called 'inconsistency' as a 'normal' manifestation of multiple and contradictory issues associated with organisational expectations and practical contexts at intake (D'Cruz 1993). Bureaucratic requirements of order and rationality implemented through statistical categorisations and "consistency" (Howe 1992; Walton 1993) ignored the disorder and unpredictability inherent to social work practice (Walton 1993; Pithouse 1987). Instead, practitioners needed organisational recognition and appropriate support, not regulation (Walton 1993). However, the report was interpreted within the organisation as "[identifying] inconsistencies . . . in what was defined and classified as 'child maltreatment' as well as responses to referrals" (Bowler 1995: 12; Mathews et al. 1995: 2).

Different factions in the debate about the meaning and practice of 'child protection' strategically deployed a major Child Protection statistical report for 1989–94 (Cant & Downie 1994). Cant & Downie (1994) reported that "allegations" were increasing exponentially, whilst "substantiation" rates remained relatively consistent over time. The increase in allegations was associated with a focus on "investigation" and minimal service provision, and an increase in cases where no investigation was conducted, this being attributed to increasing workload (Cant & Downie 1994; Mathews et al. 1995: 3). The data were accepted as valid and objective dimensions of child protection, representing problems at a level of practice, not policy.

The data confirmed one faction's concerns about net widening and inefficient use of resources, perhaps best represented as 'deficient rapacity', a juxtaposition of the polarised concepts describing child protection practice as "rapacity" or "deficiency" Dingwall et al.(1983). Simultaneously, the other faction claimed the data confirmed that an increase in resources, and increased regulation of practice, would achieve the desired levels of investigation, substantiation and service provision.

A "review of Departmental responses to child maltreatment allegations" (A Review 1995: 28–9) criticised the Guide to Practice as too prescriptive and the cause of over-classification of maltreatment. However, this review did not challenge organisational and professional assumptions that child maltreatment is an objectively real entity, nor the necessity for heavily proceduralised practice (Howe 1992; Walton 1993). Instead, these features were maintained by "the creation of greater focus, consistency and control in the way cases are taken into the Department" (A Review 1995: vii), to give greater balance to "children in families" (FCS 1996a: 2; Mathews et al. 1995: 8).

David Thorpe, a British academic and researcher on child protection, was invited to participate in the local debate, which now included academics, politicians, media and other social institutions (Mathews et al. 1995: 2–3). Thorpe's views, expressed in his book *Evaluating Child Protection* were central to the debate (Thorpe 1994). He reported on research conducted in 1987–8 for the then Department for Community Services. He criticised existing policy and practices as being too interventionist and for targeting women, particularly poor and Aboriginal women. He also challenged the practical construction of 'child abuse' as being mainly about problematised parenting, rather than "potential threats" to children (Thorpe 1994: 199).

Thorpe suggested a:

> reconceptualization rather than sharper definitions . . . which would . . . distinguish between child *welfare* (those measures which promote the care and well-being of children) from child *protection* (those measures which act directly as a barrier between children and significant harm and injury). (Thorpe 1994: 198) (original emphasis)

This suggestion was influential in constructing the New Directions, producing the third (temporary) category of "child concern report" (CCR) (A Review 1995; Mathews et al. 1995: 2–3) differentiated from their "protection". The aim was to limit the tendency to "over-classify cases as CMA [child maltreatment allegation]" or to use "more intrusive interventions . . . than necessary" with negative outcomes for clients and community (Mathews et al. 1995: 10–11). "Over-classification" was explained as a practice response to perceptions that "child protection" attracts "more" resources than "family support", or as a strategy of "risk minimisation" of "high profile errors" such as children's deaths (Mathews et al. 1995: 10).

"Concern for children" and "child protection" were represented as aims that could be achieved by "family support" as a less intrusive intervention and preferred response (FCS 1996a). Yet, in practice, the categories maintained the dichotomies between 'child' and 'family', and 'protection' and 'support'. If, for example, workers categorised a CCR, it could "become" CMA or Family Support (FCS 1996b), rather than the possibility that cases could be categorised as either CCR or CMA with preferred intervention through family support. Instead, the

CCR was a subsidiary category that would require re-categorisation into either CMA or Family Support.

Redefinitions and additional categories were not grounded in the unpredictability of practice and ongoing constructionist processes integral to it. Instead, perceived "deviations" were described as "practical difficulties in interpreting simple concepts" (Mathews et al. 1995: 23).

The New Directions represents an example of a calculated risk (Ferguson 1997; Parton 1998; 1999), balancing the potential for harm or death of children against perceptions of 'deficient rapacity' (Dingwall et al. 1993):

> The New Directions appears to be acting well within the context of current thinking in child protection, and appears to seek a balance between the different tensions inherent within child protection and family support. (Mathews et al. 1995: 8)

Risk management increasingly means surveillance of individuals/families through regulation of practitioners (Mathews et al. 1995). A range of strategies including "mentors", tutelage, surveillance (supervision and computerised systems), revised definitions linked to performance indicators, and standardised structures and procedures (Mathews et al. 1995: 103–8) aim to improve and standardise practice.

Workers are directed to implement both child protection and family support as 'high risk' and 'low risk' interventions respectively. Situated cultural rules about practice priorities, which practitioners discussed (see chapter 5), show how expectations of prioritising work in terms of levels of 'life risk' predisposes that 'child protection' will take precedence over 'family support'. Furthermore, 'sexual abuse' and 'physical abuse' are high in the "hierarchy of maltreatment" (Dubowitz 1994; Berliner 1994), whilst 'emotional abuse' and 'neglect' are not. Aboriginal children in urban locations are associated with 'low priorities' ('neglect') and therefore less likely to receive services (Thorpe 1997). These aspects of 'priorities' of intervention are explored in chapters 5 and 6 in relation to cultural dimensions of each service delivery office and in particular cases. Race-as-Aboriginality remains invisible within mono-cultural constructions of 'the family' and with gender dominating in constructing identities of 'victims' and 'responsibility'.

## CONCLUSION

This chapter has located the contemporary child protection discourse within particular historiographical and institutional relations and legitimate knowledge. Protectionist discourses have represented different meanings and practices, with different sociopolitical objectives. Constructions of the 'child' (and 'parent') are located within shifting boundaries between public and private responsibility for 'children'. Private conduct and relations are the primary focus, with lesser priority given to the inadequacies of public provision for the care and protection of children and their families and communities.

In particular, race-as-Aboriginality has been either intentionally or misguidedly deployed to produce different discourses and/or different effects for members of Aboriginal and non-Aboriginal communities. 'Protection' for the non-Aboriginal population differentiated between 'protection of (good) children/protection from (bad, female) carers', and 'protection from (bad) children/protection of the (non-Aboriginal) community'. For the Aboriginal population, 'protection' meant 'surveillance', 'discipline of (abnormal, black) bodies' and 'protection of the (white non-Aboriginal) community'. Contemporary protectionist discourses, which have submerged Aboriginality within a rhetoric of racial equality, are replaced by patriarchal (and to some extent, classist, heterosexist and disabling) protectionist practices. The hierarchy of 'types of maltreatment' intersects with race-as-Aboriginality in complex ways, producing unequal outcomes. These features are discussed in chapters 5 to 8, in how meanings and identities are constructed as sociolinguistic practices.

# 5

# Sites of practice

Child protection practitioners usually work from offices located within the communities to which they provide services. It is usually taken for granted that every office and every worker located there implements organisational policies and procedures as set out in official documents, without too much variation between them (Parton 1991; Walton 1993). Any differences between offices that may emerge through statistical summaries of intake and case outcomes, formal complaints or anecdotes are perceived as problems, described as "inconsistencies" (DePanfilis & Scannapieco 1994). These 'inconsistencies' are associated with perceived "biases" and "subjectivity" of practitioners (Jones 1993) and "idiosyncratic practice" (Tite 1993) that must be remedied. Practitioners are closely supervised and monitored, and training is offered to normalise individual practices to minimise variations. Aggregated practice outcomes, such as statistical summaries, are compared to monitor deviations (Murphy-Berman 1994; Wissow & Wilson 1992). However, this chapter shows how differences between local offices are perhaps the norm, rather than exceptional. The perspective taken is that social work practice in practice is a complex mix and interplay of situated cultural constructions of institutionally prescribed policies, and individual practices variously described as "professional judgement", "professional autonomy", "discretion", "negotiated practice" (Pithouse 1987; Scott 1989; Dingwall 1976; Dingwall 1983; Rueschmeyer 1983).

Sociological studies of organisations understand them as cultures in which participants interact to construct 'the organisation' instead of 'the organisation' being an objective entity that exists separately from the workers (Weick 1977; Hassard 1993: 4–6; Linstead 1993). In this chapter, the concept of "linguistic communities" (Bourdieu 1991) is used to understand and explore how child protection offices may appear to provide versions of a protective service that conform to what is organisationally mandated, but differ from each other sufficiently to constitute particular practice cultures.

As discussed in chapter 2, the concept of 'linguistic communities' connects 'culture' and 'language' in particular contexts. Meaning and identity construction are contextual, rather than generalisable across contexts (Foucault 1972; Dreyfus & Rabinow 1982). Each site of practice represents a particular "linguistic community" (Bourdieu 1991: 45), "a group of people who use the same system of linguistic signs" (Bloomfield 1958: 29, in Bourdieu 1991: 45). A linguistic community produces a particular culture that "anchors" and "stabilizes" words and their meanings so that they are contextually relevant (Manning & Cullum-Swan 1994: 467). Language represents a particular social and material reality through naming and categorisation. Names and categories evoke a particular meaning. Language as representation and evocation intersects with social practices (what we are legitimately allowed to do): "practice, evocation and representation interpenetrate and feed off each other in many . . . areas of life . . . (Bourdieu, 1977)" (Hodder 1994: 397).

Culture is produced through language; the ways in which the material and social world is given meaning by participants through the names that describe objects, events and experiences. The names/categories and related meanings generate rules for legitimate practice (behaviour and action) within the context and thereby also demarcate what is unacceptable practice. The meaning of 'something' in a particular context is linked to what is considered to be appropriate behaviour by participants in relation to each other and the physical context in which they interact, as a "linguistic community". Bourdieu's (1977; Jenkins1992: 30–5) representation of the Kabyle, a community in Algeria that he studied as an anthropologist, is a very useful illustrative example that has been discussed in chapter 2.

Drawing on the concept of linguistic communities, this chapter looks at how cultural rules for child protection practice were constructed at two practice sites. In particular, each office had different 'rules' (descriptive words, meanings and assumptions) about children, parents and families and the problems that were referred to them. These different rules as policy interpretations also influenced preferred practices and precluded others. The local cultures shaped individual practice by providing justifications through rules but did not necessarily restrict individual discretion. Thus, practices in particular cases that are analysed in chapters 6 to 8 are not necessarily reflective of the particular office culture at which the caseworkers were located.

The descriptions and analyses of the two offices as linguistic communities have been derived from participant observation and interviews with workers located at those sites in the mid-1990s. The policy 'content' is only relevant insofar as it structures what was expected at the time. While content might change, the sociology of professional practice in relation to policy is less related to content per se, than it is to do with how that content is interpreted for practice. Thus, it is suggested that there are important sociological issues identified in this chapter that contribute to knowledge about the links between policy (as organisationally prescribed) and practice variations that are constructed versions of policy. In this chapter, the practice variations relate to local service-providing offices whose particular cultures are understood as linguistic communities, and how meanings and identities are constructed within such communities. Chapters 6 to 8 go further by showing how individual practitioners also construct meanings and identities as "idiosyncratic" (Tite 1993) practice that may be mediated by the local cultures within which each practitioner is located. As a unique linguistic community, each site is analysed according to the cultural rules and social practices represented in/by language (the words used to describe and connote particular meaning about client groups, namely children and their parents and problems called 'child maltreatment').

A brief summary of the policy contexts and expectations that structured practice is followed by an analysis of two offices as linguistic communities. This analysis is the main focus of the chapter. The two communities have been named Urbania and Surburbia.

## CHILD PROTECTION IN PRACTICE: POLICY CONTEXTS

In chapter 4 I showed how policy as discourse operates as a politics of knowledge. Drawing on Foucault's (1971, 1978b) concept of "genealogy" as a "history of the present", I showed how the policies of 'the present' that informed practices at local offices and by individual practitioners were not a progressive and linear development over time. Instead, policies may be the outcomes of political responses to "epochal" events in the life of an organisation (Hassard 1993): for example, the death of a child (Walton 1993). A policy response to a tragedy or a public crisis might be represented as the only possible option. However, it may be an outcome of protracted political struggles between high-status participants and social institutions, including politicians, media and professionals (Parton 1991; Walton 1993; Scott & Swain 2002). Thus, a policy response at any particular time represents a particular "epistemological" position (Hassard 1993) in relation to a problem that confronts political, organisational and professional participants.

In the case of this organisation, there were different institutional (and related discursive) contexts during the two main periods of data generation for this research. In 1993 the *Guide to Practice* was the sole text representing official discourse that governed practice at both sites. By 1995, as discussed in chapter 4, there was a change in policy. The New Directions were piloted at five sites, including Urbania, from June to August 1995. This policy change reconfigured how practitioners might engage with the *Guide to Practice*, which was now complementary to the New Directions rather than being the sole policy. Workers were expected to assess referrals according to a broader set of criteria to avoid taking unnecessarily intrusive action associated with child protection. They also had options of 'family support' or 'child concern' if there were concerns for the child that were insufficient to warrant child protection intervention. However, if child maltreatment was identified as the purpose of intervention, the *Guide to Practice* continued to prescribe legitimate child protection knowledge and practice. Meanwhile, for sites that were not part of the piloting of the New Directions, such as Surburbia, the *Guide to Practice* remained the sole policy. However, the practitioners at Surburbia were quite aware of the New Directions although at that stage it had no official influence on their practice. Eventually by May 1996, after the data generation phase of this research was completed, all sites were expected to engage with both the New Directions and the *Guide to Practice*. This chapter discusses the influences of these differences and articulations for situated and individual practical constructions in September and October 1995.

## CHILD PROTECTION IN PRACTICE: PRESCRIBING PRACTICE

All child protection practitioners have specific tasks, prescribed in policy (DCS 1992; Mathews et al. 1995; FCS 1996a), which are differentiated from 'not child protection': for example, "family support" or "child concern" (Kamerman & Kahn 1993; DCS 1992; Mathews et al. 1995; FCS 1996a). Sequential stages named in particular ways maintain the separation between "child protection" and other practices: "allegation" (referral or report at duty/intake), "investigation" (assessment or follow up), and "status of the allegation" (outcome) (DCS 1992; FCS 1996a). Particular decisions arise from the "outcome", including "case [maltreatment] type", intervention and closure (DCS 1992; FCS 1996a; Murphy-Berman 1994). Statistical summaries that include profiles of children as 'victims of maltreatment', 'types of maltreatment' and 'persons believed responsible', as well as case practice (intake and outcome data), are used to monitor practice consistency in relation to policy and as a basis of professional knowledge (Cant & Downie 1994; Australian Institute of Health and Welfare (AIHW) http://www.aifs.gov.au/nch/stats/html).

### Child Protection: A Guide to Practice (1992)

This policy document was the primary influence on child protection practice until the New Directions was piloted in 1995. However, practice sites that were not part of the pilot program in 1995 relied solely on the *Guide to Practice*.

According to the *Guide to Practice*, the "central task of intake . . . is gathering and recording of information and assessing the level of risk to a child" (DCS 1992: 26). An "allegation" is "any report that suggests, or states, that a child has been harmed or is at substantial risk of harm" (DCS 1992: 26).

The investigation "aims to confirm/deny/indicate that abuse/neglect is occurring or has occurred, and if so, to what extent; assess [and ensure] safety and well being of children . . ., examine . . . family [functioning], and decide [if the case] is supportive/statutory" (DCS 1992: 33).

"Priority responses" (DCS 1992: 28–32) are organised "risk factors" against which the particular child's experiences within the family must be judged (DePanfilis & Scannapieco 1994).

The "status of the allegation" concludes the investigation, when the worker decides "whether the allegation is substantiated or not" (DCS 1992: 40). Substantiation does not have to rely on "legal evidence", but "credible evidence that harm ... has occurred ... or ... risk of further harm" (DCS 1992: 40).

### New Directions (1995)

The New Directions required workers to engage differently with the *Guide to Practice*, which was no longer the sole document. The Pilot Implementation Guidelines: A Child Protection Service as set out in Appendix 1 (Mathews et al. 1995) stated in its introduction:

> These guidelines are to assist staff determine the status of referrals received about the safety and welfare of children at the point of duty and intake (i.e. whether they constitute child maltreatment allegations requiring a child protection response) and the basis on which allegations are to be substantiated. *The guidelines are to be read in conjunction with the* CHILD PROTECTION: A GUIDE TO PRACTICE. *They will directly replace some sections of the GUIDE and will impact upon other sections.* (emphasis added)

> A child maltreatment allegation "is a referral where the information strongly supports or presents clear evidence that:

> ■ A child has been physically or emotionally harmed or injured.
> ■ A child's physical and/or emotional safety is at *severe risk of harm*, or injury is likely to occur.
> ■ A child has been the subject of an illegal act by a caregiver or other person with a duty of responsibility for the child, or
> ■ A child has been the subject of persistent actions or inactions by the caregiver or other person with a duty of responsibility to the child, that have resulted in the child's development being severely impaired (original emphasis) ...

> Situations where a referral should be categorised as a child maltreatment allegation are:

> 1  initial referrals where there is clear medical evidence of harm or injury identified by a medical practitioner or police officer

> 2  initial reports of clear disclosures of maltreatment to a hospital, medical practitioner or police officer

> 3  where information, received at the point of duty or as the result of an assessment of a CCR, provides clear information that the elements of a child maltreatment allegation are present. Where the referral source is a professional with expertise in the area, his/her assessment is considered well informed. In all

these cases, the Responsible Senior Officer must endorse the decision to designate the referral a CMA. [. . .]

Substantiation requires the confirmation of one of the following key elements of a child maltreatment allegation:

1 Illegal sexual activity by a caregiver or other person with a duty of responsibility to the child.

2 Harm or injury has resulted from persistent and/or severe actions of a caregiver or other person with a duty of responsibility for the child, or

3 There is strong evidence that the persistence and/or severity of actions or inactions will result in harm or injury to the child. This includes harm which is cumulative in its effect, i.e. past harms. [. . .]

Priority Responses to Child Maltreatment Allegations and Child Concern Reports for Use by Pilot Districts in CMA/CCR Trial are summarised in table 5.1.

| | |
|---|---|
| Priority A | A response is required immediately or within one working day: where a child is at immediate risk of harm; where a current family crisis requires immediate attention to secure the safety of the family and children – e.g. serious risk of family violence; where a child is at risk of self harm, to provide food or shelter when a family is suddenly destitute. |
| | Factors commonly associated with referrals requiring a priority A response include those . . . previously identified with priority one responses for Child Maltreatment Allegations . . . in the manual *Child Protection: A Guide to Practice*. |
| Priority B | A response is required within 2–5 working days. Where children are not at immediate risk of harm but where harm is likely to occur or reoccur. This includes factors previously associated with priority 2 and 3 responses to Child Maltreatment Allegations, . . . e.g. history of previous harm, person likely to [cause] harm, functioning and capacity of caregivers . . . In response to Child Concern Reports, these cases may include situations where there are clear indications that a quick response will prevent a serious crisis developing, e.g. parent/child conflict, impaired parental capacity to provide adequate care or has resulted in an incident of inappropriate discipline that is not severe. Relate to priority 2 and 3 responses for CMA (*Guide to Practice*). |
| Priority C | In relation to Child Concern Reports only, and where no harmful circumstances are involved . . . a response should be commenced within 10 working days. |
| | This priority response refers to cases where services are likely to help parents care appropriately for their children, e.g. where there has been no urgent situation precipitating the referral but where parents may be having difficulty with communicating with a child, setting appropriate limits or where there are concerns about emotional or social development of the child. |

*Source: Mathews et al. 1995: Appendix 1*

**Table 5.1 Priority Responses (from New Directions and Child Protection: A Guide to Practice)**

These stages and related tasks prescribe practice across all sites, but they may be implemented differently within situated meanings of child protection practice, and associated identities of the 'person believed responsible', 'child' and 'parent'. The remainder of this chapter re-presents for each site in 1995 these situated meanings and identities. The topics include situated cultural rules, their influence on how dominant versions of meanings and identities are reconstructed at the site, and their influence on situated and individual practices.

## URBANIA: 1995

I interviewed six caseworkers (Edna, Fiona, George, Helen, Ivor and Jack) about cases involving the Ibsen, Jones, Kelly, Lewis, Martini and Nicholson families respectively. I also formally interviewed Lana, the manager; Darren, Patrick and Shelley, team leaders who were previously senior social workers (child protection). I observed duty officers' practices, team meetings and case discussions and engaged in informal discussions with other workers who were not formally interviewed. My re-presentation of the situated constructions of knowledge, meanings and identities is a composite of these versions.

### Cultural rules

Urbania being a child protection/child welfare organisation, parenting practices were the main focus of intervention. However, I was surprised to hear workers expressing a common identity with 'clients' as 'parents', even though some of the parents were 'persons believed responsible for maltreatment'. I often overheard workers discussing their own problems as parents, including being called to account by professionals such as teachers, school psychologists and police. Their willingness to acknowledge their own difficulties and experiences as parents perhaps contributed to their empathy towards parents who were clients (Portwood 1998), as this example taken from my field diary shows:

> Three female non-Aboriginal Social Workers who were discussing a Child Protection investigation commented that the man (father/client) was "pissed off". This was seen as a "normal" response, as "*I wouldn't like it having a Social Worker come into the family and comment on child care.*" (emphasis added)

My observations suggested particular rules that informed the local practice culture which I have formulated as 'it's tough being a parent', and 'there but for the grace of God go I', a conclusion that was supported by many workers when I discussed it with them.

At Urbania, preferred practices were expressed as "least intrusive intervention" and "reunification of families", within "natural justice principles". Furthermore, workers were justified in "ask[ing] questions about practice", and "thinking for themselves". "Debate allows for learning and different forms of thinking" as well as "open, honest work with a family", "reflection on personal values" and a "more realistic/pragmatic involvement with the family".

## Interpreting organisational policy

### Constructing meanings and identities

Assumptions about parental normality and preferences for least intrusive intervention, described by Helen, a senior social worker as a "preventive/supportive" approach, influenced intake practices in which fewer referrals were seen as "child maltreatment". This approach was consistent with the New Directions objective of minimising categorisations of "maltreatment" so that "family support" could be offered instead.

The "third category" of CCR, seen by social workers Edna and George as a filter for referrals, limited "child saving" ways of thinking associated with 'child protection'. However, the CCR as a "temporary classification" (FCS 1996a: 13) had to be re-categorised as soon as an assessment was completed, into either "child maltreatment" (practices on behalf of "children") or "family support" (practices on behalf of "families") (FCS 1996a, 1996b; Mathews et al. 1995: 93–100).

Reports constructed as "maltreatment" were the "hard end cases". "Risk factors" which formed the basis of assessment as "investigation" offered a "simpler, narrower way of assessing families", differentiated from "family support assessment" as "more holistic, taking [poverty] into account". Family privacy as a norm at the site articulated with requirements in New Directions, but social workers George and Helen echoed general concerns that it could also "hamstring" workers in practice.

The CCR overlapped the differentiated categories of 'child maltreatment *by the family*' and 'concern for the child in the family' (FCS 1996a). Helen and George were also concerned about the implications for practice of expectations that workers would eventually make the 'correct choice' between these conceptually polarised policy categories. In their view, this created "paranoia" about "missing a CMA" because the CCR category limited intervention to "assessment". Furthermore, there was a generally expressed view that 'assessment' meant respecting 'family privacy' that therefore limited the ability to "... breach the line [of parents' rights] to get more info". 'Assessment' stopped workers from "interviewing the kid", which they were allowed to do if "investigating maltreatment".

Risk management was not just the main child protection strategy. It also aimed to meet an implicit objective of protection of the organisation, and of workers themselves, by minimising the tragedies that would otherwise create unwanted publicity. Workers negotiated a "staff guarantee/charter" (FCS 1996a) to "protect" them from blame, which Jack, a social worker, called "scapegoating". A coronial inquiry into the death of a child and associated publicity symbolised the sort of incident that risk management sought to avoid. This child's death, like so many others in recent child protection history, was seen as an outcome of procedural deviance by individual workers who felt they were blamed (Parton 1985; Parton 1991; Walton 1993).

At Urbania, the "child" was differentiated between those in need of "protection" and those who were not (for example, "young homeless"), with the meanings of both 'child' and 'protection' being defined in particular ways. I observed two such cases at duty/intake, regarding 15-year-old girls who were living independently either from choice (sexual abuse by father, mother deceased) or circumstance (unwanted by mother, father overseas). Despite their age and personal stories, they were unable to obtain relatively small amounts of financial assistance (for example, $15, $40) to secure safe housing without being subjected to extensive questioning to prove their credibility and need.

'The family' was the focus in child concern reports, unlike in child protection where the child is differentiated from the parents and there is little or no focus on 'the family'. In a CMA, the individual child as 'the client' was "sighted" to construct "what has happened" and identities of responsibility. Injuries to the child were categorised initially as a 'child concern' until further investigation determined whether the injuries were "normal childhood injuries" or likely to be a result of maltreatment, thus being re-categorised as a 'child protection' case. A worker gave me an example of a report by a school official of a child "with a bruise", believed to have "happened at home". It was "called a CCR till we could check what the bruise looked like".

Children's bodies also provided opportunities for surveillance of parental and cultural practices. An investigation of a six-month-old child with "bruising around the eyes" and "nose [with] fading bruising" as possible non-accidental injuries, revealed that marital stresses, domestic violence and isolation were contributing influences in the mother's assault on the child.

Ethnicity, cultural and racial identities were associated with language differences and affiliations as shared identities. For example, "Aboriginal" employees would facilitate access to services by marginalised "Aboriginal" families, but not necessarily challenge potentially ethnocentric constructions of problems called 'maltreatment' or how child protection practice could be culturally appropriate.

'Aboriginality' was an important identity when children's placement in alternative care was necessary, this being a policy that was fully embraced at Urbania. However, of the cases sampled at Urbania, none was categorised as 'Aboriginal', although the file about the Ibsen family ("physical abuse") showed that the child's mother was identified as "Aboriginal" after some initial confusion that she was "Polynesian", as the social worker Edna explained to me. The father was "non-Aboriginal"; this identity being extended to the child also. However, as discussed in chapter 7, patriarchal mothering assumptions (Stark & Flitcraft 1988) influenced practice and there was little consideration given to possible inequalities due to racial and cultural differences between Mr and Mrs Ibsen.

**Regulating practice**

The cultural rule of "healthy debate" constructed policy in various ways, as
- Prescriptions
- "Directions"
- "Requirements"
- "Guiding influences" for "sensible, not capricious" practice
- Allowing opportunities for "judgment"
- "Room for discretion"
- "Fair degree of freedom of interpretation"
- "Scope for professional decision making".

There was overt acceptance that workers sought to convince team leaders and senior supervisors of their practice judgments and case categories:

> If the child is at risk, I'll call it a CMA and talk the Team Leader into accepting the definition. (Shelley, Team Leader, talking about caseworkers' practices)

> Worker needs to know how to present the information and present the argument in a convincing way. (Jack, Social Worker)

> [If staff disagree with guidelines, they may] reconceptualise their work [and] beef up arguments in a particular case. (Darren, Senior Case Work Supervisor)

However, policy interpretations as "judgments" had practice consequences and related accountability. "[You] have to make judgments despite having manuals; still have to be accountable for the *actions* you take" (emphasis added) (Lana, Manager).

Statistics – for example, "numbers of duty cases, CCRs and CMAs" – regulated situated practices by comparisons across sites as "consistency" (equated with practice "quality") (FCS 1996a; Mathews et al. 1995):

> Urbania's data in relation to CMA, CCR, and CCR converted to CMA is in trend with the other districts . . . excepting [site X] . . . and in line with corporate trends. (Lana, Manager)

> The Manager agrees with the SCWS that [we] need more apprehensions in line with other districts [sites] and New Directions. (Shelley, Team Leader)

Staff did not necessarily share the Manager's views about how statistical consistency was to be achieved or even that it was important to do so:

> The staff have different views to the management [who] want the categories . . . to be consistent with other Districts. (Shelley, Team Leader)

Statistics also regulated practice by being directly linked to resource allocation by comparison of "substantiation rates" across sites, which Helen, a social worker, argued "did not really represent what you were doing". There were also the difficulties in substantiating "neglect" which was the "typical case" for the site.

Workers were overwhelmed with additional regulatory strategies that Howe (1992) calls "proceduralisation", and "bureaucratisation". They described "paper work" and "numerous meetings", different surveillance and monitoring strategies: "checking intake forms are correct and procedures have been followed", "to account for all cases" and prevent "cases falling in gaps". Nevertheless, social workers Helen and Jack resisted by "testing the flexibility of the system" and by "being difficult".

To maintain and disseminate what is considered as legitimate knowledge and to prevent 'incorrect' knowledge being learnt, professional networks are created by inculcation of those considered to be not knowledgeable by training and education, supervision, and pairing of a less knowledgeable worker with an expert. At Urbania I was told about and observed many examples of such strategies of knowledge coordination and regulation. Less knowledgeable workers such as non-social workers or "junior staff" were taught techniques for "information gathering and classification", assessment procedures and "interviewing" on the assumption that these are neutral procedures that can be applied in any situation (Fairclough 1992). "Joint interviewing" ensured all "significant information" was gathered. For example, the investigation of the Ibsen family ("physical abuse") was co-worked by Edna as Acting SSW (CP) and Ivor, a Family Welfare Officer. Similarly, the Kelly family ("neglect") was co-worked by Fiona, a new social work graduate aged in her twenties, and whoever of the SSWs (CP) was available.

**Cultural rules in practice**

The main cultural rules at Urbania were parental normality, least intrusive intervention, and healthy debate. Only 'hard end cases' were constructed as child protection cases, and workers did not deviate from what was prescribed in the *Guide to Practice* (1992). The general culture was constructed in informal conversations and formal case discussions and processes. Sometimes the rules were apparent when staff deviated from them, because they explained the reason for the deviation. However workers did not always make explicit the cultural rules for Urbania when they explained their practices in particular cases. Only the Nicholson case (chapter 8) showed, in some form, the articulation of all three rules.

The immediate categorisation of the referral in the Nicholson case as 'neglect' was the opposite of the cultural rule of 'least intrusive intervention', although Jack's intake practice complied with least intrusive intervention by "taking [the referral] as a goldy [a child concern report form]". Jack's engagement with this case showed the influences of the other two rules, parental normality and healthy debate. He debated the categorisation of neglect by describing it as "a fait accompli", as the outcome of an investigation by Crisis Care workers, hospitals and police (chapter 8), who were accepted unquestioningly as knowledge experts (FCS 1996a; DCS 1992). Jack told me:

> Because this [investigation] was done by Crisis Care it didn't get processed in the usual [. . .] a fait accompli . . . not too many questions [. . .] I guess also because you've got hospitals and police which comes under the definition of CMA [. . .].

However, within these constraints Jack exercised some discretion. His response was a version of the cultural rule of healthy debate, a preference for a CCR/family support category, and practical gender equality. Jack recognised the mother's identity as 'drug addict' and its potential consequences for her baby, yet he was able to recognise the mutually beneficial relationship she had with her child:

> [If] we can get this woman to stabilise . . . she's got some [parenting] skills and we can enhance and support them. We don't really want a baby in care just because mum uses drugs per se.

> This mum really wants her baby back [. . .] really having a meaningful life through her child at the moment, she's not able to care for herself at the moment, so realistically, she wouldn't be able to care for the baby [. . .].

The Kelly case ("neglect") also breached the cultural preference for 'least intrusive intervention'. It could be argued that it fitted the other rule of 'healthy debate', simply because alternative perspectives were allowed. Nevertheless, the social worker Fiona acknowledged the influences of her "upper middle class Catholic" positioning on her practice. She constructed all children as 'vulnerable and dependent' and held a particular cultural image of 'normal families'. Yet Ms Kelly and her children perceived Fiona's interventions as intrusive (chapter 8). Although Fiona acknowledged the potential malice from the male reporter who was known to be in conflict with Ms Kelly, the apparent 'facts' of the family's abnormality dominated. Furthermore, Fiona's practice was not seen as "idiosyncratic" (Tite 1993) or "subjective" (Jones 1993) by her colleagues. Instead, she had their full support, co-working the case with one or other of the Senior Social Workers (Child Protection). Thus, despite a stated preference for least intrusive intervention, it was difficult for practitioners to question cultural constructions of every child as 'vulnerable and dependent' even when they were pre-adolescent and demonstrably 'independent' as in the Kelly case (chapter 8).

It could be argued that three cases at Urbania were 'hard end cases', based on their categorisations as 'physical abuse' (Ibsen), and 'sexual abuse' (Jones & Lewis) (chapters 6 and 7). The processes of constructing maltreatment and identities of responsibility that are analysed in detail in chapters 6 and 7 could justify the departure from the rules of 'least intrusive intervention' and 'parental normality'. However, despite the proclaimed 'shared normality' with parents, patriarchal mothering assumptions significantly undermined notions of equality between practitioners and parents, particularly mothers. Gender differences between mothers and male workers (George and Ivor) perhaps exacerbated inequalities associated with 'client' and 'practitioner'. However, I was even more concerned to observe practices by women as practitioners/parents that appeared to show no solidarity with women as clients/parents. Women as parents were not the equals of female practitioners: for example, Edna, the social worker in the Ibsen and Jones cases. Male and female practitioners often described the mothers as 'unprotective' and therefore 'responsible' for men's 'maltreatment' of the children, even where the women's experiences of male violence were known. The mother's 'unprotectiveness' was associated with "not stopping/almost approving the hitting" (Ibsen family), "abdication of responsibility" by letting children live with their physically abusive father (Jones family), and apparent breaches of heterosexual monogamy by the mother (Lewis family).

Helen, a social worker, whose independent thinking was valued within a cultural rule of 'healthy debate', successfully exercised discretion in how she categorised particular practices as 'sexual abuse' associated with a 'person believed responsible' (Martini family). She questioned the way in which boys as young as four years could be categorised as "perpetrators" of "sexual abuse". Instead she proposed an alternative meaning of their practices as "playing" or "experimenting". She transformed the reported identity of the seven-year-old boy (see chapter 6) from 'person believed responsible for sexual abuse' to a possible 'victim of sexual abuse' by "somebody else (older boys or grown ups)". This reconstruction of identities of the children involved in the case also altered the meaning of the referral, the focus of the investigation and the outcome as "unsubstantiated sexual abuse", with no "person believed responsible".

## URBANIA AS A LINGUISTIC COMMUNITY IN 1995

Urbania in 1995 was a practice site working within two primary policy texts, namely, the *Guide to Practice* and the draft New Directions, that were to be used as complementary policies. These articulating policies influenced situated practices, but were also interpreted and contested by individual practitioners and as a collective. Whilst differences and debate were accepted as normal and essential for practice, there was also concern that 'actions' should be accountable as there were consequences for children, parents and the organisation. Procedures governing 'actions' aimed to minimise practice 'inconsistencies' and to promote accountability. However, individuals subverted these regulatory strategies in various ways to negotiate meanings and identities. In general, the opportunities for negotiation and debate, preferred practice of least intrusive intervention, and the rhetoric of parental normality minimised categorisations as child maltreatment/protection.

Particular definitions of 'child' and 'protection' included only children seen as 'maltreated', but excluded children who might need 'protection' but who were not considered to be 'maltreated': for example, 'young homeless'. Cultural rhetoric of shared 'parental' identities between workers and parents/clients minimised the potential for oppressive practices between 'professionals' and 'parents as clients/persons believed responsible'. However, uncritical assumptions about 'normal families' as heterosexually monogamous, egalitarian relationships influenced practical constructions in each case, thus undermining the rhetoric of equality with parents. In particular, patriarchal mothering practices constructed 'identities of responsibility' in which mothers were "responsible" and men remained "invisible" (Milner 1993).

## SUBURBIA: 1995

At Suburbia I observed duty officers' practices, team meetings and case conferences, and engaged in informal discussions with many practitioners. I also formally interviewed the Manager, Anna; the Senior Casework Supervisor, Eric; and Team Leaders, Jerry and Laura. I also interviewed five workers (Kim, Lyla, Morris, Carly and Olive) about the O'Keefe, Park, Quinn, Riley, Underwood and Turner families.

### Cultural rules at Suburbia

My formulation of the dominant cultural rule as 'defensive practice' (Sanders et al. 1999: 265) was strongly supported by what I heard formally and informally and observed in the physical structure and social relations at the office. For example, there was overt security using coded locks on all doors from the waiting area, and individuals often "patrolled the corridors" when a "dangerous client" was being interviewed by a colleague. The following statements encapsulate the culture of defensive practice (or resistance to it):

- Follow organisational procedures.
- Make sure you minimise workload.
- Protect workers from "mistakes".
- "Protect the political arse."

Secondly, workers believed that defensive practice was necessary because they were working with a community where "dangerous", argumentative and "loud" (verbally aggressive) parents resided, with often 'contentious' cases. There was a collective identity, voiced by many individuals who considered themselves to be 'normal', but obliged to work in a "local community like the Bronx", which "breeds violent people". Particular sub-groups in the local community were identified as examples of problem clients who populated Suburbia: women as sole parents, people in public housing and Aboriginal people. A social worker, Kim, did live in Suburbia. However, while she acknowledged her more privileged circumstances – less suffering, not unemployed, own house – she also saw herself as "apart from a lot of people in this community".

A third aspect of the rule of defensive practice was related to the sense of being the sole agency responsible for child protection. "Nobody wants to own CP any more – still defensive practice." Agencies "refer more, act less", leading to more work for "the welfare" (that is, workers at Suburbia).

## Interpreting organisational policy

### Constructing meanings and identities

The sense of siege at Suburbia was summed up by workers' descriptions of their practice context as "in a war zone" with "dangerous clients" being "out of control", "crapping on the stairs" or "pissing in the water fountain", and threatening the receptionist. Dangerous clients were "loud" and "verbally aggressive", and/or physically violent to staff. Some were "regulars" known for their "hysteria" and "aggression" or "paranoia", in response to children being placed in care or made wards.

The most dangerous people were apparently 'normal' parents, who could be seen as "reasonable people . . . with children and concerns for them". They did "not [fit] the stereotype [of the] drunken hobo who's going to pull a knife on you because you have refused him some money" (Laura, Team Leader). By contrast, the workers liked "polite and amenable" clients who were "very subdued and quiet" because they were easier to "keep under control".

Beyond coping with 'dangerous parents' who were reacting to child protection intervention that could separate them from their children, workers also considered that dangerous parents increased 'risks' to children, including death and serious injury. Thus, defensive practice was necessary to minimise such risks that could otherwise become practice 'mistakes'. 'Defensive practice' as 'protection' and 'risk minimisation' had multi-layered objectives, in which safeguarding the child's bodily integrity and normality would also safeguard workers and the organisation from unwanted publicity for 'mistakes'.

The effects for workers of one such 'past mistake', a child's death and the associated coronial inquiry, continued to influence defensive practice as "risk management/minimisation". This case and its aftermath were so pervasive on practice that the Manager, Anna, commented to me: "How long do you let it go on for, so that it forever affects your practice? Risk management is so great for staff that it's a worry."

To minimise 'mistakes', a broader construction of 'maltreatment' was preferred, one that privileged children's rights over family privacy/integrity (Fox Harding 1991). If "comprehensive information" required by the *Guide to Practice* to manage/assess risk (DCS 1992: 26) could not always be achieved, workers "played safe" by constructing "risk factors" as "what we don't know" or "looking for negatives". Preferred protective practices were "apprehensions [of children], their removal from, [or their] non-return home". Anna described these practices as "pretending to protect children" and a breach of "family privacy". "We don't march into a family and remove a child because we don't know."

'Contentious' cases also were reason for defensive practice. In such cases, parents disputed official meanings of events as 'maltreatment' and their own 'responsibility', "because they [the clients] all know their [legal] rights". These parents often engaged an external network of allies to support their positions against the department, represented by the caseworker. External allies included legal advisers engaged by the O'Keefe, Quinn and Riley families; politicians by the Riley family; the Departmental Consumer Advocate (Underwood family); "articulate friends" (Quinn family) and family members (Turner family). These temporary coalitions operated as psychological battering rams against the site, and increased 'contentiousness' and the workload that workers had to defend against.

Laura expressed the generally held view that child maltreatment was a pervasive problem that was objectively true, but only recognised by people with appropriate expertise. "People don't go around looking for bruising on children. They don't have CP eyes like we do."

Anna's comments perhaps best encapsulated the linkages between case categorisation and expected practices that had consequences for workload and organisational politics. "[I]f you go one way, it sets a whole set of processes in motion." She gave an example of foster parents who used "cold showers" as "discipline". If these practices were categorised as "abuse", she "would not have been game to ignore procedures"; that is, she would have to "... investigate, notify the Director General, prosecute foster parents". She had to "look at the bigger picture, including workload and legal implications".

Anna also contested the local cultural practice of seeing children's bodily abnormalities in a simple cause-effect relation that disregarded contextual explanations. For example, "broken bones", "bruises" per se meant 'child maltreatment'. Also, certain parts of the body were associated with particular abnormal practices described as "inappropriate touching" or "masturbation" – for example, "breasts" or "genitals". For Anna, the meaning of perceived bodily abnormalities could not be taken for granted as 'child maltreatment'. Instead, power and vulnerability of individuals involved over time were key practice considerations in constructing 'maltreatment'.

Anna also promoted "discretion and flexibility" instead of "self protective and slavish following of regulations". Her practice approach destabilised the existing power/knowledge relation in Suburbia: "people [were] positioning [them]selves within teams and [sub] cultures [of different knowledge]". Laura, on the other hand, considered that "opposition and debate" were "risky" if they disrupted compliance with policy and procedures. Instead, 'child maltreatment' was an undisputed fact that workers could not deviate from ("if something [is] clear as being CP"), and they were expected to meet "children's needs", seen as a fixed and absolute reality (Woodhead 1990).

The "hierarchy of maltreatment" (Dubowitz 1994; Berliner 1994) was strongly adhered to. "Sexual" and "physical assault" categories were either differentiated with "sexual abuse" being "worse" than "physical abuse", or as "the same" (equally problematic), because they "happened together". However, together 'sexual and physical abuse' were divided from the "most damaging emotional abuse" because they were "easier to deal with", being "more concrete".

High priority workload involved "immediate investigation" of "serious sexual assaults (rape), and serious physical assault (injuries to children)". "Hitting" children or "neglect" were not "serious enough". These lower priority cases "only happened once" and workload mainly involved writing letters to parents, "usually mums/single parents", asking them to come in and discuss the referral/concerns (Laura, Team Leader; Lyla, Welfare Officer), "finding out what's happening for mum, make a referral and close" (Laura, Team Leader). In lower priority cases, the onus was on the clients to make contact for "support services". "We won't seek them out due to workload" (Laura).

Olive, a social worker, told me that 'Aboriginal' people were associated with 'neglect', financial assistance or domestic violence that required a "supportive and preventive role" *outside* 'child protection'. They did not meet the site's priorities of "very high risk dangerous type cases".

The only investigation of "neglect" involved the Park family. This exception to the situated rule about "priorities" involved a child/family identified as "non-Aboriginal" (on file as "Vietnamese"). I have discussed the ethnocentric practices in this case in chapter 8. At Suburbia, this family gained pseudo-Aboriginal identity, because, as was explained to me by team leaders, "they have similar kinship relationships". Furthermore, these assumptions of ethnic 'otherness' meant that the case was allocated to Lyla who, being Aboriginal, would "understand" and "explain well".

At Suburbia, 'Aboriginal' identity could be described as an attachment to the dominant ethnocentric discourse, represented by the Aboriginal Child Placement Policy that was "followed religiously". This policy regulated the removal of children from their parents' care, and advocated placement with culturally appropriate caregivers. However, the likelihood of its implementation was minimal, as "most [child protection] cases are non-Aboriginal". None of the cases selected for me by senior managers involved 'Aboriginal' children/families. An Early Education Officer who identified as "Aboriginal" worked mainly with "non-Aboriginal" families (self or other referred), although ostensibly she had been appointed to work with Aboriginal families who were a substantial part of the population in Suburbia.

Some female practitioners expressed an "interest in women's place in the world, dealt with power and gender" or the "gentle side", "the nurturing side". However, in practice they were the norm against which they judged women/clients/mothers. Patriarchal mothering practices and assumptions of egalitarian family relations were taken for granted.

Interestingly, Morris, the only male social worker, seemed to have a better grasp of gender issues in child protection practice: for example, recognising male violence to women and children. He also spoke about "vanishing men", who left "most women . . . to be accountable for their performances as mothers", often "coming out worst". Morris had a more sympathetic view of 'parents as persons believed responsible'. Instead of being 'dangerous' and intentionally causing harm, he saw most parents as transgressive of their own constructions of normality, by abnormal practices, rather than intentions: "[their] main aim is to look after the welfare of the children even when their actions point in different directions".

Children were seen as vulnerable/dependent victims, along with an unspoken assumption that they were also undeveloped adults (Jenks 1996). These assumptions about children constructed parental responsibility for "supervision" of their children as care (preventing "loneliness" and "fear") and regulation ("keep them under control").

The vulnerable and 'good' child was a legitimate 'victim in need of protection'. These children were usually younger, and with limited ability due to language or social recognition of their competence to participate in constructing the meanings of their experiences. "Babies [who] got priority" were "powerless victims" of "cruel" practices, which "could have long term emotional effects", with "needs and rights to protection [by others]". Child protection workers gave "a voice to . . . the voiceless and unprotected [child]", who could also be "delightful little surprises".

Anna offered a contrasting view to the pervasive construction of children as vulnerable and dependent. She emphasised children's "resilience", and that "permanent harm" was often unlikely. The example of foster parents using cold showers as 'discipline' (discussed above) highlighted these differences. These practices could be constructed as "abuse", and also as "serious inappropriate parenting" or "a power issue – adult power over child". Laura saw the same practices as "bizarre", "deliberate and cruel".

Children who were capable of participating in the meanings of their experiences of disadvantage and oppression and who sought official help did not fit the local definition of the vulnerable/dependent child. Teenagers, for example, were seen as less vulnerable/dependent, 'bad' children and possibly not legitimate 'victims' in need of 'protection'. Laura gave the example of one teenage girl who "lived on the streets, with men, unwanted by parents or alternative carers". Laura described her as "talk[ing] as if she's 20!" which I heard as, 'she's not really a child and can look after herself'. In a second example related to me by a duty social worker, a teenage girl's report of "physical abuse" was seen as "a bit iffy, given it's only her story; she's left home to live with boyfriend and parents don't approve".

### Regulating practice

At Suburbia, the overwhelming feature of defensive practice was that collective decision-making was preferred to individual casework. The aim of collective constructions of meanings and identities was to maximise conformity with prescribed policies and procedures because "no assessment process is perfect". "No individual worker gets a case to follow up without extensive consultation, reading of files and planning what action to take."

Local strategies to coordinate knowledge and minimise deviation from prescribed practice included "team meetings", "case discussions/consultation", "joint interviewing" or "pairing" with the Senior Social Worker (CP) as the expert, teaching workers techniques to "confront parents", "investigation" and "intervention". Expertise was vested solely in the Senior Social Workers (CP) who "sight[ed] and sign[ed]" all intake forms and consulted with all duty officers to regulate intake.

Carly told me about how she valued the local collective memory of "instructions" that would prevent individuals "forgetting", becoming 'disconnected', "isolated", "paranoid" and "foolish". Ultimately, collective decision-making and regulation of individual practice would minimise "mistakes" such as children's deaths or "sexual abuse in foster care", which were controversial and publicised cases at the time.

Some workers complied with "extensive consultation", to achieve compliance with procedures [1a–b], and maximise, if not guarantee, practice outcomes [2] (and minimise risk):

> I'm told that what I did [with the Riley family] was right [1a] and that, if I had done anything differently then I would have been wrong [1b], but the outcome of what I did was wrong [2]. (Carly, Social Worker)

Others, like Morris, a social worker, contested extensive consultation as unnecessary: "intricate details of regulations"; and as "trivia", which devalued maturity and experience, and minimised individual responsibility.

Workers at Suburbia were aware that computerised statistical summaries recorded their "workloads" and the outcomes of their practices as categories whose "consistency" across sites was a measure of compliance and "quality practice". Collective responsibility defended individual practitioners from such surveillance by 'the organisation' because no one could be identified as solely 'responsible'. Similarly, workers feared organisational prescriptions for recording and auditing practice, known as "file management". As social workers, Carly, Kim, Morris and Olive, remarked, this was not about "quality standards" but "uncover[ing] something that's of concern [about workers]." These organisational strategies to regulate practice exacerbated the defensive culture. Both Kim and Morris said, "We spend a lot of time writing reports to cover our backs", which had serious practice consequences: "less time to engage with clients e.g. do home visits", "isolation" from the local community and "impersonal" practice.

Ultimately, individual compliance minimised repercussions for the organisation, including "publicity, legal action and potential compensation [to clients]". However, non-compliance and "practice mistakes" by individuals had "very serious consequences" for them, including "abandonment", "scapegoating", and "being sacked for not doing as they were told", framed in legal terms as "negligence" and abrogation of "duty of care".

## Cultural rules in practice

Cultural rules were 'defensive practice' to manage 'risk' from 'dangerous clients', 'contentious' cases and related work overload; and to minimise 'practice mistakes'.

Most of the cases selected for me by the Manager and Senior Case Work Supervisor as 'typical' for Suburbia illustrated in practice the cultural rules about 'dangerous parents' and/or 'contentiousness' associated with parental challenges to professional knowledge/power. Of the six cases sampled, only the Park family's case was my choice, but indirectly. I had wanted to interview an 'Aboriginal' worker, who happened to be the case manager for the Park family. Nevertheless, the Manager and Team Leader worked the case into the category of 'dangerousness'. They told me that "the father had 'knifed the children'. However, there was no report on file of any child being 'knifed', although 'neglect' was alleged, and there was a description on file of "physical abuse" ("hitting" with an implement). And only one child was involved.

Three cases in particular (O'Keefe, Quinn and Turner) became part of the local "myths and legends" (Pithouse 1987) as symbolic of 'dangerous parents' and 'contentious' cases. These cases were revisited almost continually at team meetings or in more informal conversations. As symbols of cultural rules, these cases justified defensive practice and, as Morris (social worker) said, they gave "mystique" to individual practitioners.

The Quinn family's case did not fit the cultural rule that preferred constructions of 'maltreatment' to other possible categories of presenting problems. This was a "long-standing" case (over four years). The problems were described on file as "chronic physical and emotional neglect" and by Morris, the caseworker, as "long term physical neglect and low level abuse" – in short, as 'deficient parenting'. The transformation to a 'child maltreatment' category, "at risk", was a response to the mother's withdrawal of 'cooperation' with the workers. Instead she contested the placement of her children and wardship she had previously agreed to. From this point on the mother, Ms Quinn, was an 'adversary' (see chapter 7). Ms Quinn's increasing distress at the children's relationship with the foster mother, including calling her "mum" culminated in Ms Quinn's assault of a support worker on an access visit with the children. She was then seen as 'dangerous' and the incident was discussed repeatedly at the site. Ms Quinn's aggressive engagement with workers and the involvement of media, lawyers and, as her caseworker Morris described them, "articulate, intelligent and better class" friends, increased the contentiousness of the case and related workload.

Patriarchal mothering assumptions (Stark & Flitcraft 1988; Milner 1993) strongly influenced practice. Female practitioners were often harsh in their judgments about women as mothers, and also were more likely to construct the mother as 'unprotective', being solely or equally 'responsible' for harm to children. Men's responsibility was either disregarded or minimised. Furthermore, the women's own experiences of violence were disregarded. Examples of patriarchal mothering practices were apparent with the O'Keefe, Riley, Stubbs and Turner families (chapters 7 and 8).

With the O'Keefe family, Ms O'Keefe's intellectual disability increased perceptions of her as an incompetent mother. Thus she was also positioned as unequal in relation to her husband and to the social workers, Kim and Laura. Ms O'Keefe's 'intellectual disability' was deployed by her husband and the workers as an explanation for her inability to parent ("control the children") (D'Cruz 1998), without hitting them and causing bruises. The workers did not contest the husband's/father's known violence to his wife and children. Laura, the Team Leader said, "He clouts her just like a school kid". Ms O'Keefe's disability was used to justify her husband's violence as "frustration". Workers reconstructed Mr O'Keefe's violence to Ms O'Keefe as a joint responsibility, with advice to them at a case discussion "to deal with their relationship". The workers also saw Ms O'Keefe's disability as a disqualification from parenting, wondering aloud: "Has she had her tubes tied?" They also saw her as a deficient woman/partner ("not a good catch for a desperate man"). Mr O'Keefe was not seriously considered as 'responsible for physical abuse'.

The Underwood family represented another 'typical' case for the site. The "complicated family system" was a frequent talking point, as the children were from the mother's and father's prior relationships as well as their current relationship. Their 'complicated family' illustrated their deviance from a socially acceptable image of normal families, mainly because of the parentage of the children. Two girls, Madeline and Penny, were from their mother's childhood sexual relationship with an adult male who was also her own mother's sexual partner. Furthermore, Mr Underwood had another child living with his former wife as well as other children living with him and his current wife.

This family was described on file as having an "extensive history". However, in line with cultural rules, none of the previous reports of 'neglect' and 'emotional abuse' was of high enough 'priority' or provided "enough evidence for statutory intervention", until 'sexual abuse' was 'disclosed', 'investigated' and 'substantiated' (chapter 6).

Also, within the cultural rules at Suburbia, five children in a sexual abuse investigation constituted overwork because of interviewing and documentary requirements to take legal action. The step/father's public identity of 'dangerousness', described by Olive, their caseworker, as "really volatile" with a "violent background", was managed to minimise the effects of his "hostility" to public officials. However, his 'dangerousness' did not alter Olive's and her colleagues' constructions of Ms Underwood as an 'unprotective mother', because she did not prevent Mr Underwood's 'sexual abuse' of the children. Constructions of Ms Underwood's unprotectiveness (and 'responsibility') were increased by workers' beliefs in the 'intergenerational transmission of sexual abuse' (chapter 8).

The Riley family's circumstances fit the rules of 'dangerous parents' and 'contentious' cases, within the very broad definition of child maltreatment recognised at Suburbia. The extreme aspects of the case that exemplified 'dangerousness' were the infant with multiple fractures made visible through a "skeletal survey". Within the dominant version of 'maltreatment', the injuries as a "constellation" were categorised as "non-accidental" by doctors, and as "physical abuse" by social workers, for which the parent(s) were "responsible" as cause, and later, as not accountable (chapter 7). Alternative explanations for the injuries, which the coalition of police and parents represented as "accidental", with different, unrelated "causes", were rejected. Workers reconstructed these explanations as parental "denials", "untruths", "discrepancies" and "blaming others", which fit the cultural willingness to construct parents as dangerous and provoking controversy. Parental challenges to the official version increased workload and the 'contentiousness' of the case. Parental 'abnormality', possibly relevant 18 months before, persisted even when Carly had become the caseworker in 1995, and new decisions needed to be made regarding reunification of a relatively older child with his family:

> It is clear that he got injured . . . what isn't clear . . . is how come, what the dynamics were that led to the injuries [. . .]. [At] the case conference, [I] said I don't think this kid should go home. (Carly, Social Worker)

The Turner family fits the profile of 'dangerousness' with its extreme and publicly sensationalised events; the death of a new born infant by his father's actions.

However, it was not this death that was the focus of 'child maltreatment' investigation, but a 'risk assessment' for the surviving older sibling. Although the father immediately acknowledged "responsibility" and pleaded "guilty" to manslaughter, the entire public image of the family was under scrutiny for the private and hidden discrepancies that could indicate risk. "Father may be shielding the mother – taking responsibility for her actions which led to the death of the baby. Was the father really the offender?" Olive and her co-workers who were conducting the risk assessment constructed Mr and Ms Turner's responses to the death of their baby as "minimisation" and "denial". Workers considered that the parents' responses were too unemotional, and were indicators of abnormality, rather than possibly their way of managing their extreme grief. A worker who suggested this explanation at a case discussion was ignored.

The Park family's circumstances are unusual in comparison with the rest of the cases that I sampled at Suburbia. First, as mentioned above, I selected it by default, by choosing the worker Lyla as a key informant. However, as also mentioned above, whilst it was the only case of 'neglect' sampled, it was reconstructed by the Manager and Senior Social Worker as another 'dangerous case'. How the version of 'dangerousness' emerged is unclear. The file reveals that the child protection worker "discovered physical abuse" when investigating a report of "neglect – school non-attendance", and there are references to the father's use of an "iron rod" or "big wooden stick", but no knife. Yet the version related to me by Lyla and the managers referred to a "knifing". It is possible the construction of the allegation as 'child maltreatment' of a 'neglect' case normally not considered a priority at Suburbia had to be reconstructed into a more serious 'type' so that it was then made consistent with cultural rules about 'dangerous parents' and 'contentious' cases. In the Park case, the father is immediately positioned as a 'dangerous adversary', described on file as "an asthmatic . . . reported to be a dogmatic type of person and has very aggressive behaviour". The construction of 'maltreatment – neglect and physical abuse' excluded contextual explanations, including the family's relationships as consequences of Vietnamese culture, war and migration (see chapter 8). The investigation appeared to breach procedures (DCS 1992: 35), including the exclusion of the father and other family members from the process and sole reliance on what the child Ho told workers. However, such practices minimised the extent of contentiousness and workload. Workers merely "informed [the father] that we had interviewed [child] at school . . . and his disclosure was substantiated, thus we are going to apprehend him".

## SUBURBIA AS A LINGUISTIC COMMUNITY IN 1995

This section has explored Suburbia as a linguistic community in 1995, as regulated by the *Guide to Practice*. 'Clients/parents/persons believed responsible' were constructed as 'dangerous' and created work by contesting official constructions of what happened to children and who was responsible. 'The family' was seen mostly in opposition to 'the child' because of the heavily child-centred approach taken and the preference for broader definitions of maltreatment. Patriarchal mothering assumptions influenced constructions of identities of responsibility, including "responsible mothers, invisible men" (Stark & Flitcraft 1988, Milner 1993). Aboriginal children and families had "different problems" than 'sexual' and 'physical abuse', which were local priorities. Thus, Aboriginal families did not receive services for problems related to poverty and material disadvantage. However, the taken-for-granted norm of white, Anglo ethnicity generated a category of ethnic 'otherness'. Aboriginal and Vietnamese families were placed into the category of 'ethnic other', justified by assumptions about similar kinship arrangements. Furthermore, potentially ethnocentric practices influenced intrusive child protection intervention for reported 'neglect' of the Vietnamese child, although 'neglect' was not normally a priority for intervention at Suburbia.

The 'child' was assumed to be both 'undeveloped adult' and 'vulnerable', constructing normal parents as good carers and regulators of their children. Child maltreatment was an objective fact and its correct assessment relied on expertise that was confined to particular professionals. Children's bodies offered material evidence, with children as objects for paternalistic protection by professionals (Fox Harding 1991). Yet when children were able to speak for themselves and ask for protection, they were treated with suspicion. 'Risk management/minimisation' was a political activity aimed at 'protecting children', 'protecting workers' and ultimately 'the organisation'.

## URBANIA AND SUBURBIA: LINGUISTIC COMMUNITIES IN 1995

As linguistic communities in 1995, Urbania and Suburbia were culturally different. This was possibly partly related to Urbania's engagement within a more complex policy context, whilst Suburbia ostensibly was contextualised within a single policy and one that had been in place at least since 1993. However, cultural rules in each community influenced the relations between knowledge and power, structuring work practices between colleagues and supervisors and between 'practitioners' and 'clients'. Thus the meaning of 'protection' and its implementation in practice was contingent upon how 'maltreatment' and the identities of 'child', 'parent' and 'responsibility' were constructed at each site.

## CONCLUSION

This chapter has given an overview of the differing cultural rules and practices at two sites from which workers interacted with each other, and children and parents, around child protection discourse. Cultural rules, expressed in language, influenced what was considered to be legitimate knowledge, as an intersection of institutionally prescribed discourses and situated interpretations, and particular priorities, and how these were implemented in practice. Situated and culturally constructed knowledge privileged and normalised particular constructions of meanings of reported events (chapter 6), and identities of 'person believed responsible' (chapter 7), child, parent and adult (chapter 8). Yet both sites shared the apolitical construction of the family and patriarchal mothering assumptions, with particular gendered consequences for meanings and identities, and with little consideration of race, ethnicity and culture. In chapters 6 to 8, I show how meanings of 'what happened' to the child and identities of 'responsibility', 'child' and 'parent' were constructed in each case, with language as a rhetorical device of power in practice.

# 6

# 'Something happened': Constructing maltreatment

This chapter explores how reports that 'something happened' to a child may become categories of 'maltreatment'. The title of this chapter, 'Something happened . . .', emerged through interviews with practitioners and from files, showing how a nebulous category of childhood experience expressed in everyday language remains officially unaccounted for until it is transformed into what is recognised as 'maltreatment'. Child protection practice involves responses to reports that 'something happened' or establishing 'what happened'.

As discussed in chapter 3, contemporary child protection discourse is structured according to a taken-for-granted, three-part rule that 'someone [1] did something [2] to a child [3]'. This rule influences and justifies child protection policy and practice, which involves an investigation of the 'truth' of each of the elements of the rule. Through child protection practice, practitioners transform the three elements of the rule into official categories. Thus, a report that 'something happened' (to a child) may become a 'type of maltreatment', aggregated into a profile of 'child maltreatment'. The 'someone' who 'did something' (to the child) may become a 'person believed responsible' or a 'perpetrator', and part of a profile of "dangerous individuals" (Hearn 1990). And the 'child' may no longer remain a particular individual with a particular set of problematic experiences, but become a 'victim' and part of a profile of other 'victims of child maltreatment'. The official categories that come to represent particular and personal experiences also become official knowledge about the dimensions of child maltreatment and how it should be responded to through protective and preventive services.

This chapter explores how 'something' that 'happened' to a child becomes categorised as a 'type of maltreatment' and how, at the end of the investigation, it becomes part of official and professional knowledge about the boundaries and dimensions of child maltreatment. 'Substantiation' of the report is not just a case of comparing a set of 'objective facts' against abstract and generalised risk assessment criteria (DePanfilis & Scannapieco 1994; Murphy-Berman 1994). Instead, substantiation begins with the categorisation of 'what happened' to the child. The concept of categorisation was discussed in chapter 2, in the section on rhetorical devices.

The relevance of categorisation for child protection practice can be shown by a parallel example from Smith (1990a). In "K is mentally ill", the categorisation that 'K *is* mentally ill' then sets in train particular ways of making a plausible case to support the identification (naming) of K *as* 'mentally ill' (Smith 1990a). Language is central to this process, as both a naming device and a device of power and strategy (Potter 1996). First, language allows us to give names or categories to events and experiences as a way of engaging in the world and in social interactions. Secondly, as a device of power and strategy, language as rhetoric is deployed to build up preferred versions of meaning, and simultaneously destroy other versions.

The process of categorisation begins by naming a particular event or person in a particular way, as for example, 'mentally ill'. Then the speaker (or writer) deploys a range of linguistic resources known as rhetorical devices by which he or she (or they) makes a plausible case for the categorisation (label), so that the category becomes 'fact' (Smith 1990a, Potter 1996). Similarly, the categorisation (naming) of 'what happened' to a child can, at the outset, set in train particular processes by which work is done to support the plausibility and legitimacy of the particular category.

Thus the person making a case for the category (meaning) they have given to 'what happened' then proceeds to substantiate their meaning by linguistic (rhetorical) devices. If there are different meanings, practitioners must decide which meaning (including their own) is the most plausible. This process is not a neutral one, but embedded in power relations whereby each participant seeks to advance their own case and resist and destroy meanings and constructions that they do not accept. For example, parents may strenuously dispute a categorisation of bruises on a child as 'physical abuse' with implications for them as 'abusers', but may be more willing to accept a meaning of 'inappropriate punishment' or 'discipline' (Graham 1981). Practitioners, on the other hand, may consider that parents are 'liars' or that they are in 'denial' of the 'facts' if they offer alternative explanations to the worker's view that 'maltreatment' has occured. The process of making meaning is complicated by often crisis-driven and volatile situations, in which children's well-being may be seriously compromised if practitioners make 'the wrong decision' (Howe 1992; Walton 1993).

Thus for professional practice, particularly in a contentious and controversial field like child protection, it is argued here that it is essential for practitioners and policy-makers to critically question official categories, as naming devices with descriptive definitions. Furthermore, it is essential that the mostly invisible and taken-for-granted practices by which private experiences and meanings become official categories are also thoroughly explored, rather than taken for granted as benign interventions on behalf of children.

This chapter also shows how the body of the child is central to the process of categorisation. Within the medico-scientific paradigm that informs contemporary policy and practice, the actual child becomes a body of evidence, an evidentiary object. That is, the physical body is seen and represented as a set of neutral characteristics that may be differentiated between what is abnormal and what is not (Parton et al. 1997). Bodily abnormalities may be further differentiated between 'normal' abnormalities, such as "congenital" conditions (Wardinsky 1995) or "accidental" injuries (Cohen et al. 1997), and those that are considered abnormal – for example, "non-accidental" or "inflicted" (Ewing-Cobbs et al. 1998; Boyce et al. 1996) – which may constitute maltreatment. The physical body as evidence may be extended by accumulation of abnormal behaviours manifested by the child, as having no other explanation but maltreatment (Rose 1989). The process of categorisation involves accumulation of a range of perceived abnormalities of the child's physical body and behaviours – in medical terminology, a syndrome – that has also come to characterise contemporary child protection policy and practice. As a discourse, definitions of child maltreatment of various types similarly operate as a syndrome where particular abnormal features may represent maltreatment (Parton et al. 1997). For example, a case where "a child exhibits medical, psychiatric, behavioural problems, unusual behaviour, and developmental delay" is "more likely to be substantiated" as "maltreatment" (Jones 1993: 252).

A particular feature of the child's body as an evidentiary object is how the body is partitioned, different body parts being associated with different types of maltreatment. The partitioning of the body allows for practical constructions of a "hierarchy of maltreatment" (Dubowitz 1994; Berliner 1994; Doyle 1996). As discussed in chapter 3, maltreatment and its types are differentiated and prioritised according to a hierarchy. This chapter shows how a hierarchy of maltreatment is maintained, whereby the complexity of children's experiences of oppression and disadvantage is reduced to only one type of maltreatment, excluding other types as being of lesser or no importance. The consequences of such practices for children and their families are also considered.

I have written this chapter with some trepidation, fearing that the critical sociological analysis of case practice presented below will suggest a betrayal of the children whose lived experiences are daily the cause of official concern. Furthermore, I am concerned that what is said in this chapter about how meaning is constructed through particular social processes may be misappropriated and misused to dismiss children's experiences of oppression or the work that is done to promote their welfare. Therefore, I emphasise that the exploration in this chapter of how reports as 'child maltreatment' of children's everyday lived experiences may become official categories of maltreatment is grounded in the complete acceptance that children experience a range of disadvantaged circumstances, problematic care and tragic outcomes. However, for the reasons outlined above, it is not enough to claim moral, ethical and legal justification for intervention on behalf of children. It is also essential to continually problematise and reflectively and reflexively (Taylor & White 2000) critique professional practices in which knowledge and power are deployed on behalf of the state. How do we know that in the cause of protecting children we as practitioners and policy-makers are not deploying official knowledge and power destructively? Is there a way in which we can protect children through a constructive engagement of knowledge and power? These are some of the bigger policy and practice questions that this chapter begins to explore, and that will be addressed in other ways in the rest of this book.

## STAGES OF CHILD PROTECTION INTERVENTION

Child protection practice is structured into sequential stages, categorised as "reporting"/"intake", "investigation" and "outcome" as "substantiation" (or not) (Murphy-Berman 1994; Kalichman et al. 1990). This structuring assumes that child protection intervention is a linear and tidy process, whereby meaning is made in a clear and rational way. Instead, the cases will show how these assumptions of practice rationality are the exception rather than the rule. The process of constructing meaning of 'what happened' to the child is often fraught with complexity and confusion, as participants struggle to advance their version of events and resist other versions. Furthermore, the process of intervention does not necessarily proceed in an orderly fashion, and in fact it may not always be clear when a report has been made and to whom, and what stage the intervention is really at.

## RE-PRESENTING THE CASES

Each case is set out as a separate contextual entity, structured according to each (nominal) stage in the intervention process. At each stage, different participants offer their versions of 'what happened'. The child protection worker coordinates the network of meaning that is constructed, whilst marginalising participants and their meanings that are deemed unacceptable, implausible or wrong. The process and outcomes of intervention are recorded on files within the "documentary reality" (Smith 1974; Zimmerman 1974) allowed by the organisation and later reconstructed to me in the interviews. The versions I have accessed on files, and even some workers' accounts, are often composites by different workers involved at different times in each case. The case analysis re-presented below is my reconstruction of these different official versions of 'what happened' to different children. Each case is offered as a separate and self-enclosed story, making visible the diverse life events glossed by the categories of maltreatment, and the processes by which life events are transformed into official categories.

Six cases selected from the total sample of 20 are presented below, to explore the processes of categorisation in constructing child maltreatment from what happened to the child. Four general themes are explored in this chapter. These are:

- Categorisation: 'sexual abuse substantiated'
- Categorisation: 'sexual abuse unsubstantiated'
- Categorisation: 'physical abuse unsubstantiated – at risk'
- Categorisation: 'hierarchy of maltreatment'.

## CATEGORISATION: 'SEXUAL ABUSE SUBSTANTIATED'

Two children, Jane Allston and Mary Constable, were connected through the man officially identified as 'person believed responsible'. Mary Constable became part of the investigation of the report about Jane Allston and, as a consequence, she was also identified as the subject of a separate report of maltreatment. Both girls were categorised as 'non-Aboriginal'. Jane was aged six and Mary 14 when each report alleging sexual abuse was made.

Jane's and Mary's cases show how 'sexual abuse' as a descriptive category or name of particular experiences and events also operates as a process of categorisation. Arguments are made at each stage of each case to support the category within its own self-contained definition, with alternative or multiple explanations being minimised or disregarded.

### Jane's case: Reporting/Intake (1) – 'talking about it in a particular way'

Jane's mother, Sarah Allston, is recorded as the "source of the allegation" on the file. However, there were other reporters and a chain of reporting before Ms Allston made her report to Urbania. According to the file, the father of the child, Peter Allston, was a client of the Correctional Services Department. He was categorised as a "sex offender" for "stealing women's underwear". Therefore, his already abnormal identity as 'sex offender' precluded any doubts when he "talked about s. a. [sexual abuse]" to the Correctional Services' female social worker, who reported a 'sexual abuse' case to the local child protection office.

However, as there was no record on file of what Mr Allston had actually said to the Correctional Services worker, I sought clarification from the caseworker:

HD: So was he definitely saying he'd done something? . . .

Worker: *He's implying to them* that . . .

HD: But he didn't come out and say?

Worker: *No it was just that the way he talked about it*, they didn't know for sure . . . (emphasis added)

This shows that a report of sexual abuse does not have to follow the precise discursive formation: 'I sexually abused my daughter'. The social and cultural taboos on talking about sexuality in general and sexual abuse in particular (Foucault 1978a; Scott & Swain 2002) are maintained in this example: by "implications" and a certain "way of talking about it", a pattern repeated in the extract of the interview above. Furthermore, these silences, absences and implications are seen as definitive of the category (the same as) 'sexual abuse'. Despite "not knowing for sure", the Correctional Services worker's construction as 'child sexual abuse' is privileged, but the man's "implied" version is not represented except by a vague claim of 'what he talked about' and 'how he talked about it' (Smith 1990a, Margolin 1992). The privileged version sets the scene for the rest of the process (Smith 1990a). As the investigation unfolded, each participant's version was a particular representation of 'child sexual abuse (or not)'.

### Jane's case: Reporting/Intake (2) – 'Jane has been sexually abused'

Ms Allston made contact with Urbania after the caseworker requested the Correctional Services worker to "get the lady [Ms Allston] to phone [him]". Ms Allston's report was recorded by the "intake" social worker as a formal report of child sexual abuse. Ms Allston said that she was:

> . . . concerned about *possible sexual abuse* [1] by . . . ex-husband [2] on her daughter [3]. [. . .] Daughter showing signs of obesity, *[mother] watches [child's] diet* [4]. [Jane] wants no contact with old house [5a]. [Jane] believes father does not love her [5b]. [Mr Allston] only wants to see [Jane], *not her brother* [6]. In the past, [Mr Allston] has sexually abused other children [7]. Ms Allston's sister about 6 years ago . . . then 7–8 years old [7a]; [also] . . . his niece [7b] and other young girls [7c]. Mr Allston recently charged with stealing women's underwear . . . involved with Corrective Services [8]. [. . .] Ms Allston worried that father wanting contact with [daughter] – he will do something [9]. (emphasis added)

In this version, the allegation is recorded according to the rule, 'someone did something to a child' [1–3], in which the specifics of Jane's case that meet the rule are stated. The mother tells the hearer/reader that her account is of 'possible [child] sexual abuse'. Her construction aggregates separate incidents of abnormalities of the child and of the alleged offender. Unexplained abnormality of the child's body [4] is emphasised by a contrast structure (Potter 1996; Smith 1990a): the "obesity" is happening despite the mother's control of the child's diet. Inexplicable behaviours [5a, 5b] are not represented as having different causes, but complete a three-part list (Potter 1996) as a set of typical features of sexual abuse [4, 5a–b].

The father's apparent preference for his daughter, whilst not wanting contact with his son, is a contrast structure [6] that suggests that the father has questionable motives regarding his daughter, and his apparent rejection of his son. Officially, such a conclusion would strengthen his possible identity as 'child sex abuser'. The mother then offers a three-part list representing her concerns, as part of a class of similar "past" practices by her ex-husband with other children [7a–c]. The association of Mr Allston's identification as a "sex offender" [8] builds up the case for child sexual abuse. The overall generalised concern, "he will do something", underlines the invisibility of child sexual abuse in terms of 'knowing what happens' and 'when' it does, and the barriers to prevention (and protection). It simultaneously gives plausibility to the mother's explanation of "worry" for her daughter, rather than her "self interested" (Potter 1996) rejection of the father's wish for "contact" following a recent marital separation. The caseworker said it was "not just a custody issue", because "Probation and Parole [helped us]". This validated the report as potentially 'about child sexual abuse', setting in train an investigation in which the child, Jane, was interviewed.

### Jane's case: Investigation (1) – 'the contradictory identity of child sexual abuse victim'

"Category entitled" knowledge (Potter 1996) is a strategic device whereby a person who is identified in a particular way may also be seen as especially knowledgeable because they have access to knowledge as a consequence of their particular identity. Thus, as an alleged victim of child sexual abuse, six-year-old Jane Allston was positioned as knowledgeable of 'what happened' to her. However, this legitimacy relied on contradictory identities of entitlement. As a '(normal) child' in this culture, she was 'not entitled' to 'sexual' knowledge (Kitzinger 1990). However, her identification as 'victim of sexual abuse' gave access to 'entitled sexual knowledge', grounded in her experience, but also disrupted her identity as 'normal child'. These contradictory identities of entitlement increased the plausibility that 'something had happened'. The caseworker said that a normal six-year-old child would not otherwise know and would "rarely lie".

### Jane's case: Investigation (2) – 'the shape of the interview'

The primary feature of the investigation that Jane Allston had been sexually abused is what I have called 'the shape of the interview'. By this I mean that the verbatim extracts from file notes of the interviews with Jane conducted by the male caseworker and a female social worker show the (out)lines of prescribed questioning (although unrecorded). Thus, the official categorisation of 'sexual abuse' defined in particular ways also prescribes what is relevant evidence, and how to elicit this evidence within legally acceptable parameters in case there is a need for legal action (protection and/or prosecution) (Daro 1991). The shape of the interview also shows what has been excluded from consideration, as 'not evidence of sexual abuse'. The positioning of the child as a body of evidence validates the child as a 'knowledgeable witness' as the victim of essentially private acts. However, the child is also positioned as potentially 'abnormal' as a 'child' because she now has access to knowledge that is normally denied to 'children' (Foucault 1978a; Kitzinger 1990), as a feature of their 'innocence'. Furthermore, there is no clear-cut distinction between these two potentially mutually exclusive identities for the child as victim of maltreatment. Instead, if the child is unable to fulfil completely the identity of 'knowledgeable witness' within the prescribed definition of sexual abuse, there is ambiguity as to the 'truth' of the allegation.

This record of the interview with the child is the workers' reconstruction of what was relevant to the investigation of sexual abuse, and has been read/re-presented as such:

> She was 'surprised about genitals' on anatomical dolls [1].

The workers used anatomically correct dolls (Kendall-Tackett 1992a, 1992b) as a forensic technique, a way of concretising the child's actual experience and told in a different context. This is intended to minimise bias and collect legally admissible evidence of 'what happened', as a description of 'who did what to whom' in relation to particular body parts:

> She [Jane] named the penis as 'doodle' and 'bottom', but had 'no name for vagina etc.' [2] 'Private parts' were 'covered by bathers' [3a]. The child said, 'some parts you are not allowed to touch' [3b]. Then 'we [workers] began on parts OK to touch – she named face, hands, feet, etc.' [3c].
>
> She then said, 'someone's touched my (pointing to vagina) down there . . . it was Carl and Emma [4a]. They used to live near us . . . I told [their mum] and my mum, but I touched theirs too.' It appeared that Carl and Emma were just friends . . . a game . . . mutually OK [4b].

This extract shows the ambiguities in Jane's category entitled knowledge as 'victim of sexual abuse'. She clearly is able to respond to entitled knowledge for a child of her age, differentiating between "private" (and 'public') body parts and related practices, such as "touching" [3a–c]. That is, the workers are trying to establish a baseline of Jane's knowledge of cultural assumptions about sexuality and the body, whereby sexuality and related body parts are designated as 'private' in terms of acceptable visibility and boundaries to access by others. This differentiation also positions other body parts as 'public' in terms of acceptable visibility and access by others. However, Jane's sexual knowledge such as names for body parts [2] was uneven, as were her accounts of different people "touching" her "down there" [4a]. One set of events was normalised by workers as "just [same age] friends", and "mutually OK" [4b].

> Asked if anyone else had touched her private parts. . . . replied very quickly 'not daddy' [5a]. . . . quickly followed by 'but it was yukky' [5b]. No further comment [5].

Had she ever seen a penis? Said 'yes'. Asked what it looked like. 'Sort of floppy . . . big . . . then it stood up . . . but it wasn't daddy.' [6] She then said 'I'm daddy's special girl, the only one . . . We play special games.' She would not comment on 'what types of games' [7].

Discussed 'good and bad touching' (good = birthday kiss on cheek; hug at bed time; bad = touch private parts); [8] 'good and bad secrets' (good = birthday surprises; bad = would not discuss bad secrets) [9].

Workers deployed a contrast structure (Potter 1996; Smith 1990a) in their record of Jane's response to questions about "anyone else touching her", building up the suspicion that 'something had happened' and implicating "daddy" as 'responsible' for it. They noted Jane's apparently voluntary and "very quick" naming and simultaneous exclusion of "daddy" from the "anyone" [5a] who had "touched her", rather than expected possible responses of 'no one', or 'yes, this is who touched me'. This conclusion was supported by Jane's association of "yukky" with "touching" [5b]. Another contrast structure was the record of Jane's description of a penis. She again apparently voluntarily named and excluded "daddy" from the penis that she had seen [6], rather than possible responses of 'No, I have never seen a penis', or 'Yes, this is whose penis I saw'. Jane's allusions to "special games" with "daddy" without elaboration [7] and refusal to discuss "bad secrets" [9] again raised suspicion (Foucault 1978a), but without any detailed narrative necessary to link practices with identities as "[legal] evidence" (Faller 1988).

The workers concluded their interview by returning to the distinction between 'private parts' (associated with 'bad touching') and 'public parts' (associated with 'good touching'). This appeared to be a preventive strategy by inculcating Jane with appropriate cultural knowledge about the body.

The final sentence of the interview record stated that Jane:

[d]rew family group including sad father 'cause he doesn't like my mum' [10].

This final statement recording the investigation did not generate a possible meaning as a child's expression of grief due to a recent parental separation and as an explanation for some of the unexplained behaviours that the mother reported [statements 5a–b], and that were associated solely with sexual abuse.

The shape of this interview suggests some features that constitute the official categorisation and definition of sexual abuse at least within this jurisdiction. First, there is a demarcation of the body into 'sexual (and private) parts' and by definition, 'non-sexual (and public) parts'. Furthermore, the 'sexual and private' parts are associated with 'bad touching', and the 'non-sexual and public' with 'good touching', thus also introducing a moral distinction. The child as victim is 'tested' on knowledge of these cultural and moral distinctions as a base for establishing the validity of subsequent claims. Apparently voluntary statements by the child must associate 'someone' who 'did something' to them within the form of the rule, but where this does not occur, legal ambiguity may be created, whilst the 'truth' of the allegation may remain in the social domain. Claims of a 'special relationship' and 'special games' become euphemisms for sexual abuse. There is limited space for more ambiguous meanings that could include, but not be confined to, sexual abuse. Ambiguity in human relationships, including those between small girls and their fathers, is not easily accommodated within the interview. Is there some way of 'protecting from yukky touching' without loss of 'specialness', assuming both these aspects are important to the child as it appeared to be in this case? Furthermore, family context and circumstances that may also explain some 'abnormalities' manifested by the child – for example, parental separation – are outside the boundaries of the interview.

### Jane's case: Outcome – 'inconclusive'

The ambiguities of the interview with Jane did not give a clear meaning of 'what happened', described by the caseworker as "not really conclusive". Jane was re-interviewed. The caseworker stated what Jane said in the subsequent interview, "She said she just played with his twinkie till it hurt him". Child protection practitioners might hear such a statement as evidence of 'sexual abuse'; however, because it did not constitute legal evidence, it was seen as "very minimal". Police also interviewed Jane, and according to the caseworker, "she didn't disclose anything".

### Jane's case: Investigation (3) – 'Mary becomes a body of evidence'

As a way of offering corroborative evidence (Potter 1996), Jane's mother, Ms Allston, advised the caseworker that ". . . her fourteen-year-old sister [Mary Constable] . . . the husband had done something to her". This statement constituted both a "report" of a new case of "sexual abuse" and a part of the "investigation" of Jane Allston's case.

### Jane's case? Mary's case? Whose case? – 'He had done something to her'

Mary Constable's mother (who was also Jane Allston's maternal grandmother) was briefly interviewed following this information. According to the file record, Ms Constable said:

> When Mary was about nine years old – stayed with sister (Ms Allston) and Mr Allston and had told her that Mr Allston had done something to her [1]. Mary didn't say what [2], but Mr Allston had come to the house half drunk [3a] at 1 o'clock in the morning [3b] and said he was sorry for what he had done to Mary [3c]. Ms Constable had not followed it through [5] . . . and Mary had since become anorexic and under a psychiatrist [4].

The first statement in the interview with Mary's mother follows the rule: 'someone did something to a child' [1]. In keeping with 'talking about it in a particular way', the invisibility of 'child sexual abuse' and the silence associated with it is maintained in how Ms Constable says 'what happened to Mary'. Euphemisms are used – for example, "he had done something to her" – that maintain the cultural taboo of talking about sexuality and sexual abuse (Foucault 1978a) [1, 2], and underline the invisibility of the range of personal experiences that are officially categorised as sexual abuse. In this case, the euphemism was the only way that Mary's mother, Ms Constable, could engage with the process, as she did not know the details of the incident [5]. Instead, Mr Allston's apparently odd behaviour at the time, which Ms Constable recollected and re-presented as a three-part list (Potter 1996) [3a–c], is seen as an explanation of his possible guilt for 'doing something (sexual abuse) to Mary'. The assumption of inexplicable behaviours is that within a child protection discourse they represent 'sexual abuse'. Ms Constable did not clarify with her daughter Mary the claim that Mr Allston had 'done something to her'. Nor did she seek an explanation from Mr Allston for his odd behaviour [5]. Furthermore, Mary's inexplicable bodily ("anorexia") and mental ("under a psychiatrist") abnormalities [4] are grouped together as support for a meaning of 'sexual abuse'.

### Mary's case: Investigation (1) – 'family secrets'

Mary Constable's version of what happened to her revealed a "five-year family secret", according to the caseworker:

> . . . when she was about 10 years old [1a], she was staying with [sister, Ms Allston] [1b] prior to their getting married [1c] . . . At about 2 or 3 am, [1d] she woke up [1e] and [Mr Allston] [1f] had come into the room [2] and removed her pyjama bottoms [3]. It went on for ages [1g]. I screamed and [Ms Allston] woke up and said, 'What's the matter?' I just said, 'I hate him'. He touched me [4a] and tried to get his fingers in me [4b]. He also touched me on the breasts through my top [4c]. I was at his [1f] house [1b] with a friend [1c] and he asked us to lift our tops [5a], saying, show me yours, and I show mine [5b]. I told mum about it [6a] and she spoke to [Mr Allston] [6b] – he said he was sorry.

Mary's detailed narrative of 'what happened to her' gives "access to the scene" and builds up its credibility (Potter 1996; Faller 1988b). First, Mary's version follows the general rule that 'someone did something to a child' and, by the detail, fills in its specific features. The description fitted the discursive formation of 'sexual abuse': her age at the time [1a], the context [1b–c, e], place [1b] and time [1c–d, e], identification of the person responsible [1f] with specific actions on separate occasions [4a–c; 5–a–b] (Faller 1988b) as invasive of private, physical space [2] (Foucault 1980; De Swann 1990: 183–94) and private bodily (sexualised) parts [3; 4a–c; 5a–b] (Foucault 1978a). Furthermore, Mary's version contradicts her mother's version, told earlier in the process, that she knew little about 'what happened'. Instead Mary says that she told her mother 'about it' [6a] and that her mother 'spoke to Mr Allston' [6b] about 'what he had done to Mary'. Therefore, the 'five-year family secret' does not seem to mean that Mary had kept her experiences to herself until revealed through this investigation, but that 'what had happened to her' was perhaps not openly discussed in her family, for reasons unknown.

### Mary's case: Investigation (2) – 'this really happened'

As discussed in chapter 3, within child protection discourse 'the child' is defined as a homogeneous identity that legally and socially covers a range of individuals, aged from birth (sometimes pre-natal) to 18 in most jurisdictions. Furthermore, it is assumed that the experiences of one child are common to all children in any context (Jenks 1996; Prout & James 1990). There is little recognition of the differences between individuals' experiences that may articulate with experiences shared within groups. These assumptions underpinned the investigation of allegations that Mary Constable had been sexually abused, so that corroborative evidence could help the investigation of 'what happened to Jane'. The caseworker for both Jane and Mary said to Mary's mother (also Jane's grandmother): "Listen, this . . . really happened and I think it might be happening to your granddaughter [Jane]". Mary herself commented: "It's likely enough to happen to her and I don't want it to happen".

Jane Allston and Mary Constable, along with other girls who had come in contact with Mr Allston, appeared to have shared experiences of some form of 'yukky touching' (to use the language of six-year-old Jane). Such 'touching' was clearly unwanted by both Jane and Mary. However, the main difference between Jane and her teenage aunt, Mary, is the nature and quality of the relationship between each child and Mr Allston. To Jane Allston he was her father with whom at best she appeared to have an ambivalent relationship, in which she did not like the 'yukky touching' but also felt 'special' to her father. Mary, on the other hand, was Mr Allston's prospective sister-in-law when he 'touched' her. Her response to Mr Allston was of outright rejection: 'hating him'.

### Mary's case: Investigation (3) – 'the contradictory identity of child sexual abuse victim'

Mary's credibility as a category entitled witness (Potter 1996) was established first by her detailed narrative of what happened to her. Furthermore, her apparent lack of self-interest (Potter 1996), described by the caseworker as "non vengeful" despite being a 'victim of sexual abuse' who could reasonably be expected to show some 'self-interest', worked in her favour. However, although Mary was credible in the social domain, the legal tests of 'truth' still had to be satisfied. The police accepted that 'what happened to Mary' was 'sexual'. However, they contested 14-year-old Mary's claim of "abuse" at age nine or 10 as 'self interested', asking,

"Did you lead him on?". Her category entitlement as 'victim' was temporarily suspended until her own possible complicity in sexual activity could be tested.

### Jane's case and Mary's case: Outcomes – 'sexual abuse substantiated'

The reports that Jane Allston and Mary Constable were sexually abused were substantiated. Because what Jane was able to say to child protection workers and police was not conclusive, the substantiation relied on medical evidence, in which her body 'spoke for her': "findings of a physical examination" at the paediatric hospital were of "penile and digital vaginal and anal penetration". This was categorised as "indecent dealings/molestation". Mary's verbal evidence, "two disclosures" to police, was categorised as "indecent dealings". Mr Allston would be charged.

### Categorisation: 'sexual abuse substantiated'

These two cases have shown how an 'implied' comment by an identified sex offender was heard within particular discursive prescriptions and re-presented as 'sexual abuse' by multiple participants throughout a rather messy and complicated intervention process. It could be argued that the initial report made by the Correctional Services social worker was indeed 'true', as supported by medical technologies of the body (in Jane Allston's case) and the corroboration by Mary Constable. However, the final outcome in six-year-old Jane's case excludes her ambiguous version, in which she simultaneously implicates and excludes 'daddy' as 'responsible for sexual abuse'. The intervention, the sole intention of which was to achieve a single and definitive categorisation of meaning (shown by the shape of the interview), did not allow for exploration of apparent ambivalence or ambiguities such as the child's 'specialness' to her father, yet wanting the 'yukky touching' to stop. It also excluded the meaning to the child of the parental separation that may have explained some of the 'abnormalities' attributed solely to sexual abuse.

As a six-year-old, Jane Allston was unable to meet the legal tests of truth (Daro 1991), but medical technologies of the body apparently provided corroboration. However, within a constructionist perspective an ethical difficulty arises. I have argued that the categorisation as 'sexual abuse', beginning with interpretations of implied remarks by the child's father and continuing within the investigative process, produced particular meaning and 'truth'. If this is so, how valid is the medical corroboration, particularly as some commentators (Adams et al. 1994; Hobbs et al. 1995) argue that the body alone does not provide infallible/conclusive evidence of sexual abuse? Furthermore, a fundamental assumption of social constructionism and the operation of discourses is that the meaning (naming category) given to an experience or an event will set in train how that category is justified and social relations associated with it. The ethical implications of this assumption highlight the difficulties of the constructionist perspective for socially problematic issues such as child maltreatment. There is a significant risk of dismissal of actual oppressive experiences, yet the question must be asked about how appropriate protection can be provided while allowing for multiple or ambiguous meanings of children's experiences.

## CATEGORISATION: 'SEXUAL ABUSE UNSUBSTANTIATED'

This case involves two seven-year-old, non-Aboriginal boys, Simon Martini and Henry Moore, who were reported as 'perpetrator' and 'victim' of 'sexual abuse', respectively. The analysis shows how meanings of 'what happened' to a child can be transformed depending upon how the specifics of the rule 'someone did something to a child' are reinterpreted in practice. In this case, these reinterpretations significantly influenced how 'what happened' was constructed, with an outcome of 'sexual abuse unsubstantiated', where a different interpretation of the rule could have produced an outcome as substantiated. Furthermore, the ambiguous identity of 'child' as both victim and perpetrator of sexual abuse is a feature.

### Reporting/Intake (1): 'Simon has sexually abused Henry'

The male school principal reported to Urbania that:

> [p]arents of a 6 y.o. boy [Henry] . . . explained that whilst at school yesterday, their son was taken into the toilets by Simon where Simon sucked his penis and licked him. Simon told the other boy, [Henry] 'what I am going to do will make you a big boy.' The . . . child told his [parents] and they went to the school this morning. That child seems fine. [. . .].

Whilst the school principal was not a witness to the reported incident, his category entitlement was associated with the "cultural credibility" (Potter 1996) given to someone of his public status. He was also described as "very caring", thus his report was not malicious or punitive, but of concern for students in his care. In his report, Henry is a 'victim' of Simon as a 'person believed responsible for sexual abuse'. The principal's primary intention was that Simon's apparent "sexual dangerousness" (Hearn 1990; Bell 1993) should be controlled. He showed less concern for the "victim" child, who "seems fine". The caseworker said that the principal "wasn't happy . . . to give me the name of the victim boy, but was happy to give me the name of the other child". He placed both children under surveillance, asking the teacher "to keep an eye on them [. . .] the teacher actually noticed that Simon was leading Henry away [. . .] this is how we [workers] found out about the next one [incident]".

The caseworker categorised the initial report as "Child Concern", a descriptive category summarising that "two six-year-old boys [were] behaving in a sexually inappropriate manner at school", where the relationship was not one of inequality between 'victim' and 'perpetrator', but of an interaction between peers. Also, as a "once off [sic] incident", "it wasn't a top priority", until the second report was received three days later.

### Reporting/Intake (2a): 'Child concern to child maltreatment'

The principal phoned again before investigation of the first report commenced. "Simon . . . again approached Henry . . . School becoming quite anxious."
The workers changed the category to "child maltreatment":

> because . . . the first one [report] was [on] Friday. This had happened again . . . on . . . Monday . . . so we decided that we really needed to look at it there and then, because it wasn't . . . a one off incident.

A second incident suggested a pattern (or accumulation) of incidents (Potter 1996), building up the concern that 'what happened' was more serious, and warranted immediate action as an investigation of sexual abuse.

### Reporting/Intake (2b): 'Who did what to whom?'

Whilst the initial report was of the form, 'Simon has sexually abused Henry', the workers did not investigate sexual abuse of Henry by Simon, particularly because the caseworker "had difficulty calling this six-year-old boy [Simon] a perpetrator of sexual abuse". Instead, her (their) interpretation of Simon's statement, "what I am going to do is make you a big boy", was that Simon had gained knowledge normally only associated with adult sexuality by being a 'victim', rather than embodying dangerousness as an 'abuser'. Thus, the workers transformed the identities and relationships of 'victim' and 'perpetrator' in the reported incident by reconstructing Simon's identity from 'perpetrator' to 'victim' of an unknown 'abuser' in a different unreported incident. The suspected incident of sexual abuse to be investigated involved Simon (as 'victim') and "somebody else" (as 'perpetrator'):

> . . . our thoughts were that children don't say those sorts of things, this kid had heard that somewhere else, so we were concerned . . . *that this child [Simon] had been abused by somebody else who had said those words to him* . . . (emphasis added)

### Investigation: 'What happened to Simon?'

The investigation was not to establish that 'what happened' was sexual abuse by Simon as 'abuser', but ". . . to investigate the child Simon who had perpetrated the act to find out if anything was happening to him". The investigation revealed how sexuality as a discourse (Foucault, 1978a) operates in, and as, a practice. This includes how sexual topics may be spoken about and who is entitled to know what in relation to sexuality. Therefore, children are entitled to know certain aspects of sexuality as a way of protecting them from what is considered to be outside their entitlement as children. Such prescribed knowledge also operates as a disciplinary strategy, by which children are instructed in what is legitimate and illegitimate in terms of knowledge and practices for them. Simon, who was possibly a victim of someone else and therefore a category entitled witness (Potter 1996), could potentially offer further details on 'who had done something to him'. However, as the workers found, the inculcation of children into sexual discourses played an important part in how Simon participated in constructing 'sexual abuse – unsubstantiated'.

Adults (parents, teachers and so on) inculcate children in what they are entitled to know about sexual knowledge and practice. In the case of Simon Martini and his school friends, this consisted of vocabulary that necessitated speaking about the unspeakable, the social and cultural taboos associated especially with childhood sexuality (Foucault 1978a). This vocabulary used language familiar to children, like "games", "touching" or "doing silly things", that were given special moral significance as deviance by association with descriptors like "rude" or "rudies"; particular locations, like "toilets", and with body parts, such as "bums and doodles". It demarcated entitled sexual knowledge for a child: and simultaneously prescribed normative conduct; that "rude games are things that you don't do" (Foucault 1978a; Goldman & Goldman 1982).

Although the workers clearly believed that "Simon had been exposed to something", he became "more and more cagey, . . . I'm not going to tell you anything . . . about anything . . . ". "[He] was the innocent child", as "having nothing to do with the rude games", and "emphatically denied that anybody had touched him ever".

Simon's self-presentation as "innocent" of all unentitled knowledge and practices, and therefore as "asexual" (Kitzinger 1990), also precluded official constructions of 'what happened' to him. This contradiction was noted by the caseworker, when the mother "described the time she [dealt with] Simon and his girl cousin at the same age . . . experimenting . . . Simon would know his actions were wrong". The caseworker said, "I agreed, but I think this is also why Simon will not tell us anything", especially as these discursive rules were enforced by attending a "Catholic school . . . he has rude bits and you aren't allowed to do this".

### Outcome: 'sexual abuse unsubstantiated'

Simon eventually told his mother "that he had touched Henry and that Henry had done it to him" and ". . . that . . . no . . . adult had touched him". The mother informed the caseworker adding, " . . . she didn't believe there was anyone else involved". "So we decided all we could say was that it was unsubstantiated . . . ", despite "feeling" that:

> . . . Simon had been exposed to something, because of . . . 'what I'm going to do is make you a big boy'. That's not six-year-old talk . . . I still feel strongly that *somewhere, something has happened to this child; he's heard it somewhere or something* . . . (emphasis added)

The silences and invisibility associated with sexual knowledge and practice so permeate child sexual abuse that it is extremely difficult for children as victims to properly represent themselves or their experiences without being confronted with the fundamental contradictions of being a 'child as victim of sexual abuse'. In this case, Simon represented himself as the asexual and innocent child, as a culturally normal child. The workers were clearly concerned that Simon's self-presentation did not account for contradictory aspects of his identity. That is, they could not explain how Simon came to know the phrase 'what I am going to do is make you a big boy' because it could not be accounted for if he was an asexual, innocent, normal child. Yet because he was inculcated into the normal identity of child, they could not ascertain from him the information that only he could know but would not reveal as it would be inconsistent with his self-presentation as 'normal child'. The secrecy and silence around sexuality and children's experiences in particular are encapsulated in the caseworker's remarks that "somewhere, something has happened [but we don't know what]".

### Categorisation: 'sexual abuse – unsubstantiated'

This case shows how a report can be transformed into different categories of meaning as 'sexual abuse', 'child concern', 'maltreatment', if the identities around 'what happened' are reconstructed and repositioned. If the initial construction of meaning which positioned Henry and Simon as 'victim' and 'perpetrator' respectively was followed, the outcome could have produced a different categorisation, namely, 'substantiated sexual abuse', with a seven-year-boy as 'person believed responsible'. However, in this case, the workers' reconstruction of identities of 'victim' and 'perpetrator' around a different set of (suspected) events also changed what was being investigated. Thus, the outcome, 'sexual abuse – unsubstantiated' referred to a suspected case in which a 'perpetrator' in the reported case was repositioned as 'victim'. It also shows how children themselves participate in social and cultural discourses of sexuality and therefore can subvert official constructions of their experiences and identities as 'normal children'.

### CATEGORISATION: 'PHYSICAL ABUSE UNSUBSTANTIATED – AT RISK'

Murray Francis was a four-year-old boy (ethnicity Unknown) who came to the attention of child protection workers following a report by a woman on a bus. The report was investigated as 'physical abuse'. This case shows a different example of how the report fitted a categorisation as 'physical abuse', even though it was not initially reported in the form: 'Murray is being physically abused by someone', unlike the report about Jane Allston discussed earlier in this chapter. In that case, the claim that 'Jane was being sexually abused' began the report, the reporter subsequently making a case to support the category of 'sexual abuse'.

In the case of Murray Francis, the rhetorical device of "extrematization" (Potter 1996) is a key feature in the initial categorisation as 'physical abuse'. However, during the investigation, different participants offered alternative explanations of the reported incident that eventually contributed to the reconstruction of the report as possibly 'not physical abuse', although apparently conditional as the child was also declared as being 'at risk'. The Eakins family is also referred to in some of the file text because Ms Francis and Ms Eakins were friends/housemates. [The worker who investigated the report was not interviewed because she had moved to another office. Instead, only the worker who had taken the initial report about Murray Francis was interviewed. This worker happened to be the caseworker for the Eakins family also.]

### Reporting/Intake: 'constructing physical abuse'

> Ms Court was travelling in a bus [1a] . . . and while it was stopped [1b], she saw Russell [adult male] dragging [2] a 13–18 month old [3] boy [ethnicity "unknown"] along by a rope [4]. Ms Court said the child was 'roped up' [5] with a piece of rope around his arm, by which he was being dragged along [6]. The child apparently fell over and Russell was seen to start smacking . . . him [7]. Ms Court seems to think [8] that Russell lives in a de facto relationship with Tammy Francis and Rosemary Eakins or both [9].

First, this report fits the general rule 'someone did something to a child' [2–4], which is later elaborated on [statements 5–7]. The detail shows how a rhetorical device, "extrematization" (Potter 1996), builds up the report as plausible and as 'physical abuse', by the image of "immediate danger" and giving a "sense of urgency" (Jones 1993: 247). Extreme actions [2, 5, 6, 7] by an adult male are associated with the apparently very young child [3], whose limited ability to walk would be assumed by his reported age (Potter 1996: 187–8). The plausibility of the report is built up by the apparently minimal self-interest of the reporter (Potter 1996), a woman in a bus [1a–b] as detached observer. The child was unknown to her, identified only as "a boy". Although she identified the man by name and commented on his private relationships [9], her distance is indicated by her lack of definite knowledge, as a surmise only [8]. An investigation of physical abuse was conducted.

### Investigation: 'from extreme incident to everyday routine'

The record of the investigation following the home visit by a social worker (not the intake worker) shows the (out)line of the questioning to meet the requirements of evidence as 'physical abuse (or not)':

> Rosemary Eakins was not home. I explained to Tammy Francis [Rosemary's flatmate] the allegation . . . regarding a child being dragged on a rope and smacked by Russell. Tammy said that it would not be Rosemary's child, but her

> son Murray [1]. Russell often walks Murray to the bus and takes him to . . . day care [2] . . . [She] is heavily pregnant and unable to walk far [3]. Russell does not live with her or Rosemary. She does not have a relationship with Russell [4]. She said that Russell gets a difficult time in the community. He has in the past been accused of child abuse, but this was unfounded [5]. [She] said Murray was out with Russell [6a]. She was not concerned about Murray being with Russell [6b] and had not noticed any injuries after the alleged incident [6c]. I asked her permission to contact . . . day care centre and she said I could do this [7]. I also asked Tammy to get Rosemary to give me a call so that I could confirm that the complaint was not about her child . . .

The process of normalising as everyday routine a potentially extreme incident categorised as 'physical abuse' was started by the mother's immediate knowledge of the child, man and context [1]. She constructed the incident and participants as a normal activity of an adult, with the man in loco parentis [2], and as helpful to her as pregnant woman [3]. This also justified and normalised her reliance on his help. However, she simultaneously constructed her relationship with the man as sufficiently distanced as 'friend', not intimate partner [4], but someone with whom she had a positive connection, by defending him from "unfounded accusations" by "the community" [5]. Normalisation of the incident was linked to the identity of the man by the mother's three-part list (Potter 1996) representing her "lack of concern" [6a–c] about his association with her son.

Her constructions were validated by the workers as "category entitlements" (Potter 1996) of a knowledgeable mother, rather than "self interested" (Potter 1996). The workers positioned the mother as a partner in the investigation, rather than adversary, by seeking her "permission" to access corroborative evidence [7] (Potter 1996), which she readily gave, thus building up her identity as 'cooperative partner'.

The other mother, Rosemary Eakins, was also interviewed in the investigation. Her version as recorded:

> confirmed that Russell is not a caregiver [1] for her daughter [2]. Her daughter does not walk on a lead [3], but is usually in a pram [4]. . .

Rosemary Eakins's "confirmation" provided corroboration (Potter 1996) of the man Russell's role and relationship to her daughter. She also skilfully minimised official surveillance of her parenting by showing that the reported incident was unrelated to her parenting practices. First, she distanced the man Russell as "not a caregiver" [1] of her child, identified as a "daughter", and not a boy as reported [2], and also as too young to be able to walk, being transported in a pram [4]. She also normalised the "rope" as a "[walking] lead" [3], often used for toddlers.

The social worker included the man identified as 'responsible' in constructing 'what happened':

Russell spoke to me and said that Tammy's son is very difficult to manage [1a] and tantrums [1b], throwing himself on the ground [1c]. He said he would not deliberately hurt Murray [2].

Russell, normalised the incident in which he was involved as 'child management', not 'child maltreatment'. He further normalised the incident and his claims of child management by showing through a three-part list [1a–c] (Potter 1996) that the child could be "difficult", thereby separating any "hurt" to the child from "intent" to do so [2].

### Outcome: 'physical abuse – unsubstantiated at risk'

The caseworker reassured the mother that the children would not be apprehended. "As I had spoken to them all about the incident, I would not pursue it further." The report was constructed as "unsubstantiated – at risk".

However, the worker who took the report for this case, and whom I had interviewed in relation to both the Eakins and Francis cases, contested this outcome. As the intake worker, who believed that parents engaged in "cover ups" when being investigated for child maltreatment, she considered that the outcome as 'unsubstantiated' was invalid because the investigating workers were 'not thorough enough':

> . . . There were two workers . . . investigated that, and I don't think they investigated that thoroughly enough, because when . . . they [parents] say, no it was just a strap thing, they should have asked to see it, and they didn't.

### Categorisation: 'physical abuse – unsubstantiated at risk'

This analysis has highlighted several issues. Firstly, it shows how reports about incidents in which children seem to be in 'immediate danger' or extreme need may generate a variety of plausible explanations that reconstruct the incident as part of an everyday routine and as 'normal'. Hence, where a categorisation of 'physical abuse' is apparently indisputable, it may be normalised by other apparently plausible versions and therefore be 'unsubstantiated'. The analysis also shows how different workers may have produced different meanings, including whether or not the report was 'substantiated', as a consequence of different assumptions about parental integrity and parents' motivation towards their children. The case also highlights the ethical contradictions posed if practitioners work with parents in a 'cooperative partnership' in establishing 'what happened' to a child as a simple category of 'maltreatment'. There is the possibility that 'cooperation' may lead to collusion and failure to address children's experiences of violence and oppressive practices. It is also possible that whilst there may not be concerns about 'maltreatment', more general assistance to parents for promoting children's welfare may not be offered if 'physical abuse' is 'unsubstantiated'.

## CATEGORISATION: A 'HIERARCHY OF MALTREATMENT'

In chapter 3, the concept of a "hierarchy of maltreatment" was discussed in some detail. The concept is a feature of contemporary child protection practice, influenced by discursive rules about the 'status' of some types of maltreatment over others (Berliner 1994; Dubowitz 1994; Doyle 1996). This 'status' regards 'sexual and physical abuse' as more serious than 'physical and emotional neglect', and furthermore regards 'sexual abuse' as more serious than 'physical abuse'. A hierarchy of maltreatment may influence what is reported and how it is categorised in terms of the 'type of maltreatment', such that some types of maltreatment do not attract the same degree of professional concern or intervention. This also has consequences for what enters the official record of the statistical profile of child maltreatment. If particular cases are given greater attention, then they are more likely to enter the record as children's current or most common experiences, whilst excluding other experiences. For example, the priority given to 'sexual abuse' followed by 'physical abuse' tends to minimise the much more widespread experience for children of 'neglect' associated with poverty and disadvantage (Wolock & Horowitz 1984; Minty & Pattinson 1994; Scott & Swain 2002). The two cases below show how the 'hierarchy of maltreatment' operates in practice. The reliance on establishing a single, 'most serious' category of 'maltreatment' significantly minimises the complexity of the children's experiences of oppression and misrepresents their experiences within the domain of organisational and professional knowledge.

## CATEGORISATION: 'SEXUAL ABUSE SUBSTANTIATED'

There were three children in the Jones family (ethnicity "Unknown"): two girls, Melissa (aged 11) and Teresa (aged 12), and their brother Peter (aged eight) at the time of the intake report at Urbania. The children's parents were separated and, through negotiation with their mother, the father had temporary custody. The children and their father were living with family friends when the woman friend reported to child protection workers her concerns about the father's behaviour to the two girls. The case was "substantiated" as "sexual abuse" at intake by the caseworker, with Melissa and Teresa as "subjects of the allegation". Their eight-year-old brother's experiences are unknown, beyond his immediate family relationships. The case shows how a hierarchy of maltreatment is manifested in the partitioning of the child's body, with different body parts representing different 'types of maltreatment'. These discursive features influenced the practical categorisation as 'sexual abuse' in this case.

### Reporting/Intake/Investigation: 'what happened to Melissa and Teresa'

The female friend, Susan, who was caring for the children:

> said that these three children and their father . . . ha[d] been living with them for about three weeks . . . Susan said on Wed. night Melissa went . . . to bed, but came out . . . later and asked her sister to come to bed now. When Susan asked why, Melissa told her that dad [1] had been touching her on the leg, first to see if she would wake up [2], and then started touching her on her private parts over her shorts [3]. Susan said Melissa was very upset about this.

The incident that precipitated the report involved Melissa's narrative of 'what happened', giving detailed access to the scene (Potter 1996), including identifying a particular individual [1], his actions and perceived intent [2], linked to 'private (sexualised) body parts' [3] (Foucault 1978a, Faller 1988b). However, the carer, Susan, continued her report by adding the corroboration provided by Melissa's older sister, Teresa:

> . . . Teresa then disclosed that approx. two months ago [1a] in [another part of the country] [1b] when they were living with their dad [2] in a caravan park, he also touched her [3]. Teresa told carer that it began by him rubbing her stomach [3, 4] and then rubbing her leg [3, 4] to see if she would wake up [3]. When she pretended to be asleep, he put his finger into her vagina [5]. Teresa told Susan that it also happened to the older sister Yolanda (now 22 years) [6] [living elsewhere]. Teresa said that Melissa was involved with the . . . welfare . . . and was put in foster care after dad [7] touched her [8]. Teresa said that he touched her under her clothing in the private parts. At this time, Melissa said to her dad [9] that she would tell her mother. [Dad] [10] picked her up by the throat threatening her not to tell her mother [11]. Teresa told carer that it was at this time the police were involved and Melissa was put into accommodation with welfare [12]. It is believed this occurred about two years ago . . .

In the above extract, Melissa's sister, Teresa, provided corroboration (Potter 1996) linking similar incidents from the 'past' into the 'present', again providing extensive detail and access to the scene (Faller 1988b). This included specific dates [1a], place (named) [1b]; particular individual ("dad") [2, 7, 9, 10] and his actions [3], connected to 'private body parts' [3, 4], each action and body part 'escalating' in degree of what I call 'sexualisation' ("touching stomach", "rubbing leg", "putting finger into vagina"). Teresa provided additional corroboration (Potter 1996), saying "it also happened to [22-year-old sister]" [6, 8]. The plausibility of Teresa's account was strengthened when she referred to previous social and legal intervention [7, 12].

Melissa and Teresa described their father's domination expressed as violence, when they tried to resist him. He "picked [his] daughter up by the throat when she said she would tell her mother" [11], "bashing", "punched in the head", leaving "bumps and bruises", and "hitting" her on various parts of the body. The children's recourse to their mother's help was limited. Firstly, she minimised (Potter 1996) her husband's practices by recategorising them as "sickness".

Secondly, she was also subordinated by his violence: "there was nothing mum could do as he . . . would just bash her up too . . .".

Mr Jones's oppressive practices extended to the "extra-familial" (Conte 1991; Fischer & McDonald 1998), involving two other 'girls/children', one aged six and the other aged 16. Their particular identities of inequality (generational, due to age and temporary disability, respectively) were features in how Mr Jones minimised their resistance to him. The six-year-old girl who refused "to sleep in his bed any more [because] he touched her private parts" was *told to get back into his bed which she did*". The 16-year-old "*was an epileptic and had a fit one day. [He] . . . took her somewhere* and proceeded to sexually abuse her by putting his finger in her vagina" (emphasis added).

### Outcome: 'sexual abuse substantiated'

Within the legal/criminal domain, the "children's disclosure" categorised only as 'sexual abuse' was sufficient to "charge" the father, although "[police] were of two minds", not having medical evidence. However, the father "denied the charges and was released from police custody". He escaped further investigation by relocating himself and disappearing: "whereabouts currently unknown". The police "would not bother with an extradition order for something so minor".

Within the social domain, substantiating 'what happened' as "sexual abuse – indecent dealings/molestation" was, for the caseworker, "a kind of combination":

> Based on what [the children] had said, and that the Police Child Abuse Unit decided to charge dad . . . and the history stuff, the moving around, are the kids possibly interfered with, previous allegations of abuse, the way the kids presented, what my hunch was . . .

### Categorisation: 'sexual abuse substantiated'

This case has shown how the hierarchy of maltreatment is manifested in the partitioning of the body, whereby particular 'types of maltreatment' are associated with particular 'body parts'. Furthermore, the priority that is given to particular descriptions of 'what happened' separates different 'body parts'/types of maltreatment' from each other. Therefore, there was no association made between "physical abuse" and 'non-sexual body parts' that were violent strategies by which the father could continue the 'sexual abuse' of his daughters and other young girls/women. The reduction of 'what happened' to Melissa and Teresa to a single category, 'sexual abuse', precluded an analysis of the inequalities of power in families, especially between adult males and young children/girls, that also extended to the "extra-familial" (Conte 1991; Fischer & McDonald 1998). The man's disappearance limited any effective 'protective' response. Further, because of the reductionist categorisation of 'what happened' to Melissa and Teresa as 'sexual abuse', there was also no overall plan for protecting the children in case their father gained access to them again. Child protection that is focused on individual cases that identify 'victims' and 'persons believed responsible' as aberrant compared to the general population tends to limit broader considerations of the generally powerless position of 'children' in relation to 'adults' in many Western societies (Freeman 1983; Franklin 1986). Child maltreatment is perhaps just a particular expression of these more general inequalities.

## CATEGORISATION: 'SEXUAL ABUSE SUBSTANTIATED'

There were five children (four girls, aged 10, nine, eight, five, and a boy aged eight) who were step and half siblings from a two-parent (heterosexual) family (ethnicity unrecorded). The Underwood family had a long history that was known to Suburbia. Both this 'history' and the incident that finally resulted in child protection intervention and a categorisation of 'sexual abuse substantiated' shows how a hierarchy of maltreatment and a partitioning of bodies operated to influence particular interventions and outcomes, and precluded others.

There were significant gaps in the statistical records and also on file relating to the report that resulted in the categorisation of 'sexual abuse'. Therefore, this analysis draws mainly upon the Particulars of the Application to the Children's Court prepared one month after the report was made, and the interview with the caseworker seven months after the report was made.

### A hierarchy of maltreatment: 'official history'

The report that was eventually categorised as 'sexual abuse' was part of an extensive official "history" – six years of "allegations" from schools, community organisations and hospitals about:

> . . . physical abuse and . . . sexual abuse, [although they] have never been substantiated. The allegations [by school and day care centres] in relation to neglect have been ongoing . . . about inadequate hygiene, clothing and lack of attention to medical conditions. [. . .]

> . . . the long term emotional abuse is of more concern . . . a consequence of a blended family with limited strengths and resources.

The problems presented did not warrant a place in the hierarchy of priorities at Suburbia. " . . . [O]n [three] occasion[s] an assessment was made that *our resources needed to respond to priorities of a higher order than chronic neglect*" (emphasis added). Nor was there "enough evidence to proceed with statutory action". These statements on file suggest that child protection intervention was perceived as a last resort in which 'statutory action', meaning legal intervention, was required. Furthermore, 'chronic neglect' was not high on the list of priorities, nor were multiple allegations of (unsubstantiated) reports of physical and sexual abuse. This statement of 'priority' is associated with the available resources, implying that child protection was a lot narrower in intent than promoting the general welfare of children.

However, a report was received that eventually was constructed as a "higher priority", with redirection of "resources" as a particular "protective response" to "child maltreatment".

Reporting: 'what happened? "sexual abuse" and/or "physical abuse"?'

The Particulars of the Application to the Children's Court state that:

> On [date one month earlier] it was reported to the Department that on [day before report was made] Madeline Underwood had disclosed that she was locked in her room for long periods of time [1]; . . . that [her step/father] came [sic] into her room [2], puts [sic] her blanket and sheets in the wardrobe [3], takes off her pyjamas and makes her feel "rude" [4]; . . . [he] takes his clothes off [5] and hits her with a stick all over her body [6], and ties her legs with a strap until they are swollen [7]; . . . in the holidays she was locked in her room until 5 pm [8a] and then had dinner and all the children were then smacked [9] and put into their rooms again [8b].

The above extract is 10-year-old Madeline Underwood's report about 'what happened' to her. It justifies to the Children's Court why child protection intervention was made and why an application for wardship was necessary. Madeline Underwood's report shows how parental/adult power may be expressed in the home and to family members, through a combination of practices. These included:

- constraints on her liberty and that of her siblings, without apparent justification [statements 1 and 8a–b]
- invasion of her personal space and time [2–3] (read as night time, in bed, asleep) (De Swann 1990)
- 'sexualised' practices [4–5] (the word "rude" is read as a euphemism for 'sexual practices', as is the nudity of both stepfather and stepdaughter, at his instigation)
- assaults upon 'non-sexual parts' of her body [6, 7] and that of her siblings [9].

On the Summary of Reasons for Apprehension, the description of the variety and combination of practices of parental/paternal power was reduced to an "allegation of sexual abuse". This distillation of the complexity of Madeline's experiences to a single category of 'sexual abuse' was repeated in the caseworker's reconstruction to me of 'what happened':

> . . . a call . . . came in from the school concerned about Madeline Underwood who had disclosed to a school [staff member] that dad had made her feel rude, that's what she said . . .

However, in practice the report was investigated initially as possibly 'physical' and/or 'sexual abuse'.

### Investigation: 'separating "sexual abuse" from "physical abuse"'

The child Madeline was interviewed at the school and restated other incidents when her stepfather had "hit her", confined her to her bedroom for long periods "each day" after school, and "put his finger and his tongue in her 'privates' [child's meaning for vagina]".

The social worker's reconstruction of the interview with Madeline indicated that the "disclosure" was "that dad had been physically abusing her, she [also] disclosed that dad digitally penetrated her . . . that dad had whispered to her that she wasn't to tell . . .". This version shows how 'physical' and 'sexual' practices of oppression operate together (Ney et al. 1994; Goddard & Hiller 1993), the former facilitating the latter.

Throughout the investigation, shifting constructions and reconstructions of 'what happened' as 'physical abuse' or 'sexual abuse' continued, often represented ambiguously. For example, in the questioning of Madeline, she was asked "if she'd seen any of the other siblings [unstated], or if she was worried about any of the other siblings and she [said] no".

> . . . we had discussions with the team leaders, the case work supervisor, the manager here, because our feeling was that *it was leading up to an apprehension of Madeline . . . for physical abuse* [father had "tied her legs with a rope", "hitting her on the head"] . . . she was saying that she was suffering by dad. (emphasis added)

The construction of 'physical abuse' was given priority, because Madeline's version was validated by the "school's experiences" of the father's "volatility" and "capability of physical violence". The workers "were told [by senior staff] to apprehend Madeline . . . and we arranged for her to go to [hospital] that day . . .".

It is at this point that there is a sudden, unexplained change in the investigation of either 'physical abuse' on its own, or in combination with 'sexual abuse'. This change occurs with the type of hospital that Madeline was taken to that day. Instead of a general paediatric examination, she attended the "child sexual abuse unit" at the paediatric hospital. The medical officer reported only on an examination of 'sexual body parts' such as the vagina to provide evidence of 'sexual abuse' (or not). This examination was "not conclusive". The 'normal' abnormalities expected to represent 'sexual abuse' "were distorted" because of existing abnormalities from a previous "gross injury to her vagina" (Bond et al. 1995). When Madeline attended the hospital for examination/treatment of this earlier injury, her father explained it as "accidental" – a "fall from a bunk bed". His explanation was accepted at the time.

### Outcome (1): 'Madeline has been sexually abused'

Despite the limitations of medical technologies in distinguishing "non-accidental genital abnormality" from "accidental genital abnormality" (Adams et al. 1994; Hobbs et al. 1995; Bond et al. 1995), Madeline was able to speak for herself, giving the hospital "a very clear disclosure of dad digitally penetrating her". Her previous injury was reconstructed by the hospital as 'non-accidental' and 'sexual abuse', this time undermining as self-interested (Potter 1996) the father's explanation of 'accidental injury'. This was "enough evidence for statutory [socio-legal] action", so Madeline was "apprehended" because of 'sexual abuse'.

### Investigation continued: 'when is a disclosure not a disclosure?'

Whilst Madeline was being medically examined, her siblings "continued to be interviewed". The contradictory use of the word "disclosures" intersecting with official and situated 'priorities' is represented in the caseworker's construction of 'what happened' to these children:

> . . . we knew at that stage that we would apprehend Madeline, but we didn't feel that we knew enough, *we didn't have any disclosures from the other children [1]*, *we had the disclosures of physical abuse at some stage [2]*, they all talked about times when they'd been hit [2a], and . . . they all told us . . . they'd . . . been locked in the bedroom each night, [2b] . . . chained across the door so they couldn't get out [2c] . . . [. . .]

> . . .*there were not disclosures [3a], like real serious disclosures [3b]* and although we knew there was lots of information on the file, we actually hadn't gone through the file at that stage because it was very difficult to put all the information together [4a], *we decided to apprehend Madeline given her clear disclosure of sexual abuse [5]* . . . we were told that we didn't have enough at that stage to apprehend the other children [4b]. (emphasis added)

The reconstruction of the meaning of 'disclosures' that constituted an official and situated 'priority' is suggested by contradictory statements [1, 2a–c, 3a–b] that there were "no disclosures" and then that there were. Statement 1 is read as implying that there were 'no disclosures of *sexual abuse*' from Madeline's siblings, for two reasons. Firstly, is the immediately *preceding* statement that Madeline was apprehended for "sexual abuse". Secondly, there is the immediately *following* statement that they did have "disclosures" for "physical abuse", represented as a three-part list [2a–c] (Potter 1996). The 'priority' given to these differentiated 'disclosures' was that those constituting "physical abuse" [2a–c] were "not [real] disclosures" and "not real serious" [3a, b]. Corroboration (Potter 1996) could not be obtained easily from the extensive file records which, according to the caseworker were "difficult to put together", being presumably a set of fractured incidents over time, rather than a unitary and coherent picture which constituted a valid 'disclosure' (Lamb & Edgar-Smith 1994; Roesler & Wind 1994).

The parents were constrained in their opportunities to offer their own version(s) of what happened to the children, particularly Madeline. As a strategy at Suburbia to manage and minimise 'dangerousness', 'contentious' cases and workload, the parents were merely "asked to come to the office". The caseworker said, "We didn't inform the parents that we were going to interview them because we felt like it would hinder the investigation [of sexual abuse] . . .", which was consistent with policy. Although "concerns that [the children] were locked in their rooms" had already been invalidated as 'not a disclosure' and excluded as a topic for investigation, this was the topic of conversation with/examination of the parents. The caseworker only informed the parents towards the conclusion of the interview with them that:

> we had interviewed all the children and that going on the information that Madeline had given, it was our assessment that she was at risk of harm at home, that she had been apprehended . . . and wouldn't return home until further investigation had been carried out. [. . .]

However, the construction was the general "risk of harm at home", rather than the specific 'sexual abuse'. The caseworker remarked that:

> [t]he father was very hostile . . . because of his past experiences . . . the allegations of possible sexual abuse . . . and all of them were unsubstantiated [. . .] he would say that the department were out to get him . . .

The other children "went home", where they continued to experience oppressive adult male power: 'hitting' them and 'confining' them to their rooms. The caseworker's construction of these practices glossed the politics of gender and generation, by equalising the responsibility for the practices as 'parental', rather than 'paternal' [1], and as benign, if misguided, practices of "control" [2] and "safety" [3]:

> . . . it sounds like mum and dad [1] were finding it difficult to cope with five boisterous children and that was a way of [keeping them under control] [2] . . . and [dad] said . . . it was for safety . . . reasons [3] . . .

Madeline's statement to the caseworker that she had witnessed her nine-year-old sister, Penny, " . . . being sexually abused by dad . . . digitally penetrating [her], mum being present, . . . not participating . . . but . . . watching what was happening", "ratcheted up" (Scott 1998) the 'priorities' from potential 'physical abuse' to 'sexual abuse' of all the children.

Documentary corroboration (Potter 1996) to support socio-legal intervention was sought:

So we had a discussion and we decided that we would read through the files, we would go through the files with a fine toothcomb and we would do a timeline on the contact we had. . . . We had a [team] meeting . . . [female social worker colleague] did a timeline and we then had a meeting with the intake team and that was the senior case work supervisor and the team manager and we looked at the pros and cons, . . . the safety issues and we debated and came to a consensus that the other children were to be apprehended . . .

### Outcome (2): 'fitting the hierarchy of priorities'

The official "timeline on contact" "put together" a coherent and unitary construction, eventually represented in the Particulars of the Application to the Children's Court. However, it still required a "debate" between colleagues about "the pros and cons" and "safety issues", before there was "consensus" about "sexual abuse" of the other children. There was now "enough evidence to proceed with statutory action", meaning wardship and alternative care.

### Categorisation: 'sexual abuse substantiated'

This case has shown how the hierarchy of maltreatment represented in the partitioning of bodies intersected with priorities at Suburbia in constructing what happened to all five children as 'sexual abuse'. This was despite an extensive official 'history' of 'neglect', 'emotional abuse', poverty and disadvantage, as well as 'allegations' of 'physical abuse' and 'sexual abuse', for which the 'lack of evidence', particularly of the latter, precluded official intervention. Instead, the discursive priority given to 'sexual' practices as most dangerous to children excluded their other experiences, including violence by their step/father, from constructions of justifiable 'protective' intervention. Furthermore, priority given to some 'types of maltreatment' excluded the representation of all experiences of these children's oppression/disadvantage.

This limits the extent of official knowledge of the complexity of children's experiences and minimises the more pervasive and entrenched oppressive practices associated with poverty and generalised violence, including those that may be better seen as the responsibility of 'the state' rather than solely parental dangerousness and/or incompetence. The self-perpetuating knowledge maintained by hierarchies of maltreatment is also an issue because there is a circularity in how policy and practice priorities maintain the hierarchy of maltreatment in public and private knowledge about 'child maltreatment'.

## CONCLUSION

In this chapter, I have analysed how reports that 'something happened' to a child may be substantiated (or not) and become official 'types of maltreatment'. The analysis in each case is structured according to the prescribed linear stages organising 'child protection' intervention, named as 'reporting'/'intake', 'investigation' and 'outcome' (as to whether or not the report is 'substantiated'). This is intended to show how prescribed 'child protection' intervention is assumed to be a simple set of stages whereby reports that 'something happened' to a child can be given official meaning as a 'type of maltreatment' or not. However, in practice, the intervention process is messy and the apparently discrete linear stages often overlap or run parallel. Some 'reports' may be simultaneously 'investigations' (for example, the Allston and Constable cases and the Underwood case) and some 'outcomes' may constitute 'reports' in another context ( for example, the Allston and Constable, and the Jones cases), connecting cases across place and time, or across time and place within the same case. These practice realities in regard to process also significantly influence how meaning is constructed.

Usually, there is only a single 'reporter' recorded, which may not fully account for multiple 'reporters', hidden influences and contexts for 'reporting'. These aspects were apparent in several cases discussed in this chapter, and especially those of Jane Allston, Mary Constable, and the Underwood and Jones children.

The 'investigation' stage allows for the child protection worker's engagement of multiple participants in ascertaining 'what happened', including the child and parents, and sometimes the 'person believed responsible': for example, in the Francis case. However, in other cases – for example, in relation to the Allston/Constable and Jones children – the 'person believed responsible' was not interviewed as part of the child protection investigation, although the police may have done so in a separate but related investigation.

The 'outcome' stage is the consolidation of multiple versions, represented as a single category of 'substantiation' or not; and 'type of maltreatment'. Versions that do not contribute to the construction of a single category – for example, ambiguities or contradictions – are excluded. For example, the Allston case showed how the interview that sought to substantiate (or not) whether or not the child had been sexually abused tended to exclude multiple or alternative explanations for perceived abnormal behaviours by the child Jane. Yet when investigating the Martini case, workers reconstructed the meaning of the 'sexual abuse' category to explore possible alternative explanations for the child Simon's alleged 'sexual abuse' of another child of the same age.

However, the main point of the chapter is how meanings of what happened to a child are constructed throughout the process and may be transformed at different stages, through the deployment of rhetorical devices. I have analysed each case separately because the practical and official meaning of 'what happened' to a child is only appropriately understood within its context of construction.

The analysis is informed by Foucault's conceptualisation of the body as a site of knowledge/power. I have re-presented different examples of how the body of the child is central to constructions of meaning as 'reported', 'investigated' and the eventual 'outcome' within discursive prescriptions of how to see and say 'what happened' to a 'child'. The cases also show how the official hierarchy of maltreatment is organised from 'highest priority sexual abuse', through 'physical abuse', with minimal attention given to 'neglect' and 'emotional abuse': for example, the Underwood and Jones children. These cases showed how partitioning of the body is related to the hierarchy of maltreatment and its types, and is a significant feature of the construction of meaning. Challenging discursive prescriptions can also alter constructionist processes and outcomes: for example, as in the Martini case and to a lesser extent the Francis case.

This chapter has shown how child protection discursive categories of 'type of maltreatment' are not unitary and homogeneous. The official categories gloss over unique sets of events and processes of construction, involving different participants with differentially validated knowledges. This suggests that existing categorisations of 'what happened' ought not represent unproblematic and definitive knowledge claims that are instead simplistic labels for diverse experiences with potentially different meanings for participants, including those identified as 'victims' and 'persons believed responsible'.

The next chapter analyses the construction of the official identity, 'person believed responsible', showing how the meaning of 'responsibility' is entwined with 'what happened' and with particular constructions of identity of the person identified as 'responsible'.

# 7

# Identities of responsibility

As discussed in chapter 3, contemporary child protection discourse is structured according to a taken-for-granted rule that 'someone did something to a child'. In the previous chapter, we explored how the 'truth' of reports that 'something happened' to a child is accomplished in practice. The outcomes of practical constructions in each case were represented by the official categories of 'maltreatment' and whether or not they were 'substantiated' within the rules of what constitutes 'substantiation' (or not) in child protection discourse. In this chapter, we explore how the official identity of the 'person believed responsible' is constructed in practice. This identity is important in the discursive rule because 'something' that happens to a 'child' must be associated with 'someone' who is responsible, by acts of either commission or omission.

This chapter shows how the identity of the person believed responsible is structured within discourses of "dangerous individuals" (Hearn 1990) from whom the child in the particular case, all children, and the community must be protected. Through practical constructions in each case, private identities are transformed into public categories of abnormality. The 'person believed responsible' was not always individually identified, but remained a shadowy 'someone'.

The dominant assumption that identities of responsibility are fixed and meaningful across contexts and social relationships produces particular complications for child protection practice. This is because participants with an interest in the case may not share perceptions of individual responsibility associated with dangerousness. Differences between participants' perceptions of responsibility are contingent upon the relationships between the person identified as responsible and others in the case network, including the child protection practitioner. For example, a man identified officially as a person believed responsible for sexual abuse may not be seen as such by friends or female partners, to whom he may be a pillar of the community and a loving father and husband. Whether or not these are misguided perceptions is not at issue for this chapter. Instead, such perceptions are shown to be particular constructions associated with the 'self' who is presented in those relationships and contexts, and are perhaps no more misguided than the official perception of responsibility and dangerousness. However, what is important for this chapter is how the positioning of participants within the case may limit each participant's personal construction of the individual to the identity that they 'know', precluding engagement with other possibilities for identity, including alternative, complementary or even competing identities.

Another important feature of child protection policy and practice discussed in this chapter is how gender and responsibility are related (Stark & Flitcraft 1988; Milner 1993; Thorpe 1994; Minty & Pattinson 1994; Korbin 1989; Hetherton & Beardsall 1998; Hetherton 1999). This chapter shows how such gendered outcomes, conceptualised as "responsible mothers, invisible men" (Milner 1993), are consequences of sociolinguistic practices in each case. The cases show how discourses of the patriarchal, heterosexual family as the implicit norm in child protection policy structure practice, with consequences for how responsibility is constructed as a gender issue. Feminist concepts of "the politics of the family" and "patriarchal mothering" (Stark & Flitcraft 1988) provide the tools for unpacking dominant discourses of 'normal families' and paternalist protection of children, by which women become "responsible" and men "disappear" (Milner 1993).

## RE-PRESENTING THE CASES

The cases presented below show different aspects of identity discussed above, and how these aspects are implicated in the eventual categorisation of 'person believed responsible' in each case. Eight cases will be presented, (anonymised through pseudonyms and with identifying details altered). Each case will show how the practical construction of the identity of the person believed responsible is accomplished. The analysis will focus on how language represents versions of knowledge through linguistic devices as strategies of power. Thus, language and the knowledge it represents about identity is not neutral, but is deployed strategically through particular resources to construct identity as versions of normality or abnormality. The particular resources that are deployed in each case, such as categorisation and three-part lists (Potter 1996), have been explained in chapter 2.

The themes explored in this chapter through different case examples are:
- 'Dangerousness' and the identity of the 'person believed responsible'
- Identity as contextual, partial and multiple
- Responsible mothers, invisible men: both parents are reported, father officially 'disappears'
- Responsible mothers, invisible men: father is reported, he officially 'disappears'

- Responsible mothers, invisible men: 'the unprotective mother' and 'the dangerous man'
- Responsible mothers, invisible men: patriarchal mothering and disabling practices
- Responsible mothers, invisible men: father is reported, mother is suspected, both 'responsible'
- Responsibility for emotional abuse: the cultural idealisation of motherhood
- Constructing versions of maternal responsibility to meet case objectives.

## 'DANGEROUSNESS' AND THE IDENTITY OF THE 'PERSON BELIEVED RESPONSIBLE'

This case shows how dominant policy assumptions of 'dangerousness' associated with 'abuse' or 'maltreatment' influenced how a particular man was identified as "person believed responsible for sexual abuse", although the allegations were "unsubstantiated". Official knowledge of 'other' cases in which this man was also alleged to be maltreating the children with whom he was associated was significant in giving greater legitimacy to the referring agency's general suspicions.

Alan Eakins, aged four years, was reported to the intake worker[1] at Urbania by a specialist 'Aboriginal' organisation, presumably because Alan was identified on file as 'Aboriginal' (his biological father's identity). However, the child's racial, ethnic and cultural identity were incidental to case processes. All participants engaged within the dominant discourse, as shown by the record of the report at intake, which is re-presented by indented segments interleaved with my readings of them.

The report by the referring organisation began by constructing 'what happened' to Alan as 'abuse', through the rhetorical device of categorisation (Potter 1996; Smith 1990a):

> They feel he may be being abused [1] as he soils [2a], wets [2b], he is very underweight [2c] for his age [3] – 12 kilos [3a], four years [3b] and very small [3c]; his language development [4] appears to be very delayed [4a]. He has few words [4b].

The construction as "abuse" [1] is supported by a cumulative list (Potter 1996) of bodily and language abnormalities associated with Western conceptions of "(child) development" [2a–c, 3a–c, 4a–b]. However, the main features for this

---

[1] Note that the intake worker for the Eakins' case was not the worker who took on case management and whom I interviewed for this study. The intake worker was not interviewed as she had left the site.

chapter relate to how the identity of 'person believed responsible for (sexual) abuse' is constructed, in statements that follow immediately from the categorisation as 'abuse':

> He [Alan] appears to be afraid of Aboriginal men [5a] . . . he is OK with white men [5b]. [Organisation] believe Russell [adult male] [6a] is living with one of the girls [6b] (probably Tammy who shares a flat with Rosemary [mother of Alan]) [6c]. They believe something is not right with Alan's behaviour and development [7]. [. . .] The child's poor behaviour reflects the parent's poor management skills [8a]. Alan said he was hit in the stomach on access with mum [9a]. [Mum] said he had fallen over [9b]. [Mother] has said when she cannot handle Alan she locks him in his room all day [8b].

The commencement of the process of constructing abnormal identity begins by offering a generalised profile of dangerousness. A contrast structure [5a–b] (Potter 1996; Smith 1990a) that the child is "afraid of Aboriginal men" whilst he is "OK with white men" first differentiates "men" of the child's acquaintance according to their apparent visibility as "Aboriginal" or "white". Secondly, the contrast structure suggests that it is "Aboriginal men" whom the child fears. This contrast implies that the child's 'fear' of "Aboriginal men" in general is due to him being 'abused' by a particular "Aboriginal man", whilst feeling safe ("OK") with "white men". The next statement [6a] gives specificity (Potter 1996) to the general profile of dangerousness by naming a particular man, Russell, and linking him to the child's immediate context [6b–c] as "living with" [6b] the child's mother's female friend/flatmate [6c]. More generalised concerns repeat the process of constructing 'abuse' as embodied abnormalities [7]. The dangerousness of the child's context and associates [9a] is contrasted (Potter 1996) with his mother's explanation [9b]. This is achieved by destroying the mother's category entitled knowledge (Potter 1996) (what she would normally be expected to know as the child's mother) by a prior comment on her "poor (child) management skills" [8a]. An extreme example (Potter 1996) of her poor child management skills is given: "locks him in his room all day" [8b].

The intake report continued (the section in italics is the intake worker's recollections of her previous involvement with this family):

> [Organisation] concerned about Russell [10a] without being able to make any specific allegation [10b]. *[Ms Eakins and Ms Francis] informed me in conversation recently that Russell had been accused of sexually abusing some children and that this had been investigated (I don't know what children were involved . . .).* [11] Alan also has a drooping eyelid and a slight scar below his eye. The . . . carers are going to take [child] to a medical appointment to have him checked out. . . . [12] *There was a recent report that Russell had tied a male child up with a rope and dragged him along [street]. This turned out to be [Tammy Francis's] son. Russell walks [Murray Francis] to the bus on a lead to take him to day care centre. Murray*

*the son is said to tantrum and throw himself on the ground. They use a harness . . . not a rope* [13a]. *Both [women] deny that Russell is living with them in the flat because they don't want to lose their Social Security benefits* [13b]. *When I was investigating the incident re Murray*[2], *his mother informed me that Russell was not living in the flat* [13c]. *Both [mothers] are aware that allegations of the sexual abuse of children have been laid against Russell in the past* [13d]. *They feel there are certain people . . . out to get Russell* [13e]. [13] Alan is still in . . . placement . . . (emphasis added)

The reporter specifically identified a particular man as being 'responsible' for 'abuse' of Alan [10a], but was "unable to make any specific allegations" [10b] beyond generalised concerns about the child. However, the intake worker's prior knowledge of these families introduced the specificity that was lacking in the reporter's statements (Potter 1996). The intake worker interleaved situated official knowledge of other cases [11, 13a–e]. First, she mentioned that the mothers of the children, Ms Eakins and Ms Francis, "informed her" of a "recent investigation" of Russell for "sexually abusing some children" [11]. Thus, the existence of a prior case of this man's identity of 'responsibility for sexual abuse' lends specificity to the report about Alan Eakins. However, the specificity is limited because the identities of the children are unknown to this worker. After she records details of other concerns by reporters regarding the Eakins family [12], she continues with the accumulation (Potter 1996) of knowledge about the man identified as responsible through prior involvement by herself or her colleagues. Statement 13 aggregates this worker's personal/professional knowledge of the Francis family, which she had previously investigated [13a, 13c], identifying Russell as "person believed responsible" for extreme (Potter 1996) practices, yet which she categorised as "unsubstantiated" (see chapter 6). The mothers' alternative versions of Russell's identity of 'responsibility' are re-presented as self-interested (Potter 1996) [13b], and at the same time justified this worker's categorisation of the report about Murray Francis as 'unsubstantiated' [13c]. The worker repeats that the mothers are aware of public constructions of Russell's identity as 'responsible for sexual abuse' [11, 13d], and concludes by re-presenting the mothers' alternative version of Russell's identity as 'victim' of "certain people" [13e].

The report about Alan Eakins was referred for investigation. The investigating worker whom I interviewed commented on her prior knowledge that influenced her engagement with the family. The "third case" that she refers to below was the same case referred to by the intake worker in statements 11, 13d and 13e in the extract above:

---

2   This worker is referring to her investigation of the Francis case discussed in chapter 6. The investigating worker for the Eakins case was the intake worker for the Francis case.

> . . . Our particular concerns in this case [Eakins family] actually related to a third case. . . . there'd been a child [1] who'd been *anally raped* [2] in a block of flats [3] and. . . *the man who'd done it . . . was the de facto of one of these women here* [4] . . . (emphasis added)

The man's 'responsibility' is built up by the association of a specific (Potter 1996) and extreme (Potter 1996) category of action [2] to a generalised child [1] in a generalised location [3] by an identifiable 'person responsible' [4]. Thus, he is constructed as 'dangerous' to all children.

The investigating worker's "personal belief" in this man's abnormality for extreme "cruelty" towards children and his generalised "strangeness" and "dangerousness" was influenced by her role as intake worker in regard to a report about a child, Murray Francis (chapter 6), involving the man later reported in the Eakins' case:

> . . . I personally believe it would have been a rope because I actually took that duty call . . . the woman who rang me was extremely distressed, she said she'd never seen anyone be so cruel in all her life . . .

Although the reported 'physical abuse' of Murray Francis alluded to in the above extract was 'unsubstantiated', the man was officially categorised as "person believed responsible" (see chapter 6). The extreme images portrayed in that report marked this man as 'dangerous'. This knowledge was incorporated into the culture of Urbania, influencing the processes of identity construction in regard to allegations relating to his maltreatment of another child, Alan Eakins, and constructing him as "person believed responsible for sexual abuse". This categorisation was made despite the allegations being "unsubstantiated", "in view of no medical evidence, no disclosures and no police conviction", because the children's mothers refused to allow the workers to interview the children or to have them medically examined at the paediatric hospital. The mothers disputed the official view that the man was 'responsible for sexual abuse', and resisted the workers' intervention by preventing access to their private relationships. The next section shows the different positionings by Ms Eakins and Ms Francis, and the investigating worker, in relation to the man's identity, and how these different perspectives in an adversarial relationship were counterproductive to ensuring the children's welfare.

## IDENTITY AS CONTEXTUAL, PARTIAL AND MULTIPLE

The official construction of responsibility of the man Russell in the Eakins case, also showed how this identity may be contested, a familiar feature of child protection practice. The analysis here shows such contestation as a consequence of context and the relationships relevant to that context. Both Ms Eakins and Ms

Francis, the mothers of the children of concern in related cases, offered alternative versions of Russell's official identity, as "person believed responsible for sexual abuse".

The worker and both mothers' different positionings in relation to the man identified as 'responsible' influenced their differing constructions of his identities as 'person believed responsible' and 'not responsible', respectively. Three sub-themes show these different positionings and their overall consequences for identity construction.

### Sub-theme one: 'the truth about identity'

For the worker, social facts [1, 2a–b] were not always legal facts [3]:

> a past incident of a child who was *sodomised* [1] by a man identified as Russell. He denied assaulting the child [2a], *although the child had clearly identified him* [2b]. He was not charged with any offence, and so we cannot say he assaulted the child [3].(emphasis added)

Nevertheless, this was 'true' in the social domain: "... the department operates on different principles to the police or law. [...]".

However, this was 'not true' for the mother. She "knew of allegations regarding a four-year-old child who was assaulted in the block of flats". However, she undermined the allegations as being outside her category entitled knowledge as direct witness (Potter 1996) – "no assault took place in her flat", as only "allegations" about an unidentified child in an unspecified location.

The worker validated the social truth of the child's experience. Lack of 'legal' corroboration was explained to the mother as a feature of the child's inability to meet the requirements of "fact" (Daro 1991) within the legal domain, rather than as an invalidation of the child's actual experience. "I [worker] explained ... that often charges were not laid when child was too young to make a statement to the court or withstand questioning ...".

### Sub-theme two: 'relationships between child and abuser'

The official version of these relationships, represented by the worker, was that "children are often abused by people close to them". This was countered by the mothers' response that "the children show no fear of Russell" and the apparent contradiction of the children "liking someone who assaulted them". For the worker, this contradiction was entirely feasible: as an "odd thing – abusers are often close to children, the children ... can like them as well as dislike them ...".

### Sub-theme three: 'contexts of identity construction'

During the investigation, the primary worker and her co-worker:

> discovered through the police that he [the identified man] had been convicted and had gone to jail before for offences committed against . . . the child of a previous de facto . . . [. . .].

They "discussed [with the mothers their] concerns for the children in view of Russell's past record of sexual assault on a young child", demonstrating dominant assumptions that the identity of "paedophile" transcended time/place. It was generalisable through the association between a particular 'dangerous man' with the particular and simultaneously generalised 'child':

> We, you can work on the assumption that because he abused children in the past, it was highly possible knowing how perpetrators work, paedophiles work, that these children were certainly at risk, and if not, had been interfered with, it would happen in the future . . . you have to assume that it's going to be . . .

This identity of "dangerousness" obscured all other possible identities, and was contested by the mothers.

> We actually then tried to get these women to realise that the man that they had been living with . . . posed a risk to their children . . . we requested that they have medical examinations . . . they saw no evidence that the children had been sexually abused . . .

The mothers' responses demonstrated that their (and their children's) relationships with this man competed with and obscured the official construction. Officially, Russell was seen as Ms Francis's "de facto" and as Ms Eakins' male "friend/neighbour".

To Ms Francis, Russell was 'partner/parent':

> [Ms Francis] denied this was so and . . . admitted to being upset at the allegations against Russell *who is the father of [her two children]*. (emphasis added)

To Ms Eakins he was 'surrogate dad' to her child:

> [Ms Eakins] denies that Russell has ever hurt [son], she says *[son] likes him and calls him 'dad'* (emphasis added).

The mothers' construction of Russell was as a 'victim', "persecuted" and "accused" by "certain people in the community out to get [him]" because he was "handicapped". This precluded their abilities to see, hear or say his official identity as 'dangerous'.

The grain of truth in the mothers' versions that Russell was being 'persecuted' was minimised (Potter 1996) by the worker, who legitimated 'persecution' as 'protection of the community':

> We didn't have anything to go on. We were going on a supposition that this man was a known abuser, had abused children in the past, but we had no disclosure, ... so it was very difficult for us to act, and *I guess that there was a ... vendetta ... that this man was a danger to the community, and we had to try and ... nail him somehow ...* (emphasis added)

The worker's construction of Russell as "dangerous to the community" precluded her engagement with the mothers' alternative constructions of him as 'vulnerable'. His potential vulnerabilities as seen by the mothers were minimised (Potter 1996) and dismissed in the worker's generalised and unspecific language (Potter 1996): "he had *a bit of brain damage or something like that ...*" and, "*I'm not certain if he doesn't experience some sort of epilepsy, I can't even recall to be honest ...*" (emphasis added)

The worker's task to demonstrate to the mothers the 'truth' about Russell's identity required social and medical examination of the children. The mothers refused access to their children and attempted to construct their own knowledge network about 'what, if anything, happened' and Russell's role in it, by arranging examinations with their own GPs. No conclusive evidence of "genital abnormality" was found, and no further medical assessment was conducted "because of trauma associated with this".

This case has shown how official/public versions of identity are constructed, which then may compete with and even contradict private versions, if seen, heard or said from a realist perspective. The child protection practitioner gave legitimacy only to the official version of the man's identity as 'dangerous' and therefore 'responsible for sexual abuse'. However, the validation of identity, as only one possibility precluding the potential plausibility of other possibilities, set up an adversarial relationship between the worker and the mothers, the mothers being seen as misguided, intransigent and unprotective and the worker being seen as unnecessarily intrusive. The mothers' strong resistance to the worker's version that disregarded theirs created barriers to further engagement with the mothers and their children. The question for child protection policy and practice is how workers could engage with their own and alternative versions of identity, to allow for the productive deployment of knowledge/power in realising 'protection' of children.

## RESPONSIBLE MOTHERS, INVISIBLE MEN: BOTH PARENTS ARE REPORTED, FATHER OFFICIALLY 'DISAPPEARS'[3]

The Gilman case shows how, in practice, gender differentiated identities of responsibility are constructed. In this case, only the mother was officially categorised as 'person believed responsible for physical abuse – excessive corporal punishment', and the father became 'invisible'. The family's ethnicity as "Aboriginal" appeared to be coincidental to the engagement between the worker and family members, with all participants interacting within the dominant assumptions relating to child protection. Family members did not make claims for the relevance of "Aboriginal" identity to the case, presenting instead as a 'normal' urban, settled, heterosexual and non-Aboriginal (white) family. The worker did not formally record their identity as "Aboriginal" but informed me of this during the interview: "Did you know that this is an Aboriginal family?"

Mr and Mrs Gilman's teenage daughter Laurel reported to Suburbia:

> that she is being hit at home: (1) [date] she was hit with the wooden handle of the broom across the arm, back and behind her right ear . . . by mum (2) [previous night] hit by mum across her face as mum thought she had hit her sister across her face [in keeping with] the [family] rule [. . .] (3) a week after the last school holidays ended, dad hit her with a strap across her face . . .

Laurel represented one of the incidents when her mother hit her as "punishment" for "hitting her younger sister". This description was reconstructed within discursive formations (prescribed language and related meanings) by the female caseworker and her colleagues as "*allegations* that mum hit her" (emphasis added). The word "allegations" indicates a construction of the problem as child protection, rather than the alternative of family support (parent–teen conflict) available to the workers.

"Patriarchal mothering" assumptions (Stark & Flitcraft 1988), played out in mundane detail, show how this mother was constructed as 'responsible' for the 'care' and 'control' of the children, and as 'responsible for physical abuse', whilst the father's disconnection from child care/control maintained his invisibility from public surveillance.

The mother contextualised the "hitting". She was "tired", caring for a "newborn baby awake during the night", with "household jobs" and "[seven other] children to care for during the day". She was also responsible for

---

3   This case has been discussed in a published article: D'Cruz, H (2002) 'Constructing the identities of "responsible mothers, invisible men" in child protection practice', *Sociological Research Online*, vol. 7, no. 1 http://www.socresonline.org.uk/7/1/d'cruz.html

controlling the "conflict" between the girl, described as "particularly difficult", and her sister. Nevertheless, she had tried some "solutions", which relied on 'care' strategies, including "paying more attention to [Laurel] . . . and less to [sister]" and "telling [Laurel] . . . to talk to her [about problems]". However, as Laurel's behaviour became worse, she resorted to "control" strategies: "discipline", which escalated from "screams and yells" to "swearing", "frustration" and "hitting".

While 'normal' mothers are 'responsible' for "family rules" and their enforcement (Donzelot 1988), this must occur within limits dictated by the state:

> Their family rule is . . . you did that . . . that's what you get . . . Whether you agree . . . [or disagree] with the family rule . . . *the stance that we take is that if you hit a child and it leaves a mark, then you've gone too far. That's the kind of benchmark that I use* . . . So while I'm not saying that it's an appropriate . . . thing to do, it didn't leave a mark. Mum had . . . there's a family norm about . . . the consequences [of actions]. (emphasis added)

This mother was under examination from the first phone call to her final contact with the social workers:

> [Mrs Gilman] responded very well . . . when I phoned her, in contrast to the . . . case I described earlier where . . . everything else was more important. . . . She said, 'I'll get someone to baby sit [the] kids . . . and I'll be there as soon as I can.' She responded very quickly . . . and that sort of gives you an idea about . . . whether it's accurate or not . . . the priority that their children take in their lives . . .

Judgments of the mother's normality were redeeming features that limited the extent of public surveillance. She was a "reasonable" person who "reflected on what she was doing . . . she didn't seem angry . . . [This] was . . . an opportunity . . . to reflect on . . . what had happened . . . talking about it, she was crying". Furthermore, she "responded very well [to the request to come in]. Everything else wasn't more important." She even got someone to baby sit the children so she could attend the interview.

Having noted that at the conclusion of this case only the mother was categorised as "person believed responsible for physical abuse", although both parents had been reported, I was curious about the practical construction of "responsible mothers, invisible men" (Stark & Flitcraft 1988; Korbin 1989; Milner 1993):

> HD: The girl . . . identified three separate incidents where she was hit by both her parents . . . So is it the most recent incident that you would investigate in terms of person responsible? [Note that the worker's response to this question took 305 lines (2146–2451) which I have interpreted as her extreme discomfort with a question that dealt with an aspect of her practice that was taken for granted. I have only included the 'relevant' lines, not the 'digressions'.]

> Worker: ... In terms of dad, *I don't remember* [1] what I did with dad. I suppose I focused primarily on ... the incidents with mum [...]. *When I phoned, mum was home* [2a]. ... *Mum answered the phone* [2b] and she agreed to come in. ... I suppose ... I could have got sidetracked in that the focus of [girl's] *concerns* [3a] were mum. This *stuff* [4a] to do with dad was not the primary thing she talked about ... and there was an *incident* ... *that day* [5a] ... mum had been *cross* [3b] with her ... the *stuff* [4b] to do with dad got lost in the *conflict* [3c] with mum. [...] ... the conflict between the two children, the pressure that puts on mum and how she responds [6]. ... The *issue* [4c] with dad was *not a current concern* [5b] ... and it got lost.
>
> HD: ... Maybe mum was the person ... primarily responsible for the daily care of the children?
>
> Worker: Certainly [...] I suppose my assessment was that the [family] conflict [was] ... parent–teen stuff ... the primary issue ... *that was the thrust of the intervention with mother and child* [7]. (emphasis added)

This extract clearly demonstrates how assumptions of "patriarchal mothering" (Stark & Flitcraft 1988) intersect with the discursive formation that 'someone did something to the child', constructing "responsible mothers, invisible men" (Stark & Flitcraft 1988; Milner 1993). The mother did "confirm" that 'she had hit the girl'. The invisibility of the father is suggested by his apparent disappearance from the worker's consciousness [1], colloquially, 'out of sight, out of mind'. The mother's 'place' at home [2a] and as gatekeeper [2b], and assumptions that she was primarily "responsible" for "the daily [child] care" and "responding to family conflicts" [6, 7], also increased her visibility to public examination as 'person believed responsible' for 'hitting' her daughter. The immediacy of the incident with the mother [5a], unsurprising as she had most responsibility for the children, contrasted (Potter 1996) with the father's "issue" [4c] as "not current" [5b]. The more generalised description (Potter 1996) of the father's actions, as "stuff" [4a, 4b] and "issue" [4c], contrasts with specific vocabulary (Potter 1996) for the mother's actions [3a–c]: "concerns", "cross", "conflict". Although both parents were identified by their daughter as 'equally responsible', taken-for-granted assumptions about gendered roles and responsibilities increased the mother's accessibility and public visibility, with consequences for her official identity construction as solely 'responsible for physical abuse', with the father 'invisible'.

## RESPONSIBLE MOTHERS, INVISIBLE MEN: FATHER IS REPORTED, HE OFFICIALLY 'DISAPPEARS'[4]

Following the intake report at Urbania, Mr Ibsen was identified as "person believed responsible for physical abuse" of his teenage daughter. The case analysis shows how he repaired this identity to a more positive one, 'concerned, frustrated parent punishing his daughter'. His sociolinguistic practices, as strategies of resistance, were central to reconstruction of his identity, subverting ongoing official surveillance of his practices of domination. However, the case analysis also shows that Mr Ibsen's strategies to achieve both normality and invisibility were facilitated by the workers' own patriarchal practices and assumptions of gender equality in families. Although the official outcome of the case recorded the father as "person believed responsible for physical abuse – excessive corporal punishment", the mother, perceived as 'equal parent/partner', was held equally responsible, as 'unprotective'.

This case shows two sub-themes in constructing identities of 'responsibility'. The first is the father's strategic deployment of sociolinguistic resources to repair his identity as "person believed responsible for physical abuse". The second theme is the construction of the mother's identity of 'responsibility' associated with 'unprotectiveness'.

### Sub-theme one: the father repairs his identity of 'responsibility'

The father was clearly 'responsible' within the discursive formation: 'he had hit the girl'. The 15-year-old daughter ("non-Aboriginal" – her father's identity; her mother was "Aboriginal") "had visible bruising on inner thighs [pink and raised, from electric cord] . . . caused by . . . father, . . . during argument last night when [Judy] returned home two hours late from her boyfriend's".

Two workers (male and female) visited the family, following their interview with Judy and physical examination of her injuries. The father, Mr Ibsen, immediately began an active reconstruction of himself as compliant and a 'concerned parent', as this account by one of the workers shows:

> They greeted [1a] us, let us in [1b], and the father said he was aware of why we were there [2a]; it was because he had hit [daughter] last night and he said he knew he should not have done it [2b], and he would have contacted the department but he didn't do it [2c]. [. . .] we didn't even have to present ourselves . . . he said it all before we got through the door [3a] . . . which is an acknowledgement [3b] and good that at least he's not denying he's done it [3c] . . . the first thing really is that you acknowledge you have done something before you

---

4   See D'Cruz (2002), ibid.

*can actually make some changes. He was willing to talk about it . . . we said that people would listen to his version* [4] . . . (emphasis added)

The apparent willingness of 'the family' ("they") to allow official entry into the home [1a–b] set the scene for a generally compliant surface engagement, strategically managed by the father to ensure official recognition of "his version" [4]. His self-presentation as compliant (and simultaneously 'concerned parent') was achieved by taking control of the interview. He prevented the workers from questioning him [3a] by instead immediately volunteering the basic information, which was undisputed by all participants: making explicit the reason for official contact [2a–c], and acknowledging his transgressions [2b–c]. This minimised (Potter 1996) the adversarial, inquisitorial relationship in which he was positioned as defendant, and defused professional knowledge/power. His strategic dominance impressed the workers as "co-operativeness" (DePanfilis & Scannapieco 1994: 238), an important 'risk-assessment criterion'.

Through telling "his version", he simultaneously "acknowledged" his "hitting", but reconstructed it as "punishment", and his identity as 'concerned parent' – "he would have contacted the department [for help]", and "there is no way he would choose that form of punishment again".

His self-presentation as compliant and concerned parent relied on undermining his daughter's identity as 'victim' and 'vulnerable child'. His concerns were expressed as a three-part list (Potter 1996): his daughter's boyfriend, her associations with 'drug dealers', and "smoking dope", identifying her in the private domain as the black sheep. "I've brought up six children . . . and most of them have all done quite well, except for this one." However, the transformation of Mr Ibsen's identity from (sole) 'person believed responsible for physical abuse' to 'concerned parent' also involved the transfer of some 'responsibility' to the mother/wife, Mrs Ibsen, as the section below shows.

## Sub-theme two: the mother becomes 'responsible'

The second theme is the articulation of the mother's identity of 'responsibility' with the father's. Although the daughter had alluded to "domestic violence", the workers' assumptions of equality within the heterosexually partnered/parented family positioned both parents/partners as 'equals'. At the 'joint interview', which involved both partners, the female worker asked Ms Ibsen about "physical violence" to her by her husband, which she "denied". This "denial" was taken at face value, rather than recognised as the only possible response for a woman who was being asked about violence to her in the presence of the man who might be responsible for it. Nor did the workers appear to recognise that the possible threat of violence to the mother could constrain her ability and/or willingness to offer an alternative construction, by criticising her husband's/the children's father's self-presentation as 'concerned parent'.

Instead, the equalisation of gendered identities of 'husband' and 'wife', 'father' and 'mother' reconstructed both as 'concerned parents'. Gendered identities of 'responsibility' positioned the father solely as 'responsible for hitting', and related to the single reported incident. However, the mother's 'responsibility' was more complex, seen by the female and male workers respectively as follows.

Female worker:
- "not preventing it", "not stopping him"
- [whilst she] "did not like it when her husband took physical action . . . she could not work out . . . another way of getting daughter to see their point of view".

Male worker:
- "saying nothing"
- "not trying to protect her daughter" and "almost approving of the punishment".

### The implications of 'responsible mothers, invisible men' for this family

The intersection of the father's strategic dominance and the workers' engagement within an egalitarian construction of 'the family' maintained the oppressive relations and father's domination. His prior "history" of many similar and previously unreported incidents of "punishment" did not undermine his identity as a 'concerned parent'.

The workers observed his practices of domination in their presence:

> Issues of control . . . *dad talked over other members of the family and both [workers]* . . . I think he has got a *pivotal role in the family* and . . . *the discipline.* (emphasis added)

However, they did not see these practices as signs of oppression of family members, all of whom were women (his wife and two daughters). Instead, workers' perceptions that he was "very judgmental . . . quite domineering in some things" were contrasted with (Potter 1996; Smith 1990a) ". . . at the same time also quite concerned about his daughter". Yet, his 'control' and 'dominance', even over public officials, did not construct the single reported incident in the family, as a glimpse of private relations of oppression associated with gender and generation.

The reconstruction and repair of the father's identity from 'person believed responsible for physical abuse' to 'concerned parent' influenced the withdrawal of public surveillance of the family and an 'agreement' for "family counselling". 'Person believed responsible' was reduced to a set of actions ('causes') with particular 'effects' manifested in the girl's physical body. Whilst this construction fitted the discursive rule, 'someone did something to a child', it minimised the relevance of gendered and generational inequalities and oppressive relations of the heterosexual family, and their implications for the construction of identities of 'responsibility'.

## RESPONSIBLE MOTHERS, INVISIBLE MEN: 'THE UNPROTECTIVE MOTHER' AND 'THE DANGEROUS MAN'[5]

Constructions of mothers as 'unprotective', immediately positions their male associates as 'person(s) believed responsible'. For example, the man identified as 'responsible for sexual abuse' of the four Lewis children was constructed as 'person believed responsible' as a logical outcome associated with constructions of the 'irresponsibility' of 'unprotective [heterosexual] mothers' as associates of 'dangerous men'.

This case shows the articulations between social class, patriarchal mothering and monogamous heterosexuality, in constructing the identity of the 'unprotective' mother. Particular male identities of 'dangerousness' (sexual predators) are positioned in relation to 'unprotective' mothers, who are 'responsible' for giving these men access to their children. Four "non-Aboriginal" children (two girls, aged four and two; and two boys, aged five and three) were subjects of an investigation for "sexual abuse". Judgments of their mother's 'responsibility' as social security recipient, heterosexually promiscuous and financially profligate facilitated the construction of an official identity as 'person believed responsible' of the man reported for 'sexual abuse'. The man identified remained invisible from official investigation, although not escaping an officially recorded, if nominal identity of "person believed responsible for sexual abuse".

The intake record on file at Urbania shows the rather complicated reporting process for this case.

The police:

> called with concerns over Pam's four children. Constable Care said that [when] issuing a restraining order against Pam's ex-[male] partner, Steven, he spoke to Steven's mother, [who] informed him that there was a possibility that Pam's children were being sexually abused by [her] current partner, a 19 y.o. man known only as Claude. [Steven's mother] said that she had also spoken with a neighbour of Pam's who claimed that the children had told her that 'Claude is doing things to us'. [Steven's mother] said that the children had recently been to hospital for treatment for oral [sic] herpes. [. . .]

Doubts about the legitimacy of this report were documented on file. Firstly, police saw it as "third hand", through a "friend of a friend" (Potter 1996). Secondly, the

---

5   see D'Cruz (2002), ibid.

conflictual context of reporting suggested "self-interest" (Potter 1996). Thirdly, there was doubt whether 'herpes' necessarily represented 'sexual abuse'. The (male) caseworker received medical clarification that 'herpes' was not a conclusive indicator of sexual abuse. Despite the formally expressed doubts about the report, he considered there was significant likelihood the children had been sexually abused by their mother's male friend. This he attributed to the consequences of the mother being 'unprotective' and therefore 'responsible' for her male associate's suspected sexual abuse of the children.

The worker began the construction of the mother's abnormal identity of 'unprotectiveness', and therefore 'responsibility', by examining her compliance with monogamous heterosexuality, marked by the paternity of the four children [1, 2]:

> . . . She's got four children. . . . they were all by the same father [1] . . .
>
> [. . .] I've asked her . . . whether the children were all her ex partner's [2], she was actually married to this fellow. She said yes [2]. They all look the same . . .

Her perceived transgressions of heterosexual monogamy through her association with "a number of fellows, various fellows", gave access to the children by these "many males" [3a], who would "prey upon" them [4]. However, the identity of heterosexually promiscuous woman intersects with male/female relations as material exchange [5, 5a]. In this case, she is financially (and sexually) attractive to 'predatory males':

> . . . I would be very surprised if Carol hasn't been sexually abused. . . . There has [sic] been so many males [3a] in the family's life and because of [mother's] lifestyle [3b] and the environment she lives in [3c], she's quite open to being preyed upon by various males [4] who see her as a source of income [5] with the kids. She gets reasonable money . . . from Social Security [5a].

Furthermore, the 'unprotective' mother, as Social Security recipient, was one of "those women". Her image of socioeconomic dependency is painted through "cheap accommodation" [6a], associating material deprivation as "welfare mothers" with heterosexual [6b] and financial [7] profligacy and a lack of sobriety [6c]. Although this mother "doesn't drink alcohol", she is guilty by association with those that do:

> [. . .] When you are on Social Security . . . you live in cheap accommodation [6a] and a certain number of *those women* like to have a man around [6b]; probably drink alcohol [6c], drugs [6c] . . . I don't think she drinks alcohol, but . . . I don't know where her money goes. She's got lots and lots of minor debts . . .the money just trickles through her fingers [7] [. . .] (emphasis added)

The caseworker then makes a direct association between the many "transient [males]" [8a, 8b] as "uninvolved users" [9], and their "sexual abuse" of the children [8c]:

> Worker: She has a lot of transient people . . . going into her house [8a] [. . .] I've been around there and there's been two or three males in the house [8b] [. . .] There is a high likelihood because of the number of people going in and out of the house, the children will possibly be abused, because of the transient population [8c].
>
> HD: Most of the transient people are males?
>
> Worker: Yeah [8] [. . .] they look upon [mother's] place as somewhere to crash for the night [. . .] There's no involvement or anything, the place is just used as a flop house [9].

However, the mother's attraction to "transient males" as an "income source" is transformed into a sordid material 'dependency' [12] on these males as 'fools' or 'users', in exchange for material and possibly sexual favours [11a, 11b, 11c1–11c3]:

> I was really quite concerned that there seemed to be a lot of money being spent by her and she's still in debt. . . . she's still in debt [10a], . . . A lot of transient males [11a], no washing machine [10b], . . . never any food in the place [10c] [. . .] She picks up with drongo ["fool, simpleton" (*Australian Oxford Dictionary*, 1988)] fellows who . . . are not doing anything [11b] and are virtually using her [11c]; somewhere to sleep [11c1] and someone to sleep with perhaps [11c2]; someone who's got a roof over their heads [11c3] and might toss her a bit of money . . . to buy food [12] . . . she's just stuck in that cycle . . .

The sub-text of the relationship(s) between mother and the man/men involved was a commentary on her/their transgressions of monogamous heterosexuality as material exchange. The mother's 'protectiveness' of the children was judged according to unspoken images of 'the normal (heterosexual) mother', polarised against 'the (heterosexual) welfare mother'. Thus, the mother's apparent 'irresponsibility' constructed her as 'responsible' for the practices of abnormal heterosexual men.

In constructing the 'protective mother' as contingent upon monogamous heterosexuality, the image of the 'normal man' emerged in relation to 'wife': "she was actually married to this fellow". The normal monogamous heterosexual man as 'father' would not 'prey upon' the woman or the children. The mother's perceived transgressions through her association with "a number of fellows, various fellows", and therefore "being open to being preyed upon by [them]", identified her as 'unprotective mother', whose children were "sitting ducks" to be "sexually abused".

The caseworker did not interview the man alleged to be 'doing things' to the children, thus maintaining the individual man's official invisibility. However, the combination of his assumptions about the mother's 'responsibility' and 'unprotectiveness' through her particular 'lifestyle' and her male associates influenced his construction of the particular male as 'person believed responsible'.

## RESPONSIBLE MOTHERS, 'INVISIBLE' MEN: PATRIARCHAL MOTHERING AND DISABLING PRACTICES[6]

The O'Keefe family's involvement with child protection intervention shows how both patriarchal mothering and disabling practices were directly implicated in constructing Ms O'Keefe as responsible for physical abuse, whilst her husband became 'invisible'. He participated strategically in these processes of identity construction, facilitated inadvertently by the two female caseworkers, whose sociolinguistic practices replayed patriarchy, in which the mother's intellectual disability was also a feature.

A boy aged five and a girl aged three years at the time of the report, (ethnicity "Unknown"), and identified as "intellectually disabled" were reported to Suburbia by the school because of multiple bruises noticed on at least 15 separate occasions over seven months. Initially, both parents were perceived as 'equally responsible', and were asked to explain the injuries. Previous reports had been received that Mr O'Keefe was "hitting" his wife, and "leaving large bruises". Ms O'Keefe had also reported that he was "throwing the children across the room", and Mr O'Keefe "admitted" to a male doctor that he had hit the children with a belt. Two interconnected sub-themes show the processes by which the father 'disappears' and the mother becomes responsible.

### Sub-theme one: the adult male's 'disappearing act' – hiding behind the intellectual disability of women and children

Mr O'Keefe was able to 'disappear' from official surveillance by his own strategic engagement within the process of constructing 'responsibility'. However, he was facilitated in this by the two (female) workers who were apparently unaware of family relations of inequality and their discriminatory assumptions about people with intellectual disabilities. The workers normalised Mr O'Keefe 'hitting' his wife as his frustration with a (disabled) woman, who "can't do things or keep up to his standard". When he was called to account for the injuries to the children, he

---

6     A version of this case was previously published as ' "Taking responsibility" for "physical abuse": gender and disability' in 7th Australian Women's Studies Association Conference Proceedings, 16–18 April 1998, Adelaide, South Australia, pp. 18–27

"repeated[ly] deni[ed] . . . knowledge of how bruising occurred". He also shifted the official gaze from himself by two strategies. First, he normalised the bruises by abnormalising the children. They were "clumsy" or "bruise easily". "Adam does not notice bruises as they are so common." He also claimed that the children were "difficult to manage".

His second strategy was to shift the official gaze to his wife as 'responsible' for 'child care' and 'child maltreatment'. He mitigated his claims of her abnormality by strategically deploying her 'developmental disability' as a normal explanation for her 'parenting' difficulties. The mother "remained silent, unless . . . specifically asked".

### Sub-theme two: constructing the mother as 'responsible'

Ms O'Keefe was marginal to the workers' engagement with the family, and Mr O'Keefe in particular, "remaining silent, unless specifically asked", thus reinforcing his dominance and opportunities to transfer responsibility to his wife. The official construction of the mother as 'responsible' was reinforced by additional reports and observations from various women, who could ostensibly have been allies, but who instead acted as agents of surveillance.

A female neighbour reported that "she had been told . . . that Mr O'Keefe bashes his wife and when he is not at home, Ms O'Keefe bashes the children". Within the discursive formation linking 'what happened' to 'person responsible', the mother was clearly 'responsible'. Her intent was also built up, as "bashing" them only when the husband was "not at home". He was constructed as their protector, whilst simultaneously ignoring reports of his violence to his wife and children.

I asked about the possibility of the father's 'responsibility' for the bruises on the children and the mother's reluctance to say so. The female caseworker replied:

> We don't know . . . *in the beginning we leant towards . . . dad that was hitting the kids*, but then *afterwards* and *it's my belief now* . . . of course, I've got nothing tangible to hang this belief on, . . . *it's really [mother]* . . . *that was hitting the kids, especially [son]*. I've observed her on *a number of occasions*; she will sit there *very, very passively, not saying a word*. I remember one day, it was about getting the children to day care and they were wanting us to supply transport. . . . . I said to [mother], it's not that far away, you can walk up to day care with the children, and she says, I get headaches!! I get headaches when I walk!! and *up she got and ran out of the room* . . . *it was just* . . . *like a real uncontrollable outburst of anger, so I believe that's probably the way she'd operate with the kids*. All the file notes say . . . [mother] *takes a lot from the kids*, . . . *she will sit there* and [son] will beat up on her and she'd . . . say, no don't [son], . . . go away, *and take a whole lot of stuff until all of a sudden she probably snaps, so that's my belief* . . . (emphasis added)

In constructing 'responsibility', this worker preferred to exclude known evidence of the father's/husband's violence, while relying on a "belief" based on an accumulation (Potter 1996) of single incidents as typifying the mother's 'responsibility': as "(sudden) uncontrollable outbursts" of pent-up "anger", contrasting with her usual "passivity" and "silence". Her identity construction as apparently 'irrational' ("all of a sudden she probably snaps") was less justifiable, being contrasted with the husband's apparently 'rational' violence, as a response to a woman who was a 'sub-standard (intellectually disabled) mother'.

Further evidence of the mother's 'responsibility for physical abuse' was offered by a specific (Potter 1996) incident in which a disability support worker "overheard [mother] smacking [son] for about six minutes very hard". In a discussion of the incident with the parents, the mother was a "problem" for the husband, and 'responsible' for "hitting the kids".

The caseworker said:

> [. . .] another of the reasons why we think [Ms O'Keefe] was hitting the kids . . . there was one worker who did hear her hitting . . . [Adam] for quite some time and when I spoke to them, . . . [Mr O'Keefe] said, . . . you know what I have to deal with now, this is the problem that I've got . . .
>
> There's no doubt . . . that she's the nurturer of these children . . . but she's unable to set any limits on their behaviour . . .

The mother's public visibility continued through normalising techniques, including "parenting programs" and "social training". The father maintained his invisibility from public scrutiny by resisting engagement, "refusing to talk" or be available when 'parent training' workers made contact. He also strategically deployed the category of 'intellectual disability' to emphasise his wife's inability to comply with techniques.

The husband was not seriously considered as 'responsible for physical abuse'. His violence to his wife was justified in terms of her failure to 'meet his standards' of 'normal mothering' which she clearly was unable to do, due to cognitive limitations. Her 'inability' to parent ('mother'), in particular through 'appropriate control' as a cognitive and "conceptual" activity, was seen as a feature of her disability.

The children, through their "developmental delays" and ability to "verbalise [only] in unintelligible cries", were excluded from processes of identity construction.

The mother's public visibility and 'responsibility for physical abuse' was a product of public and private patriarchy (Fox Harding 1996), intersecting with "disabling practices" (McMahon et al. 1996), which simultaneously rendered the father 'invisible' and therefore, 'not responsible' (Milner 1993; Stark & Flitcraft 1988).

## RESPONSIBLE MOTHERS, INVISIBLE MEN: FATHER IS REPORTED, MOTHER IS SUSPECTED, BOTH 'RESPONSIBLE'

The Riley case is a special example of official practices of identifying mothers as 'responsible', leaving men 'invisible'. In this case, the father claimed 'responsibility' for the reported "accidental injury", which was officially redefined later as "non-accidental" (maltreatment). The sub-text of the process clearly identified the mother as primarily, if not solely, 'responsible' for the 'non-accidental' injuries. However, the couple's refusal to identify self or other as 'responsible' disrupted the official requirement to identify unequivocally a particular individual as 'responsible'. The only option apparently possible was identification of "both parents", as "persons believed responsible for physical abuse". The actual child was a male about ten weeks old at the time of the report (ethnicity "Unknown"). He had a 17-month-old sister.

### Sub-theme one: father is responsible for 'accidental injury'

Mr and Ms Riley took their baby John to the paediatric hospital because "they were concerned about his right arm".

Mr Riley immediately claimed responsibility for the injury:

> [He] caused the injury [1] . . . after he found [child] vomiting and choking in his pram [2] . . . and grabbed [baby's] arm [3] to turn him on his side [4]. [Father] said he had panicked [5].

In this record taken from the file, the father's 'responsibility' as 'cause' of the injury [1] is constructed as 'normal', as a response to a potentially life-threatening, but single incident [2]. His reaction to crisis, as "grabbing" the child's arm [3], is explained as first aid [4]. The entire incident is contextualised and normalised as one of "panic" [5]. It was an 'accidental injury'.

However, this apparently straightforward identification of responsibility for accidental injury was transformed when the meaning of the single injury was changed to 'non-accidental injury' following medical intervention, as the next section shows.

### Sub-theme two: who is responsible for 'non-accidental injury'

The transformation of the single visible injury to the child's arm occurred through medical examination of the less visible parts of the body, through technology like a skeletal survey.

> On [date] a skeletal survey was carried out [1] and [male consultant] found [2] . . . approximately 13 [3] fractures [4] in different areas [5] of [baby's] body.

This quasi-medical report is presented as a scientific technique of knowing [1] (Potter 1996). It is also presented as a disinterested discovery ("found") [2] (Potter 1996), suggesting that this is an 'objective' and therefore indisputable 'fact'. Through quantification [3] (Potter 1996), medical categorisation [4] (Potter 1996) and distribution [5] of hitherto invisible bodily abnormalities, this version contested the father's version as 'accidental', transforming the meaning of the single injury into an example of 'non-accidental injuries'.

The consequence of the medical construction of the injuries as "non-accidental" was that the 'person believed responsible' needed to be identified. Within the dominant discourse, this meant that it could not be taken for granted that the father was the "person believed responsible". The investigation that followed shows how the father as 'person responsible for a single injury' came to acquire a sub-text that cast suspicion on the mother.

### Sub-theme three: the mother is suspected

The medical social worker's file record described the identities, roles and relationships in this family:

> Mr Riley works as a milkman.[7] He has two jobs [1] and works seven days a week [2]. He has taken a significant amount of time off work since [baby's] birth in order to help his wife cope [3]. Her mother . . . stays overnight midweek to help too [4].

This apparently neutral description of family relations shows the comparison with the "breadwinner/carer" model as the norm (Gatens 1998). It also operated as the justification for constructing primarily the mother, but eventually both parents as 'responsible' (as 'cause' and 'not accountable') for the injuries to the child.

First, the father is super-normalised as a good provider, perhaps overworking by having two jobs and working seven days a week [1, 2]. The mother is represented as a less than capable primary carer, because the husband has been interrupting his 'normal' role to "help" with hers [3]. Her mother also assists with the care of the children, sometimes staying overnight [4].

These extreme parental/partner roles of 'overworked husband/father' and 'incompetent (not coping) wife/mother' are repeated throughout the investigation, precluding consideration of the injuries to the child as possibly 'accidental' *and* 'non-accidental', with differing identities and degrees of 'responsibility'.

In particular, there were significant differences between how medical practitioners and social workers understood the injuries, and how the police and parents explained them. The parents offered many explanations for the injuries,

---

7   The father's occupation has been changed to safeguard the family's privacy.

including a naturopath who had been treating the child for colic and a clinician who took the baby's blood for testing. Both could have been responsible for 'accidental, unintentional' bruising and some broken bones. Other explanations in support of 'accidental, unintentional' injuries related to family members being over enthusiastic in playing with or hugging the baby. The multiple injuries were explained by medical practitioners and social workers as "a constellation of injuries" (a syndrome) with a single cause. This explanation was supported by "the theory of doctor hopping" (Gelles 1987b), because the mother was taking the children to different doctors. The medical reports from these different doctors did not indicate any concerns for the baby, although they commented that the mother was anxious and needed reassurance. Two paediatricians interviewed the naturopath. The paediatricians reported that the naturopath was "confident he could not have caused the injuries: it did not cross his mind". The paediatricians cleared him as a possible 'cause' of the injuries, describing him as "a witch doctor (in its nicest sense)" and a "reasonable chap". There was "no way he could have done the injuries". When the police interviewed the naturopath three days after the paediatricians did, they reported that the naturopath had "acknowledged that he may . . . have caused the rib fractures . . . [paediatric consultant's] dating of them coincides with his treatment". Therefore, the police tended to see the injuries as outcomes of separate, unrelated incidents, including the naturopath's treatment. The police did not see that their approach would ignore the multiple injuries, just that "they'd . . . have to identify the cause of each one". However, the apparent contradictions in this evidence recorded on file were not given due consideration. These competing explanations influenced different conclusions: with the medical/social version as "non accidental injury, maltreatment" given legitimacy and the police/parents' version, "accidental injury", "unintentional" or multiple causes dismissed.

The mother's "distress" during the investigation, expressed as "tired and stressed" and "crying", represented accumulated evidence of her abnormality, rather than an opportunity for engagement with her experience of being investigated for child maltreatment. Her acts of resistance were seen as abnormal, represented in two three-part lists [1a–c, 2a–c] (Potter 1996): "variations in attitude . . . from defensive [1a], to appealing [1b], to angry [1c]. She has felt accused [2a] and blamed [2b], and has consistently protested her innocence [2c] [. . .]". Her escalating resistance and contestation of professional knowledge/power were transformed into an increasingly abnormal identity as 'mother' and as 'responsible for physical abuse'.

### Sub-theme four: both parents are responsible

The parents "denied" that they had caused the injuries, instead proposing alternative identities of 'responsibility' associated with 'accidental' injuries. The mother identified a range of possibilities, including a natural health worker who was massaging the baby, a clinician who did a blood test on the baby, or family members who were overenthusiastic when playing with or hugging the baby. The father considered that he may have accidentally and unintentionally "hurt" the child by "being too strong when squeezing him". Alternatively, his wife could have "hurt" the baby, but this was qualified as "unintentional" ('accidental'), attributing it to "stress". He had seen her "put [baby] down roughly and gone away to cry". However, in his view, his wife was always a good mother.

The meaning of 'responsibility' broadened from 'direct cause' (at the start of the investigation) to include 'accountability' (at the time of apprehension of the child pending a Care and Protection Application). Both parents, but especially the mother, resisted "acceptance of responsibility" as 'causal' and as 'accountable'. Each was expected to identify self or other as 'responsible' (as "cause of injuries" or "accounting for the cause, responsible for safety"). This did not allow for exploration of the parents' differential and shared meanings of 'accepting responsibility', and implications for their identities as 'mother' and 'father'. For example, the female worker commented on "[mother's] and her extended family's high expectations of her parenting ability". The couple's perceived unwillingness to identify self or other as 'direct cause' represented their failure as parents "to provide a reasonable explanation of how the injuries were caused or by whom".

The magistrate "accepted without qualification the unequivocal medical evidence [that] [serious non-accidental injuries] . . . were inflicted while [the child was] in the care of one or both respondents [parents] . . .", and, in doing so, invalidated the alternative constructions of 'responsibility' associated with 'accidental injuries', offered by police and parents.

The case conference summed up the social construction of both parents as 'responsible':

> Neither parent accepts responsibility [for the injuries]. The only available conclusions are that one parent or both . . . were responsible . . . If only one parent caused the injuries, then the non-injuring parent is colluding by covering up. . . . The only possible way to respond . . . is to act as if both parents were equally responsible . . . On that basis, work with the family will focus on each parent individually satisfying us that they do not present a significant risk to [baby] and that . . . we would not have to fear that parental collusion would . . . present a risk.

'Protective' intervention which depended upon the parents 'accepting responsibility', defined by the female worker as "opportunities to explore the frustrations of parenting [read as mothering]", and the "many indicators of stress in the family", was "not successfully . . . addressed . . . because the couple has devoted all their energies to denying any degree of responsibility".

## RESPONSIBILITY FOR EMOTIONAL ABUSE: THE CULTURAL IDEALISATION OF MOTHERHOOD

This case shows how perceived transgressions by women as mothers are examined against images of normality: the "cultural idealization of motherhood" (Rose 1989) and "patriarchal mothering" (Stark & Flitcraft 1988). The shared enculturation of Ms Hamilton, a sole parent, and (female) social workers at Suburbia seamlessly constructed the identity of "person believed responsible". The conflation of 'mothering' with 'person believed responsible for emotional abuse' excluded multiple explanations for perceived breaches of normal mothering.

Ms Hamilton participated in the official construction of her identity as "person believed responsible", by judging her normality against cultural prescriptions of "idealized motherhood" (Rose 1989; Phoenix & Woollett 1991). She sought to place her three children in foster care because she considered that she was an unfit parent. Her construction of personal abnormality was shared by the intake (female) social worker, who had constructed Ms Hamilton as 'person believed responsible for emotional abuse' by the end of the intake interview.

Ms Hamilton's self-representation at intake, as simultaneously compliant with and resistant to cultural expectations, relied on a variety of rhetorical devices to position her simultaneously as 'reporter', 'mother' and 'person believed responsible':

> . . . wants all three kids in foster care [1a] . . . *she has too many financial problems* [1b]; she does not love [son] [2a] and hits him a lot [2b] . . . *does not leave bruises* . . . but feels like flogging him [2c]. [described son as] aggressive [3a], a bully with the girls [3b], whinges all the time [3c] . . . she has never bonded with him [4a], and feels no love for him [4b], does not care how this affects him [4c]; *loves the girls* [5a], but really does not want them [5b], never cuddles them [5c] or tells them she loves them because she cannot feel this [5d]; [six-year-old daughter] very attention seeking . . . [mother] feels this is because of her parenting style; [6] recently, neighbours have begun accusing her of molesting the . . . kids and of physically abusing them. . . . denies this, *but said she . . . calls them 'little shits' all the time and does hit [son] with a stick* [7]. (emphasis added)

Statement 1a is represented/heard as an abnormal request from a mother, contextualised by an explanation of "financial problems" [1b]. At best, this offered ambiguous constructions of identity as 'materially impoverished' and 'bad money manager'.

Statement 2 gives extreme examples (Potter 1996) of her 'bad mothering' [2a–c] as a three-part list (Potter 1996), whilst simultaneously minimising (Potter 1996) her abnormality by "not leaving bruises". However, the immediately following statement, "feels like flogging him", indicates an extreme (Potter 1996) intention, consistent within local constructions of "maltreatment".

Statements 3a–c contain a three-part list (Potter 1996) in which presentation of the son as a 'problem' ("aggressive", "bully", "whinges") offers a possible justification for her wish to "flog him". However, the repairs of her abnormal identity are undone by juxtaposing this with statements 4a–c, a three-part list (Potter 1996) of her own perceived abnormalities as 'mother'. The "modalizing terms" (Potter 1996) of "never"; "no" and "does not care" make her perceived transgressions extreme.

The mother then offered a contrast structure in statement 5: she "loves the girls". However, despite this 'love', she made a contrastive assertion (Potter 1996; Smith 1990a) expressed as a three-part list [5b–d] (Potter 1996) of perceived, unfulfilled tasks of the 'normal mother'. She further represented her "parenting style" as abnormal, as a 'cause' of the daughter's perceived inappropriate behaviour, "attention seeking" [6].

Finally, in statement 7, while she contested the "neighbours' accusations" of "molestation" and "physical abuse" by a "denial", she also continues to represent herself as a bad mother through the clause, "but she calls them 'little shits'" and "hits son with a stick". The conjunction "but" suggests a refutation of 'molester' or 'physical abuser', as extreme identities with which she did not identify (Graham 1981). However, Ms Hamilton offered alternative negative descriptions, as 'name caller' and 'hitter with stick', confirming her identity as 'person believed responsible for emotional abuse'. These cumulative examples of her abnormality fitted the discursive and situated meanings of "classic emotional abuse".

The identity of 'person believed responsible' was constructed solely within cultural images of motherhood (Rose 1989), and excluded other possible identities additional to or instead of 'mother responsible for emotional abuse'. Instead, her "personal problems" and experiences were solely conditions for 'bad mothering':

> Was raped . . . believes this is why she hates [son] because he is 'male'. . . . in financial debt . . . needs help with financial management, would like a [housing] transfer as neighbours are harrasing [sic] her . . . no support . . . from her family, except . . . [youngest child's] dad. . . . feels suicidal . . . she has O.D. twice before . . . a very heavy drinker in the past. . . .

As "classic emotional abuse", perceived maternal abnormalities are 'causes' of "harmful" effects on children – the "therapeutic familialism" (Rose 1989: 175), in which "the mundane tasks of mothering come to be rewritten as emanations of a natural and essential love" (Rose 1989: 157).

"Emotional state" (Stark & Flitcraft 1988) was assumed to be an accumulation of 'past' experiences and deterministic of the woman's 'present' identity. The mother's:

> preoccupation with . . . long standing childhood issues clearly affect[ed] care of the children and communication with them. Any human being so preoccupied with personal issues has very little to offer a child (or adult). [. . .]
>
> *Substantiation . . . at intake – mother describing her own behaviour and concerns, admitted everything. . . . Clear presentation of information from the mother that [the] children were at high risk.* (emphasis added)

The primary feature of this case was the practical construction of abnormal motherhood (and the unspoken norms against which it was constructed). The undisputed acceptance of the mother's apparent self-representation as 'abnormal' by the female social workers involved at intake and later, problematises the assumptions that they are in fact shared meanings (and identities of responsibility). 'Emotional abuse' is the abnormal manifestation of women's cultural transgressions as mothers. The official construction of 'mothering' as a primary identity for women reconstructed a range of problematised experiences solely as 'causes' of 'bad mothering', precluding other possible identities for 'woman', and 'responsibility' beyond 'mothering'.

## CONSTRUCTING VERSIONS OF MATERNAL RESPONSIBILITY TO MEET CASE OBJECTIVES

The Quinn children were seen to be 'at risk'. This case shows how discourses of normality and abnormality articulate and are deployed strategically within different official objectives. The mother's identity as 'deficient but not responsible mother' is transformed into "person believed responsible" for placing her children "at risk", showing how positionings of participants as contextual, influence identity constructions.

There were two children (ethnicity unrecorded, but read from the file as "non-Aboriginal") in the care of their mother. These children, a girl aged nine and a boy aged seven were subjects of a wardship application about four years after the initial referral.

The "history of involvement" with the mother and children was of:

> repeated and numerous [substantiated] complaints in relation to the [mother's] care of her children . . . allegations [of] neglect, poor and inadequate supervision, inadequate care and physical abuse (file summary of 18 reports over four years).

This was constructed as a 'parenting issue', a "case of long-term physical neglect and low level abuse", and *not* a 'protective issue'. As 'family support', the mother was identified as 'parent in need of support'.

At a case conference, the official objective was to achieve placement of the children in care with their mother's consent. Her transformation two months later to "person believed responsible for risk" ("long-term chronic physical and emotional neglect") was associated with different official objectives, and a reconstruction of her relationship with the social workers as adversaries. This time the mother's withdrawal of consent required legal strategies that contested her normality as mother, and justified placement of the children in alternative care. The transformation of her identity to 'person believed responsible' and the adversarial relationship also identified her as one of the 'dangerous' clients assisted by Suburbia.

### Sub-theme one: constructing the identity, 'mother in need of support'

The following extract demonstrates the process of identity construction as 'mother in need of support':

> The [female, Social Worker] case manager is certain that [mother] *loves her children very very much* [1a] and *wants the best* [1b] for them. [Mother] is very insightful [1c] into her problems and her dilemma has always been knowing that the *very severe abuse she endured in her own childhood affects her ability to cope and to parent* [2] . . . [Her] love for the children means she wants them with her [3a] [but] then she becomes completely overwhelmed, [3b] without meaning to [4a] she neglects their welfare, [4b] and makes frantic attempts [5a] to have others take care of them for her [5b] . . . realistic [6a] and unselfish [6b] in requesting wardship . . . a chance in life [for the children] [6c] . . . [. . .] [Decision voluntary long-term permanent care].(emphasis added)

The mother was present at the case conference where she heard this official construction of her identity as 'normal'. She was not just a ('normal'), loving and insightful mother, whose children were a priority; she was better than normal, as the three-part list of "modalizing terms" (Potter 1996) suggests [1a–c]. Her childhood experiences were also extreme (Potter 1996) ("very bad") [2], diverting and minimising (Potter 1996) "blame" (and 'responsibility') for 'present' parenting difficulties. Her 'responsibility' was further minimised by a three-part list (Potter 1996) of contrasts (Potter 1996; Smith 1990a) between seemingly normal parental intentions [3a, 4a, 5a] with seemingly unintended effects [3b, 4b, 5b]. She "loves the children" and at the same time, becomes "overwhelmed" by them; she "doesn't mean to", but 'does in fact' "neglect their welfare". She wants to have someone care for them, but does so "frantically" – as both unseemly abrogation of motherhood and as seeker of suitable alternative carers. Finally, her official positive image is enhanced by a three-part list [6a–c] (Potter 1996): as "realistic", "unselfish" and "child centred" – and normal mother.

Her (super)normality, constructed by various rhetorical devices such as three-part lists, extrematisation and contrast structures usually deployed to construct abnormality (Potter 1996), offered at least two possible readings. The surface representation was of 'normality', which the mother heard. However, the sub-text was a power strategy deployed by caseworkers to maintain the mother's compliance and cooperation in protecting the children without legal action.

However, this fragile partnership was shattered by a "letter [from the mother] giving formal notice that the children's . . . placement was no longer acceptable . . . she wanted them moved . . . if this was not done, she would . . . resume care herself [. . .]."

The mother's actions were explained by the male caseworker as a surface compliance with expectations of 'normal' mothers' responses to the loss of their children:

> A month previously, [mother] had been co-operative and had been seeing the children whenever she wanted, . . . and had no plans to take them back. [. . .] She had come to terms . . . that she couldn't cope with the children [. . .] When she was faced with the reality of that, . . . with the backing of friends, *she felt she ought to put up as much of a fight as possible because she thought that to be the appropriate thing to do* . . . (emphasis added)

### Sub-theme two: constructing the identity 'person believed responsible for placing children at risk'

The male social worker, as new case manager, responded to the mother's "formal notice" by a case discussion. This time, the mother who was now an adversary, was excluded, unlike at the case conference held two months previously in which she had been included. Wardship would replace "voluntary placement":

> [Caseworker] felt that [mother's] comments had been prompted by *a sense of guilt and loss, after . . . deciding to relinquish the children* [1] . . . *reflective of . . . past history of ambivalence* [2] and tendency to make *decisions based on her own needs* [3] . . . the following risks and issues were identified: . . . long history of . . . *inadequate and neglectful parenting* [1a] . . . at times . . . *physically abusive* [4b] and placed the *children at risk* [4c]; attempts to redress parenting deficits over many years have failed [5] . . . impact of [mother's] parenting . . . has had observable negative consequences [on children's behaviour] [6] . . . [. . .] decision to support and protect placement by wardship . . . (emphasis added)

This extract shows the transformation of her identity to 'person believed responsible'. The first statement seems to construct the mother's actions as 'normal' emotions associated with "relinquishment of children". However, the subsequent statements abnormalise these feelings as this mother's "history of ambivalence" added to her perceived selfishness ("her own needs") [2, 3]. This is particularly interesting in its contrast with her image as 'unselfish' in the previous extract. Furthermore, where the previous extract diverted 'responsibility' away from the mother, the descriptive categories of her abnormality in this extract, as a three-part list [4a–c] (Potter 1996), are child protection vocabulary denoting 'responsibility'. Her construction as abnormal mother was confirmed by the failure of official normalising strategies [5], and by constructing her as 'responsible' for (as 'cause of') "observable negative consequences" for the children [6], consistent with the discursive formation, 'someone did something to a child'. With the mother now an adversary, the legal domain offered a site for contestation of 'responsibility', to justify 'protection' of the children.

This case has shown that identities of 'responsibility for maltreatment' are fluid and dynamic within particular contexts – in this case, to meet particular official and private objectives. Identities may be strategically constructed so that while the sub-text clearly communicates to knowledge experts the intended version of identity, this may not always be heard, seen or said by those who are less knowledgeable of these strategies. However, the effects of such knowledge are shown in this case when the mother gained access to the linguistic code. She contested the original decision and her superficial positioning as 'cooperative', continuing instead as adversary. She was eventually constructed as 'dangerous', following her physical assault on a worker, and her engagement with media in seeking to equalise power relations with workers at the site.

## CONCLUSION

In this chapter I have analysed the processes by which the official identity of 'person believed responsible' is an outcome of different practical constructions. A variety of participants engage in these processes. The analysis shows that the identity of 'person believed responsible' is integral to how 'what happened' to a child is constructed. The meanings given to the reported events thus position the identities of 'responsibility' as 'cause' of particular visible and/or invisible 'effects' embodied in the child. Particular constructions of identity are thus legitimated and others de-legitimated. Therefore, the official category of 'person believed responsible' is not transcendent and unproblematic, but may be represented by parallel, alternative and sometimes shared versions, embedded in contexts of place, time and relationships.

The cases show the overwhelming influences of public and private patriarchy (Fox Harding 1996; Stark & Flitcraft 1988), which produce official and unofficial identities of "responsible mothers, invisible men" (Stark & Flitcraft 1988; Milner 1993), within apolitical analyses of the heterosexual family. Thus, women were frequently identified as 'persons believed responsible' primarily because they had main or sole 'responsibility' as child carers. In four of these cases, Gilman, Ibsen, O'Keefe and Riley, the 'type of maltreatment' was substantiated as 'physical abuse'.

With the Gilman family, where the woman was in a heterosexual partnership and along with her husband was reported for 'hitting' their daughter, the husband/father became invisible and therefore not identified as 'person believed responsible'. In the O'Keefe family's case, the father was never considered seriously as 'responsible' for hitting the children. Instead, he skilfully engaged with the workers' patriarchal mothering assumptions and disabling practices, to shift responsibility onto his intellectually disabled wife. In the Riley case, a heterosexual partnership where there was doubt about the 'cause' of a child's injuries, the mother was suspected as being responsible. However, because neither parent could or would 'accept responsibility' (as 'cause') or 'explain cause' (as 'accountability'), "both parents" were 'equally responsible'. Identities of 'unprotective (heterosexual) mother' also constructed women as 'equally responsible' for male oppressive practices: for example, the Ibsen and Lewis families. In the Ibsen case, the father strategically managed his identity construction as 'responsible for physical abuse' by presenting himself as a 'concerned parent'. The workers' patriarchal mothering assumptions and their engagement with 'the family' as a network of 'equals' greatly facilitated the transformation of the father's identity to a more benign one, and the mother's responsibility was constructed as an expression of 'unprotectiveness'.

The only cases in which men were clearly identified as 'dangerous sexual predators' (Eakins and Lewis families) also had consequences for the mothers. In both instances they were held 'responsible' for the degree of 'protectiveness' they showed towards their children. This protectiveness was defined according to how they cooperated with the investigating workers in giving access to their children and rejecting their male associates (Eakins case); or in how their 'lifestyle' gave access by 'dangerous men' to their children (Lewis case).

Dominant cultural prescriptions of mothering are often shared by mothers-as-clients and by women-as-caseworkers. This was especially apparent in the case of the Hamilton family where the mother's self-evaluation as a 'bad mother' led her to seek help within this negative self-definition with a consequent identification as 'person believed responsible for emotional abuse'.

Finally, professionals may use language strategically to communicate about client identities in ways that further case objectives without clients necessarily being aware of the intent of what they hear or read about themselves: for example, the Quinn case.

In the next chapter, I analyse the remaining part of the generalised rule 'someone did something to a child'. I look at how the identities of 'child' (as related to 'parent' and 'adult'), which are central to constructing 'what happened' and 'person believed responsible'. They are also embedded in micro-practices of knowledge/power, and are contextually constructed.

# 8

# Who is a child? Who is a parent?

Chapters 6 and 7 explored how official meaning as 'maltreatment' is constructed following a report that 'something happened' to a child, and the complexities of constructing 'responsibility' when 'someone' is identified as having 'done something' to that child. This chapter explores the identity of the 'child' who is the focus and justification of protective intervention. It is through the particular child that a report that 'someone did something' becomes relevant for public intervention into the private space of 'the family'. If no 'child' is involved, the 'someone who did something' remains unknown and of no official interest. Furthermore, both the 'someone' and the 'something' do not acquire official categories of 'responsibility' and 'type of maltreatment', respectively.

The focus of the analysis in this chapter differs from that of the previous two chapters. In those chapters I looked at how, in particular cases, official categories of maltreatment and identities of responsibility were constructed. In this chapter, the analytical focus is on how the identities of 'child', 'parent' ('mother', 'father') and 'adult' are implicated in how official categories of 'maltreatment' and identities of 'responsibility' are constructed. The analysis shows how identities of the 'child' and 'parent' are stereotypical images whereby abnormality is constructed against taken-for-granted assumptions of what is considered normal.

As with the previous chapters, a selection of cases will illustrate examples of the construction of identity as a feature of social and linguistic practices by child protection workers. Whilst the categorisation of the cases according to 'type of maltreatment' anchors the analysis, it is not the primary issue. However, the categorisation of maltreatment is relevant in how the identities of child, parent and/or adult were implicated in the constructionist process.

Three issues are featured in the analysis. Firstly is the focus on the shifting practical constructions of 'child', as relational to 'parent', ('mother' and 'father'), and 'adult', by unpacking the discursive and cultural assumptions associated with these identities.

Secondly, the analysis explores the positioning of the child in the particular case as a body of evidence that operates as knowledge about the normality (competence) of the parent and/or adult in relation to the child. Thus, as a body of evidence that constitutes official knowledge, the child is not solely the subject and object of protection. Instead the particular child as a body of knowledge also becomes evidence to justify the operation of professional power to discipline and regulate persons believed responsible/parents/adults.

Thirdly, the cases show how dominant assumptions about 'the family' influence constructions of identities. This theme was also explored in chapter 7. The case analysis showed how "patriarchal mothering" assumptions (Fox Harding 1996; Stark & Flitcraft 1988) and a disregard for the "politics of gender and generation" (Stark & Flitcraft 1988; Frost & Stein 1989) tended to significantly influence how identities of responsibility are constructed. In this chapter, the focus of the analysis is on how these patriarchal assumptions and apolitical practices are implicated in constructions of identities of 'child', 'parent' and 'adult'.

Intersecting with these three analytical dimensions is the assumption in developmental psychology that the child is civilised as "a future citizen" (Rose 1989). The link between the 'child' in the present and as a future citizen informs a key child protection concept, "the intergenerational transmission of (sexual) abuse" (Bagley 1991; Smith & Saunders 1995), discussed in chapter 3. In the case of women, their experiences as victims of abuse as children, particularly sexual abuse, predetermines their competence as mothers. The 'unprotective mother' is a direct consequence of childhood abuse and possibly other maltreatment and, furthermore, such mothers expose their own children to maltreatment as a replication of their own childhood experiences. Men's childhood experiences do not appear to have the same deterministic quality in relation to their roles and responsibility as fathers. Ethnocentric assumptions about 'normal families' and roles and responsibilities that underpin child protection may be another form of oppressive practice akin to patriarchal mothering.

## RE-PRESENTING THE CASES

The cases analysed below are selected from the total sample of 20. Four of these cases (Eakins, Francis, Quinn and Underwood) have been analysed in chapters 6 and 7, where the construction of maltreatment or identities of responsibility, respectively, were the primary foci. However, in this chapter the focus of the analysis is on how the identities of 'child', 'parent' and 'adult' articulate in each case and their influence in constructing maltreatment and responsibility.

The following themes will be explored:
- The gendering of victimisation and dangerousness, and the identity of the 'child'

- The 'child' as a body of evidence: constructing 'physical abuse' – protecting children or regulating mothers?
- 'Child protection': differentiating 'normal families' from 'welfare families'?
- 'Home Alone' – constructing 'the normal child', 'the good mother' and 'happy families'
- The 'child' as a body of evidence: constructing 'neglect' – legitimating surveillance of mothers?
- Normal and abnormal mothers – foster mother and biological mother
- 'The intergenerational transmission of sexual abuse' – a concept and its practical meaning
- Girls: born mothers; boys: more than a father
- Child protection – ethnocentric meanings of 'the family'.

## THE GENDERING OF VICTIMISATION AND DANGEROUSNESS, AND THE IDENTITY OF THE 'CHILD'

This case poses questions about how child sexual abuse is defined and categorised within the complicated world of childhood, including sexual expression and the relations of power that exist between children, even when they 'play' (Lamb & Coakley 1993). The case also offers insights into the different ways in which the identity of 'child' may be complicated by gendered identities of '(girl as) victim' and '(boy as) offender' in child sexual abuse cases (Prout & James 1990; Jenks 1996).

According to the file, a 14-year-old non-Aboriginal girl, Petra Blake, reported to the Police Child Abuse Unit that she was "age[d] [between] seven [and]11 . . . when abuse [rubbing breasts and vaginal area; penetrated penis into vagina] happened". Her report was accepted and categorised as "sexual abuse". Petra's cousin Robert was identified as the "person believed responsible". No adult "corroboration" (Potter 1996) was recorded, in contrast with normal child protection practice in which 'adults' mediate on behalf of the 'child', on the assumption that children's testimony on its own is invalid. However, perhaps the girl's age at the time of the report and her category entitled knowledge (Potter 1996) as the principal witness, being a victim of the reported incidents, did not require further corroboration. Furthermore, the Police Child Abuse Unit might have been more responsive to Petra Blake's report, given their role in and awareness of child protection.

The report on file at Urbania did not elaborate beyond the bare details following the rule that 'someone did something to a child'. We are not told whether more than one incident occurred between Petra and Robert when Petra was aged between seven and 11 years. It is unclear whether this age range is Petra's attempt to give a context to her experiences as a younger child, but cannot be more specific due to the delay in reporting. It is also unclear whether a single incident occurred within the stated time-frame, or whether multiple incidents of various 'types', including what was reported, occurred within that time-frame.

Furthermore, I noticed from the file that the police stated that Robert was a "minor" at the time of the "offence". Curious as to what Robert's 'minority' status might mean, particularly in relation to a categorisation as 'sexual abuse' of an event that had happened possibly between three and seven years previously, I searched the file for further information. The reason for my curiosity was to explore how age differences between 'children' as 'victims' and 'offenders' operated to construct 'what happened' as 'child sexual abuse', and how this categorisation might relate to childhood play (Lamb & Coakley 1993). However, Robert's age at the time of the incident(s) reported by Petra was unknown and shrouded in confusion as the following exchange between the male caseworker and myself shows. [The discussion relates to a form where Robert's age was indecipherable. Someone had amended the initial entry by writing a different age over the first entry.]

Worker: He was 17.

HD: The CPIS [Child Protection Information System] form says he was 16 when he was charged. He was a minor when it happened.

Worker: . . . That's 19, he's currently 19 . . . he was 17 at the time . . . When I got his name, I was looking back on the computer . . . it was when he was about 16 or 17 when it happened.

HD: She was only seven or 11 when it happened?

Worker: Yes, seven.

HD: Nineteen when he was charged. . .

Worker: Eighteen or 19 . . .

HD: She's 14 now. . .

Worker: She's 14 now . . . that will make him 12 [when the incident occurred].

The facts of the case as to Petra's reported experiences are not in question here. However, the case does raise some critical questions for policy and practice. First, the assumptions that the 'sexual abuse' category encapsulates all experiences, regardless of age – for example, 'seven to 11 years' – must be considered. It does not help us understand the differences between experiences of events which had happened some years before between children when they were much younger, and how they might be perceived when older, especially by 'victims', influencing reports of 'sexual abuse' as criminal acts (Ferguson 1997). Furthermore, an older child's increased knowledge may, in retrospect, re-cast past experiences involving peers in a different way, with ambiguity related to both perceived 'consent' *and* 'resistance'.

Similarly the dearth of contextual detail surrounding the reported incidents of the structure 'someone did something to me [a child]' limits professional knowledge in terms of policy development and ethical practice. Contexual detail would include access and the extent of perceived 'coercion' and 'consent' (Bell 1993) that may allow for some account to be taken of "sexual play" ('normal childhood behaviour') and "sexual abuse" (abnormal) (Lamb & Coakley 1993). The case also raises questions about whether child protection policy and practice strictly demarcate the meaning of 'child' in relation to social and legal rights. The 'child' Petra, as 'female victim', is afforded 'care and protection' that her male cousin Robert is not. Nonetheless, he was also legally and socially a 'child' at the time of the reported incident(s). However, according to the male caseworker, Robert had forfeited any rights to care and protection as a 'child' as he had 'become an offender', a person believed responsible for 'child sexual abuse'. "Any kid [boy] over the age of 10 you can have for sexual abuse." His socio-legal status as 'child' at the time of the reported incidents was minimal if not irrelevant. These concerns about age between 'victims' and 'offenders' who are 'children' are important when considering how 'what happened' between them is officially categorised. It seems an extreme response to construct 'sexual abuse' without contextual information as outlined above.

More pragmatically, with regard to the statistical profiles of 'victims' and 'offenders' in relation to 'child sexual abuse', it would seem important to record details like age as relevant at the time of the incident(s) and not at the time of the report of those incident(s). Otherwise there is potential for misleading knowledge claims about the profiles of 'victims' and 'persons believed responsible' for 'child sexual abuse'.

This case has posed critical questions for child protection policy and practice in regard to 'child sexual abuse'. There are insights offered into how there may be different socio-legal statuses accorded to 'children', influenced by cultural assumptions about sex, gender and sexualities of 'children'. It shows there is potential for more complicated understandings of both 'victim' and 'offender' identities as they relate to 'children' in order to ensure that the rights to care and protection are properly extended, rather than privileging the 'girl child victim' to the exclusion of the 'boy child offender'.

## THE CHILD AS A BODY OF EVIDENCE: CONSTRUCTING 'PHYSICAL ABUSE' – PROTECTING CHILDREN OR REGULATING MOTHERS?

The case of Stuart Davis shows how the child as a body of evidence operates as much to regulate women as mothers as it does to protect children. The analysis illustrates the "politics of the family" and how assumptions of "patriarchal mothering" (Stark & Flitcraft 1988), including conflicting social identities, relationships and allegiances, produced identities of 'unprotective mother' and "responsible mothers, invisible men" (Stark & Flitcraft 1988; Korbin 1989; Milner 1993). This section will explore in detail the sub-themes related to this process.

### The child as a body of evidence: constructing 'physical abuse' – The case of Stuart Davis

This case illustrates how the child represented a body of evidence whereby professional knowledge that sees and defines bodily abnormalities in particular ways operated with professional power to enforce that definition (Foucault 1972, 1980) and to regulate the mother rather than the male offender who had been identified as 'responsible'.

The actual child, Stuart Davis, an "Aboriginal" male aged one year, lived with his mother, Kathleen, and her de facto, John, described on file as a "blending family". Stuart was brought to official attention when family friends and relatives contacted the Crisis Care Unit, reporting perceived bodily abnormalities as indicators of "risk": "a bite mark to the face, and bruising to his body", "very distressed and quite listless".

Although the family's ethnic identity was recorded on file as 'Aboriginal', the relevance of this identity for the child's family and friends, and for child protection workers, appeared to be minimal. Lay people were able to engage with the official child protection discourse, reporting through shared language (Ferguson 1997), and by a non-Aboriginal family friend, Ms Albers, bridging the gap between private 'Aboriginal family' and public 'non-Aboriginal' officials.

The child's body as an object of evidence and a source of professional knowledge/power depended on the visibility and definition of abnormalities in constructing the category of 'physical abuse'. The body appeared to operate as a living map, analogous to the two-dimensional paper body maps maintained on case files. "Injuries" were sighted/sited and mapped from the bodily surface, as table 8.1 shows.

| Mapping bodily abnormality – knowledge devices | The particular body – Stuart Davis, a body of evidence |
| --- | --- |
| Bodily sites – where are abnormalities sited/sighted on the body? | "left cheek", "right buttock", "top left of thigh", "top right of thigh", "front of left foot", "below left of shin bone" |
| "Quantification" (Potter 1996) – number of abnormalities sited/sighted | "two", or "one" (stated as "a", or in singular) |
| Categories ('type') of injury – typology | "bruises", "scratch", "scratches", "cut" |
| Modalities (Potter 1996) – colour | "blue/brown", "red", "brown", "blue/red" |
| Modalities (Potter 1996) – shape of abnormalities | "oval" |
| Modalities (Potter 1996) – dimensions of abnormalities | "size of a ten cent coin", "tiny", "approx 1 cm", "small", "approx the size of a pea", and a pen drawing to represent the size of scratches |

Table 8.1 Mapping bodily abnormalities – 'physical abuse'

The bodily abnormalities set out in table 8.1 were constructed as 'physical abuse'. Other bodily abnormalities such as a "very distended stomach" were differentiated as 'normal abnormalities' by child health nurses, as a "birth problem", a "kidney problem", and therefore not maltreatment (neglect).

### The child as a body of evidence to regulate women as mothers

The construction as 'physical abuse' of the set of abnormalities with no 'normal' explanation seen on Stuart Davis's body facilitated the deployment of professional power to achieve 'child protection' through the regulation of the child Stuart's mother, Kathleen Davis. The workers at Urbania who were asked to "follow up" with an investigation, after Crisis Care workers had advised them of their assessment of the previous night, expected to visit Stuart at Ms Albers's home. Ms Albers was the friend to whom family members had taken Stuart the night before with their concerns about his well-being. Ms Albers had agreed to care for Stuart overnight until the workers at Urbania could visit next morning. However, before the workers could arrive at Ms Albers's home, Stuart's mother, Kathleen, had called at the house. She then took Stuart home with her, as Ms Albers could see no reason to stop her from doing so. (There was no court order preventing it.) The workers were annoyed with Ms Albers for letting Stuart go home with his mother because they could not "operate" in a particular way; that is, to ascertain Kathleen Davis's competence as a 'protective mother', despite her partner, John, being identified as 'responsible' for Stuart's injuries:

> Ms Albers had released the child [to his mother] and it changed the whole way we could operate . . . had we put [him] in care *until we'd ascertained whether the mother was going to act protectively towards [him]* . . . (emphasis added)

Furthermore, Ms Albers's contact with Kathleen Davis was seen as warning her of the pending child protection investigation and she could therefore concoct a story to refute the workers' questions about the physical abuse of Stuart. In the caseworker's words: "she [Kathleen] was well prepared for us coming".

In addition to the bodily mapping as set out in table 8.1, the worker whom I interviewed and her colleague "viewed" the child Stuart at his mother's home to "follow up" the construction of "physical abuse". The file indicates a retrospective account of the home visit, with workers' observations ("bruise on left cheek") and interpretation ("indicative of having been bitten by an adult").

The workers' construction of Kathleen Davis as an 'unprotective mother' relied on three main aspects of Kathleen's responses to their adversarial investigation. Firstly, her version of the injuries was 'childhood accident', thus disputing the official version as 'physical abuse'. Secondly, Kathleen was perceived as 'protective' of her partner John by "hot denials" that he had "injured" her son. Thirdly, she refused to identify John amongst a crowd of people in the house. Hence the workers were unable to interview him. Therefore, Kathleen Davis was an unprotective mother who 'chose' to protect her male partner at the expense of her son.

It seemed that Kathleen Davis's 'choices' did not encompass possible "inconsistencies and complex allegiances" (Doane & Hodges, 1992: 79, in Featherstone 1996: 185) towards her son Stuart as a 'maltreated child' and her 'abusive partner' John. For example, there was evidence on file that the John was violent to Kathleen: "a fair amount of arguments" and the child Stuart "caught in the middle". Also the caseworker had sighted a bruise on Kathleen's cheek. However, both these instances of the mother's experiences as a potential victim of violence were minimised (Potter 1996). The worker did not pursue the possibility of violence to Kathleen and therefore the implications for her ability to protect Stuart from John. Instead, ". . . she was just denying that there was a problem really". The possibility of Kathleen's ambivalence towards (dependence on/fear of) her partner (Stark & Flitcraft 1988; Gary 1991) was also not considered.

Kathleen's fear of loss of Stuart into care if she accepted the official version of his injuries as 'physical abuse' – "No one was taking Stuart from her" – was not acknowledged, yet this had been considered as a preferred intervention at the outset of the investigation:

> Ms Albers had released the child [to his mother] and it changed the whole way we could operate . . . had we put [him] in care until we'd ascertained whether the mother was going to act protectively towards [him] . . . (emphasis added)

As a version of "responsible mothers, invisible men" (Milner 1993), this mother was 'responsible' for regulating the man's private conduct (Donzelot 1980, in Hirst 1981): "we [workers] told Kathleen we would not be taking Stuart but that she needed to protect him from harm". The 'adult male', John, who was identified officially as 'person believed responsible for physical abuse', nevertheless remained 'invisible' from public regulation, partly owing his invisibility to his partner Kathleen's apparent 'protectiveness'.

However, the child Stuart remained the justification of official and public surveillance of his mother through the engagement of public child health services to monitor Stuart's well-being: "she was having contact [with child health], not hiding the child away". The child health nurse acted as an agent of surveillance of maternal conduct whilst focusing on the child: the nurse "advised that if Kathleen did not come into the Clinic tomorrow, she would follow her up at home". Furthermore, as Foucault (1977, 1980) points out, the governance of the self involves an awareness that one is under surveillance by others in an institutional hierarchy. The caseworker said that Kathleen Davis "was aware that we were aware and . . . monitoring the situation . . . she was following up with Child Health . . . really couldn't hide anything".

This case has shown how a child's bodily abnormalities constructed as 'physical abuse' operated primarily as an examination of the mother's normality as 'parent', despite her male de facto being identified as 'person believed responsible'. 'Child protection (adult male regulation)' was primarily a private (and maternal) responsibility, enforced by public surveillance and examination. Patriarchal mothering assumptions expected the woman to 'choose' her child as a 'protective' mother, disregarding the complexities of heterosexual family politics. The mother remained publicly visible and therefore 'responsible' for private conduct, whilst the man 'responsible for physical abuse' remained "invisible" (Stark & Flitcraft 1988; Milner 1993) from public regulation.

## 'CHILD PROTECTION': DIFFERENTIATING 'NORMAL FAMILIES' FROM 'WELFARE FAMILIES'?

A report that 'something happened' to a particular child has ramifications beyond the particular case. Profiles or patterns that define and describe 'maltreatment' of various 'types', 'persons believed responsible' and 'children as victims' are constructed from individual cases and become official and professional knowledge of a problem called 'child maltreatment' and a response, 'child protection'.

The cases of Murray Francis and Alan Eakins have been explored in chapters 6 and 7, focusing on how reports may be constructed as 'types of maltreatment' and 'identities of responsibility' respectively. In particular, chapter 6 showed how the report about Murray Francis and the man reported as 'responsible for physical abuse' influenced the construction of the same man as 'responsible for sexual abuse' in a subsequent report about Alan Eakins, discussed in chapter 7. The analysis that appears below explores how children as bodies of evidence of physical and sexual abuse operate to regulate women as mothers. The analysis shows how cultural assumptions about 'normal family functioning' and 'normal mothers and children' informed the assessment of both the Eakins and Francis families. The mothers, Rosemary Eakins and Tammy Francis, are assessed for their 'protectiveness' towards their children in relation to the 'dangerous' man Russell with whom they were associated. The aim of 'child protection' allowed scrutiny of the women as mothers and their relationships, which normally would be deemed as 'private' and out of bounds to 'outsiders' to 'the family'.

### Gaining entry to the family: the child as an opportunity

The wide-ranging focus of child protection, which began with the children as bodies of evidence, is suggested in the caseworker's concerns:

> We had a concern about these other children . . . [Alan Eakins and Murray Francis] . . . *where two young women . . . share a flat . . . the partner of [Tammy Francis] . . . [she] has had another child of his* . . . (emphasis added)

Child protection workers were unable to discover detailed information about the family arrangements and relationships in the Eakins and Francis households because the mothers would not grant access to the children and there were not sufficient legal grounds to demand access. Therefore, child protection workers used the opportunity of protective concerns in relation to Alan Eakins to find out more about the Francis family, with whom Alan Eakins and his family were associated:

> Mother [Rosemary Eakins] had difficulty handling [Alan] and she . . . placed him in care, and that's where we had the opportunity to interview him personally, because we just couldn't get into this other family [Francis family], into the house itself, to interview the other children . . . (emphasis added)

### 'Normal families', 'welfare families': assessing risk

In conducting their risk assessment, the workers seemed to rely on implicit images of 'normal' mothers, families and children, against which they compared the actual people. Their assessment, as recorded on file and related to me in the interview with the caseworker, relied on contrast structures (Potter 1996; Smith 1990a) and three-part lists (Potter 1996) to construct abnormality. The workers expected the mothers and children and their living circumstances to conform to implicit stereotypes about families reported for child maltreatment, which contrasted with stereotypes of 'normal families'. Instead, the families challenged these stereotypes of abnormality, as these extracts from the files and interviews illustrate:

> They [the mothers] work well together [1a] . . . the [male] partner [Russell, alleged abuser] is not always there . . . he's got a separate residence [1c] . . . it's an ideal situation [2] . . . they're very supportive [1b] and the home, when we went early one morning [3], the kids were beautifully dressed [3a], and sitting at the breakfast table [3b] eating their meal [3c] . . . there were no squabbles [3d], it was all very calm and controlled [4] . . . [. . .].

> The home was a surprise [5a], *because you had an image of what to expect* [5b]. (emphasis added)

> The flat was extremely tidy [6] and the overall impression was one of good order and harmony [4].

As the above extracts show, the overall image the Eakins and Francis families presented to the workers at their apparently unexpected visit early one morning was "ideal" [2], "calm and controlled", "orderly and harmonious" [4], rather than the expected chaos and conflict stereotypically associated with families investigated for child maltreatment. The mothers were in a supportive partnership with each other that did not rely on the presence of an adult male [1a–c], particularly someone like Russell, who had been identified as 'dangerous and cruel' in relation to his alleged treatment of Murray Francis (see chapter 6). Contrast structures (Smith 1990a; Potter 1996) show how the mothers' conformity with images of the 'normal family' disrupted workers' expectations of their abnormality as a 'child protection family' [5a, 5b].

Despite it being "early in the morning" [3], the children were not just "dressed", but the "modalizing term" (Potter 1996), "beautifully", shows that they surpassed expectations [3a]. The children were behaving normally, "eating their meal" [3c] at the "breakfast table" [3b] again, appropriate for the time of day, but also impressive, because of the "calm and control" at the "early" hour.

These mothers and their family circumstances clearly disrupted the official stereotypes of chaos and conflict, and dirty, unkempt, unfed children. In an attempt to reconcile the conflict between what they expected when they visited and what they observed, the caseworker reconstructed these 'ideal' circumstances as public (surface) images, possibly designed to impress the workers. ". . . [The interesting thing is that when you go into [these women's home] is that *outwardly they . . . run a very good family set up*. [. . .]" (emphasis added).

The caseworker continued her reconstruction of what she considered the mothers were 'really like' behind their 'outward very good set up'. She disrupted their 'outward' public image of normality by reconstructing the mother's identities within images of abnormality consistent with (her) expectations, and designed to reveal their abnormal, ('true'), 'inward' or private 'set up':

> Worker: Very, very *quietly aggressive [1], these women* [laugh] [2] you know *they're assertive, but aggressive* [3] in terms of their . . . they can be quite manipulative, they're both *welfare wise* [4], . . . this *lack of protectiveness towards their children, they protect the perpetrators* [5].
>
> HD: How much do you think that this thing about 'women needing a man' has anything to do with it?
>
> Worker: It's just unbelievable how many times you see it here, *they'd bend over backwards to protect the man to the detriment of their children* [6] . . . (emphasis added)

Through the use of contrast structures (Smith 1990a; Potter 1996) [1, 3], the worker associated the mothers' 'outward' images of "quietness" and "assertiveness" with an 'inward' opposite of "aggression". Their "wisdom" is contrasted with and confined to "welfare" [4] as manipulative and "welfare frauds" (Jamrozik 1991: 231–57). Through statements 5 and 6, also contrast structures, the mothers are constructed as 'unprotective': their "protection of the man" operates to the "detriment of their children". The caseworker further distanced herself from the mothers, as "these women" [2], representing herself as the norm of good woman/mother.

However, the caseworker found that these mothers did not match her images of 'unprotective (welfare) mothers' and 'unprotective (desperate, heterosexual) mothers' that are part of the stereotype of women who 'choose' their male partners over their children, as this extract from an interview shows:

> From what I've heard about these women, I found it really quite funny, because the police had described [Tammy], the mother of Murray . . . then when we went out there she was completely different. I remember them saying, she's really fat [1], and she's really ugly [2], and she's really hard [3], and *I think that she'll have trouble getting a man, and she's desperate, and that's why she's hung on to this bloke* [4] . . . and we went out there and . . . she's quite plump [overweight (on file)], but she's very pretty [5] and very softly spoken [6] and very . . . neatly presented [7] . . . She didn't appear rough [8] or common [9] or hard [10] in any way at all . . . she wasn't at all what we expected [11] . . . (emphasis added)

The stereotypes of 'normal' and 'abnormal' women/mothers that operated in the risk assessment are set out in table 8.2.

| Mapping Tammy Francis – 'what she was not' [that is, 'welfare mother'] | Mapping Tammy Francis – 'what she was' [that is, 'normal mother'] |
|---|---|
| Police description of Tammy Francis told to workers prior to their home visit – two three-part lists (Potter 1996):<br>■ "fat" [1], "ugly" [2] and "hard" [3]<br>■ "she'll have trouble getting a man [1] and she's desperate [2], and that's why she's hung on to this bloke [3]" | Worker's description following the home visit – contrast structure (Potter 1996; Smith 1990a): "She [Tammy] is quite plump [overweight (on file)], but she's very pretty . . . |
| Worker's description following the home visit – a three-part list (Potter 1996): "She [Tammy] didn't appear rough [1] or common [2] or hard [3] in any way at all" | Worker's description following the home visit – a three-part list (Potter 1996): "She [Tammy] is quite plump, but she's very pretty [1] . . . and very softly spoken [2] and very neatly presented [3]" |
| "she wasn't at all what we expected" | "she wasn't at all what we expected" |

Table 8.2 'She wasn't at all what we expected' – Constructing the 'heterosexual welfare mother' in a 'child protection family'

Contrary to expectations of 'welfare mothers' and families being investigated for child protection reasons, table 8.2 shows the simultaneous operation of images of 'abnormal, heterosexual, welfare mothers' and 'normal, heterosexual, not welfare, mothers' during the risk assessment. The worker's concluding statement summarises the tension between these two sets of opposing stereotypes and shows that these particular mothers disrupted expectations of what they would be like as 'welfare mothers'. The mothers embodied 'normal' (heterosexual) femininity (Smith

1990b), represented by two three-part lists, strengthened by a contrast structure of what they were and what they were not.

### Protecting children: responsible mothers

The identification of the mothers as 'protectors' of their children positioned them as 'responsible' for the conduct of their male associate, Russell, towards their children. Russell himself remained 'invisible', partly through the women's alternative constructions of his identity (see Alan Eakins, chapter 7) and partly also through their resistance to child protection workers' investigations of their family circumstances and relationships.

However, there was no doubt that Tammy Francis and Rosemary Eakins were being held responsible for the care and protection of their children, as the comments on file indicate following the investigation and case closure:

> As both Tammy and Rosemary have been made aware of [Russell's] past offences [sic] against other children, it is hoped that this will see these mothers acting in a protective manner towards their children in the future.

The case examples of Alan Eakins and Murray Francis have shown how children as bodies of evidence facilitate entry by child protection workers into the private space of 'the family', and the examination of identities, relationships and practices. In particular, the analysis presents an example of "responsible mothers, invisible men" (Stark & Flitcraft 1988; Milner 1993), influenced by assumptions of "patriarchal mothering" (Stark & Flitcraft 1988) and "femininity as discourse" (Smith 1990b). Furthermore, Tammy Francis and Rosemary Eakins were expected to conform to stereotypes of 'welfare mothers' whose family circumstances were under investigation due to child maltreatment allegations against their male associate. While child protection was ostensibly the primary focus of public intervention, assumptions of patriarchal mothering enforced 'protection' as a private and maternal 'responsibility'. Furthermore, child protection investigation allowed the regulation of women as mothers and surveillance of the private space of 'the family' that would otherwise be out of bounds to 'non-family' or 'the state' (Donzelot 1980, 1981).

## 'HOME ALONE' – CONSTRUCTING 'THE NORMAL CHILD', 'THE GOOD MOTHER' AND 'HAPPY FAMILIES'

The case of the Kelly family and the child protection intervention for 'neglect' may be described as a real life 'Home Alone' scenario. It shows a number of features of 'constructing neglect' that rely on cultural assumptions of the care and protection of 'children' and the role of parents, particularly mothers in achieving this. It demonstrates the intersection of public and private patriarchy (Fox Harding 1996) in constructing the mother Lisa Kelly as "responsible for neglect – [lack of]

supervision". It shows how 'neglect' is a special example of child maltreatment where omissions of expected parenting/mothering practices carry a great deal of power to regulate women and intervene in families. It also shows how 'neglect' may be the opposite side of the coin of what is considered 'normal mothering': as 'neglecting' to undertake what is expected. This feature perhaps explains, at least partially, why women/mothers are overwhelmingly represented as 'persons believed responsible' for 'neglect' in contrast to the pattern of "responsible mothers, invisible men" (Milner 1993) in physical and sexual abuse cases (Forbes 1993; Carlson 1992; Hearn 1990). The case also shows how carefully crafted expressions about the care and protection of children may be strategically deployed by private individuals in conflict with women to 'set the welfare on them' as a way of taking revenge or otherwise punishing them. There is a good chance that a child protection investigation can be set in train as long as the referrals conform to the language of danger and risk to children. Once started, an investigation may maintain sufficient momentum to cause distress, whether or not more benign objectives may be achieved for the children. "Patriarchal mothering" assumptions (Stark & Flitcraft 1988) "discipline and punish" (Foucault 1977) those women who do not conform to cultural expectations of 'normal mothering'. The enforcement of norms, known as the "cult of domesticity" (Rose 1989) and "familialisation" (Rose 1989) in assessing/constructing 'neglect', are summed up in this case by the female social worker's "strong beliefs in the way a family should be". Patriarchal mothering practices were supported by cultural assumptions about "children's needs" (Woodhead 1990) and 'parental (maternal) responsibility' for meeting them.

The Kelly children were "non-Aboriginal", a boy, Peter, aged 15 and a girl, Sarah, aged 12. The caregiver/family structure was described on file as "single parent female". Their mother, Lisa, was away from her usual residence because she was engaged in resolving problems associated with her business activities – her main source of income. When she was away, Lisa Kelly arranged for friends and neighbours to visit the children regularly. She also provided sufficient food and gave the children access to money through a cash card. Despite these arrangements, the case turned on disputes about the legitimacy of Lisa Kelly's business activities, and her absences from home were seen as 'neglecting her children'.

### Reporting 'neglect': concern for children or regulation of women/mothers? The case of Peter and Sarah Kelly and their mother, Lisa

Two reports were received about the care of these children, who were "left alone at home". The first report, made by an anonymous male to police, was investigated by Crisis Care workers and immediately closed. The "children [were] OK [safe] and their mother will return during the weekend". The very next day, a man (possibly the same man who made the first report) made a second report. This second report was made to the caseworker at Urbania whom I interviewed.

> We got another call [1] . . . from another person [2] who again [3] said that the children were being left alone [4] for long periods of time [5] . . . he said that the children were a lot younger . . . eight and 11 [6], *and that really changed the urgency of the case* [8].
>
> Also he [caller] made connotations of her being in [an] illegal sort of business [7] [. . . .] and that also made me think that we definitely needed to look into it . . . (emphasis added)

The man used extreme images to communicate a sense of risk and danger to the children, which seemed to achieve the effect he desired; namely, the official investigation of Lisa Kelly for the neglect of her children. The suggestion of cumulative evidence (Potter 1996) represented by the second report ("another call" [1]) begins the process of building up the sense of risk to the children. According to the caseworker, the second report was by an apparently independent witness [2] (Potter 1996), who was apparently a different person from the man who had made the first, 'unsubstantiated', report, and who repeated the concerns expressed in the first report [3]. Furthermore, the 'second' caller's use of extreme images (Potter 1996) of the children's vulnerability [4–6] built up the version of risk and danger to them and of their mother's failure to properly care for them [8]. Additionally, this second caller strengthened the plausibility of his report by making extreme allegations against the mother herself. There were "connotations" of her "illegal" practices [7], which increased the chances of a child protection investigation.

Although there was no proof on file of the reporter's identity each time, based on my own practice experience, I read the two reports as being by the same man who, being thwarted from his unstated objective on the first occasion, made a second report the following day. His first report about these two children, 'home alone', apparently did not achieve the desired effect because his second report relied on the device of "extrematization" (Potter 1996) to build up the sense of danger and risk to the children. The success of the second report in engaging the attention of child protection workers is suggested by the caseworker's explanation to me, in response to my enquiry about the possibility that the complaint was malicious:

> Worker: At first there was the anonymous stuff . . . then I took the next one [call], and he did give me his name, but no identifying information . . . so we don't know what his connection was to her . . . he just said that she owed him money and that was all.
>
> HD: So there could have been some malice?
>
> Worker: Definitely, definitely.

The worker did not know what the caller's relationship was to Lisa Kelly and her family. Although she acknowledged the "definite" possibility that the caller was "malicious", the worker nonetheless gave the report greater credibility than her doubts about it.

## Constructing 'neglect': 'what were you worried about?'

This section explores the cultural assumptions about the care and protection of children and how 'neglect' is constituted through absences of various expectations about 'normal' parenting/mothering and family life. After reading the file I sought to clarify what were the basic concerns that maintained the worker's tenacious involvement in the case. In my perception, there seemed to be an overreaction, particularly given that the children seemed to be well provided for. At the very worst, it was an example of a mother needing support rather than policing. I sought to make explicit the assumptions informing practice in this case.

In response to my question, "What were you really worried about?", the worker said:

> An intruder [1a] . . . I don't know the boy [brother/son, Peter] from a bar of soap whether or not he has his mates around for raging parties or not, [2] . . . and just who they would let in to the house [1b] . . . and just the emotional stuff for the kids being left at home and alone all the time, how that was affecting them [3] . . .

In this extract, the absent mother, Lisa Kelly, was placing her children at risk in several ways, characterised by potential and imagined worst case scenarios. Firstly, there was the possibility of a generalised 'intruder' [1a] and expected 'irresponsible' behaviour of the children by letting just anyone into the house [1b]. Next, there are more specific and detailed concerns where the children are differentiated according to gender: the girl, Sarah, a potential 'victim of maltreatment' and the boy, Peter, a 'perpetrator' of 'maltreatment' either on his own, or by his [male] friends against his own sister. Thus, Lisa Kelly owed a primary responsibility to her daughter, Sarah, to protect her from her older brother and other 'dangerous', 'out of control' young males, and for both children to be protected from unknown 'intruders'. Finally, there is the assumption that being 'home alone' constitutes emotional damage [3] – an absent mother is responsible for damage which leaves no visible, bodily traces but which culturally has a reality for 'the mind' and "the soul" of the child (Rose 1989).

In further anticipation of a worst case scenario, the caseworker imagined Sarah as a potential victim of her older brother, Peter:

> If there are problems between her and [brother] and *one night* [1] they have a *big fight* [2] and he *locks her outside* [3] . . . and mum's away for three weeks [4] . . . (emphasis added)

The worst case scenario is built up by extreme descriptions (Potter 1996) that encapsulate a very particular Western lifestyle where service provision is normally confined to set office hours and there are few people available to assist outside these hours. Hence, the worker's concerns about "one night" – unpredictability and a time of day when there are minimal services and people to help [1], not just a "fight" but a "big" one [2], and where Peter "locks her outside" [3]. This scenario relates to assumptions about 'the family (home)' as a "haven in a heartless world" (Frost & Stein 1989), particularly "at night" [1]. For the caseworker, this worst case scenario would culminate in an "unexpected tragedy" for which the mother would be 'responsible' through her 'neglect' (as absence) [4]. The caseworker sought to prevent such a tragedy.

### Constructing 'neglect', contesting 'neglect': the identity of 'the child' and 'maternal responsibility'

In this section, the caseworker's assumptions about children in general as dependent, vulnerable, incompetent and irresponsible, and therefore requiring a parent/adult to care for and protect (supervise) them, are disrupted by the two actual children, Peter (15 years old) and Sarah (12 years old).

The mother's competence as a 'parent' relied on the extent to which she was 'child centred', a dominant cultural expectation of 'parenting':

> Her work should not have come . . . before leaving her children alone, unsupervised, and she made it very clear that's what she had to do, and would keep on doing it regardless . . .

Hence she was '(ir)responsible', being 'responsible for neglect' through her irresponsibility, as 'self', not 'child centred'.

Further evidence of her '(ir)responsibility' was associated with the importance of parental presence and availability to their children at all times. This mother failed dismally, according to the caseworker, who identified three features of maternal absence:

> Yes, she had made a lot of provisions, a lot of people wouldn't have as many [1a], but just the fact that they [the children] were being left alone [2a] a lot [2b] and that they were quite young [2c] [1b]. (emphasis added)

The caseworker acknowledged that Lisa Kelly had 'made a lot of provisions' [1a] for the children through organising a trusted friend to call around to see them, providing food and access to money. As material provisions, the mother has surpassed expectations [1a], described by "modalizing terms" (Potter 1996): "a lot", "as many". However, the mother's provisions for the children's material and personal security did not compensate for an absence that was entirely 'self centred' and therefore unseemly. Through a contrast structure (Smith 1990a; Potter 1996) and a three-part list (Potter 1996), the caseworker emphasised the mother's transgressions (Potter 1996). The clause [1b] operates as a contrast structure to nullify the material provisions [1a]. The mother's extended absence is described by using extreme features (Potter 1996) to strengthen the contrast structure [1b]: leaving "quite young children", "home alone", "a lot" [2a–c].

These three central features, influenced by cultural constructions of 'childhood' and constructed as a problem of 'neglect – lack of supervision', had different meanings for the children:

> [The children] said they could look after themselves [1], they had been left alone before [2], they said not as many times as we said [3].

The children represented themselves as 'independent' and 'capable' and not requiring 'adult'/'parental' supervision/care [1]. Being "left alone" facilitated these abilities [2], rather than the opposite. They also disputed the official claim of being 'left alone a lot', claiming it was a lot less frequent (Potter 1996).

The worker conceded that "it was a lifestyle they were quite used to". However, rather than reconstructing the problem of 'neglect' and her assumptions of incompetent, dependent and irresponsible children, the worker instead saw the children as adapting to abnormal parenting practices: "They didn't conceive of it as a problem". 'Normal children' were dependent and vulnerable, and needed the 'supervision' of an 'adult'/'parent' (Jenks 1996).

I explored whether the age of the 'child' mattered in how the parent's responsibility for 'supervision' is constructed, as in this case there was a 15-year-old and a 12-year-old. The worker differentiated between the 15-year-old as being able "to stay there" [on his own] whereas the "11- [sic] year-old would be of concern . . . at risk". I then explored whether gender mattered in constructing vulnerability amongst children.

> HD: Would it have mattered if the 11-year-old was a boy?
>
> Worker: I don't think so. I think it was just the age not the different sex [sic].

However, when I explored her previous constructions of the girl 'at risk' from her brother, "who would bring all his [male] friends around", the worker said:

> Yeah for me that was, but as far as placing them and having supervision . . . it was just the age and that one [Sarah] was too young.

Furthermore, there were culturally defined age-appropriate tasks and responsibilities: ". . . a 15-year-old was very young to be looking after an 11-year-old full time as well". Beyond what was age appropriate, the worker differentiated between what were 'normal jobs' amongst family members and 'parenting' as 'looking after younger siblings' was not the 'normal job' for a 'child' (who was 'not an adult' and 'not a parent'): "It shouldn't have to be his job".

### Child protection and 'neglect': 'rescuing the abandoned'?

The worker's tenacity in working with the Kelly family was a rescue of the abandoned, by "not giving up on . . . a family like this". She continued to construct the roles and relationships of the Kelly family as transgressions of 'normal family' identities and practices, particularly as the children did not conform to official expectations of 'children neglected by their mother'. She considered that the 'transgressions' of family identities were perhaps related to temporary "struggles": "they will probably all get through whatever this is and she [mother] could be genuinely struggling . . . to get a better life for her and her children". However, the construction of the family's problems as 'child maltreatment' cast 'child protection' as helping the mother "to get through it and the kids are left a little more [sic] [emotionally] unscarred than they will be".

This case has shown how constructions of 'neglect' are so interwoven with patriarchal mothering assumptions intersecting with images of the (normal) 'child' as 'vulnerable and dependent', that it is almost impossible to separate them. Furthermore, it shows how women as mothers are over-represented as 'persons believed responsible for neglect' as social practices that replay cultural images of normal mothering, childhood and family life.

## THE CHILD AS A BODY OF EVIDENCE: CONSTRUCTING 'NEGLECT' – LEGITIMATING SURVEILLANCE OF MOTHERS?

This case illustrates how mothering as a primary role for women is represented by 'children' – at all stages of development, manifested by the pregnant woman (pre-natal), the new-born infant, and the developing child. It is almost impossible to set out a case analysis in which childhood and motherhood feature as separate entities because the extent of perceived 'normality' of one is a commentary on the other.

In particular, mothering as a privatised activity is regulated through panoptic surveillance (Foucault 1977, 1980) of women, through official examination of their children's bodies as sites of knowledge/power. The baby's body was a site of coordinated knowledge/power of medical, social and legal domains, by which the woman's private conduct as 'mother' could be examined and normalised (Lupton 1999b; Phoenix & Woollett 1991). The mother was caught in a web of surveillance constructed from coordinated professional knowledge/power, and was unable to extricate herself as anything other than a 'bad mother'. The 'child', Belinda Nicholson, (ethnicity "Unknown") was a female, whose caregiver was her mother, Alana, a "single parent". Belinda was aged six weeks when she was apprehended as a child in need of care and protection, with an application for transfer of guardianship from her mother to the state.

## Constructing 'neglect', constructing 'children', 'policing mothers'

There have been examples in this chapter of the ways in which the body of the child is a marker of parental, particularly maternal, competence. The extent of bodily abnormality, especially that which cannot be explained 'normally' – for example, as congenital or accidental – is then constructed as 'child maltreatment' and, more often than not, women as mothers are held solely or equally responsible for it. This case shows how the 'child' became an object of evidence representing her mother's competence, as a consequence of entwining of women's primary responsibility for children associated with biological parenthood, through pregnancy and childbirth, and social parenthood, through expectations of "domesticity" (Rose 1989).

The ongoing surveillance of the woman, Alana Nicholson, as 'mother' was an accumulation (Potter 1996) of diverse instances, where her practices of mothering were examined legitimately by medical, legal and social knowledge domains, and recorded on file. The web of professional surveillance began with the medicalisation of pregnancy and childbirth (Rose 1989; Lupton 1999b). The female social worker at the maternity hospital reported Alana Nicholson and baby Belinda to Myopia, a child protection office, when Belinda was nine days old and ready for discharge. The maternity hospital social worker's concerns related to identifying Alana as a "drug addict", which was seen as incompatible with the identity of 'normal mother', particularly as mothering/child care in most Western societies remains an individualised, private responsibility, with minimal public and community responsibility for children (Fox Harding 1996).

However, the maternity hospital social worker only requested that preventive and support services be offered to Alana Nicholson to help her to care for Belinda. She justified this under a broad interpretation of the child protection organisation's "statutory" responsibility for children. However, the practitioners and their supervisor at Myopia had a different construction of 'child protection'. "There were no CMA concerns." In the light of this conclusion, they discussed with the maternity hospital social worker that "there was no role for [their department]". It was also a way of managing a "lack of resources" at their office, implying that the referral was not sufficiently extreme to warrant their involvement. However, they suggested services from non-government family agencies and alcohol and drug organisations.

Therefore, to ensure that Alana Nicholson discharged her responsibilities of care and protection of her baby, the state was permitted to place her under surveillance in the guise of social and medical service provision. Services such as "drug counselling" and "rehabilitation" offered to assist Alana, 'the drug addicted *woman*,' seemed to operate primarily as strategies of surveillance of Alana 'the drug addicted *mother*'. For example, the drug counsellor reported "concerns about the care of the baby" and "mother falling asleep whilst breast-feeding". Child health services provided to ensure Belinda's well-being, such as "sighting" and "weighing" her, operated as strategies of surveillance of Alana's performance as a "drug addicted mother". For example, the child health nurse reported on baby Belinda's progress, saying that Alana Nicholson was "not attending court" for drug offences and was "living chaotically".

Although there was no formal involvement by child protection workers in assisting Alana and Belinda, their files included reports from various agencies expressing their concerns about Alana as a mother as discussed above. Furthermore, whilst social and medical services ostensibly provided various forms of assistance to Alana to care for baby Belinda, they combined within legal parameters to examine the mother's normality through the body of her baby. In addition to the weaving of professional knowledge about Belinda Nicholson and her mother following Belinda's birth, it seemed that Alana had been under surveillance as a mother even before Belinda was born. For example, a security guard in a shopping centre reported that he had noticed Alana as 'pregnant woman (mother to be)', and that "she was drug affected as she was nodding off".

The decision to take legal action to transfer Belinda's guardianship from her mother Alana to the state came about when police notified Crisis Care workers that there were no suitable caregivers for Belinda when Alana went into police custody pending a court appearance for drug offences. Crisis Care workers gained Alana's permission to place Belinda in emergency foster care and to be checked at the children's hospital because she "seemed extremely small for her age and seemed to have laboured breathing and a temperature".

Following the examination of Belinda at the children's hospital, the Crisis Care worker reported:

> The Doctor said that she was undernourished [1] and appeared to have a fungal infection above the anal region [2]. It was also unclear as to whether Belinda was undergoing any treatment due to her mother's heroin addiction [3].

> The Doctor felt that due to Belinda being undernourished [1], having a fungal infection [2] and the lack of information on Belinda's medical history [3], that she should be admitted for observation [4]. [Hospital] awaiting contact from [maternity hospital] for any background information regarding Belinda's medical history. [. . .]

This medical assessment reported by Crisis Care workers shows the operation of a syndrome, by the combination of observed bodily abnormalities [1, 2 and 3] in the two excerpts above. One possible alternative of treating each abnormality as a separate problem with a separate meaning and solution does not appear in the text.

The Crisis Care worker's report continued:

> Crisis Care workers requested that Belinda not be returned to the care of her mother. A holding order was also discussed . . . The mother was notified verbally that the child had been apprehended because of concerns for its well-being . . . and that she could not remove her from [hospital].

The outcome of the medical examination of Belinda as a body of evidence was central in providing grounds to proceed with legal action under a child protection intervention. The initial involvement as a response to a 'temporary lack of suitable caregivers' for an infant was reconstructed as a more serious intervention ('child maltreatment – neglect'). This reconstruction set in train various processes by which Alana Nicholson would lose guardianship. The case was referred by the Crisis Care Unit to Urbania.

The initial social crisis, redefined as 'child protection', engaged a coordinated network of medical, social and legal practitioners and their respective knowledge to construct the "reasons for apprehension" of the baby as documented on file:

> Whilst in mother's care . . . found to be malnourished and not receiving adequate medical input; . . . separate reports . . . mother . . . using drugs . . . unable to feed Belinda properly; . . . on one occasion [was] found passed out by police . . . Belinda in her care. No other responsible adult . . . related to Belinda to provide adequate care . . .

Furthermore, the network of professional surveillance of Alana as 'mother' included selective knowledge from 'the past' to build a case for transfer of guardianship of Belinda from Alana Nicholson to the state:

> Worker: The hospital Social Worker . . . [maternity hospital] [1] [3] . . . [paediatric hospital] medical staff [1], . . . Police [2], . . . CIB [2], . . . they saw her nearly dropping her baby and not feeding her and the kid being underweight. . . . Crisis Care because they saw the baby and saw her [3] . . . we've got a *list of witnesses*.
>
> HD: All the official kinds of people, not somebody off the street . . .
>
> Worker: No *they were fairly reasonable witnesses* . . .
>
> HD: It wasn't . . . one event was it . . . it was a series . . .
>
> Worker: *They were different times*, . . . *a cumulative thing* . . . (emphasis added)

The accumulated medical [1], legal [2] and social [3] knowledge (Potter 1996) of the baby's body over time and place represented an uncontestable site of knowledge/power about Alana's competence as a parent/mother (Donzelot 1980, in Hirst 1981). The caseworker at Urbania told Alana that "[she would] lose this [case]".

Alana Nicholson could not resist the weight of constructed professional knowledge attesting to her as a 'neglectful mother'. Public responsibility for the 'care and protection' of Belinda Nicholson was primarily to ensure that the private responsibility by her mother was discharged within culturally acceptable standards that were set down by professionals representing social, medical and legal institutions.

This case has shown how cultural constructions of normal mothering are legitimised and implemented by professionals representing social, medical and legal knowledge. The 'child' may be objectified as a body of knowledge/body of evidence that is read as a commentary of a woman's competence as a parent, to the extent that the 'child' comes to represent a sort of mirror in which the competence of the 'mother' is seen. In the process, the identity of 'mother' dominates to the extent that the 'woman' and her needs are lost.

## NORMAL AND ABNORMAL MOTHERS – FOSTER MOTHER AND BIOLOGICAL MOTHER

The Quinn family's story was very complex and long standing. It presents many possibilities for understanding how the identities of 'child', and 'parent' as 'mother', are constructed, within particular meanings of 'child protection'. The case analysis below is taken from files and my interviews with the caseworker. It provides a glimpse into some very complex cultural assumptions and official practices, and their effects for this family. The case was also analysed in chapter 7, as an example of the contextual construction of identities of responsibility.

The two children involved as subjects of the incidents reported in the mid-1990s are the focus of this analysis: a girl, Susan, aged seven or eight years, and a boy, John aged five. The children's ethnicity was unrecorded, but I assumed this to be "(white) English" or "Anglo Saxon", because the file recorded that their mother, Louise, a "single parent", was an immigrant from England and their fathers were either English or "Anglo Australian".

### Achieving the care, protection and discipline of the 'child': Differentiating 'good mothers' and 'bad mothers'

In this section the analysis shows how actual people involved in a child protection case may come to represent cultural images of 'good' and 'bad' mothers. This case shows how a foster mother and the children's biological mother represented these identities. In constructing the respective identities of 'good (foster) mother' and 'bad (biological) mother', the children became bodies of evidence – not just as physical bodies that could be examined medically, but also as social bodies whose behaviour and its acceptability reflected upon the women and their competence as 'mothers'. In this case, child protection goes beyond the physical care and protection of children. The usually unspoken requirement that parents must also regulate/discipline children, 'tame the savages' (Jenks 1996; Prout & James 1990) and prepare them as "future citizens" (Rose 1989) is a feature of 'age and stage' theories of child development.

All the extracts presented are taken from the Particulars of the Care and Protection Application made to the Children's Court. The Particulars re-present previous documents and reports on file, interweaving them into a set of facts that compare the care of the children by their mother and by the foster mother. The official intention is to demonstrate that the children are in need of state "care and protection". In these documents, the '(biological) mother' and '(social) foster mother' are referred to as the "Respondent" and "Ms Pell" respectively, suggesting that Louise Quinn, the children's mother, is on trial and must 'respond to' accusers about her incompetence. In contrast, by identifying the foster mother by her name rather than an anonymous label, her official standing as a 'good mother' is affirmed.

The first extract shows how the 'child protective' strategy of placement with a single female foster parent is a commentary on 'normal' and 'abnormal' mothers. John Quinn becomes a site of knowledge/power, in which judgments about his behaviour operate as judgments about the competence of his mother and foster mother as 'parents':

> [Carer, Ms Pell] reported that John was *still* bed-wetting [3a] [//] *but that his behaviour on entering her home (urinating on the bedroom floor* [1], *soiling* [2a] *and smearing* [2b] *and writing his name in faeces* [2c] *on the bathroom wall and toilet seat) had improved when he had been told this was unacceptable* [3b] [. . .] [Ms Pell] reported no concerns about Susan [John's sister] . . . (emphasis added)

In this extract, the child John is the focus of the official gaze. However, he is simultaneously represented/read as a commentary on the contrasting competencies of 'biological mother' and 'foster mother'. Because of the parallel processes of identity construction, this analysis will be considered as two readings.

John's misbehaviour as a feature of expectations of 'age and stage' is represented by his failure to keep 'toileting rules', in terms of:
- the wrong time: "still" in relation to his "bed-wetting" (the "age appropriate child" of developmental psychology) (Rose 1989)
- the wrong place: "on the bedroom floor" in relation to "urinating", rather than a toilet,
- the wrong behaviour, set out in a three-part list (Potter 1996) [2a–c].

However, the foster mother, Ms Pell's description of John's extreme abnormality also constructs her identity as 'normal mother', contrasted with the 'biological mother' as 'incompetent'. Ms Pell's qualifier "still" in relation to John's bed-wetting is not just a commentary about John. Ms Pell is also commenting on her own 'competence' as a 'mother'. Whilst the bed-wetting is clearly inappropriate for 'age and stage' [3a], there is a complicated use of language to criticise John's mother's competence in raising him, and to praise Ms Pell's own competence in improving John's behaviour. Firstly, the apparently abnormal bed-wetting [3a] is followed by a contrast structure (Smith 1990a; Potter 1996) (in italics in the extract). This very complicated statement does several things. The conjunction "but" is usually used to express a comment that contrasts with a preceding claim in the same sentence. In this case, the "but" is related to the clause that John's "behaviour has improved" since coming to live with Ms Pell. Sandwiched between the "but" and the statement of John's improved behaviour is a three-part list (Potter 1996) of John's extremely abnormal behaviours [2a–c] when he first came to live with Ms Pell. These behaviours are attributed by implication to his mother's incompetence because they stopped as soon as he entered Ms Pell's care. Ms Pell indicated that she was able to achieve these "improvements" in John's behaviour by simply telling him what was "unacceptable" [3b]. The apparent simplicity of Ms Pell's achievement further underlines John's mother's incompetence because she was unable to undertake a simple parenting task.

In a second extract, an unnamed "caller" compared the "respondent's [Louise Quinn's] care of the children" and their care with the foster mother, "noting a change for the better in the children's behaviour".

> John . . . is 150% better behaved [1]. He does not throw tantrums [2a], head bang [2b], is not rude or aggressive [2c] and this is a wonderful thing to see [2]. Susan is 100% more secure [1] as she did not . . . know where her next 'feed' was coming from [3a]. She is able to relax now [3b]. . . and be a little girl [3c].

The strength of the caller's claims about the children's improvement since entering foster care relies on quantification [1] (Potter, 1996), and using examples of 'normal' 'good behaviour' expected from children in two three-part lists [2a–c, 3–c] to support these claims of improvement. John is now a 'disciplined child' [2], represented by a three-part list (Potter 1996) of "improvements" [2a–c], and therefore an achievement for the foster mother as 'good mother'. Susan is now the 'age appropriate child', dependent on 'adults' for basic survival, her "next 'feed'" [3a], she can 'be a little girl' [3c].

A case conference report incorporated the "caller's" comments, and recorded these comparisons of the apparent success of the 'protective' strategy:

> John whilst in the care of the Respondent soiled [1a], smeared [1b], urinated [1c], tantrumed [1d], was aggressive [1e] and non-compliant [1f]. Susan whilst in the Respondent's care had acted as caregiver to the children [2] and experienced chronic bed-wetting [3]. John and Susan's behaviour had improved markedly whilst in the care of Ms Pell. [4]. Susan has stated clearly she does not wish to return to the Respondent's care and has been anxious and scared [with this

> possibility] [5]. John has stated that he is happy where he is, *but wishes to return to the Respondent's care* [6]. (emphasis added)

A three-part list (Potter 1996) is a common rhetorical device to construct abnormality. In this example, a double three-part list (Potter 1996) emphasises the extent of John's abnormality whilst in his mother's care [1a–f]. Susan's abnormality in her mother's care is suggested by a description of an inappropriate role for her age and identity as 'child': "acting as caregiver to the children" [2] and with inappropriate consequences for her: "chronic bed-wetting" [3]. Statement 4 relies on the children's behaviour to compare the respective competencies of the two 'mothers'.

While Susan appears to express a preference for her foster mother's care [5], her brother John expressed a preference for his mother's care, rather diplomatically. This is reported as a contrast structure (Smith 1990a; Potter 1996), where John apparently links his "happiness" in foster care by the conjunction "but" to a contradictory "wish" [6]. However, possibly because she was older than John, Susan's wishes were privileged as expressions of the 'children's best interests'. The worker's description to me of Susan as "very articulate and mature for her age, and she knows her own mind and has been very clear from the beginning … about her mother, removing her from where she was" lends support for this conclusion.

Susan's "maturity" was used to support the case conference decision to maintain the children in foster care. However, the same description was used as further evidence of her mother's poor parenting. The caseworker told me that "part of the reason she's so mature is because that role was forced on her by her mother well in advance of her years".

## Constructing 'maternal incompetence'

Child protection in this case was a commentary on the '(biological) mother's' "incapability" in discharging the normal tasks of 'parenting':

> She was incapable of providing a stable and safe home for the children [1] who in numerous incidents over the years [2] … seemed to be neglected [3a] and were left uncared for [3b] and left alone [3c] …

Louise Quinn's "incapability" to meet the norm of "stable and safe home" [1] was built up by quantification (Potter 1996) of incidents too "numerous" to mention, and as an accumulation of such incidents (Potter 1996) over time [2]. Louise Quinn's incompetence is emphasised by a three-part list (Potter 1996) [3a–c].

However, her greatest transgression in not fulfilling her 'care' of the children was intensified by her abrogation of the role/identity of 'parent' ('mother'):

> The older girl was left in the role of mother [1] … when she was seven … [2].

> Part of the reason she's so mature is because that role was forced on her by her mother well in advance of her years [1] [2] and she was and acted as a parent to her two siblings [1].

First, Susan as the eldest 'child' was "forced" into culturally unacceptable identities of 'parent' [1] and 'adult' [2] where normally 'child' and 'parent', and 'child' and 'adult' are assumed to be mutually exclusive. If she was not forcing a parenting role onto her young daughter, Louise Quinn involved "other people", which transgressed the cultural expectation of 'mothering' as a private and sole responsibility (Fox Harding 1996) usually of a woman who is biologically related to the children in her care.

> [She] spent a lot of energy finding other people to mind the children [1], she spent very little time caring for the children over the years [2] and was consistently looking for respite care [3a] or organising baby sitters [3b] or leaving the children on their own [3c] . . .

Louise Quinn's preparedness to "spend a lot of energy [read as 'time']" looking for "other" child minders [1] is contrasted with her preparedness to "spend very little time [read as 'energy'] "doing so herself [2]. Her abrogation of her responsibility as child minder was demonstrated through a three-part list (Potter 1996) of 'how she spent her energy/time' as mother [3a–c] instead, which was considered to be inappropriate.

The children became bodies of knowledge that were judged in terms of 'normality', as 'civilised' and 'age appropriate' (Gittins 1998; Prout & James 1990), as a commentary on their mother's 'normality' as 'parent'. The yardstick for judging normality of children and their mothers relied on comparisons of "previous" (as 'past') with 'present', and as a predictor of the 'future', a version of the linearity of 'protective' outcomes for the "child as future citizen" (Rose 1989).

This case has shown how child protection discourse is an examination and differentiation between 'normal' and 'abnormal' 'children' and 'parents', primarily women as mothers. The objectives of protective practice contextualise particular dividing practices (Foucault 1977, 1980) by which discursive and cultural images of normal children, parents/mothers and families provide the template for the hierarchical examination and constructions of (ab)normality. Diffuse categories of 'risk' may rely on images of 'normal childhood, parenting/mothering and family life'.

## 'THE INTERGENERATIONAL TRANSMISSION OF SEXUAL ABUSE' – A CONCEPT AND ITS PRACTICAL MEANING

"The intergenerational transmission of sexual abuse" (Bagley 1991; Smith & Saunders 1995) is an influential concept in child protection policy and practice. It assumes that women's childhood experiences of 'sexual abuse' tend to determine how they will protect their own children, including giving access by 'dangerous men' to their children and 'choosing' those men in preference to their children. This assumption clearly influenced child protection practice with the Underwood family.

However, an exploration of the family circumstances, as documented on file and related to me in interviews with the caseworker, offers some insights into what this concept might mean in particular cases. The lived experiences of various family members, including the mother, Beryl Underwood and her children, tend to disrupt assumptions of maternal 'responsibility for child (sexual) abuse' that somehow are predetermined and inevitable consequences of childhood experiences. Instead, the analysis shows how identity and biography are not linear and coherent (Stanley 1992), such that there are deterministic consequences for the "child as future citizen" (Rose 1989). Instead, 'child sexual abuse' may be understood as a "(particular) politics of a (particular, heterosexual) family" (Stark & Flitcraft 1988) in which family-specific examples of inequalities of gender and generation are practised.

The Underwood family's case shows that the politics of each family is a particular set of identities and relationships of 'child' and 'parent'/'adult', embedded in different strategies of power and resistance, complicating official constructions of 'what happened' and identities of 'responsibility'. This aspect was explored in chapter 6. The case also allows comparison of differences in 'family' politics represented through the 'sexual abuse' of the 'children' and that of their step/mother Beryl when she was a 'child'. These differences also suggest that the identities of 'child', 'parent' and 'adult', and the meaning of 'sexual abuse' may be more fluid than assumed, as a feature of the particular 'family' context, practices and relationships. As known from the file, there were five children (ethnicity unrecorded): four girls, Madeline (9), Penny (8), Joanna (10) and Alice (5); and a boy Thomas (8). These children were "step" and "half siblings". Madeline and Penny were Beryl Underwood's biological children from a previous relationship; Joanna and Thomas were Steven Underwood's biological children from a previous relationship, and Alice was Beryl and Steven's biological child.

## The step/mother as 'victim of child sexual abuse'

Beryl Underwood, the step/mother of the five children identified as victims of 'sexual abuse', was 'sexually abused' as a 'child'. The "person believed responsible" was a biologically unrelated 'adult' male, Jacob, who was Beryl's mother's live-in partner (de facto). The culturally 'normal' relationships between an 'adult' and a 'child' usually constituted by biology (as 'parent'), or a social identity by which appropriate 'adult'/child' relationships are named – for example, step parent, aunt, uncle or similar – were absent in the relationship between Beryl and Jacob. In this 'family', age as a defining category for relationships was absent.

Instead gender and heterosexuality constituted the main relationships between 'family' members. Thus Jacob as 'male' (and an 'adult') had sexual relationships with Beryl's mother, a 'female' (and an 'adult'), and with Beryl, a 'female' (and a 'child'), apparently with her mother's knowledge.

These invisible, private practices may have remained so, except that the 'child' Beryl became pregnant at 14. The sudden visibility of her active sexuality through her pregnancy could have given her an identity of 'adult, female'. However, this identity was disallowed to the 'girl child' as defined socially and legally. Instead, as a 'girl child', her experience was constructed solely as "child sexual abuse" and "carnal knowledge". While the 'girl child' could be a 'parent'/'mother', she could not also be 'adult, woman'.

The man 'responsible' was jailed for 'carnal knowledge' ('child sexual abuse'). Teenage Beryl and her mother continued to visit him in jail. On his release, he resumed a sexual relationship with both of them, whilst living in their house. Beryl, the 'child/mother' now aged 15 or 16, became pregnant again.

There are apparent differences between the official and private constructions of 'what happened' to this 'child'. First, the 'child' Beryl and Jacob, the 'person responsible', gave different versions of "when it started". Beryl said she was aged 13 and Jacob said she was aged nine. This is all the more surprising as one would expect that there would be some agreement between those with "category entitled knowledge" (Potter 1996) as 'victim' and 'person responsible' about a potentially 'objective fact' of their relationship. However, the discrepancy suggests that what is and is not 'sexual abuse' may not always be shared by participants.

These events also raise questions about the meaning of "coercion/consent" of the 'child' Beryl (and her 'mother') in this particular 'family' (Stark & Flitcraft 1988; Forbes 1993; Bell 1993). Within stereotypical constructions of 'coercion/consent', the girl may be expected to state the younger age, emphasising generational inequality and her relative powerlessness. Similarly, the man's claim that Beryl was nine years old (rather than older) is surprising, given that he was more likely to suffer greater penalties for this. It also suggests that despite social, legal and cultural taboos on sexual relations between individuals called 'children' and those called 'adults', some private arrangements may not accept such institutionalised rules. This comment is not intended to advocate for 'child sexual abuse' but to raise critical questions for professional practice and how interventions might be made appropriately, especially when family members, including the 'child', may not perceive that there is a problem.

In Beryl's case, before she became Ms Underwood and 'mother' of several children in a blended family, these considerations were relevant to child protection intervention on her behalf. Becoming a 'mother' whilst still a 'child' was a marker of the illegitimacy of the sexual practices in which she was engaged as a 'girl child' with an 'adult man' and with her own mother's knowledge. Hence, the categorisation as 'child sexual abuse/carnal knowledge'. Social workers later involved with Beryl as a 'step/mother' and her 'children' drew on their assumptions about 'the intergenerational transmission of sexual abuse' by defining 'sexual abuse' the same experiences for every child in which sexualised body parts and particular are always involved, bu t with the context and nature of relationships disgarded. Thus, because Beryl had been 'sexually abused' as a 'child', it was concluded that her own children were also being 'sexually abused'. She was 'responsible' for the "generations of sexual abuse . . . in that family". In doing so, caseworkers did not locate Beryl's step/children's experiences of 'sexual abuse' within the particular politics of their 'family', in which Beryl, their 'mother', was now an 'adult female', not a 'girl child'. Furthermore, the children's father, Steven, was not held 'responsible' (culpable) nor was his 'intergenerational responsibility for sexual abuse' explored. Instead Beryl became 'responsible', while Steven remained 'invisible' (Milner 1993; Stark & Flitcraft 1988).

### The Underwood 'children' as 'victims of sexual abuse'

In Beryl Underwood's current heterosexual partnership, her children's experiences of 'sexual abuse', as told by them, were part of an overall context of adult male oppression and domination, which the caseworker called "terror". However, through "hierarchies of maltreatment" (Dubowitz 1994; Berliner 1994) manifested in the partitioning of the body to signify 'sexual' parts and 'non-sexual' parts, 'sexual' practices were given priority over 'physical' practices of domination and oppression (see chapter 6).

Power associated with 'parents' as 'adults' operated to suppress the children's experiences from being made known. It also limited gender solidarity between Beryl and her daughters, in relation to 'sexual abuse'. Instead, 'parental'/'adult' power reconstructed as "lies" Madeline's witnessed statements of her father's domination of her sister Penny: "finger in her privates" and "biting" her. Furthermore, Steven Underwood's domination of his family through "terrorism" and a system of surveillance discouraged the children from "talking about home" ("making disclosures") to anyone outside the family. For example, the caseworker told me about one of the girls who had been "removed [from home] for two weeks a couple of years ago . . . because she had a black eye and she [said] dad did it". She told the school, "I cannot talk to you again, I'm not allowed to talk about home". The caseworker's "feeling [was] that . . . she had been threatened in some way . . . this really nasty terror", because the child was "really afraid to talk about home and she's tried to stop the . . . siblings saying anything" by saying, "I'm going to dob [tell] on you". This child "did dob on [her brother Thomas] . . . and he ended up with a black eye . . . dad had given him because he talked about mum and dad rooting in the shower".

Each child responded very differently to the 'terror' they lived with. Madeline resisted by 'talking about home', increasing the public visibility of private practices. However, the caseworkers' apolitical construction of the heterosexual family intersected with their assumptions about a hierarchy of maltreatment (Berliner 1994; Dubowitz 1994). As the analysis in chapter 6 showed, through greater priority being given to 'sexual abuse', Madeline's siblings' experiences of physical domination and oppression were minimised as "not real serious disclosures" and therefore less worthy of protective intervention.

As can be seen from the above analysis of the Underwood's children's experiences that were categorised as 'sexual abuse', there are distinct differences between their experiences and those of their step/mother Beryl when she was a 'child'.

### The intergenerational transmission of sexual abuse – the girl child as 'victim', the girl child becomes an 'unprotective mother'

Caseworkers' assumptions about the 'intergenerational transmission of sexual abuse' and an apolitical analysis of 'family' relations also influenced their construction of the mother, Beryl Underwood, as 'unprotective'. The extract below is taken from an interview with the caseworker and a genogram on file:

> There are lots of reasons for mum staying with him and . . . if you look at the pattern with intergenerational abuse [1] and she's very dependent [2a], often in a relationship with people who dominate her [2b] and she hasn't dealt with her own sexual abuse issues anyway [2c] and doesn't realise or . . . believe that she's non-protective of her own children [3].

Beryl Underwood was constructed as an abnormal 'mother' in relation to her 'children'. She was 'responsible for their sexual abuse', as a consequence of her own similarly categorised 'childhood' experiences (statements 1 and 2c). Possible differences between her experiences and those of the children, including presence or absence, or extent of physical domination, were excluded. Statements 2a and 2b identify her as abnormal, 'adult female', "dependent" and "dominated". Yet her identity as 'adult female' and experiences of oppression are only relevant in constituting her as abnormal ('unprotective mother') (statement 3). There is no construction of adult males' power (Frost & Stein 1989; Stark & Flitcraft 1988; Featherstone 1996, 1997) and 'responsibility' for various forms of 'abuse' in either of Beryl's 'family' contexts: in her family of origin where she was both 'girl child' and 'mother' and in her new family arrangements as 'mother' and 'adult woman'.

While it appears from the file that Beryl Underwood did not experience aggressive forms of coercion as part of her childhood sexual relationship with the man Jacob, there was substantial evidence on file about her husband Steven's violence to her and their children. For example, it was known that Steven

Underwood had been convicted of a violent assault on another man. The school teachers were afraid of his "volatility" and avoided confronting him as much as possible. The female caseworker at Suburbia also experienced Steven Underwood's expressions of anger, as "storming out of the room", "slamming doors" and "doing a song and dance". The closest he came to physical violence to the worker was the symbolic "just about bit off my head". However, the caseworker, unlike Steven's wife and children, was able to resist him through her greater power associated with professional knowledge: "asking questions several times because she got [no] answer", and "just bringing him back [into the room when he stormed out]".

Yet the caseworker's experiences of Steven Underwood's power, expressed as physical aggression, did not increase her understanding of Beryl Underwood's daily, lived experiences with an extremely violent man. From an entirely child-centred construction of 'what happened' and identities of 'responsibility', Beryl was constructed as 'unprotective', while taking for granted Steven's dominance of his family:

> HD: Would mother say something different if she was interviewed separately?
>
> Worker: I honestly believe that if I did talk to mum I wouldn't get anything I could actually work with and I believe he wouldn't allow it to happen.
>
> HD: Will he not allow her to talk to anyone separately? She must be in a very vulnerable position . . .
>
> Worker: And it's very sad to watch her [. . .]
>
> HD: . . . How much freedom does she have to slip out and come and see you, or ring you up . . . how much does he watch her and control her?
>
> Worker: He's a very controlling person and very forceful, he's quite frightening.

In this case analysis, I have shown how identities of 'child', 'parent (mother and father)' and 'adult' may be differently constructed within the politics of the heterosexual family. While there are clear differences in power associated with gender and generation (age), the politics of the particular family may produce different experiences of these power relations and their outcomes for 'children' and 'parents', with different meanings of 'maltreatment (sexual abuse)'. This case shows how unitary constructions of the socio-legal child may need further exploration in regard to the 'relative' meanings of discursively problematised practices, and how 'children' resist and negotiate the power relations of their experiences. However, the thorny problem of 'children's' "consent/coercion" (Bell 1993) as the 'realist' dimension of generational inequality, expressed in some cases as 'sexual' practices between 'adults' and 'children', must also be explored. Furthermore, the category of 'sexual abuse' does not account for the variety of children's (and women's) experiences within 'the family'. The analysis also disrupts the linearity of maternal 'responsibility' associated with the 'intergenerational transmission of (sexual) abuse', and simultaneously challenges official exclusion of the adult male's biography in constructing 'responsibility' for oppressive practices.

## GIRLS: BORN MOTHERS; BOYS: MORE THAN A FATHER

The Turner family's case shows how the identities of 'mother' and 'father' are differently constructed in relation to the 'child'. The main theme could be encapsulated as 'girls, born mothers; boys, more than a father'. The case shows how an expectation of mothering as a preferred (or sole) identity for women seems to obliterate additional identities for women, to the extent that even their experiences as girls are seen as predetermining their competence as mothers. Every experience that Karen Turner had from childhood throughout her womanhood, pregnancy and motherhood became legitimate sources of evidence about her competence as a 'mother'. On the other hand, Greg Turner's competence as a 'father' was confined to his particular relationship with his child in the immediate family context.

The child Stanley, who became the focus of the risk assessment, was the two-year-old brother of a dead baby boy, Arthur, one month old at the time of his death. Karen and Greg Turner were the children's biological parents/caregivers. The ethnicity of family members was recorded as "Unknown" but possibly Anglo-Celtic or Anglo-Saxon Australian.

The main focus of the child protection intervention was to conduct a "risk assessment" to ensure Stanley Turner's safety in his parents' care. The risk assessment followed a report that baby Arthur had died as a consequence of his father's actions late one night, when he was feeding Arthur. The baby was screaming and, in frustration, his father shook him so severely that it caused serious cranial and spinal injuries and almost immediate death. However, Arthur's parents did not discover his death until the next morning.

### 'Parenting': gender and responsibility in relation to 'children'

Greg Turner "accepted that his actions killed [the baby]", and pleaded guilty to manslaughter. Doctors and police found evidence that corroborated (Potter 1996) Greg Turner's acceptance of guilt. However, the caseworker and senior supervisors at Suburbia doubted Greg's claims of responsibility for Arthur's death. Instead, at a case discussion, Greg Turner's "acceptance of responsibility" was seen as possibly "shielding the mother [from] her actions that led to the death of the baby. Was the father really the offender?"

In keeping with the suspicion voiced in the case discussion, the worker's risk assessment to ascertain Stanley's safety in his parents' care focused almost exclusively on Karen Turner. The 'risk assessment' assumed that Karen Turner's biological/reproductive capacity, constituting her as 'mother', would offer knowledge about her competence, and therefore 'risk' to the 'child' Stanley. However, Karen Turner's identity was not a simple biological and social relationship with her actual children. Instead, her entire life as documented in various official records in the child welfare department, the hospital and other organisations became an 'open book' in seeking to assess her competence as a mother on the suspicion that she, rather than her husband, Greg, had killed baby Arthur. The evidence of Karen's responsibility for Arthur's death would also indicate the risk she posed to two-year-old Stanley.

### The 'girl child' is the mother of the woman . . . and of her own 'child'

Karen Turner's official 'past', as a "long history of conflict with her mother", "alleged sexual abuse by stepfather, history of running away from foster placement, . . . ward 15 to 18 years" became a possible risk factor in her competence as a mother. However, the caseworker "didn't pick anything up that had alarm bells ringing that could be significant in the death of this baby". The assumption in child protection is that the 'past' is connected to the 'present' in a simple linear and deterministic understanding of life history and biography (Stanley 1992). This assumption influenced the conclusion that Karen Turner's teenage 'past' constituted her as potential and actual 'mother' (Cole et al. 1992; Casanova et al. 1994; Banyard 1997), a version of the intergenerational transmission of child abuse (Bagley 1991). The identity of 'child' is an abstraction when the future mother is still a child herself. However, there is an implicit cultural expectation that the girl child is being groomed for motherhood, as "the future citizen" (Rose 1989).

### The 'adult woman' as potential and actual 'mother' in relation to the potential and actual 'child'

When a girl 'child' reaches legal and social 'adult' identity as 'woman', the implicit expectation that she will become a 'parent'/'mother' continues. In Karen Turner's case, her identity as a woman is subsumed within judgments of competence as a mother. The 'child' is less of an abstraction, less of a potential purpose for a girl child/adult woman, but becomes a more tangible presence through Karen Turner's pregnancy (antenatal) and then more strongly, postnatal (Phoenix & Woollett 1991). Throughout these processes of 'becoming mother', Karen Turner is placed under professional surveillance (Lupton 1999b) to assess her competence as a 'mother' as the extracts below show.

A 'pregnant woman' ("antenatal") constitutes the 'child' as 'unborn', but no longer an abstraction, thus allowing official surveillance of the potential mother:

> She kept all her antenatal appointments and she was referred to the social work department which is normal procedure with any history of depression and chose not to follow that up. The hospital were saying that they wouldn't be concerned . . . because not everyone does.

Despite unresolved debates on the appropriate naming of the biological entity as 'child', for example in 'pro-life'/'pro-choice' campaigns or infertility treatments (Albury 1998; Charlesworth 1989; Moore 1996), the woman as mother remains a site of medical and social knowledge of 'future risk' to the 'unborn child'. As the worker explained:

> What are the factors we need to take into consideration that we didn't have knowledge of before Arthur's death, there were not concerns. I checked the hospitals, if she became pregnant again, if we were still involved . . ., I guess we would be a touch concerned and would probably monitor the situation quite closely.

The identity of 'mother' shifts again following the birth of the 'child' (as "post natal"), qualified by the number of previous 'children', and its association with 'risk'. This woman's identity as a 'new (first time) mother' [1] was compared with that of 'second time mother' [2]:

> I [worker] had a talk to . . . the hospital that Arthur [second child] [2] and Stanley [first child] [1] were born in, and the hospital was saying that they had not had any concerns [1] [2] and that mum had Stanley in hospital and she was on early discharge, but there was nothing on the file that was concerning [1] [3] . . . when she had Arthur and again with an early discharge [2] [3]. She filled in the self referral form . . . which is normal procedure at the hospital [4] . . . one of the questions, have you ever been depressed after the birth of a child and she said yes, after Stanley, [5] it was difficult to cope [5] and that . . . raised alarm bells in me [1] [5]; another question was that she had a difficult sex drive, a slow sex drive [6], and her doctor diagnosed her as depressed . . . with Arthur [7] . . . and she was on some medication [7], that's new information for us [2] [7].

With both children, the hospital "had no concerns". Karen had discharged herself "early", on both occasions, an unusual occurrence and implied indicator of "concern" (or "risk"). The contrast (Smith 1990a; Potter 1996) with "nothing on file" normalised this feature as specific to this mother [3]. Karen's completion of a "self referral form" was normalised as compliance with "procedure at the hospital" [4]. However, her potential risk as mother, in relation to the death of Arthur, her second baby, is suggested by the comparison of her as 'new' and 'second-time' mother. "Depression" [7] and "difficulty coping" as a 'new mother' [5] "raised alarm bells"; as did her "difficult" and "slow sex drive" [6], "depression" and "medication" [7] when her second child was born.

## 'Planned' and 'unplanned' pregnancy, 'wanted' and 'unwanted' children – assessing risk

The medical and social regulation of reproduction through "planned" or "unplanned pregnancy" (Gelles 1987a: 57) constructs the 'mother' as instrumental in achieving 'parenthood' for at least heterosexual couples, and their intent as 'parents' towards the 'child'. The child's corresponding identities as categories of risk are "wanted" or "unwanted" (Gelles 1987a: 57). An 'unwanted child' and an 'unplanned pregnancy' were predictors of higher risk (Gelles 1987a: 57), yet these simplistic categories were disrupted by the events in this family:

> Stanley [first child] was not a planned baby *and he was described by them as being the perfect child* [1] and Arthur [second child, deceased] was planned *and he was described by them as being a screamer [2]*. (emphasis added)

Each child's abnormality was a feature of particular cultural and private expectations represented as contrast structures (Potter 1996; Smith 1990a). The first child, Stanley, was "not planned" ('unwanted'), suggesting potential 'imperfection' and 'high risk'. Instead, he was "perfect" [1]. Conversely, the "planned" and therefore 'wanted [second] child' Arthur did not live up to private expectations – of cultural myths of planned pregnancies and wanted children, and his "perfect" older sibling. He was a "screamer" [2] and, by implication, a private disappointment whose tragic death retrospectively symbolised a public face of 'high risk'.

The "perfection" of the first child, Stanley, partly indicated that he might not be "at risk", and also that he was older and had survived beyond infancy:

> My [worker's] gut feeling after this amount of time is that Stanley is not at risk.

> Clearly Stanley is a special child in the family, where boys are generally a special child, labelled as the 'perfect child', looking at their coping, another baby that isn't screaming. [HD: Why is Stanley special, unplanned?] He ate, he slept, and he did all the right things, had a pleasant nature, eats and sleeps at the right times. *He wasn't planned, but he gave them no trouble* . . . (emphasis added)

## Risk assessment – family privacy and the myth of predicting risk

A fundamental assumption of risk assessment in child protection practice is that sufficient information can be gathered about family circumstances – identities, roles and relationships – to be able to predict whether or not the safety of small children can be ensured in the home. The issues explored so far in assessing risk to two-year-old Stanley Turner, following the death of his baby brother Arthur by his father's actions, show how suspicion and uncertainty about 'what happened' and 'who was responsible' is a significant part of the process. In particular, the mother Karen Turner became the focus of the risk assessment despite her husband Greg taking full responsibility for the child's death. This section shows how risk assessment is more to do with managing uncertainty (Parton 1998, 1999; Kemshall 2002; Joffe 1999) where the legal and social requirement is to respect 'family privacy', while effectively 'protecting' children. Much of what is 'known' by workers amounts to a guessing game and judgments about what is 'normal' in the particular family. In the Turner family's case, uncertainty about 'parental' roles and relationships and family circumstances influenced a decision that Stanley Turner was "at risk": ". . . We don't really know what happened, what was going on surrounding the death of the other child."

The worker's construction of risk was based on an assessment of the Turner family against what was considered 'normal', both culturally and also as expressed to her by Greg and Karen Turner, who had apparently accepted these cultural expectations of 'normal' families and parenting (Rose 1989):

> What they're saying is, we have this perfect relationship [1], we really support one another [2a], we work 50/50 [2b], everything's shared 50/50 [2c], yet mum does all the night time feeding [3].

The worker's assessment (above) acknowledges that the parents have an understanding of what is required of them as a couple and as good parents [1, 2a–2c]. Their idea of a (contemporary) 'perfect relationship' is one that is expressed in popular media, where there is an equal partnership in the parenting role. However, in the worker's assessment, expressed as a contrast structure [3] (Potter 1996; Smith 1990a), they do not have a 'perfect relationship' because, despite their claims, the 'mum does all the night time feeding'.

Furthermore, the worker's risk assessment considered that the mother's breach of her usual role in doing the night-time feeding may have contributed to the death of baby Arthur.

> And one of the questions I thought about [was], I wonder if anything significant happened, before giving that feed, on that night. Mum saying, I can't do this any more [1a], I'm going to bed [1b], you'll have to deal with it [1c], and he was angry [2].

The 'significant event' that the worker sought that precipitated Arthur's death was associated with the possibility that Karen Turner reneged on her role. Karen Turner's suspected 'responsibility' is constructed through a three-part list (Potter 1996) [1a–c] and its consequences, the father's "anger" that contributed to Arthur's death [2].

The worker's suspicion of the 'significance' of the night of Arthur's death continued, encapsulated in a single sentence:

> Everyone [1] making such a deal [2] about this one night [3].

A global category, 'everyone' [1], referred to the extended family as well as Karen and Greg Turner. The importance that they gave [2] to that one night [3] increased the worker's suspicions that the family was hiding something and therefore increased the possibility of risk to the surviving child.

### 'Risk assessment': patriarchy in practice?

'Risk assessment' is a central feature of contemporary 'child protection' practice. In this case, there are two main elements. The first element is about identities of responsibility. Despite the father willingly accepting responsibility for causing his infant son's death, child protection workers' suspicions brought the mother into primary focus as 'really responsible'. A significant amount of time in the risk assessment focused on the mother's personal history for clues as to her competence as a mother. Furthermore, the risk assessment also examined family relationships with the mother's transgressions of agreed roles as the main focus. Suspicions remained about her responsibility in precipitating events that caused her husband's expressions of anger and frustration that killed baby Arthur. The analysis shows how the identity of the 'child' shifts as a relationship with 'adult' and 'parent', and more specifically, 'man' and 'woman', 'father' and 'mother'. It is clear that the identities of individuals categorised as 'female' become not just 'women', but 'mothers', as a primary identity. There is little room for any identity other than girl/woman/mother, with the 'child' as an abstraction or as a physically real individual always present. For individuals categorised as 'male', there are greater options for identity beyond 'father'. As this case showed, despite the father being primarily responsible for the death of his infant son, the mother became the primary focus of attention and he 'disappeared' (Milner 1993).

## CHILD PROTECTION – ETHNOCENTRIC MEANINGS OF 'THE FAMILY'

So far in this chapter and indeed chapters 6 and 7, there has been a focus on how patriarchal mothering assumptions strongly influence child protection practice. The almost predetermined outcome in most cases is to construct the mother as equally or solely 'responsible' for maltreatment, while the man who may be actually responsible, 'disappears' (Milner 1993; Korbin 1989; Stark & Flitcraft 1988). The Park family's experiences show how patriarchal mothering assumptions may have a more complex relationship with the monocultural image of 'the family' within child protection discourse. The image of the 'normal family' tends to influence risk assessment and protective responses, whereby those considered to be 'abnormal' are constructed into a 'typical profile' of child maltreatment as a social problem. The focus solely on the child as a body of evidence of 'what happened' and associated 'identities of responsibility' takes for granted how 'normal families' ought to care for and protect the child. There are particular assumptions about members who constitute 'the family', and their roles and relationships towards each other and, particularly, the 'child'. The Park family's experiences of child protection intervention make explicit the ethnocentric constructions of 'the family' that influenced child protection workers. The files and interview transcripts are notable contexts for the experiences, practices and identities of members of the Park family, and a lack of awareness of alternative 'protective' responses.

The Park family, whose ethnicity was recorded as "non-Aboriginal", was from Vietnam. They had come to Australia as refugees from the Vietnam War. The constitution of this 'family' was exacerbated by experiences of being refugees and from a different culture, and was fundamental to the protective issues that precipitated child protection intervention. None of these contextual factors appeared to be taken into account in the intervention.

The school reported to Suburbia about eight-year-old Ho's:

> regular absenteeism at school (adopted father does not allow the child to attend school while the child loves to go to school). The child hasn't been fed . . . school staff are feeding him.

From intake, the case was categorised as 'child maltreatment – neglect' without an awareness of very complicated family circumstances in which Ho's relationship with his 'adopted father' was categorised as 'neglect'. The relationships in this family were complicated primarily by war and refugee status as the section below shows.

### Constructing the Park family

The story of 'mother', 'child' and 'father' as migrants and refugees has two overlapping versions that I am aware of. The first version [version 1] was told by a female Vietnamese teacher and recorded on file. A female Aboriginal caseworker told me the second version [version 2] when I interviewed her about the case. She became involved long after the initial investigation was completed by 'white Anglo-Australian' child protection workers.

Both versions give as context the separation of family members through the Vietnam War and subsequent movement as refugees and migrants. In this case, there is the existence of a previously unknown 'family member' (a child/young boy):

> [Mother and child] were sponsored by [child's] mother's husband . . . and her [adult] son . . . who were already in Australia . . . [version 1]

> What I know about this case is that the [husband] and some of his family came over to Western Australia first and left the mum back in Vietnam . . . and when she came over she had this young boy [Ho] with her . . . [version 2]

When Truc arrived in Australia, she sought to restore her relationship with her husband Huong after their long separation. As part of this process she needed to explain the existence of a child who was clearly not her husband's. In doing so, she attempted to reconcile potentially conflicting identities as 'mother' of a child biologically unrelated to her husband and yet remain a '(heterosexually monogamous) wife':

> When [Ho] was about two months old, his adopted mother . . . found him in a basket on [sic] her front door . . . She sought [sic] pity on [him] and brought him up as her own son [version 1]

> She told the father that somebody had left him on her doorstep when he was two months old, but the birth certificate says that she's the natural mum and it had father unknown . . . [version 2]

In both versions, the child is a relatively newborn infant, and represented as a 'doorstep foundling'. In version 1, Truc's identity as 'social' (not 'biological') mother is emphasised by the qualifier "adopted", and her relationship as "pity" for a "child", not as an intimate connection to an unknown adult male who is the child's "father". In version 2, the identity of social/adopted mother is contested by the legal identity of "natural (read as biological) mother", thus disrupting Truc's attempt to normalise and reconcile her identities as 'wife' and 'mother' in relation to a single adult male partner Huong as 'husband' and 'father'. The "unknown father" emphasised her transgression as 'non-monogamous wife'.

Truc's attempts to reconcile and represent two potentially conflicting identities to her husband Huong were unsuccessful:

> [Ho's] mother has been subjected to continual verbal abuse and misunderstanding from her husband about the origins of [Ho] . . . he criticised her [for] having previous affairs [as] the reason for the birth of his adopted son [1] [2] [. . .] . . . husband thinks [Ho] is a thorn in his life and a burden on his shoulders. [3] . . . [mother wanting] to divorce her husband in her choice between husband and son [4]. [version 1]

> So the father thought . . . she had this child through another relationship [2] and . . . that caused a lot of problems with mum and dad . . . there was a lot of domestic violence [1] . . . she was on the point of leaving [4] [version 2]

The focus of the husband's violence to Truc was her actual or imagined transgressions as 'wife', made visible by the 'child' Ho's existence [1]. Furthermore, the adult male Huong had no biological relationship as 'father' to the 'child' [2], and appeared unwilling to be a social parent [3]. The only difference is that in version 1, the relationship between the unwilling 'father' and his 'son' [2] is qualified by the adjective, "adopted". Truc was unable to reconcile the identities of 'normal' wife (as sexually monogamous) and mother. The violent relationship forced her to make a "choice" between her husband and her son [4].

However, before Truc could leave her husband, an intruder who broke into the house murdered her, leaving the child Ho in the care of the unwilling "adopted father". In this context of conflict about 'parent' and 'child' identities and relationships, an older son Tran, known as Ho's "adoptive brother", became recognised socially and legally as Ho's 'parent' through "legal guardianship". This newly constituted relationship complicated the family's existing biological and social relationships, intensified by the ethnocentric construction of 'protection'.

## Constructing 'neglect' and 'physical abuse'

In addition to the school's reports that Ho was absent regularly from school and was often not fed properly, child protection workers 'discovered' that Ho was also being 'physically abused' by Huong, his adopted father. Ho informed the workers who interviewed him that he was afraid of Huong, who used to hit him with a stick. It was clearly necessary to ensure that the child Ho was not being physically injured due to violence. However, the workers did not explore the context for the violence that had its origins in Ho being a child of his deceased mother's (suspected) extra-marital relationship in Vietnam. Furthermore, Huong's reliance on Ho to assist him at home because of his extreme ill health meant that he often prevented Ho from attending school. By taking a narrowly child-centred focus, Huong, as the "adopted father" ("parent"), was identified as 'dangerous', and a 'person believed responsible for neglect and physical abuse', who was unfit to care for Ho.

However, while the brother Tran, as legal guardian, "provided for daily needs including money, clothing, school lunches", he was unable to "interfere" with their father's "neglect" of Ho. " 'Father is the head of the family. They have to respect him.' [. . .] He had tried to reason with his father . . . regarding caring for [child] [without] success."

## A 'protective' response – disrupting the family?

'Protection' in this case may be seen as a disruption of 'the family', as this extract shows:

> Tran, by making such an arrangement demonstrated his commitment to the ongoing care of his adopted brother [1]. It does not entirely relieve him of the pressures of having failed to stay at home and take care of his father [as the youngest unmarried 'child' in his family, culturally is expected to look after his father] [2], but is certainly less problematic for him than remaining under one roof [3].

Ho was placed, with his "brother" as "legal guardian" [1], in separate accommodation, because Tran could not guarantee Ho's safety in the shared home with Huong, the 'father'. However, although less problematic than living together [3], the relocation intensified the conflict of identities for Tran, who was expected to fulfil certain obligations within a prescribed cultural relationship [2] as a "son" to his "father".

The precariousness of this 'protective' strategy that ignored the social and cultural context for the child and his family apparently could only be maintained by protective intervention described as a "buffer", a divisive force and a cushion to minimise family pressures:

> [. . .] Ho's circumstances have improved significantly as a result of Departmental intervention, *but it is important that we continue to be involved in order to provide the buffer against pressure which may be exerted on Tran. . . . to resume living in his father's home* [. . .] The only difficulty Tran identified was the pressure that he may come under to have his father return to live in his household. He knows that this would not be acceptable to the Department and will consult us if pressure is brought to bear on him. (emphasis added)

> Tran would choose the father over Ho because he's the father's natural son, *so we have to make sure now* . . . (emphasis added)

### Ethnocentric child protection

Experiences as migrants/refugees from long-standing and more recent sociopolitical upheavals in Vietnam and family separations were played out in this family. Yet these experiences did not constitute a context for exploration of the 'allegations' involving a 'child' and a male adult, identified as 'parent/person believed responsible', yet 'othered' as 'caregiver'. The complex naming of identities and relationships in this particular sociopolitical context called 'family' seemed to represent the confusion of the macro sociopolitical context in which it was embedded and produced.

'Protection' contributed to the disruption of particular social and cultural relationships. It did not address the complexities of contextual identities and relations that necessitated or initiated public intervention into that 'family' on behalf of a 'child'. Instead, 'child protection' was a set of culturally oppressive sociolinguistic practices of knowledge/power that in this case constructed 'adult' males as 'responsible for neglect'.

### CONCLUSION

This chapter has shown how the general categories of 'child' and 'parent' (and 'adult'), as lived identities of actual people, are particular to the contexts in which they are given meaning by the individuals involved, and in relation to particular experiences and circumstances. These insights challenge professional knowledge based on the profiles of 'victims of maltreatment' and their circumstances, derived from statistical aggregations of case information. Instead, the analysis offer a critique of the assumptions of statistical profiling that all children's experiences categorised as 'maltreatment' are exactly the same. More fundamentally, there is a critique that the identity of 'child' denotes a generalisable set of features and experiences that relate to any individual who is culturally, legally and socially defines as a 'child'.

Children may also be differentiated as legitimate subjects of child protection, particularly in relation to age and gender. Small children, regardless of gender, were seen as vulnerable and innocent and in need of protective intervention. However, gendering in relation to girls as victims and boys as offenders is simplistic, needing a more complex understanding of childhood and relationships between children, including coercion.

Additionally, this chapter has shown how the identities of 'child', 'parent' and 'adult' are constructed in relation to each other. Normally, no one can be a 'child' unless in a relation to a 'parent' and/or 'adult' as separate identities (Jenks 1996). However this chapter has shown that although a 'child' can become a 'parent' as shown in the Underwood family case study, this actuality immediately deems the illegitimacy of the two identities being occupied simultaneously. Furthermore, it is impossible for a 'child' to simultaneously be an 'adult', as identities allowed to those identified as 'adults' such as 'parenthood' are disallowed to 'children'.

The 'child' in child protection legitimates the access by public officials into the normally private domain of the family. Whilst the ostensible purpose of child protection intervention is to secure the well-being of children in the care of their families, the 'child' becomes a body of evidence that operates as a judgment of the competence of parents, particularly mothers: for example, the Davis, Eakins, Francis, Nicholson, Turner families. This feature of patriarchal mothering (Stark & Flitcraft 1988) that strongly influences how responsibility for maltreatment is constructed was discussed in chapter 7 and was again a key aspect of the relationship between the identities of 'child', 'parent' and 'adult'. In many cases it was difficult to separate the construction of the identity of the 'child' and its normality from that of the mother and her competence. This entwinement of the identities of 'child' and 'mother' was also a dominant pattern in the cases discussed in this chapter, particularly in cases categorised as 'neglect': for example, Kelly, Nicholson, Quinn.

Risk assessment relied on stereotypes of 'normal families' and 'welfare families' and the expected roles and behaviours of members of each 'family type'; as shown, for example, by the interventions in the Eakins and Francis families, the Quinn family, the Turner family and, to some extent, the Davis family. The Quinn family's case also showed how foster mothers embody 'normal mothers' and become the standard of competence against which biological mothers are compared. The assumption has been challenged that risk assessment is a rational and foolproof method of predicting risk and minimising harm to children. The case studies showed that risk assessment is built on uncertainty and uncritical generalisations about families and their circumstances, as a consequence of balancing 'family privacy' with 'child protection': for example, the Turner and Kelly families. Furthermore, risk assessment relies heavily on patriarchal and ethnocentric assumptions about the roles and responsibilities of family members. In particular, women's identities are so closely bound up with motherhood and children that there is little room for alternatives, whereas men have a greater range of options and their identities are more than 'just fatherhood': for example, in the Turner case. Whilst there was only one case involving a family of Vietnamese heritage (the Park family), the lack of awareness of cultural and political influences on family circumstances and allegations of 'neglect' emphasised the ethnocentrism of child protection policy and practice.

The chapter has shown that the privileged position of professional knowledge/power in child protection discourse takes for granted the cultural assumptions of normal identities of 'child' and 'parent' (mother and father) and family relations as heterosexual, Anglo and apolitical. In the next chapter I draw together the main points of the book, discussing the implications of unreflexive practices of knowledge/power for protection of children. The concluding chapter considers how cultural assumptions of normality influence meanings of 'what happened' to children and identities of 'responsibility' for those events. These processes of construction are embedded in taken-for-granted identities of 'child' and 'parent' (and 'adult'). Proposed alternatives juxtapose the 'realist' objectives of social work in addressing inequality, manifested as bodily abnormalities and represented as 'child maltreatment', with 'relativist' positions of the meaning of events and associated identities. The importance of reflexivity to achieve productive knowledge/power in child protection practice is also discussed.

# 9

# Constructing meanings and identities in child protection practice

This book has made a case for validating and supporting professional discretion, not as an unaccountable and "idiosyncratic" (Tite 1993) approach to child protection practice, but one that is critically aware of the assumptions of professional knowledge, its exercise through professional power, and the implications for people's lives. An analysis of 20 cases has shown how professional discretion is exercised in child protection work with children and families, as a process by which meanings and identities are negotiated outcomes of social interactions. Additionally, the analysis has shown the dynamic connections between professional practice and knowledge.

This analysis has relied on an original methodology that I have called a 'fractured lens'. The fractured lens, which I have constructed primarily from Foucault, Bourdieu and Potter's work, has centralised language in how meanings and identities are constructed, not just in each case, but within the different layers of social organisation that contextualise child protection practice. Language is a resource that represents knowledge and is also a device of power by which some versions of knowledge become legitimate and other versions are dismissed. A sociological analysis through social constructionism has shown how taken-for-granted knowledge in contemporary child protection is not an objective fact or an absolute truth and something that can be achieved by regulation of practice. Instead child protection knowledge is an outcome of negotiation of different meanings and versions represented in language that simultaneously operates as representational of knowledge and an exercise of power.

This analysis has extended similar sociological critiques (Dingwall et al. 1983; Thorpe 1994; Parton et al. 1997) of the assumptions in child protection that child maltreatment is an objectively 'real' entity, one that can be identified easily by knowledgeable persons. A social constructionist position takes the view that all knowledge is 'relative' and makes a somewhat contradictory assertion that there can be no absolute truths. Furthermore, knowledge communicated through language and images is a representation of 'reality', but does not reflect it as a direct, one-to-one correspondence. Representations of knowledge are relations of power; as struggles between competing versions of what is considered as 'legitimate' knowledge. However, as a social worker, it seemed quite problematic to take an entirely sociological approach, especially through social constructionism that can appear to trivialise children's very real lived experiences, including disadvantage, serious injury and death. Hence, through a "dualist" (Heap 1995) position I have sought to maintain a connection to the lived realities of children, whilst taking a sociological analysis of how these lived realities become problems of a particular kind and not another. This analysis also has explored how different explanations (as 'relative' meanings) of lived 'realities' become particular versions of truth and other versions do not. Thus, the analysis has held in tension the 'social' and the 'sociological' aspects of 'child protection' – on the one hand, as a necessary response to promote children's well-being and, on the other, as a process that is implicated in the relations of professional knowledge and professional power. The complexities of child protection practice have been represented by a recognition of the layers of social organisation that structure practice in cases, each layer itself socially constructed within a particular set of knowledge/power relations. Hence, 'literature', 'policy' and 'situated' constructions of meanings of maltreatment, and identities of 'responsibility', 'child', 'parent' and 'adult' represent networks of knowledge that influence each other and case practice in a dynamic way.

## CONSTRUCTING MEANINGS AND IDENTITIES: THE SOCIAL ORGANISATION OF CHILD PROTECTION

Social constructionism emphasises the importance of context in the construction of knowledge; in this analysis, of meanings and identities central to child protection. Hence, this research has focused on a particular legal jurisdiction, Western Australia, as a self-regulating organisational context. A "genealogical analysis" (Foucault 1971, 1980) of 'protectionist' policies in Western Australia that relate to 'children' has given insights into how policies may change, not as progressive developments but as political responses to various events, major and minor. The concepts of "epochal" (key events) and "epistemological" (ways of understanding and responding to key events) (Hassard 1993: 16–20) have been helpful in understanding policies as discourses, the example of Western Australia being illustrative of similar processes elsewhere.

The articulations of race-as-Aboriginality and gender in constructions of 'child protection' from the time of colonisation, through self-government, Federation and beyond, are meaningful only in Australia. 'Race' and 'gender' associated with 'child protection' in other contexts – for example, Britain or the United States –

must be understood within the particular historiographies and lived experiences of different populations; within different social, cultural, political and legal structures and agendas.

While an apparently globally shared and homogeneous discourse represented by 'the literature' appears to be unproblematically incorporated into local jurisdictions, this research suggests that global and local, however defined, must be held in tension, with one informing the other. A social problem, called 'child maltreatment', and a policy response, called 'child protection', need to be contextually reconstituted so that locally appropriate meanings and identities, and public responses, may be constructed, without precluding an international political agenda for children as citizens.

Policies are implemented in practice, usually by practitioners located at community-based offices. This research has shown how each office in the city environs, Urbania and Suburbia, as "linguistic communities" (Bourdieu 1991: 45) were different cultures. The construction of meanings and identities at each site as a linguistic community shows how policies may be interpreted but nonetheless be sufficiently like the prescribed version to be acceptable. At Urbania, one of the cultural rules was 'healthy debate', which legitimated relativism and individuals who overtly contested policy prescriptions, as well as those who complied with them. Debate was encouraged and individual strategies of resistance were overtly acknowledged. Furthermore, the possibilities for relative meanings that did not deny the realities of reported incidents were encouraged by policy changes (New Directions) and situated constructions of 'parents' and 'workers' as 'equals', expressed as 'there but for the grace of God go I!' These assumptions positioned 'child protection' as a necessary, but usually unlikely category of practice, so fear of 'mistakes' such as children's deaths/coroner's inquiries was managed within cultural rules.

At Suburbia constructions of 'parents' as 'dangerous' and 'out of control' elevated 'child protection' as a primary category of practice. Institutional prescriptions of how to see and say 'child maltreatment' were enforced, excluding alternative versions. Fear of 'mistakes' pervaded the site, which had previously been the subject of a coroner's investigation. Individual practice was regulated to prevent 'practice mistakes' – not just from concern for the child, but as 'protection' for practitioners and "the political arse" (field notes). The broader definition of 'child maltreatment' was part of 'defensive practice' (Sanders et al. 1999) to ensure nothing was missed. Individuals did not engage in debates about practice, unless their organisational statuses offset penalties for doing so. Debates were confined to and managed by coalitions.

The notion of 'practice consistency' tends to preoccupy administrators whose belief is that quality and effectiveness are related to uniformity and conformity. However, acknowledging that the cultures of practice differ may offer opportunities for dialogue about the assumptions and purpose of practice and the meanings of 'effectiveness' and 'quality'.

The analysis of each case as a separate contextual entity has also generated significant insights into the social organisation of practice. The overall pattern of practice was to 'prove' or 'disprove' official versions of 'what happened' and identify 'who was responsible', by "risk assessment". The official version had sole legitimacy. Alternative versions were incorporated into the discourse of 'risk' as 'lies', 'denial', or other abnormal practices by individuals whose 'self interest' cast them as 'dangerous', 'incompetent' or 'unprotective'.

This research also challenges assumptions that heavily regulated practice (Howe 1992; Walton 1993) will maximise 'correct outcomes', represented by statistical "consistency" (DePanfilis & Scannapieco 1994; Murphy-Berman 1994; Deisz et al. 1996; Mathews et al. 1995). Firstly, the prescribed 'stages of intervention' were not the same in each case. Reporting/intake, investigation and substantiation could happen simultaneously (Hamilton family); the outcome of an investigation in one context could be a report in another (Blake, Constable, Davis, Kelly and Nicholson families). The artificiality of recording as a 'report' only when a case comes to the attention of departmental child protection does not recognise the influences of the multi-staged process of 'reporting' through both public and private networks. This was the rule rather than the exception (Allston, Constable, Davis, Ibsen, Jones, Kelly, Lewis, Martini, Nicholson, O'Keefe, Riley, Underwood and Turner families). This process could offer the potential for multiple re-workings of 'what happened' and identities of 'responsibility', the 'child' and the 'parent(s)', before the 'case' is reported to the responsible department. Secondly, within the messiness of daily child protection practice, the myriad participants in each case who might or might not be engaged in the process, from 'reporting' through 'investigation' and an 'outcome', is also diverse and unpredictable. Thirdly, each case also shows different processes of construction within the chaos of practice, simply because the differences between each case precluded any other option. Some cases, for example, Francis, Martini, Nicholson and Riley, gave opportunities to glimpse the connections between different workers' perspectives and the potential for different practices and outcomes.

The analysis of each case as a separate entity shows that the categories of 'maltreatment' and identities of 'person believed responsible', 'child' and 'parent' gloss the diversity of private events, practices, identities and relationships. The cases also show that meanings and identities are specific to particular private networks, which generally offer alternative or parallel versions to the official version. However, the distinction between 'public' and 'private' meanings and identities is not clear-cut (Conte 1991; Ferguson 1997; Fischer & McDonald 1998). Some parents/members of the public apparently did engage with the so-called public discourse, through appropriate language and/or shared meanings of normal/abnormal parenting (mothering) (Ferguson 1997). For example, the representation of Ms Allston's categorisation of her report of her ex-husband's 'sexual abuse' of their daughter, and her ability to offer appropriate descriptions in support of her categorisation. Or Ms Hamilton, who was recorded as representing herself as a bad mother, which was uncontested by the female social worker with a resulting categorisation as 'substantiated emotional abuse' of the children. Or the strategic deployment of the language of concern for children by a (possibly malicious) male reporter to mobilise public scrutiny of Ms Kelly as a mother, and 'substantiation [of her] neglect' of the children. 'Children' who were 'able to speak for themselves' (Ferguson 1997), rather than 'adults' reporting on their behalf, were able to engage child protection services: for example Petra Blake, Laurel Gilman, Judith Ibsen, Teresa and Melissa Jones, the Lewis and Underwood children, receiving 'protective' services with varying degrees of effectiveness.

The key features of 'child protection' are the identification of 'type of maltreatment', 'person believed responsible' and the identity of the 'child'. These three features are defined in literature and policy and have particular practical constructions in each case. Outcomes of each case are aggregated and represented as statistical profiles that contribute to policy and professional knowledge about 'child maltreatment' and 'child protection'. The construction of these three elements as meanings and identities is discussed below.

## CONSTRUCTING MEANINGS IN CHILD PROTECTION PRACTICE

Definitions of 'types of maltreatment' in literature and policy associate physical bodies with particular problematic practices and outcomes manifested in the child's body. Through categorisation, a word, concept or category represents 'something' and the associated definition draws the boundaries of what the category means and what is excluded, and how to make a case in support of a particular category (Potter 1996; Smith 1990a). Categorisation as a process and a linguistic practice has been explored in chapter 6, showing how reports that 'something happened' to a child are transformed into 'maltreatment' (or not) of a particular 'type': for example, 'sexual abuse' in the Allston and Constable cases, and 'physical abuse' in the Francis case.

The general category, 'child maltreatment', does not take into account the specific and diverse contexts in which such practices occur. Contexts did influence the extent of surveillance and normalising strategies – for example, in relation to the Davis, Gilman, Ibsen and O'Keefe families – but rarely reconstructed 'what happened' as 'something other than maltreatment'. However, there were some exceptions.

The report that used extreme language to describe 'what happened' to Murray Francis was transformed by information about a context of parent/child interaction, and was categorised as 'unsubstantiated', although Murray Francis was 'at risk'. A report about six-year-old Simon Martini as a 'perpetrator of sexual abuse' against another six-year-old boy relied on context that transformed the focus of the investigation. The worker disagreed with identification of a six-year-old boy as a 'perpetrator', instead repositioning him as a 'possible victim of someone else'. The outcome was 'unsubstantiated' with no 'person believed responsible'.

'Types of maltreatment' are associated with body parts. The partitioning of the body intersects with an increasing emphasis on "hierarchies of maltreatment" (Berliner 1994; Dubowitz 1994; Janko 1994) which give priority to 'sexual abuse' over 'physical abuse', and 'sexual abuse/physical abuse' over 'neglect' and 'emotional abuse'. The case analysis also offers support for the claim of the "neglect of neglect" (Wolock & Horowitz 1984) due to a "hierarchy of maltreatment" (Berliner 1994; Dubowitz 1994; Janko 1994). The hierarchy of maltreatment was a cultural rule at Suburbia in 1995, and practised in relation to the Underwood children. The hierarchy of maltreatment was not expressed as a cultural rule at Urbania in 1995, and there was a cultural preference for only "hard end" (thus, fewer) cases (field notes) being categorised as 'child maltreatment'. Nonetheless this rule was practised in relation to the Jones children in 1995. The Jones and Underwood children's cases were discussed in chapter 6. Both cases were categorised as 'sexual abuse', despite the children's reports of a range of experiences of oppressive practices in relation to other body parts. Furthermore, these categories included as outcomes of 'substantiated maltreatment', call into question the meaningfulness of statistics representing 'types of maltreatment'.

The connections between definitions, body parts, hierarchies and processes of categorisation generate a circular relationship between formal knowledge and discourses, and social and linguistic practices. Expectations and prescriptions that certain 'types of maltreatment' are of greater importance than others create a practice context that maintains these priorities. The greater attention given in practice to particular 'types of maltreatment' that are then included in statistical profiles about the dimensions of child maltreatment continues to justify the formal hierarchies of maltreatment. Through this circular process, the discursive hierarchy produces a statistical hierarchy, which in turn justifies the claims of particular distributions of 'maltreatment types'.

The hierarchy of maltreatment associated with individual responsibility tends to exclude the complex problems of 'social class' and 'race'. 'Social class' is interpreted from the descriptions of recipients of 'welfare' or 'social security', described as living in poverty, or material deprivation relative to social and cultural norms. For example, no shoes, dirty clothes, in public housing, debts, unemployed, no toys, no washing machine in many of the families: Eakins, Francis, Hamilton, Ibsen, Lewis, Nicholson, Park and Underwood. 'Neglect', as a 'child maltreatment' category that encapsulates these 'class' distinctions (FCS 1996a; DCS 1992; Janko 1994; Thorpe 1994) is low in the hierarchy of intervention.

'Neglect' is also associated with 'Aboriginal' identity, expressed in cultural rules for practice and in the cases in various ways. Despite the claims in the literature that Aboriginal Australians are over-represented in child protection cases compared with their relative representation in the total population. (HREOC 1997; Thorpe 1994), this research has found rather more complex patterns that are possibly attributable to the cultural rules for practice and also practitioners' assumptions about child maltreatment and priorities. "Cultural relativism" (Channer & Parton 1990), as a form of reverse discrimination and its influences on exclusionary practices, may be one possible explanation. However, a "hierarchy of maltreatment" (Dubowitz 1994; Berliner 1994) and the "neglect of neglect" (Wolock & Horowitz 1984) were complicated by various other issues.

The first issue appears to be the problem of categorisation of 'Aboriginal' identity. As discussed in chapter 4, the categories available are 'Aboriginal', 'non-Aboriginal', and 'Unknown'. In practice, 'Aboriginal' people were not clearly identified in the client groups, much of this due to confusion about the categories, whether practitioners used the categories at all, and how they used them. The practical meaning of 'Aboriginal' identity may be contingent upon how workers choose from 'non-Aboriginal', 'Aboriginal' (Tyler 1993: 331) and 'Unknown'. For example, Alan Eakins's identity as 'Aboriginal' was related to his father's identity, whilst Judy Ibsen's ethnicity as 'non-Aboriginal' was related to her father's identity, not her mother's as 'Aboriginal'. There was also considerable confusion about the mother's ethnicity. She was initially identified as 'Polynesian'. Furthermore, with the Davis and Eakins families, despite identification as 'Aboriginal' in 'high priority' cases ('physical abuse' and 'sexual abuse', respectively), 'Aboriginal' identity did not seem to influence case practice significantly. In two 'high priority' cases categorised as 'physical abuse', the family's/child's ethnic identity either was not formally recorded, being only mentioned to me by the worker (Gilman family), or read as part of the file notes (Francis family).

In addition to how 'Aboriginal' identity is categorised in practice, situated cultural rules at practice sites supported practices where Aboriginal children and families experiencing material deprivation categorised as 'neglect' were less likely to receive services. This outcome was discussed in chapter 4 and is partially supported by Thorpe (1997). His "ranking of service distribution" (Thorpe 1997: 71) showed that of ten categories, organised by Aboriginality, family structure, service type and 'type of maltreatment', Aboriginal families came sixth and ninth, receiving home-based services for 'neglect' or 'risk' (Thorpe 1997: 75). In addition to the complex engagement with 'Aboriginal' children and their families in child protection practice, this research has shown how monocultural versions of "familialization" (Rose 1989) and family politics may influence case practices and their outcomes: for example, in the Park family (chapter 8).

Women as sole parents are over-represented as 'responsible for neglect' or 'emotional abuse' or for placing children 'at risk', as a consequence of class and gender assumptions (Thorpe 1994; Thorpe 1997; Smokowski & Wodarski 1996; Swift 1995; Janko 1994). This research has shown that categorisations of 'neglect' (Kelly and Nicholson families) 'emotional abuse' (Hamilton family), and 'at risk' (Quinn and Turner families) are less overtly associated with 'class' than with gender, as a consequence of "patriarchal mothering" practices (Stark & Flitcraft 1988) and the "cultural idealization of motherhood" (Rose 1989). Perhaps 'class' 'disappears' because it is so pervasive amongst the families who are reported for 'child maltreatment', and gender instead becomes the focus of practice as claimed in the literature (Swift 1995; Gordon 1986).

## CONSTRUCTING IDENTITIES IN CHILD PROTECTION PRACTICE

How are identities of 'responsibility' (chapter 7) and those of 'child', 'parent' and 'adult' (chapter 8) constructed in practice? Identity in the dominant discourse is fixed, unitary and transcendent, whereas the position taken in this research is that identity is fluid, multiple and contextual (Foucault 1972, 1980). Individualisation is a central feature in child protection, whereby "dangerous individuals" (Hearn 1990) can be identified and separated from 'normal people', allowing their "discipline and punishment" (Foucault 1977). Furthermore, child protection works by focusing on individual children as 'victims of maltreatment' that is defined as a problematic interaction between a 'dangerous individual' and an individual child, thus excluding a range of other forms of oppression and disadvantage that children experience.

### Identities of 'responsibility'

The 'person believed responsible' is seen as a 'direct cause of maltreatment' and "individual dangerousness" (Hearn 1990; Bell 1993). In practice, this is a simplistic category. Instead, what I call 'identities of responsibility' articulated within each case. These identities were associated with versions of public and private patriarchy (Fox Harding 1996), and constructions of the 'normal (monocultural, heterosexual) family' as egalitarian, rather than political relations between gender and generation (Frost & Stein 1989; Stark & Flitcraft 1988).

The assumption that a 'dangerous individual' is a fixed identity that crosses all contexts influenced the constructions of 'person believed responsible' in several cases. The man Russell's identity as 'person believed responsible' for 'sexual abuse' of Alan Eakins was constructed through the interweaving of his identities between a previously investigated and 'unsubstantiated' report of his 'physical abuse' of Murray Francis, and 'a third case'. However, whilst practitioners tried to convince the children's mothers that Russell was 'dangerous', the mothers had their own constructions of his identity influenced by their contextual relationship with him. Hence, in the adversarial relationship that claims only one truth, none of the participants was able to engage with the possibilities that their version of 'truth' could co-exist (perhaps uncomfortably) with other versions. Perhaps recognising the possibilities for competing or multiple versions of identity, their benefits and limitations could offer ways for constructive practice with children and parents, which the contemporary adversarial approach precludes.

Identities are situated and relate to the purpose of interactions. The Quinn case showed how in two different social work contexts, with different purposes and participants, the mother's identity was first constructed as 'deficient parent' ('not responsible for placing her children at risk'), and then transformed into 'person believed responsible'.

Rather than the taken-for-granted assumption in child protection that there is a single person believed responsible who can be identified, the case analysis (supported by policies and situated cultures) showed identities of 'responsibility' as a feature of articulating gender identities (Milner 1993; Stark & Flitcraft 1988). This research shows how these gendered identities of responsibility were outcomes of patriarchal mothering practices and assumptions of 'equality' between women and men as partners/parents. These practices and their outcomes differ in each case, as has been shown in chapter 7.

For example, Mr Gilman and Mr O'Keefe were reported as 'responsible' for 'hitting' their children and/or wives. However, in both cases, only the women/mothers were identified as 'person believed responsible for physical abuse', as 'cause' of the injuries to the children. Mr Gilman's 'responsibility' was not investigated, whilst mundane details of mothering made Ms Gilman more visible to public scrutiny. Her primary 'responsibility' for care/protection/regulation of children positioned her as solely 'responsible for maltreatment'. An apolitical analysis of the heterosexual family minimised the inequalities between Mr O'Keefe, Ms O'Keefe and their two children, which in this case was expressed as physical domination. Within a discourse of individual 'responsibility' and patriarchal mothering, Ms O'Keefe was positioned as 'responsible' and Mr O'Keefe became 'invisible'. The case also shows, as an example of "interlocking oppressions" (Yeatman 1995), how Ms O'Keefe's 'intellectual disability' exacerbated patriarchal mothering practices, thus constructing her as 'responsible' for 'physical abuse'.

The Ibsen case showed another version of identities of 'responsibility'. Mr Ibsen's strategic 'cooperation' with workers minimised his identity as 'person believed responsible for physical abuse'. Instead, the workers' construction of the heterosexual family as 'equal' relations between men and women repositioned Mr Ibsen as a 'concerned parent'. Simultaneously, Ms Ibsen's perceived 'equality' and expectations that she could 'stop the hitting', positioned her as 'unprotective' and therefore increased her 'responsibility'.

The Lewis case showed how a mother's identity as 'unprotective', and therefore 'responsible', was sufficient to construct a particular man reported as 'responsible for sexual abuse'. Heterosexuality as the norm underpins material relations between women and men. The 'unprotective' mother on social security attracts 'dangerous men' for financial and/or sexual engagement. 'Dangerous men' are then given access to the children through the 'unprotective mother'.

Mothers may be constructed as 'equally responsible', because patriarchal mothering allocates primary 'responsibility' for children to them, increasing opportunities for 'maltreatment'. With the Riley family, Mr Riley was initially identified as 'responsible for the baby's fractured arm'. However, the 'discovery' of 'multiple fractures' precluded a categorisation of 'accidental injuries' by social and medical professionals because each injury could not be seen as a separate incident with a different 'cause' as the police were prepared to do. Identities of responsibility were constructed within strongly contested versions of the meaning of 'what happened' to the child as 'accidental, not maltreatment', or 'non-accidental, maltreatment', and did not consider that perhaps both were possible. 'Responsibility' was reconstructed as both 'cause' and 'accountability' for bodily abnormalities defined solely as 'maltreatment'. There were suspicions that Ms Riley was 'responsible', but because neither parent would identify the other as 'responsible', or account for the injuries, both parents were identified as 'persons believed responsible'.

Finally, 'responsibility for emotional abuse', as it was constructed by Ms Hamilton and the social worker, is an examination by 'self' and others (often women) against the "cultural idealization of motherhood" (Rose 1989). The pervasiveness of cultural images of 'normal mothers' excluded alternative or parallel constructions of responsibility. Ms Hamilton's many problems were seen solely as risk factors related to 'emotional abuse'.

## Constructing the 'child', 'parent' and 'adult'

Contemporary child protection policy and practice construct 'the child' as a single, fixed identity, despite the age range from birth to whatever is legally, socially, and culturally prescribed. Furthermore, those defined as 'children' are assumed to be vulnerable and dependent "waifs", and simultaneously undeveloped adults or "savages" (Prout & James 1990; Jenks 1996; Scott & Swain 2002). 'Adult'/'parent' identities are privileged. Child protection discourse, which aims to reverse generational inequality by privileging the 'child', nonetheless maintains the contested relations between 'child' and 'parent'/'adult', with 'the state' as arbitrator (Fox Harding 1991).

The focus on how 'intrafamilial' identities and relationships are constructed in each case gives a different view of how constructions of normality and abnormality articulate with meanings of 'what happened' to the children and identities of 'responsibility'.

There were two cases that involved 'children' as 'victims of sexual abuse' and 'persons believed responsible': Petra Blake and her cousin Robert; and Simon Martini and his friend Henry Moore. The latter case has been discussed above in Constructing meanings in child protection practice, showing how the worker's reconstruction of the children's identities transformed the meaning of 'what happened', with consequences for what was investigated and its outcome. Petra Blake's case shows, in practice, dominant assumptions that 'children's' experiences, named in particular ways, are shared across contexts. These assumptions include that the child's experiences at one age are given the same meaning when they are reported as 'sexual abuse' many years later. There are questions about how practices between 'children' categorised as 'sexual abuse' may limit understanding of how both coercion and consent may operate in 'children's' "sexual play", making it difficult to distinguish from "sexual abuse" (Lamb & Coakley 1993). The case example also gives insights into how children's identities may be gendered, privileging the identity of '(female) child' as a 'victim of sexual abuse', but disallowing the 'protections' afforded to the 'child' who may be identified as '(male) person believed responsible for sexual abuse'.

The 'child' also represents a body of evidence, as a text from which to read 'types of maltreatment'. Additionally, as a body of evidence, the child also represents a commentary on the normality (competence) of parents/mothers. The Davis and Underwood families show how the dominant construction of the egalitarian (heterosexual) family and patriarchal mothering practices produce versions of 'responsible mothers', as 'unprotective', although the men's 'invisibility' may vary. Kathleen Davis's identity as 'unprotective' of her son articulated with her 'protectiveness' of her male partner. Workers' expectations that Ms Davis should/could 'protect' her son by regulating the man's conduct disregarded her experiences of his violence. Furthermore, her 'protectiveness' of him through her reluctance to identify him to the workers maintained his 'invisibility' to public regulation, simultaneously constructing her as 'unprotective' mother, and therefore '(indirectly) responsible' for 'what happened' to the child.

The Underwood case shows a different version of the mother's 'responsibility', through the discursive formation, "the intergenerational transmission of sexual abuse" (Bagley 1991; Gilgun 1991; Wurtele & Miller-Perrin 1992; Zuravin et al. 1996; Kreklewetz & Piotrowski 1998). There were two articulating versions of 'responsibility'. Firstly, the mother was 'responsible' for the 'transmission of sexual abuse' to her step/children, because her own experiences as a child, categorised as 'sexual abuse', were constructed as predetermining conditions for her children's experiences of their step/father's oppressive practices, also called 'sexual abuse'. The case analysis shows instead how 'child sexual abuse' is associated with the "politics of the family" (Stark & Flitcraft 1988, Forbes 1993, Featherstone 1996), and disrupts the linearity of 'intergenerational transmission' by showing how the politics of each family differs, including children's experiences of coercion/consent. The expectation that Ms Underwood could 'protect' her children from her husband's 'sexual abuse' (Donzelot 1980 in Hirst 1981; Stark & Flitcraft 1988) ignored his violence, described as "terrorism" within the family. The context of extreme coercion differed considerably from Ms Underwood's experiences of 'sexual abuse' in her family of origin, where 'coercion' and 'consent' seemed less clearly defined. This case also raises the question of why and how women are consistently held 'responsible' for men's violence to the extent that women's biographies are investigated for 'risk factors', whereas men's are not.

The 'protection of children' sometimes justifies public scrutiny of private relationships and identities that may otherwise be out of bounds. This feature was demonstrated in the Eakins and Francis cases, which were connected by the same man reported as 'responsible for sexual abuse' and 'physical abuse', respectively. The cases showed how the image of 'child protection families' constructs 'the child protection mother'. This identity constructs women's 'responsibility' as their 'willingness' to give access to their children by 'dangerous males', associated with assumptions about 'desperate (heterosexual) women' and 'welfare mothers'. Hence, workers concluded that the mothers Tammy Francis and Rosemary Eakins were unwilling to claim a close association with the particular man, partly to 'protect' their social security eligibility as sole parents, and partly to 'protect' their sexual interests by partnership with any man.

Both the Kelly and Nicholson families showed how 'mothering' is a private performance of competence conducted within the public space. Children, as bodies of evidence, offered a commentary on the normality of 'mothering'. Their mothers were 'responsible' as 'direct cause' of 'neglect'. The regulation of women as an intersection of private and public patriarchy is constructed in webs of public surveillance of the child's body as the primary site for knowledge of the mother and her regulation. Generalised images of 'children's vulnerability' position the mother as 'neglectful' if she transgresses prescriptions of "children's needs" (Woodhead 1990). Public 'responsibility' for children is limited to surveillance of private and individualised competencies, particularly women as mothers.

The Quinn and Turner cases show how the mothers are constructed as 'responsible' (abnormal). In both cases, the child represented a body of evidence of the mother's competence. Ms Quinn is compared with the foster mother, representing the 'normal mother'. Ms Turner's various life experiences are compared over time as an assessment of risk she posed to her children, while Mr

Turner's biography is of little interest, despite his claim of culpability in the death of their baby. Furthermore, Ms Turner's identity is constructed solely as a potential and actual mother, but Mr Turner's identity as a father is related only to a specific child and also more broadly than 'father'.

The only deviation from the almost overwhelming focus on women/mothers in relation to 'children' is the Park family. Their complex family arrangements and circumstances, related to cultural differences, immigration and refugee status, created the conditions for 'neglect' and 'physical abuse', but were not taken into account in the investigation. It is the only case where men were 'responsible' as carers and 'persons believed responsible' for 'neglect'.

The discussion above has made a case for professional discretion in child protection practice. The case analysis has shown that despite the assumption that increasing proceduralisation of practice is a guarantee of 'effectiveness', no amount of regulation can address the complexities of people's lives and the unpredictabilities of child protection practice. The assumption that tragic deaths and serious injuries can be predicted or prevented by procedures is not supported (Sanders et al. 1999), although many public inquiries do identify 'practice problems' (Parton 1991; Dingwall 1986; Sanders et al. 1999). The analysis of each case as a separate contextual entity has shown that practice is messy, unpredictable and complex. Statistics, which represent as factual accuracy the outcomes of child protection practice, the boundaries and dimensions of 'child maltreatment', and associated identities (Eckenrode et al. 1988; Finkelhor et al. 1990; Ards & Harrell 1993; Angus et al. 1996) are only vague representations of these complex and unpredictable processes.

The section below addresses an alternative to the administrative regulation of child protection practice. This alternative approach does not offer a 'solution' or a 'model' for practice, because theories and models can and do change, as do political and ideological agendas. Besides, I have no particular 'solution' for the complexity of practice, or the problems that practitioners grapple with daily. However, this research does suggest that practitioners are probably best served by adaptability, not by blindly following new approaches but by critically engaging with all approaches, espoused through formal theories and/or practice generated theories (Fook 1996, 1999; Sheppard et al. 2000). The approach explored below offers a way for practitioners to critically engage with 'knowledge', as a metatheory (Weinstein & Weinstein 1992), by addressing ontology and epistemology, which are neglected in social work theorising (Mass 2000). The concepts relevant in developing a metatheory of practice knowledge, which are discussed below, influenced my engagement with this research, which has been a dynamic process linking formal and emergent theories. Hence, they may also be appropriate as a way of enhancing practice discretion by offering an expanded repertoire for practice.

## REFLEXIVE AND REFLECTIVE CRITIQUES: LOOKING THROUGH A FRACTURED LENS

Reflexivity is an important feature of social constructionism, which recognises the positioning of participants as active agents in constructing knowledge. It is an ethical practice that requires each participant to continually critique how his/her positioning influences knowledge as an outcome of social processes that involve relations of power (Horsfall, Byrne-Armstrong & Higgs 2001: 11). The knower is therefore not a neutral and innocent participant (Hassard 1993: 16; Stanley & Wise 1993). Reflexivity has been central to this research and has been discussed in chapter 2, in reference to how this research was conceptualised and engaged with. In particular, the ethical and methodological position taken, of "dualism" (Heap 1995), which underpins the analysis, has emerged through a reflexive process (D'Cruz 2001) that rejects neither "realism" (associated with the risk paradigm) nor "relativism" (associated with social constructionism) (Edwards et al. 1995). The construction of my 'fractured lens', represented in chapter 2 as a neat process, is recounted elsewhere in all its messiness, as another example of reflexivity as a dynamic connection between knowledge and my place in constructing it (D'Cruz 2001). Furthermore, an organisational position in relation to policy as discourse has been addressed as both the "empirical" reality (Gergen 1989, in Hassard 1993: 16–17) of "epochal" events, and the "epistemological" approach to responding to these events as a political position. For example, mandates to respond to children's experiences of disadvantage and oppression, whilst engaging with "epistemological" perspectives, as how and why particular responses of a "fragile nature" (Hassard 1993: 20) are generated, reproduced and changed.

As discussed in chapter 2, this research has also relied on concepts related to 'research as knowledge/power in practice': namely, representation, the de-centred subject, *'différance'*, and "writing" (Hassard 1993). Combined understandings of reflexivity, representation, the de-centred subject and 'différance' influenced my engagement with the literature, policy documents, case files and interviews with key informants through "active interviews" (Holstein & Gubrium 1995) and the recognition of documents as "socially constructed realities" (Smith 1974). All these 'sources' offered representations of knowledge, not as an accurate reflection of 'truth' and 'reality', although from a dualist position the 'facts' of the case, particularly descriptions of children's experiences, were treated as 'real'. I also did not dismiss what I was told or read as 'merely representations', because it was necessary for me to engage with how knowledge was understood in the context. However, the differences in explanations of these experiences ('relativism') and how the 'facts' came to be constructed in particular ways was of interest to this research.

The case analysis has shown in some ways how reflexivity was practised, although there has been greater scope for such discussions elsewhere (D'Cruz

2000, 2002a). I took on the identity of 'curious inquirer', expecting the theoretical position I espoused to be challenged even in my own mind. I also engaged with the social constructionist approach, imagining myself trying to justify the process and outcomes to an entirely hostile audience.

Whilst the new theoretical language influenced how I read the texts (including transcripts) and engaged with informants, relativism was a more important influence as a constructive deployment of knowledge/power. My interpretation was not particularly privileged (was de-centred), and this allowed me to engage with other versions (as *'différance'*), without necessarily accepting them. I tried to understand why and how the other version(s) might be 'true' for the person offering them, and what the limitations of each version might be. Also, I explored whether or not it was possible to hold many versions at the same time, and what the benefits and limitations of this approach might be. Even in my own mind there was a political engagement of different versions, with me trying to shift to each position and understand it as if it were my own. I also scrutinised my emotional, ethical and intellectual agreement with, and resistance to, different versions. For example, the analysis of "categorization" (Potter 1996; Smith 1990a), as a way of seeing children's bodies and a rhetorical device in constructing meanings (chapter 6), highlighted the problems of realism/relativism. For example, Jane Allston and Mary Constable's cases show how categorisation as 'sexual abuse' excluded other (including parallel) possibilities, although eventually 'substantiated' by medical technologies, which the social domain could not do 'conclusively'. The conflict I faced was a dismissal of medical knowledge as 'merely' an outcome of 'categorisation' (as a way of seeing and naming 'what happened'), with the potential for dismissing the child's 'real' experience. However, in my reading of the file and transcripts, practices of categorisation clearly excluded other possibilities as explanations in addition to 'sexual abuse', and so perhaps are also problematic for the narrowness of defining 'what happened to a child'.

I was obliged to engage with the common vocabulary of child protection, even when I wanted to contest what I saw/heard. For example, my critical questions emerged from how I saw/read/heard? through my fractured lens (the visual metaphor falls down here!), but I had to translate these questions into a shared vocabulary through "active interviews" (Holstein & Gubrium 1995) with practitioners. The possibilities for 'misunderstanding' 'questions' and 'answers' are enormous, opening up debates about knowledge claims. Allowing multiple versions was not always easy to do. When I realised I was 'taking sides' (even in my own head) in regard to a particular version, I would reflect on my assumptions in that moment and generate possible explanations for my reactions. This was particularly easy to do if I was just a curious inquirer, focusing on how different versions were legitimated or not by different rhetorical devices. However, this fascinating intellectual engagement still challenged me to include the ethical and legal imperatives of child protection practice, through an emotional connection. My concerns remained for children where there were reports of extreme practices and/or tragic outcomes, or where they lived in materially deprived conditions. Mitigating circumstances for extreme parenting did not alleviate these concerns. At other times I was angry and frustrated with practitioners whose practices seemed unjustifiable or unnecessarily oppressive: for example with the Davis, Hamilton, Park and Riley families. 'Protective' practice seemed to be surveillance and policing, with little regard for children's material and power inequalities, nor for the problems of parenting. However, a continuing focus on the child's experiences as reported provided an ethical compass for engaging with difference. For example, through "active interviews" (Holstein & Gubrium 1995) with key informants, I posed questions as a naïve inquirer, seeking to discover their views while being aware of my own and the possibilities for disruption that entailed. When reading the files or transcripts, I took on the identity of 'practitioner', imagining alternative ways of engaging with different perspectives or strategies of resistance. I also reflected on ways in which I might transform resistance into a productive deployment of knowledge/power on behalf of the child. Gergen (1989, in Hassard 1993: 19) suggests that engagement with knowledge as representations is with "pragmatic implications" (consequences), not with the "truth value" of claims, which cannot be resolved easily because of strongly held ideological positions.

Nonetheless, I was removed from the uncertainties and imperatives of daily child protection practice, and was engaging with these cases retrospectively. I did not have to make almost immediate decisions about the future safety and well-being of often, small children, when intellectual interest in different versions becomes a mere luxury, and a practitioner is obliged to choose 'who is telling the truth'.

The benefits of the approach taken are that it fosters an interest in perspectives other than one's own. It also encourages reflexivity, as an approach to practice that transforms the 'self' into both subject and object in the process of knowledge/power construction in practice. My experience of reflexivity is as an ongoing participant observer of mundane social interactions that nonetheless are complicit in generating the wider structural patterns of inequality (Young 1990). Thus, by questioning my own assumptions when I was dismissive of particular versions, I gained a greater self-understanding and an opportunity to explore other possibilities.

"Writing" is understood as a way of structuring knowledge as representations within space and time (Cooper 1989, in Hassard 1993) and from the positioning of the writer. This is an extension of the de-centred subject in which meaning is not a fixed and authoritative version. It is important for social work/child protection practice because much of what is legitimated as realist knowledge is written and read from files as "managed" versions and a "social construction of documentary reality" (Pithouse 1987; Cicourel 1974; Garfinkel 1974; Smith 1974). For example, the cases show that 'the full picture' from workers' investigations is usually incomplete and selective, but represented as coherent by piecing together disparate events/incidents, and sometimes even inter-weaving text from one case into another into a linear, chronological 'case history' (Stanley 1992). In several cases, I read such summaries, variously named as Summary of Previous History, Particulars in the Application for Care and Protection, Case Conferences and Case Reviews, and even intake and investigation reports (Allston, Constable, Davis, Eakins, Nicholson, O'Keefe, Park, Quinn, Riley and Underwood families). I wondered often in reading these versions of lives what had been excluded and whether and how it would make a difference to the image of abnormality represented. The pragmatics of practice are that it would be impossible to gather all relevant information, apart from more fundamental questions of what is 'relevant' and what is not. There are of course parallels with my own selective representations of the cases and themes. I have presented what I have considered to be 'relevant', along with my own constructions of processes and practices. However, what I have excluded is also important, and positions the reader in a particular way in relation to the analysis and the claims I have made. I could also argue that I did not selectively search the cases for themes to present. I am certainly not conscious of doing so. I know that many themes 'emerged' through multiple readings, but how I read cannot be separated from these claims of my apparently innocent readings. I do acknowledge my selectivity amongst the multiplicity of themes – and the cases I chose to represent them. However, the access given to readers of the case material offers opportunities for different readings and conclusions from mine.

My 'writing' about the contributions made by this book reflects the outcomes of seeing through a fractured lens, as what is/was seen and re-presented is itself fractured and lacking coherence around a single theoretical theme. The analysis of each case as a separate contextual entity has added to an overwhelming sense of incoherence, slipperiness and incompleteness (Linstead 1993; Marcus 1994). However, these apparently negative attributes underline the complexity and unpredictability of child protection practice, in which workers are confronted daily with diverse and multi-faceted events, practices, identities and relationships, which they are expected to reduce to a limited number of categories of 'maltreatment' and identities of 'responsibility'. The ever increasing "proceduralisation" and "bureaucratisation" (Howe 1992; Walton 1993) as organisational responses to 'practice inconsistency' (represented as statistical distributions) and 'practice mistakes' (children's deaths/coroner's inquiries) are instead an irrational quest.

## RECONNECTING THE 'SOCIOLOGICAL' TO THE 'SOCIAL'

This research has taken a sociological analysis from a social constructionist perspective that has sought to address how a social problem called 'child maltreatment' is constructed through social processes in which language is central. The sociological analysis has treated social processes as a topic for research, subjecting to critique the ethical, political and theoretical assumptions underpinning 'child protection'. In this section a reconnection is made between the sociological analysis and its relevance to the social dimension of 'child protection'. The suggested approach draws upon sociological concepts about knowledge and power, which have informed this research and have been discussed above.

The proposed approach explores how two potentially opposing sociological perspectives, the realist, risk paradigm, and the relativist, social constructionist critique, and related policy and practice philosophies could be integrated conceptually and in practice. The familiar practice parallel is described colloquially as 'the grey areas' in cases that are the rule rather than the exception, where practitioners can and do negotiate complexities of actual cases that do not fit easily within single policy categories. The proposed approach explores a way of combining in practice what are usually seen as mutually exclusive concepts, expressed as "juxtaposing seeming incommensurables" (Marcus 1994: 566) in post-modern thought (Hassard 1993: 19–23). The applicability of this approach has been demonstrated in this research by the concept of dualism (Heap 1995).

The critical question is how to incorporate and explore key features of apparently oppositional paradigms, that is, risk and social constructionism, to enhance practice options that take account of the diversity of children's experiences of disadvantage and of family life that do not necessarily conform to the standardised risk paradigm. Policy and practice informed by only one paradigm as a single preferred approach significantly narrows how the complexity of family life and the problems of child welfare may be perceived and responded to. The proposed approach considers the possibilities for understanding abstract and polarised concepts as two ends of a continuum that in practice may allow practitioners to position themselves somewhere along the continuum as they draw on the necessary concepts in various combinations for practice in specific cases.

### Concepts for critically engaging with professional knowledge: how we know what we know

It is proposed that concepts about professional knowledge for practice that are normally presented as mutually exclusive may be combined in practice as set out in table 9.1. Questions for practitioners would include 'In what sorts of cases might I work entirely from one position or another and why?', 'In what sorts of cases might I be able to combine approaches and why?', 'What may be barriers to working from one position or another and why?'

| Concept | Contemporary approach (risk paradigm) | Critique (social constructionism) |
|---|---|---|
| Expectations of practitioners; policy/practice paradigms | **Instrumental rationality**, rules and procedures | **Reflexivity**[1], reflection-in-action, critique of the self and position in relation to knowledge and meanings in the situation |
| Views of 'reality'[2] | **Realism:** objective and absolute facts | **Relativism:** different versions depending on the individual |
| 'Truth' and knowledge in relation to perceived expertise and authority (or perceived lack thereof) | Truth and knowledge as absolute, known by **experts**, **privileged** knowledge | **De-centred subjects and 'différance'**[3]: knowledge as contextual, separate knowledge from 'authority' of speaker; recognise **power** related to expertise |
| Views about 'knowledge' | Knowledge as **reflecting** reality, **neutral** | Knowledge as a **re-presentation**[4] of reality, legitimacy as a **political** process |
| Views about organisational policies and expectations[5] | Organisational policies as **'epochal'** – as **neutral** and reasonable, the only possible responses to key events | Organisational policies as **'epistemological'** – as outcomes of power and political agendas |

1. Hassard, J (1993) 'Postmodernism and organizational analysis: an overview', in J Hassard & M Parker (eds) *Postmodernism and Organizations, Sage:* London, pp. 1–23; Taylor, C & White, S (2000) *Practising Reflexivity in Health and Welfare: Making Knowledge,* Open University Press: Buckingham, UK
2. Edwards, D, Ashmore, M & Potter, J (1995) 'Death and furniture: the rhetoric, politics and theology of bottom line arguments against relativism', *History of the Human Sciences,* vol. 8, pp. 25–49
3. Hassard (1993) op cit
4. Hassard (1993) op cit
5. Hassard (1993) op cit

Table 9.1 Combining concepts about professional knowledge for practice

The possibilities for an expanded repertoire in relation to professional knowledge may also offer expanded understandings of key practice skills: interviewing and writing/reading documents (case files and similar). The approach proposed in regard to skills extends the idea of a conceptual and practice continuum.

### Reconstructing professional skills

The realist, forensic understanding of interviews and case recording in the risk paradigm is placed alongside the social constructionist understanding, represented by "active interviews" (Holstein & Gubrium 1995) and "socially constructed documentary realities" (Smith 1974). These concepts have influenced the research process and have been discussed above in relation to their application and their relevance in constructing knowledge. The interview process would recognise the need for legally valid evidence and allow for an active process between practitioner and client(s). This process could enhance the information gathered so that appropriate legal and social interventions may be implemented. Similarly, case records and other documents would be written in ways that appreciate the difference between observation/description and interpretation. Writers of documents would become more aware of the multiple ways in which 'facts' can be and are represented and the political agendas associated with 'writing'. Practitioners would be required to justify their practice as recorded and discussed by recognising their underlying assumptions for particular interpretations. As readers, they may also engage with official documents reflexively and with critical awareness (Stanley & Wise 1993).

This second dimension of the proposed approach for practice is set out in table 9.2. Questions for practitioners would include: 'How might I understand the interaction between 'reflecting facts' and "representing facts" in interviewing and case files or other documents?'

| Concept | Contemporary approach (risk paradigm) | Critique (social constructionism) |
|---|---|---|
| Skills: information gathering – interviewing | Interviewing in children's protection policy and practice is seen as an information gathering technique with an aim of meeting truth claims valid in law. It is based on a view of knowledge that assumes absolute truths, a realist version of reality and that 'professional' knowledge is superior to 'lay' or 'private' knowledge. From this perspective **interviews are forensic techniques**. | **The Active Interview**[1]: An alternative view of interviews as **'active'** is that they are processes of interaction between the 'interviewer' and the 'informant'. Therefore truth and knowledge are constructed in the process of the interview and there is no absolute reality. This position relates to assumptions about knowledge as relative and as versions that have gained legitimacy. |
| Skills: information sharing – case recording | Case recording, for example on files, is usually regarded as **absolute truths/facts**. This perspective is consistent with views of reality as absolute and information as facts to support dominant versions of 'truth'. | **Case recording as "documentary reality"**[3]: This is an alternative view of case records. It takes into account taken-for-granted influences on how case records are constructed. These influences include the particular requirements by organisations of what is relevant information, of what is told and how it is told, and what is recorded and how it is recorded. Therefore considerable information may be excluded and what is recorded is reorganised into an apparently coherent and chronological 'whole' **as if** it is an unbroken social history of a person or family[3]. |

Table 9.2   Professional skills: interviewing and case file recording

1   Holstein, J & Gubrium, J (1995) 'The active interview', *Qualitative Research Methods Series*, vol. 37, Sage: Thousand Oaks, California

2   Smith, D (1974) 'The Social Construction of Documentary Reality', *Sociological Inquiry*, vol. 44, pp. 257–68

3 Cicourel, A (1974) 'Police Practices and Official Records', in R Turner (ed.) *Ethnomethodology*, Penguin: Harmondsworth, pp. 85–95; Garfinkel, H (1974) ' "Good" Organisational Reasons for 'Bad' Clinic Records', in R Turner, op. cit, pp. 109–27; Zimmerman, D (1974) 'Fact as a Practical Accomplishment', in R Turner, op. cit. pp. 128–43

The expanded conceptual repertoire and associated skills are related below to roles for child protection practitioners. Drawing on Bauman (1987), practitioners with a legal, ethical, and moral responsibility for children, who must bridge gaps between 'public' and 'private' knowledge, may conceptualise their roles as "legislators" and/or "interpreters".

### Reconstructing professional roles

Professionals as "legislators" "make authoritative statements" and "arbitrate" in controversies about legitimate knowledge (Bauman 1987: 4). This role definition would be consistent with the existing and undisputed ethical, legal and moral mandates in children's protection practice, associated with the "empirical reality" of organisations (Hassard 1993) and the "realist" perspective (Edwards et al. 1995). However, an articulating identity, the "interpreter", shifts from "legislators" with "authority to arbitrate" from a position of "superior (objective) knowledge" (Bauman 1987: 4) to "facilitating communication between autonomous . . . participants. It is concerned with preventing the distortion of meaning in the process of communication" (Bauman 1987: 5). Interpreters work by "translating statements, made within one communally based tradition [that is, professional and organisational], so that they can be understood within the system of knowledge based on another tradition [that is, the family]" (Bauman 1987: 5). The interpreter role would be consistent with the "epistemological" (Hassard 1993) transformations in regard to organisational and professional knowledge, and the "relativist" perspective of knowledge (Edwards et al. 1995). These roles and their connection to the proposed approach as begun in tables 9.1 and 9.2 are summarised below in table 9.3 Questions for practitioners would include: 'In what sorts of cases might I be able to work entirely as a legislator and when as an interpreter?', 'In what sorts of cases might I be able to combine these roles and why?', 'What may be some barriers to working as either a legislator or an interpreter in different cases?'

| Concept | Contemporary approach (risk paradigm) | Critique (social constructionism) |
|---|---|---|
| Views about professional roles[1] | **Legislator:** professionals who "make authoritative statements" and "arbitrate" in controversies about legitimate knowledge. Professional knowledge is perceived as "superior and objective". Legislators work from formalised legal mandates. | **Interpreter:** "facilitate communication between autonomous... participants. [They] are concerned with preventing the distortion of meaning in the process of communication." This is achieved by "translating statements, made within one communally based tradition, so that they can be understood within the system of knowledge based on another tradition". |

1   Bauman, Z (1987) *Legislators and Interpreters: On Modernity, Post-Modernity and Intellectuals*, Polity Press: Oxford, pp. 4–5

Table 9.3   Expanded professional roles: legislators and interpreters

Interpreters' roles in making explicit the assumptions embedded in child protection discourse would not preclude their action as legislators in 'protecting children'. Transforming 'investigation' from a 'legislative' practice to an 'interpretive' and (inter) "active" process (Holstein & Gubrium 1995) would reconstruct interviews as an exploration of versions relevant to context. Ongoing questioning of, and reflexive engagement with, the contradictions of professional knowledge/power in practice would be integral to ethical child protection practice. Difference from an 'interpreter' position would be normalised primarily as opportunities for understanding. This would be one strategy in a repertoire that aims to maximise constructive deployment of knowledge/power on behalf of 'children' and their 'parent(s)'. Difference as a site of conflict, and oppressive and coercive relations, may be the last resort.

This re-conceptualisation of professional roles and discretion in child protection practice would not dismiss the very 'real' professional, organisational and political concerns for individuals called 'children'. Instead, a focused negotiation around the meanings of bodily abnormalities, and engagement with descriptions of 'what happened' to the 'child', would be central (Bauman 1987). An example of this is suggested by Gough & Reavey (1997), in which practitioners' engagement with parental narratives of "physical punishment" as "discourses of dis/empowerment" focuses on their "pragmatic implications", rather than their "truth status" (Hassard 1993).

The danger of stalemate associated with a multiplicity of relative meanings with potentially dire 'real' consequences for the child would be addressed by an explicit statement by practitioners to parents and children of professional knowledge/power and its purpose, as a practice strategy: for example, as argued by Wise (1985). Another issue to consider is the questionable value of adversarial relationships where the disputes usually relate to naming (categorising) 'what happened' to a child. If there is sufficient engagement about the contextual meaning linked to materially real concerns about/for the child as "pragmatic implications" (Hassard 1993), does it really matter if an injury through being hit is categorised as 'physical abuse' or something else, as long as agreement is negotiated that the practices ('hitting') stop?

It may be constructive to assume initially that the parent(s) also share concerns for the child's welfare, rather than positioning them immediately as adversaries, which is the current approach where the sole purpose is to discover a single, undisputed 'truth' and apportionment of 'responsibility'. Adversarial relations solely as 'legislators' escalate unproductive power/knowledge. Interpreters may engage with resistance – for example, 'distress', 'fear', 'denial', 'ambivalence', or 'transience' – as normal responses to the experience of the child protection investigation, its implications and repercussions, including threats to identity and destruction of personal networks: for example, the loss of children into care.

Ethical practice which allows working with contradictions rather than binaries or dichotomies (Berlin 1990) would problematise the apparent binary – for example, as 'person believed responsible'/'not responsible' – and allow multiple versions of meaning and identity which may give limited 'truth' to both 'sides' of the binary. The articulation of multiple versions could give opportunities for negotiated settlements with non-negotiables being the explicit expression of social work knowledge/power as advocates for less powerful individuals or groups such as children (Wise 1985). Accountability and ethical practice would be situated within the case (Wise 1995): for example, through "reflection-on-action" and "reflection-in-action" (Schon 1988), "critical reflection" (Fook 1996, 1999), "reflexivity" (Taylor & White 2000; Sheppard et al. 2000), and "dialogue" (Parton & O'Byrne 2000). The proposed approach may contribute to child protection practice that is accountable to the organisation (instrumental accountability) and to clients (substantive accountability).

The proposed approach outlined above is clearly extremely complex. Its appropriateness and limitations have been explored in collaborative research with government and non-government child and family welfare and child protection organisations in Victoria, Australia, in 2002 and 2003. The research, Developing a practice-generated approach to policy implementation, has been documented in unpublished reports to the participating organisations and practitioners/participants while the analysis of the extensive data generated is proceeding (D'Cruz 2002b, D'Cruz 2003; D'Cruz et al. 2002). An important outcome is that practitioners who have been key informants have appreciated the approach and its contributions and challenges to their practice. Early analysis indicates that practitioners have welcomed the possibilities for an expanded practice repertoire, although there are clearly interesting questions about the connections between 'theory' and 'practice' (Fook 1996, 1999).

However, the approach espoused here may be disrupted by legal expectations of establishing unequivocal 'truth' (Daro 1991; Morison & Greene 1992; Myers 1993; Kerns 1998). Protection of individual children's rights exacerbates the shifting yet conflictual relationship between state, parent(s) and child, and maintains the adversarial approach (Fox Harding 1991). Reconstruction of children's relationship to the state from paternalism to liberation as citizenship (Franklin 1986; Freeman 1983) raises other complex questions about the state's role in relation to the vulnerability of actual children, as opposed to theoretical critiques of the social construction of the 'child'.

Child protection practice as an ethical engagement and productive deployment of professional knowledge/power with 'children' and their 'families' is seriously limited within contemporary organisational and political/ideological economic neo-liberalism, of which privatisation is a central tenet. The ultimate expression of privatisation is the withdrawal of state/public responsibility for children, instead concentrating this within 'the family', and most especially the woman as mother, as "private and public patriarchy" (Fox Harding 1996). The transformation of 'the family' from 'private' to 'public' institution (Gatens 1998) would strengthen the perennial argument for better resources for all parents in caring for children, including income security, housing and child care (Janko 1994; Thorpe 1994). The contemporary role of social workers as social police could be transformed by reclaiming social work's emancipatory objectives, as political critiques of relations of inequality 'within' 'the family', and between 'the family' and 'the state'.

## CONCLUSION

This chapter has expanded on claims made with regard to the contributions of this research in support of practice discretion and the place of professional practice in relations of power and knowledge in the service of the state. Through a methodological fractured lens, and an ethical position that acknowledges both the 'realist' and 'relativist' perspectives of child protection practice, I have shown how language as symbolic representation, social practice and the currency of power is central to the construction of knowledge. The diversity and unpredictability of daily child protection practice is normalised as "creative confusion" (Gergen 1989: 26, in Hassard 1993: 22). An alternative approach informed by the ethical and methodological perspective taken has also been discussed, along with new research to investigate its appropriateness and limitations as judged by child protection practitioners.

# References

Abrahams, N, Casey, K & Daro, D (1992) 'Teachers' knowledge, attitudes, and beliefs about child abuse and its prevention', *Child Abuse and Neglect*, vol. 16, no. 2, pp. 229–38

Ackerman, P T, Newton, J E O, McPherson, W B, Jones, J G & Dykman, R A (1998) 'Prevalence of post traumatic stress disorder and other psychiatric diagnoses in three groups of abused children (sexual, physical and both)', *Child Abuse and Neglect*, vol. 22, no. 8, pp. 759–74

Adams, J A & Wells, R (1993) 'Normal versus abnormal genital findings in children: How well do examiners agree?' *Child Abuse and Neglect*, vol. 17, no. 5, pp. 663–76

Adams, J A, Harper, K, Knudson, S & Revilla, J (1994) 'Examination findings in legally confirmed child sexual abuse – it's normal to be normal', *Pediatrics*, vol. 94, no. 3, pp. 310–17

Agathonos-Georgopoulou, H (1998) 'Commentary: Future outlook for child protection policies in Europe', *Child Abuse and Neglect*, vol. 22, no. 4, pp. 239–47

Ajdukovic, M & Ajdukovic, D (1993) 'Psychological well-being of refugee children', *Child Abuse and Neglect*, vol. 17, no. 6, pp. 843–54

Albrechtsen, J (2003) 'The decade of squalor', Opinion: *The Australian*, Wednesday, 18 June 2003, p. 11

Albury, R (1998) 'The status of human embryos', *Journal of Australian Studies*, no. 59, pp. 129–38

Almqvist, K & Brandell-Forsberg, M (1997) 'Refugee children in Sweden: Post-traumatic stress disorder in Iranian preschool children exposed to organized violence', *Child Abuse and Neglect*, vol. 21, no. 4, pp. 351–66

Anderson, P (1989) 'The origin, emergence, and professional recognition of child protection', *Social Service Review*, June, vol. 63, no. 2, pp. 222–44

Angus, G, Dunn, C & Moyle, H (1996) *Children under care and protection orders Australia 1994–5*, Australian Institute of Health and Welfare Child Welfare Series no.15, Australian Government Publishing Service, Canberra, Australia

Arber, S (1993) 'Designing samples', in N Gilbert (ed.), *Researching Social Life*, Sage: London, pp. 68–93

Ards, S & Harrell, A (1993) 'Reporting of child maltreatment: A secondary analysis of the National Incidence Surveys', *Child Abuse and Neglect*, vol. 17, no. 3, pp. 337–44

Ariès, P (1962) *Centuries of Childhood*, Penguin Books, Harmondsworth, UK.

Armytage, P & Reeves, C (1992) 'Practice insights as revealed by child death inquiries in Victoria and overseas', in G Calvert, A Ford & P Parkinson (eds), *The Practice of Child Protection: Australian Approaches*, Hale and Iremonger: Sydney

Atkinson, P (1990) *The Ethnographic Imagination: Textual Constructions of Reality*, Routledge: London

Atkinson, P & Hammersley, M (1994) 'Ethnography and participant observation', in N Denzin & Y Lincoln (eds), *Handbook of Qualitative Research*, Sage: Thousand Oaks, California, pp. 248–61

Austin, J (1975) *How to do things with Words*, Oxford University Press: Oxford, 2nd edition

Australian Institute of Health and Welfare (AIHW), *Child Protection Australia Statistical Reports*, 2000–1, 2001–2 www.aihw.gov.au/publications/welfare.html (website accessed 21 July 2003)

*Australian Oxford Dictionary* (1988), Herron Publications/Oxford University Press, Melbourne, Australia

Bacchi, C (1998) 'Policy as discourse: What does it mean? Where does it get us?' presented to the *Postmodernism in Practice Conference, the Discursive Construction of Knowledge Group*, 25 February–1 March 1998, Adelaide, Australia, unpublished

Back, S & Lips, H (1998) 'Child sexual abuse: Victim age, victim gender, and observer gender as factors contributing to attributions of responsibility', *Child Abuse and Neglect*, vol. 22, no. 12, pp. 1239–52

Bagley, C R (1991) 'Preventing child sexual abuse: The state of knowledge and future research', in C R Bagley & R J Thomlison (eds), *Child Sexual Abuse: Critical Perspectives on Prevention, Intervention and Treatment*, University of Calgary Press: Toronto, Ontario, pp. 9–26

Bagley, C, Wood, M & Young, L (1994) 'Victim to abuser: Mental health and behavioral sequels of child sexual abuse in a community survey of young adult males', *Child Abuse and Neglect*, vol. 18, no. 8, pp. 683–98

Baker, M (2001) *Families, Labour and Love: Family Diversity in a Changing World*, Allen and Unwin: St Leonards, Australia

Ball, M D (1972) *The Alice Mitchell Baby Farm Case of 1907 as a Major Cause for the Establishment of the State Children's Department of Western Australia*, University of Western Australia, Perth, Western Australia, unpublished Master's degree thesis

Ballenden, N, Laster, K & Lawrence, J (1993) 'Pathologist as gatekeeper: Discretionary decision-making in cases of sudden infant death', *Australian Journal of Social Issues*, vol. 28, no. 2, pp. 124–41

Banyard, V (1997) 'The impact of childhood sexual abuse and family functioning on four dimensions of women's later parenting', *Child Abuse and Neglect*, vol. 21, no. 11, pp. 1095–108

Barn, R (1994) 'Race and ethnicity in social work: Some issues for anti-discriminatory research', in B Humphries and C Truman (eds), *Re-thinking Social Research*, Avebury: Aldershot, pp. 37–58

Barnum, R (1997) 'A suggested framework for forensic consultation in cases of child abuse and neglect', *Journal of the American Academy of Psychiatry and the Law*, vol. 25, no. 4, pp. 581–93

Barrett, M (1987) 'The concept of difference', *Feminist Review*, vol. 26, pp. 29–41

Bauman, Z (1987) *Legislators and Interpreters: on modernity, post-modernity and intellectuals*, Polity Press: Oxford

Bauman, Z (1991) *Postmodernity: Chance or Menace*, Centre for the Study of Cultural Values, Lancaster University, Lancaster, UK

Bauman, Z (1993) *Postmodern Ethics*, Blackwell Publishers: Oxford, UK

Baumrind, D (1994) 'The social context of child maltreatment', *Family Relations*, vol. 43, pp. 360–8

Bays, J (1990) 'Are the genitalia of anatomical dolls distorted?' *Child Abuse and Neglect*, vol. 14, no. 2, pp. 171–6

Bays, J & Chadwick, D (1993) 'Medical diagnosis of the sexually abused child', *Child Abuse and Neglect*, vol. 17, no. 1, pp. 91–110

Bean, P & Melville, J (1989) *Lost Children of the Empire*, Unwin Hyman: London

Beck, U (1992) *Risk Society: Towards a new modernity*, Sage: London

Bell, V (1993) *Interrogating Incest: Feminism, Foucault and the Law*, Routledge: London

Bendixen, M, Muus, K M & Schei, B (1994) 'The impact of child sexual abuse – A study of a random sample of Norwegian students', *Child Abuse and Neglect*, vol. 18, no. 10, pp. 837–48

Benson, D E, Swann, A , O'Toole, R & Turbett, J P (1991) 'Physicians' recognition of response to child abuse: Northern Ireland and the USA', *Child Abuse and Neglect*, vol. 15, nos. 1 and 2, pp. 45–56

Berlin, S (1990) 'Dichotomous and complex thinking', *Social Service Review*, vol. 64, pp. 46–59

Berliner, L (1994) 'The problem with neglect', *Journal of Interpersonal Violence*, vol. 9, no. 4, p. 556

Betz, P & Leibhardt, E (1994) 'Rib fractures in children – resuscitation or child abuse', *International Journal of Legal Medicine*, vol. 106, no. 4, pp. 215–18

Bhopal, K (2000) 'Gender, "race" and power in the research process: South Asian women in East London', in C Truman, D Mertens & B Humphries (eds), *Research and Inequality*, UCL Press, Taylor and Francis, London, pp. 67–79

Biskup, P (1973) *Not Slaves Not Citizens: The Aboriginal Problem in Western Australia 1898–1954*, University of Queensland Press: St Lucia, Queensland

Blainey, G (2000) 'Positives outweigh the negatives in the past 100 years', Speech given to the Samuel Griffith Society, November 2000, published in *The Australian* and reprinted with permission, www.mrcltd.org.au/uploaded_documents/MCR_News3_Pt6_Positives Outweigh Negatives.htm (accessed 14 June 2003)

Boat, B W & Everson, M D (1994) 'Exploration of anatomical dolls by non referred pre-school-aged children: Comparisons by age, gender, race, and socioeconomic status', *Child Abuse and Neglect*, vol. 18, no. 2, pp. 139–54

Bogdewic, S (1992) 'Participant observation', in F Crabtree & F Miller (eds), *Doing Qualitative Research: Multiple Strategies*, Sage: California, pp. 45–69

Bond, G R, Dowd, M D, Landsman, I & Rimsza, M (1995) 'Unintentional perineal injury in prepubescent girls – A multicenter, prospective report of 56 girls', *Pediatrics*, vol. 95, no. 5, pp. 628–31

Botash, A S, Babuts, D, Mitchell, N, O'Hara, M, Lynch, L & Manuel, J (1994) 'Evaluations of children who have disclosed sexual abuse via facilitated communication', *Archives of Pediatrics and Adolescent Medicine*, vol. 148, no. 12, pp. 1282–7

Bourdieu, P (1977) *Outline of a Theory of Practice*, Cambridge University Press: Cambridge, UK (translated from the French by Richard Nice)

Bourdieu, P (1990) *The Logic of Practice*, Polity Press: Cambridge, UK (translated from the French by Richard Nice)

Bourdieu, P (1991) *Language and Symbolic Power*, Polity Press: Cambridge, UK, (translated from the French by Gino Raymond and Matthew Adamson)

Bourdieu, P & Passeron, J-C (1990) *Reproduction in Education, Society and Culture*, Sage: London 2nd edition

Bowler, G (1995) 'New Directions in child protection and family support', *Focus on Families and Children*, (August), Family and Children's Services, Perth, Western Australia, p. 12

Boyce, M C, Melhorn, K J & Vargo, G (1996) 'Pediatric trauma documentation – Adequacy for assessment of child abuse', *Archives of Pediatrics and Adolescent Medicine*, vol. 150, no. 7, pp. 730–2

Boyden, J (1990) 'Childhood and the policymakers: A comparative perspective on the globalization of childhood', in A James & A Prout (eds), *Constructing and Reconstructing Childhood: Contemporary Issues in the Sociological Study of Childhood*, The Falmer Press: London, pp. 184–215

Brah, A (1992) 'Difference, diversity and differentiation', in J Donald & A Rattansi (eds), *'Race', Culture & Difference*, Open University Press/Sage: London, pp. 126–45

Brassard, M R, Hart, S N & Hardy, D B (1993) 'The psychological maltreatment rating scales', *Child Abuse and Neglect*, vol. 17, no. 6, pp. 715–29

Brayden, R M, Altemeier, W A, Yeager, T & Muram, D (1991) 'Interpretation of colposcopic photographs: Evidence for competence in assessing sexual abuse?', *Child Abuse and Neglect*, vol. 15, nos. 1 and 2, pp. 69–76

Brazier, J & Carter, J (1969) 'Coordination of social work services for the maltreated child in Western Australia', *Australian Journal of Social Work*, December, vol. 22, no. 4, pp. 14–21

Briggs, F & Hawkins, R M F (1996) 'A comparison of the childhood experiences of convicted adult male child molesters and men who were sexually abused in childhood and claimed to be nonoffenders', *Child Abuse and Neglect*, vol. 20, no. 3, pp. 221–34

Broad, B (1994) 'Anti-discriminatory practitioner social work research: Some basic problems and possible remedies', in B Humphries and C Truman (eds), *Re-Thinking Social Research*, Avebury: Aldershot, pp. 164–84

Bross, D C (1991) 'The rights of children and national development: Five models', *Child Abuse and Neglect*, vol. 15, Supplement 1, pp. 89–98

Browning, D C (ed.) (1978) *Roget's Thesaurus: The Everyman Edition*, Pan Books: London

Bryman, A (1988) *Quantity and Quality in Social Research*, Routledge: London

Burgess, R (1982) 'The practice of sociological research: Some issues in school ethnography', in R Burgess (ed.), *Exploring Society,* British Sociological Association: London, pp. 115–35

Burgess, R (1984) *In the Field: An Introduction to Field Research*, Routledge: London

Burrell, B, Thompson, B & Sexton, D (1994) 'Predicting child abuse potential across family types', *Child Abuse and Neglect*, vol. 18, no. 12, pp. 1039–50

Butler, J (1993) *Bodies that Matter: On the Discursive Limits of "Sex"*, Routledge: New York

Butler, S, Atkinson, L, Magnatta, M & Hood, E (1995) 'Child maltreatment: The collaboration of child welfare, mental health, and judicial systems', *Child Abuse and Neglect*, vol. 19, no. 3, pp. 355–62

Byrne-Armstrong, H (2001) 'Whose show is it? The contradictions of collaboration', in H Byrne-Armstrong, J Higgs & D Horsfall (eds), *Critical Moments in Qualitative Research*, Butterworth-Heinemann: London, pp. 106–14

Caliso, J A & Milner, J S (1992) 'Childhood history of abuse and child abuse screening', *Child Abuse and Neglect*, vol. 16, no. 5, pp. 647–60

Cameron, P & Cameron, K (1998) 'Homosexual parents – a comparative forensic study of character and harms to children', *Psychological Reports*, vol. 82, no. 3, part 2, pp. 1155–91

Campbell, B (1988) *Unofficial Secrets: Child Sexual Abuse, the Cleveland Case*, Virago: London

Cant, R & Downie, R (1994) *A Study of Western Australian Child Protection Data 1989 to 1994*, Department for Community Development, Perth, Western Australia

Carabine, J (1996) ' "Constructing women": Women's sexuality and social policy' in D Taylor (ed.), *Critical Social Policy: A Reader,* Sage: London, pp. 113–26

Carballo-Dieguez, A & Dolezal, C (1995) 'Association between history of childhood sexual abuse and adult HIV-risk sexual behavior in Puerto Rican men who have sex with men', *Child Abuse and Neglect*, vol. 19, no. 5, pp. 595–606

Carlson, B (1992) 'Questioning the party line on violence', *Affilia*, vol. 7, no. 2, pp. 94–111

Casanova, G M, Domanic, J, McCanne, T R & Milner, J S (1994) 'Physiological responses to child stimuli in mothers with and without a childhood history of physical abuse', *Child Abuse and Neglect*, vol. 18, no. 12, pp. 995–1004

Chandler, J (1990) 'Researching and the relevance of gender', in R Burgess (ed.), *Studies in Qualitative Methodology: Reflections of Field Experience*, JAI Press: Greenwich, Connecticut, pp. 119–40

Channer, Y & Parton, N (1990) 'Racism, cultural relativism and child protection' in The Violence Against Children Study Group, *Taking Child Abuse Seriously: Contemporary Issues in Child Protection Theory and Practice*, Unwin Hyman: London, pp. 105–20

Charles, N (2000) *Feminism, the State and Social Policy*, Macmillan: Basingstoke, UK

Charlesworth, M (1989) *Life, Death, Genes and Ethics: 1989 Boyer Lectures*, Australian Broadcasting Corporation, ABC Enterprises, Crows Nest, New South Wales

Cicourel, A (1974) 'Police practices and official records', in R Turner (ed.), *Ethnomethodology*, Penguin: Harmondsworth, UK, pp. 85–95

Cohen, H A, Matalon, A, Mezger, A, Benamitai, D & Barzilai, A (1997) 'Striae in adolescents mistaken for physical abuse', *Journal of Family Practice*, vol. 45, no. 1, pp. 84–5

Coldrey, B (1993) *The Scheme: The Christian Brothers and Childcare in Western Australia*, Christian Brothers Congregation: Argyle-Pacific Publishing, O'Connor, Western Australia

Cole, PM, Woolger C, Power TG & Smith, KD (1992) 'Parenting difficulties among adult survivors of father–daughter incest', *Child Abuse and Neglect*, vol. 16, no. 2, pp. 239–50

Cole, R (1991) 'Participant observer research: An activist role', in W F Whyte (ed.), *Participatory Action Research*, Sage: Newbury Park, California, pp. 159–64

Collins, M (2002) 'Home alone – worried children swamp headlines', *Sunday Mail* (Queensland), 6 January 2002, p. 1

Conte, J (1991) 'Child sexual abuse: Looking backward and forward', in M Q Patton (ed.), *Family Sexual Abuse: Frontline Research and Evaluation*, Sage: Newbury Park, California, pp. 3–22

Cooper, R (1991) *Technologies of Representation*, Department of Behaviour in Organizations: Lancaster University, UK, unpublished

Corby, B (1987) *Working with Child Abuse: Social Work Practice and the Child Abuse System*, Open University Press: Milton Keynes, UK

Coulter, K (1997) 'Physical signs of child abuse – A colour atlas – Hobbs, C J & Wynne, J M', *Journal of Developmental and Behavioral Pediatrics*, vol. 18, no. 6, pp. 425–7

Cousins, M & Hussain, A (1984) *Michel Foucault*, Macmillan: London

Crenshaw, W B, Crenshaw, L M & Lichtenberg, J W (1995) 'When educators confront child abuse: An analysis of the decision to report', *Child Abuse and Neglect*, vol. 19, no. 9, pp. 1095–114

Cumming, F (2002) 'IVF case bill A "disgraceful" waste', *Sun Herald* (Sydney), 9 June 2002, p. 26

Cunningham, R M, Stiffman, A R, Dore, P & Earls, F (1994) 'The association of physical and sexual abuse with HIV risk behaviors in adolescence and young adulthood: Implications for public health', *Child Abuse and Neglect*, vol. 18, no. 3, pp. 233–46

Currie, B & Brown, R (1993) *Child Protection Information System: State Report, Western Australia*, Department for Community Development, Perth, Western Australia

Dale, P, Davies, M, Morrison, T, & Waters, J (1986) *Dangerous Families: Assessment and Treatment of Child Abuse*, Tavistock: London

Daro, D (1991) 'Commentary: Child sexual abuse prevention: Separating fact from fiction', *Child Abuse and Neglect*, vol. 15, nos. 1 and 2, pp. 1–4

Davey, R I & Hill, J (1995) 'A study of the variability of training and beliefs among professionals who interview children to investigate suspected sexual abuse', *Child Abuse and Neglect*, vol. 19, no. 8, pp. 933–42

Davies, B (1991) 'The concept of agency', *Social Analysis*, vol. 30, pp. 42–53

Davies, C (1983) 'Professionals in bureaucracies: The conflict thesis revisited', in R Dingwall & P Lewis (eds), *The Sociology of the Professions: Lawyers, Doctors and Others*, Macmillan: London, pp. 177–94

D'Cruz, H (1993) *An Exploration and Description of Decision Making with regard to Child Protection at Duty and Intake in Northern Metropolitan Region*, Department for Community Development, Perth, Western Australia

D'Cruz, H (1998) ' "Taking responsibility" for "physical abuse": gender and disability', in *Proceedings of the Australian Women's Studies Association Seventh Conference*, Adelaide, South Australia, 16 to 18 April, 1998, pp. 18–27

D'Cruz, H (1999) *Constructing Meanings and Identities in Practice: Child Protection in Western Australia*, PhD thesis, Department of Applied Social Science, Lancaster University, Lancaster, UK, unpublished

D'Cruz, H (2000) 'Social work research as knowledge/power in practice', *Sociological Research Online*, vol. 5, no. 1, www.socresonline.org.uk/5/1/dcruz.html (16 pages)

D'Cruz, H (2001) 'The fractured lens: Methodology in perspective', in H Byrne-Armstrong, J Higgs & D Horsfall (eds), *Critical Moments in Qualitative Research*, Butterworth-Heinemann: Oxford, pp. 17–29

D'Cruz, H (2002a) 'Constructing the identities of "responsible mothers, invisible men" in child protection practice', *Sociological Research Online*, vol. 7, no. 1, www.socresonline.org.uk/7/1/d'cruz.html (19 pages)

D'Cruz, H (2002b) *Research on developing a practice-generated approach to policy implementation: end of project report (December 2002)*, unpublished report, Deakin University, Social Work

D'Cruz, H (2003) *Research on Developing a practice-generated approach to policy implementation: end of project report (July 2003)*, unpublished report, Deakin University, Social Work

D'Cruz, H, Gillingham, P, Christoe, D & Cuff, C (2002) 'Building bridges: a case study of collaborative research between "the academy" and "industry", "government" and "non government", "theory" and "practice"; and yet other unknown possibilities', *Working Across Borders*, Australian Association of Social Workers and Welfare Educators and the Australian Association of Social Workers (Western Australia) Joint Conference, 29 September to 2 October 2002, Perth, Western Australia (conference abstract, pp. 20–1)

Deacon, A (2002) *Perspectives on welfare: ideas, ideologies, and policy debates*, Open University Press: Buckingham, UK

Dean, J & Whyte, W (1978) 'How do you know if the informant is telling the truth?' in J Bynner & K Stribley (eds), *Social Research: Principles and Procedures*, Longman: London, pp. 179–88

Deisz, R, Doueck, H J, George, N & Levine, M (1996) 'Reasonable cause: A qualitative study of mandated reporting', *Child Abuse and Neglect*, vol. 20, no. 4, pp. 275–87

Delgado, W (1992) 'Self-reported childhood and adolescent sexual abuse among adult homosexual and bisexual men', *Child Abuse and Neglect*, vol. 16, no. 6, pp. 855–64

DePanfilis, D & Scannapieco, M (1994) 'Assessing the safety of children at risk of maltreatment – decision-making models', *Child Welfare*, vol. 73, no. 3, pp. 229–45

Department for Community Development (DCD) (1993) media release, *Newsflash: The Melissa Inquiry*, 12 August, Perth, Western Australia

Department for Community Development (DCD) (1993–5) *Annual Reports*, Perth, Western Australia

Department for Community Development (DCD) (1995) media release, *Newsflash: Reforms and New Directions for the Department*, 6 April, Perth, Western Australia

Department for Community Services (DCS) (1985–1992) *Annual Reports*, Perth, Western Australia

Department for Community Services (DCS) (1992) *Child Protection: A Guide to Practice*, Department for Community Services, Perth, Western Australia

Department for Community Welfare (DCW) (1973–84) *Annual Reports*, Perth, Western Australia

Department for Community Welfare (DCW) (1979) 'A history of the Department for Community Welfare', *Annual Report*, pp. 9–20

Department of General Studies (DGS) (1965) *Child Welfare: Outline of History of Department from 1907 to 1937*, Family and Children's Services, Perth, Western Australia (library)

Department of General Studies (DGS) (undated) *Child Welfare: Children's Courts, WA History of Establishment*, Family and Children's Services, Perth, Western Australia (library)

Department of General Studies (DGS) (undated) *Child Welfare: Review of Child Welfare* (Extract taken from *The Civil Service Journal*, Jubilee Number 1902–52), Family and Children's Services, Perth, Western Australia (library)

Department of Native Welfare (1965) *Instruction Manual*, Western Australia (loaned by J Priestley, Department for Community Development, Perth, Western Australia, 1993)

Department of Native Welfare (DNW) (undated, circa 1964) *Functions and Services*, Aboriginal Affairs Planning Authority, Perth, Western Australia (library)

De Swann, A (1990) 'Intimate relations and domestic arrangements', in *The Management of Normality: Critical Essays in Health and Welfare*, Routledge: London, pp. 182–94

Devaux, M (1994) 'Feminism and empowerment: A critical reading of Foucault', *Feminist Studies*, Summer, vol. 20, no. 2, pp. 223–45

Dingwall, R (1976) 'Accomplishing Profession', *Sociological Review*, vol. 24, pp. 331–49

Dingwall, R (1983) 'Introduction' in R Dingwall & P Lewis (eds), *The Sociology of the Professions: Lawyers, Doctors and Others*, Macmillan: London, pp. 1–13

Dingwall, R (1986) 'The Jasmine Beckford Affair', *The Modern Law Review*, vol. 49, no. 4, pp. 488–518

Dingwall, R & Eekelaar, J (1988) 'Families and the state: An historical perspective on the public regulation of private conduct', *Law and Policy*, October, vol. 10, no. 4, pp. 341–61

Dingwall, R, Eekelaar, J & Murray, T (1983) *The Protection of Children: State Intervention in Family Life*, Basil Blackwell: Oxford

Doek, J E (1991) 'Management of child abuse and neglect at the international level: Trends and perspectives', *Child Abuse and Neglect*, vol. 15, Supplement 1, pp. 51–6

Doll, L S, Joy, D, Bartholow, B N, Harrison, J S, Bolan, G, Douglas, J M, Saltzman, L E, Moss, P M & Delgado, W (1992) 'Self-reported childhood and adolescent sexual abuse among adult homosexual and bisexual men', *Child Abuse and Neglect*, vol. 16, no. 6, pp. 855–64

Dominelli, L & Hoogveldt, A (1996) 'Globalization and technocratization of social work', *Critical Social Policy*, vol. 16, no. 2, pp. 45–62

Donzelot, J (1980) *The Policing of Families*, Hutchinson: London

Donzelot, J (1988) 'The Promotion of the social', *Economy and Society*, vol. 17, no. 3, pp. 395–427

Doueck, H J (1995) 'Screening for child abuse – problems and possibilities', *Applied Nursing Research*, vol. 8, no. 4, pp. 191–8

Doueck, H J, English, D J, DePanfilis, D & Moote, G T (1993) 'Decision-making in child protective services: A comparison of selected risk-assessment systems', *Child Welfare*, vol. LXXII, no. 5, pp. 441–52

Doueck, H J, Levine, M & Bronson, D E (1993) 'Risk assessment in child protective services: An evaluation of the child at risk field system', *Journal of Interpersonal Violence*, vol. 8, no. 4, pp. 446–67

Downing, J D, Wells, S J & Fluke, J (1990) 'Gatekeeping in child protective services: a survey of screening policies', *Child Welfare*, vol. LXIX, no. 4, pp. 357–69

Doyle, C (1996) 'Current issues in child protection – An overview of the debates in contemporary journals', *British Journal of Social Work*, vol. 26, no. 4, pp. 565–76

Drake, B & Pandey, S (1996) 'Understanding the relationship between neighbourhood poverty and specific types of child maltreatment', *Child Abuse and Neglect*, vol. 20, no. 11, pp. 1003–18

Dreyfus, H L & Rabinow, P (1982) *Michel Foucault: Beyond Structuralism and Hermeneutics*, Harvester Wheatsheaf: New York

D'Souza, N (1993) 'Aboriginal child welfare: framework for a national policy', *Family Matters*, August, no. 35, pp. 40–5

Dubowitz, H (1994) 'Neglecting the neglect of neglect', *Journal of Interpersonal Violence*, vol. 9, no. 4, pp. 556–60

Dutt, R & Phillips, M. (1996) 'Race, culture, and the prevention of child abuse', in Report of the National Commission of Inquiry into the Prevention of Child Abuse,

(Chairman: Lord Williams of Mostyn), *Childhood Matters*, vol. 2, Background Papers, The Stationery Office: London

Eckenrode, J, Powers, J, Doris, J, Munsch, J, & Bolger, N (1988) 'Substantiation of child abuse and neglect reports', *Journal of Consulting and Clinical Psychology*, vol. 56, no. 1, pp. 9–16

Edwards, D, Ashmore, M & Potter, J (1995) 'Death and furniture: the rhetoric, politics and theology of bottom line arguments against relativism', *History of the Human Sciences*, vol. 8, pp. 25–49

Eekelaar, J, Dingwall, R & Murray, T (1982) 'Victims or threats? Children in care proceedings', *Journal of Social Welfare Law*, pp. 68–82

Elbedour, S, Baker, A M & Charlesworth, W R (1997) 'The impact of political violence on moral reasoning in children', *Child Abuse and Neglect*, vol. 21, no. 11, pp. 1053–66

Elbedour, S, Tensensel, R & Bastien, D T (1993) 'Ecological integrated model of children of war: Individual and social psychology', *Child Abuse and Neglect*, vol. 17, no. 6, pp. 805–20

Elliott, M (ed.) (1993) *Female Sexual Abuse of Children: The Ultimate Taboo*, Longman: Essex, UK

Elvik, S L, Berkowitz, C D, Nicholas, E, Lipman, J L & Inkelis, S H (1990) 'Sexual abuse in the developmentally disabled: Dilemmas of diagnosis', *Child Abuse and Neglect*, vol. 14 no. 4, pp. 497–503

English, D (1998) 'The extent and consequences of child maltreatment', *The Future of Children: Protecting Children from Abuse and Neglect*, vol. 8, no. 1, pp. 39–53

Everitt, A, Hardiker, P, Littlewood, J & Mullender, A (1992) *Applied Research for Better Practice*, Macmillan/BASW: London

Everson, M D & Boat, B W (1994) 'Putting the anatomical doll controversy in perspective: An examination of the major uses and criticisms of the dolls in child sexual abuse evaluations', *Child Abuse and Neglect*, vol. 18, no. 2, pp. 113–30

Ewing-Cobbs, L, Kramer, L, Prasad, M, Canales, D N, Louis, P T, Fletcher, J M, Vollero, H, Landry, S H & Cheung, K (1998) 'Neuroimaging, physical, and developmental findings after inflicted and noninflicted traumatic brain injury in young children', *Pediatrics*, vol. 102, no. 2, pp. 300–7

Facey, A (1981) *A Fortunate Life*, Penguin: Ringwood, Victoria

Fairclough, N (1992) *Discourse and Social Change*, Polity Press: Cambridge

Faller, K C (1988a) 'Decision-making in cases of intrafamilial child sexual abuse', *American Journal of Orthopsychiatry*, January, vol. 58, no. 1, pp. 121–8

Faller, K C (1988b) 'Criteria for judging the credibility of children's statements about their sexual abuse', *Child Welfare*, September–October, vol. LXVII, no. 5, pp. 389–401

Family and Children's Services (FCS) (1996a) *New Directions in child protection and family support: Interim guidelines, standards and implementation package*, Family and Children's Services, Perth, Western Australia

Family and Children's Services (FCS) (1996b) *New Directions Steering Committee Meeting Minutes* (19 June), Family and Children's Services, Perth, Western Australia

Fanshel, D, Finch, S J & Grundy, J F (1994) 'Testing the measurement properties of risk assessment instruments in child protective services', *Child Abuse and Neglect*, vol. 18, no. 12, pp. 1073–84

Fargason, C A, Barnes, D, Schneider, D & Galloway, B W (1994) 'Enhancing multi-agency collaboration in the management of child sexual abuse', *Child Abuse and Neglect*, vol. 18, no. 10, pp. 859–70

Farinatti, F A S, Fonseca, N M, Dondonis, M & Brugger, E (1990) 'Child abuse and neglect in a developing country', *Child Abuse and Neglect*, vol. 14, no. 1, pp. 133–4

Farmer, E & Boushel, M (1999) 'Child protection policy and practice: Women in the front line', in S Watson & L Doyal (eds), *Engendering Social Policy*, Open University Press: Buckingham, pp. 84–101

Featherstone, B (1996) 'Victims or villains? Women who physically abuse their children', in B Fawcett, B Featherstone, J Hearn & C Toft (eds), *Violence and Gender Relations*, Sage: London, pp. 178–89

Featherstone, B (1997) 'What has gender got to do with it? Exploring physically abusive behaviour towards children', *British Journal of Social Work*, vol. 27, pp. 419–33

Feldman, K W, Brewer, D K & Shaw, D W (1995) 'Evolution of the cranial computed tomography scan in child abuse', *Child Abuse and Neglect*, vol. 19, no. 3, pp. 307–14

Femina, D D, Yeager, C A & Lewis, D O (1990) 'Child abuse: Adolescent records vs. adult recall', *Child Abuse and Neglect*, vol. 14, no. 2, pp. 227–32

Ferguson, H (1997) 'Protecting children in new times: child protection and the risk society', *Child and Family Social Work*, vol. 2, pp. 221–34

Finkelhor, D (1995) 'The victimization of children: A developmental perspective', *American Journal of Orthopsychiatry*, vol. 65, no. 2, pp. 177–93

Finkelhor, D, Hotaling, G, Lewis, I A & Smith, C (1990) 'Sexual abuse in a national survey of adult men and women: Prevalence, characteristics, and risk factors', *Child Abuse and Neglect*, vol. 14, no. 1, pp. 19–28

Fischer, D G & McDonald, W L (1998) 'Characteristics of intrafamilial and extrafamilial child sexual abuse', *Child Abuse and Neglect*, vol. 22, no. 9, pp. 915–29

Fischer, G (2000) 'Mis-taken identity: Mudrooroo and Gordon Matthews', in J Docker & G Fischer (eds), *Race, Culture and Identity in Australia and New Zealand*, UNSW Press: Sydney, pp. 95–112

Fleming, J, Mullen, P & Bammer, G (1997) 'A study of potential risk factors for sexual abuse in childhood', *Child Abuse and Neglect*, vol. 21, no. 1, pp. 49–58

Fook, J. (1996) 'Preface', in J Fook (ed.), *The Reflective Researcher*, Allen and Unwin: St Leonards, Sydney, pp. xii–xv

Fook, J (1999) 'Critical reflectivity in education and practice', in B Pease & J Fook (eds), *Transforming Social Work Practice: Postmodern critical perspectives*, Allen and Unwin: St Leonards, Sydney, pp. 195–208

Forbes, J (1993) 'Female sexual abusers: The contemporary search for equivalence', *Practice*, vol. 6, no. 2, pp. 102–11

Foucault, M (1965) *Madness and Civilization: A History of Insanity in the Age of Reason*, Random House: Cambridge (translated from the French by Richard Howard)

Foucault, M (1971) 'Orders of discourse', *Social Science Information*, vol. 10, no. 2, pp. 7–30

Foucault, M (1972) *The Archaeology of Knowledge*, Tavistock: London (translated from the French by Alan Sheridan)

Foucault, M (1977) *Discipline and Punish: The Birth of the Prison*, Penguin (translated from French by Alan Sheridan)

Foucault, M (1978a) *The History of Sexuality: volume 1 An Introduction*, Random House: Cambridge, (translated from the French by Robert Hurley)

Foucault, M (1978b) 'Politics and the study of discourse', *Ideology and Consciousness*, no. 3, pp. 7–26

Foucault, M (1980) *Power/Knowledge: Selected Interviews and Other Writings 1972–1977*, (edited by Colin Gordon), The Harvester Press (translated by Colin Gordon, Leo Marshall, John Mepham & Kate Soper)

Foucault, M (1983) *This is not a Pipe* (translated and edited by James Harkness), University of California Press: USA

Fox Harding, L (1991) *Perspectives in Child Care Policy*, Longman: London

Fox Harding, L (1996) ' "Parental responsibility": The reassertion of private patriarchy?' in E B Silva (ed.) *Good Enough Mothering? Feminist Perspectives on Lone Motherhood*, Routledge: London, pp. 130–47

Fox, K M & Gilbert, B O (1994) 'The interpersonal and psychological functioning of women who experienced childhood physical abuse, incest, and parental alcoholism', *Child Abuse and Neglect*, vol. 18, no. 10, pp. 849–58

Frankenberg, R (1993) *White Women, Race Matters: The Social Construction of Whiteness*, Routledge/University of Minnesota Press, USA

Franklin, R (1986) *The Rights of Children*, Blackwell: London

Franklin, R (1989) ' "Wimps and bullies": Press reporting of child abuse', in P Carter, T Jeffs & M Smith (eds), *Social Work and Social Welfare Yearbook One*, Open University Press: Milton Keynes, pp. 1–14

Franklin, B & Parton, N (1991) 'Media reporting of social work: A framework for analysis', in B Franklin & N Parton (eds), *Social Work, the Media and Public Relations*, Routledge: London, pp. 7–52

Fraser, N (1997) *Justice Interruptus: Critical Reflections on the 'Postsocialist' Condition*, Routledge: New York

Freeman, M D A (1983) *The Rights and Wrongs of Children*, Francis Pinter

Frosh, E & Lewandowski, L (1998) 'Psychological issues associated with acute physical injury – after the pediatric emergency department', *International Review of Psychiatry*, vol. 10, no. 3, pp. 216–23

Frost, N & Stein, M (1989) *The Politics of Child Welfare: Inequality, Power and Change*, Harvester Wheatsheaf: London

Fuller, R & Petch, A (1995) *Practitioner Research: The Reflexive Social Worker*, Open University Press: Buckingham

Gallmeier, T M & Bonner, B L (1992) 'University-based interdisciplinary training in child abuse and neglect', *Child Abuse and Neglect*, vol. 16, no. 4, pp. 513–22

Garbarino, J. (1993) 'Challenges we face in understanding children at war: A personal essay', *Child Abuse and Neglect*, vol. 17, no. 6, pp. 787–94

Garfinkel, H (1974) ' "Good" organisational reasons for "bad" clinic records', in R Turner (ed.) *Ethnomethodology,* Penguin: Harmondsworth, pp. 109–27

Gary, L T (1991) 'Feminist practice and family violence', in M Bricker-Jenkins, N Hooyman & N Gottlieb (eds), *Feminist Social Work Practice in Clinical Settings*, Sage: Newbury Park, California, pp. 19–32

Gatens, M (1998) 'Institutions, embodiment and sexual difference', in M Gatens & A MacKinnon (eds), *Gender and Institutions: Welfare, Work and Citizenship*, Cambridge University Press: Cambridge, UK, pp. 1–18

Gelles, R (1987a) 'Child abuse as psychopathology: A sociological critique and reformulation', in R Gelles, *Family Violence*, Sage Library of Social Research, vol 84, Sage: Newbury Park, California, pp. 49–61

Gelles, R (1987b) 'Community agencies and child abuse: Labeling and gatekeeping', in R Gelles, *Family Violence*, Sage Library of Social Research, vol. 84, Sage: Newbury Park, California, pp. 62–77

Gilbert, N (ed.) (1997) *Combating Child Abuse: International Perspectives and Trends*, Oxford University Press

Gilgun, J F (1991) 'Resilience and the intergenerational transmission of child sexual abuse', in M Q Patton (ed.), *Family Sexual Abuse: Frontline Research and Evaluation*, Sage: Newbury Park, California, pp. 93–105

Gittins, D (1998) *The Child in Question*, Macmillan: Hampshire, UK

Goddard, C & Hiller, P (1993) 'Child sexual abuse: Assault in a violent context', *Australian Journal of Social Issues*, vol. 28, no. 1, pp. 20–33

Goddard, C, Liddle, M J & Brown, T (1990), 'A fresh or flawed approach to child protection in Victoria, Australia?', *Child Abuse and Neglect*, vol. 14, no. 4, pp. 587–90

Goldman, R & Goldman, J (1982) *Children's Sexual Thinking*, Routledge and Kegan Paul: London

Goldson, E (1996) 'The effect of war on children', *Child Abuse and Neglect*, vol. 20, no. 9, pp. 809–20

Gordon, B N & Follmer, A (1994) 'Developmental issues in judging the credibility of children's testimony', *Journal of Clinical Child Psychology*, vol. 23, no. 3, pp. 283–94

Gordon, L (1985) 'Single mothers and child neglect', *American Quarterly*, Summer, vol. 37, no. 2, pp. 173–92

Gordon, L (1986) 'Family violence, feminism and social control', *Feminist Studies*, Fall, vol. 12, no. 3, pp. 452–78

Gough, B & Reavey, P (1997) 'Parental accounts regarding the physical punishment of children: Discourses of dis/empowerment', *Child Abuse and Neglect*, vol. 21, no. 5, pp. 417–30

Graham, H (1981) 'Mothers' accounts of anger and aggression towards their babies', in N Frude (ed.) *Psychological Approaches to Child Abuse*, Billing: Guildford, pp. 39–51

Greenstock, J & Pipe, M-E (1996) 'Interviewing children about past events: The influence of peer support and misleading questions', *Child Abuse and Neglect*, vol. 20, no. 1, pp. 69–80

Greenwald, E, Leitenberg, H, Cado, S & Tarran, M J (1990) 'Childhood sexual abuse: Long term effects on psychological and sexual functioning in a nonclinical and nonstudent sample of adult women', *Child Abuse and Neglect*, vol. 14, no. 4, pp. 503–14

Groenveld, L P & Giovannoni, J M (1977) 'Disposition of child abuse and neglect cases', *Social Work Research and Abstracts*, Summer, vol. 13, no. 2, pp. 24–30

Guba, E & Lincoln, Y (1982) 'Epistemological and methodological bases of naturalistic inquiry', *Educational Communication and Technology*, vol. 30, no. 4, pp. 233–52

Hacking, I (1990) *The Taming of Chance*, Cambridge University Press: Cambridge, UK

Hacking, I (1991) 'The making and molding of child abuse', *Critical Inquiry*, Winter, vol. 17, pp. 253–88

Haebich, A (1992) *For Their Own Good: Aborigines and Government in the South West of Western Australia: 1900–1940*, University of Western Australia Press: Perth, Western Australia

Haffejee, I E (1991) 'Sexual abuse of Indian (Asian) children in South Africa: First report in a community undergoing change', *Child Abuse and Neglect*, vol. 15, Supplement 1, pp. 147–52

Hall, D & Hall, I (1996) *Practical Social Research: Project Work in the Community*, Macmillan: London

'Halstead' (1938) 'Child Welfare Department. Activities in Perth over 30 years', Women's Realm: *The West Australian*, Monday, 10 January, Family and Children's Services, Perth, Western Australia (library)

Hansen, D J, Bumby, K M, Lundquist, L M, Chandler, R M, Le, P T & Futa, K T (1997) 'The influence of case and professional variables on the identification and reporting of child maltreatment – A study of licensed psychologists and certified masters social workers', *Journal of Family Violence*, vol. 12, no. 3, pp. 313–32

Haraway, D (1991) *Simians, Cyborgs and Women*, Free Association Books: London

Haskett, M E, Marziano, B & Dover, E R (1996) 'Absence of males in maltreatment research: A survey of recent literature', *Child Abuse and Neglect*, vol. 20, no. 12, pp. 1175–82

Hassard, J (1993) 'Postmodernism and organizational analysis: An overview', in J Hassard & M Parker (eds), *Postmodernism and Organizations*, Sage: London, pp. 1–23

Heap, J L (1995) 'Constructionism in the rhetoric and practice of fourth generation evaluation', *Evaluation and Program Planning*, vol. 18, no. 1, pp. 51–61

Hearn, J (1988) 'Commentary: Child abuse: Violences and sexualities towards young people', *Sociology*, vol. 22, no. 4, pp. 531–44

Hearn, J (1990) 'Child abuse and men's violence', The Violence Against Children Study Group, *Taking Child Abuse Seriously: Contemporary Issues in Child Protection Theory and Practice*, Unwin Hyman: London, pp. 63–85

Heiman, M, Leiblum, S, Esquilin, S & Pallitto, L (1998) 'A comparative survey of beliefs about "normal" childhood sexual behaviours', *Child Abuse and Neglect*, vol. 22, no. 4, pp. 289–304

Helfer, R (1991) 'Child abuse and neglect: assessment, treatment, and prevention, 21October, 2007', *Child Abuse and Neglect*, vol. 15, Supplement 1, pp. 5–16

Hellinckx, W, Colton, M & Williams, W (eds) (1997) *International Perspectives on Family Support*, London, Arena

Hemenway, D, Solnick, S & Carter, J (1994) 'Child-rearing violence', *Child Abuse and Neglect*, vol. 18, no. 12, pp. 1011–21

Henderson, I (1992) *The Bureaucratic Construction of Aborigines: A Textual and Discourse Analysis*, BA (Hons) thesis, Murdoch University, Perth, Western Australia, unpublished

Hendrick, H (1990) 'Constructions and reconstructions of British childhood: An interpretative survey, 1800 to the present', in A James & A Prout (eds), *Constructing and Reconstructing Childhood: Contemporary Issues in the Sociological Study of Childhood*, The Falmer Press: London, pp. 35–59

Herrenkohl, E C, Herrenkohl, R C, Rupert, L J, Egolf, B P & Lutz, J G (1995) 'Risk factors for behavioral dysfunction: The relative impact of maltreatment, SES, physical health problems, cognitive ability, and quality of parent–child interactions', *Child Abuse and Neglect*, vol. 19, no. 2, pp. 191–204

Hetherton, J (1999) 'The idealization of women: Its role in the minimization of child sexual abuse by females', *Child Abuse and Neglect*, vol. 23, no. 2, pp. 161–74

Hetherton, J & Beardsall, L (1998) 'Decisions and attitudes concerning child sexual abuse: Does the gender of the perpetrator make a difference to child protection professionals?', *Child Abuse and Neglect*, vol. 22, no. 12, pp. 1265–83

Hewitt, M (1991) 'Bio-politics and social policy: Foucault's account of welfare', in M Featherstone, M Hepworth & B Turner (eds), *The Body: Social Process and Cultural Theory*, Sage: London, pp. 225–55

Hibbard, R A & Zollinger, T W (1990) 'Patterns of child sexual abuse knowledge among professionals', *Child Abuse and Neglect*, vol. 14, no. 3, pp. 347–56

Hibbard, R A & Zollinger, T W (1992) 'Medical evaluation referral patterns for sexual abuse victims', *Child Abuse and Neglect*, vol. 16, no. 4, pp. 533–40

Hicks, S (1996) 'The "last resort"? Lesbian and gay experiences of the social work assessment process in fostering and adoption', *Practice,* vol. 8, no. 2, pp. 15–24

Himelin, M J (1995) 'Childhood sexual abuse and the academic adjustment of college women', *Child Abuse and Neglect*, vol. 19, no. 6, pp. 761–4

Hirst, P (1981) 'The genesis of the social', *Politics and Power*, no. 3, pp. 67–82

*History of the Department for Community Welfare, 1842–1972*, (undated) Family and Children's Services, Perth, Western Australia (library)

Hobbs, C J, Wynne, J M & Thomas, A J (1995) 'Colposcopic genital findings in prepubertal girls assessed for sexual abuse', *Archives of Disease in Childhood*, vol. 73, no. 5, pp. 465–9

Hobbs, J (1995) 'Letters to the editor', *Child Abuse and Neglect*, vol. 19, no. 3, pp. 385–6

Hodder, I (1994) 'The interpretation of documents and material culture' in N Denzin & Y Lincoln (eds), *Handbook of Qualitative Research*, Sage: Thousand Oaks, California, pp. 393–402

Hodge, R & Kress, G (1993) *Language as Ideology*, Routledge: London, 2nd edition

Holmes, G & Offen, L (1996) 'Clinicians' hypotheses regarding clients' problems: Are they less likely to hypothesize sexual abuse in male compared to female clients?', *Child Abuse and Neglect*, vol. 20, no. 6, pp. 493–502

Holstein, J A & Gubrium, J F (1994) 'Phenomenology, ethnomethodology and interpretive practice', in N Denzin & Y Lincoln (eds), *Handbook of Qualitative Research*, Sage: Thousand Oaks, California, pp. 262–72

Holstein, J A & Gubrium, J F (1995) *The Active Interview*, Qualitative Research Methods Series, vol. 37, Sage: Thousand Oaks, California

Hon. Attorney General (1972) *Community Welfare Act 1971: Second Reading Speech to the Western Australian Parliament (Legislative Assembly)*, 11 May, Family and Children's Services, Perth, Western Australia (library)

Honigman, J (1982) 'Sampling in ethnographic fieldwork', in R Burgess (ed.) *Field Research: A Sourcebook and Field Manual*, George Allen and Unwin: London, pp. 79–90

Hood, M (1997) *The Social Construction of Child Abuse in Australia and South Australia*, PhD thesis, University of South Australia: Adelaide, unpublished

hooks, b (1981) *Ain't I a Woman: Black Women and Feminism*, Pluto Press: London

Horowitz, S & Chadwick, D L (1990) 'Syphilis as a sole indicator of sexual abuse: Two cases with no intervention', *Child Abuse and Neglect*, vol. 14, no. 1, pp. 129–32

Horsfall, D, Byrne-Armstrong, H & Higgs, J (2001) 'Researching critical moments', in H Byrne-Armstrong, J Higgs & D Horsfall (eds), *Critical Moments in Qualitative Research*, Butterworth-Heinemann: Oxford, pp. 3–13

Howe, D (1992) 'Child abuse and the bureaucratisation of social work', *Sociological Review*, vol. 40, no. 3, pp. 491–508

Howe, D, Brandon, M, Hinings, D & Schofield, G (1999) *Attachment Theory, Child Maltreatment and Family Support*, Macmillan: London

Huberman, A M & Miles, M B (1994) 'Data management and analysis methods', in Denzin, N K & Lincoln, Y S (eds), *Handbook of Qualitative Research*, Sage: Thousand Oaks, California, 2nd edition, pp. 428–44

Huddleston, R (1988) *English Grammar: an Outline*, Cambridge University Press: Cambridge, UK

Hugman, R & Phillips, N (1992/93) ' "Like bees round the honeypot": Social work responses to parents with mental health needs', *Practice*, vol. 6, no. 3, pp. 193–205

Human Rights and Equal Opportunity Commission (1997) *Bringing Them Home: Report of the National Inquiry into the Separation of Aboriginal and Torres Strait Islander Children from their Families*, Sterling Press: Commonwealth of Australia

Humphreys, C (1995) 'Whatever happened on the way to counselling? Hurdles in the interagency environment', *Child Abuse and Neglect*, vol. 19, no. 7, pp. 801–10

Humphreys, C (1996) 'Exploring new territory: Police organizational responses to child sexual abuse', *Child Abuse and Neglect*, vol. 20, no. 4, pp. 337–44

Humphries, B & Martin, M (2000) 'Disrupting Ethics in Social Research', in B Humphries (ed.), *Research in Social Care and Social Welfare: Issues and Debates for Practice*, Jessica Kingsley Publishers: London, pp. 69–85

Hutchby, I & Wooffitt, R (1998) *Conversation Analysis*, Polity Press: London

Hutchison, E D (1989) 'Child protective screening decisions: An analysis of predictive factors', *Social Work Research and Abstracts*, September, vol. 25, no. 3, pp. 9–15

Ingram, D L, Everett, V D, Flick, L A R, Russell, T A & Whitesims, S T (1997) 'Vaginal gonococcal cultures in sexual abuse evaluations – Evaluation of selective criteria for preteenaged girls', *Pediatrics*, vol. 99, no. 6, pp. E81–E84 (URL: pediatrics.org/cgi/content/full/99/6/e8)

Ingram, D L, White, S T, Lyna, P R, Crews, K F, Schmid, J E, Koch, G G & Everett, V D (1992) '*Ureaplasma urealyticum* and large colony mycoplasma colonization in female children and its relationship to sexual contact, age, and race', *Child Abuse and Neglect*, vol. 16, no. 2, pp. 265–72

Ito, Y, Teicher, M H, Glod, C A & Ackerman, E (1998) 'Preliminary evidence for aberrant cortical development in abused children – A quantitative EEG study', *Journal of Neuropsychiatry and Clinical Neurosciences*, vol. 10, no. 3, pp. 298–307

Jack, G (1997) 'Discourses of child protection and child welfare', *British Journal of Social Work*, vol. 27, pp. 659–78

Jackman, C, Shanahan, D, Balogh, S & Kaszubska, G (2003) 'Axe hangs over baby tax bonus', *The Australian*, 10 June 2003, p. 4

Jackson, H & Nuttall, R (1993) 'Clinician responses to sexual abuse allegations', *Child Abuse and Neglect*, vol. 17, no. 1, pp. 127–44

Jamrozik, A (1991) *Class, Inequality and the State*, Macmillan: South Melbourne

Janko, S (1994) *Vulnerable Children, Vulnerable Families: The Social Construction of Child Abuse*, Teacher's College Press: New York

Jenkins, R (1992) *Pierre Bourdieu*, Routledge: London

Jenks, C (1996) *Childhood*, Routledge: London

Joffe, H (1999) *Risk and 'the Other'*, Cambridge University Press: Cambridge, UK

Johnson, C F (1993) 'Physicians and medical neglect: Variables that affect reporting', *Child Abuse and Neglect*, vol. 17, pp. 605–12

Johnson, J (1990) *What Lisa Knew: The Truth and Lies of the Steinberg Case*, Bloomsbury: UK

Jones, D P H (1994a) 'Editorial: Autism, facilitated communication and allegations of child abuse and neglect', *Child Abuse and Neglect*, vol. 18, no. 6, pp. 491–4

Jones, D P H (1994b) 'Editorial: Assessing and taking risks in child protection work', *Child Abuse and Neglect*, vol. 18, no. 12, pp. 1037–8

Jones, L (1993) 'Decision making in child welfare: A critical review of the literature', *Child and Adolescent Social Work Journal*, June, vol. 10, no. 3, pp. 241–62

Jumper, S A (1995) 'Meta-analysis of the relationship of child sexual abuse to adult psychological adjustment', *Child Abuse and Neglect*, vol. 19, no. 6, pp. 715–28

Jupp, V & Norris, C (1993) 'Traditions in documentary analysis', in M Hammersley (ed.), *Social Research: Philosophy, Politics and Practice*, Sage: London, pp. 37–51

Kadish, H A, Schunk, J E & Britton, H (1998) 'Pediatric male rectal and genital trauma – Accidental and nonaccidental injuries', *Pediatric Emergency Care*, vol. 14, no. 2, pp. 95–8

Kalichman, S C, Craig, M E & Follingstad, D R (1990) 'Professionals' adherence to mandatory child abuse reporting laws: Effects of responsibility attribution, confidence ratings, and situational factors', *Child Abuse and Neglect*, vol. 14, no. 1, pp. 69–78

Kamerman, S & Kahn, A (1993) 'If CPS is driving child welfare – where do we go from here?', *Public Welfare*, Winter, vol. 51, no. 1, p. 41

Kaplan, E A (1992) *Motherhood and Representation: The Mother in Popular Culture and Melodrama*, Routledge: London

Kasim, M S, Shafie, H M & Cheah, I (1994) 'Social factors in relation to physical abuse in Kuala Lumpur, Malaysia', *Child Abuse and Neglect*, vol. 18, no. 5, pp. 401–8

Kaufman, J, Jones, B, Stieglitz, E, Vitulano, L & Mannarino, A P (1994) 'The use of multiple informants to assess children's maltreatment experiences', *Journal of Family Violence*, vol. 9, no. 3, pp. 227–48

Kaufman, K L, Wallace, A M, Johnson, C F & Reeder, M L (1995) 'Comparing female and male perpetrators' modus operandi: Victims' reports of sexual abuse', *Journal of Interpersonal Violence*, vol. 10, no. 3, pp. 322–33

Kean, R B & Dukes, R L (1991) 'Effects of witness characteristics on the perception and reportage of child abuse', *Child Abuse and Neglect*, vol. 15, no. 4, pp. 423–36

Kemshall, H (2002) *Risk, social policy and welfare*, Open University Press: Buckingham, UK

Kendall-Tackett, K A (1992a) 'Use of anatomical dolls by Boston-area professionals', *Child Abuse and Neglect*, vol. 16, no. 3, pp. 423–8

Kendall-Tackett, K A (1992b) 'Professional standards of 'normal' behavior with anatomical dolls and factors that influence these standards', *Child Abuse and Neglect*, vol. 16, no. 5, pp. 727–35

Kendall-Tackett, K A & Eckenrode, J (1996) 'The effects of neglect on academic achievement and disciplinary problems: A developmental perspective', *Child Abuse and Neglect*, vol. 20, no. 3, pp. 161–70

Kent, A & Waller, G (1998) 'The impact of childhood emotional abuse – An extension of the child abuse trauma scale', *Child Abuse and Neglect*, vol. 22, no. 5, pp. 393–9

Kerns, D (ed.) (1998) 'Special issue: Establishing a medical research agenda for child sexual abuse', *Child Abuse and Neglect*, vol. 22

Kessen, W (1983) 'The child and other cultural inventions', in F S Kessel & A W Siegel, (eds), *The Child and Other Cultural Inventions*, Houston Symposium 4 (1981), New York: Praeger Special Studies, pp. 26–47

Khan, N Z & Lynch, M A (1997) 'Recognizing child maltreatment in Bangladesh', *Child Abuse and Neglect*, vol. 21, no. 8, pp. 815–18

Kinard, E M (1998) 'Classifying type of child maltreatment – Does the source of information make a difference', *Journal of Family Violence*, vol. 13, no. 1, pp. 105–12

Kincheloe, J & McLaren, P (1994) 'Rethinking critical theory and qualitative research', in N Denzin & Y Lincoln (eds), *Handbook of Qualitative Research*, Sage: Thousand Oaks, California, pp. 138–57

King, L J (1972) *Community Welfare Bill, Speech by Minister of Social Welfare to the South Australian House of Assembly* (reprinted from *Hansard*) (1 March), Family and Children's Services, Western Australia (library)

Kinzl, J F, Mangweth, B, Traweger, C & Biebl, W (1996) 'Sexual dysfunction in males: Significance of adverse childhood experiences', *Child Abuse and Neglect*, vol. 20, no. 8, pp. 759–66

Kitzinger, J (1990) 'Who are you kidding? Children, power and the struggle against sexual abuse', in A James & A Prout (eds), *Constructing and Reconstructing Childhood: Contemporary Issues in the Sociological Study of Childhood*, The Falmer Press: London, pp. 157–83

Korbin, J (1989) 'Fatal maltreatment by mothers: A proposed framework', *Child Abuse and Neglect*, vol. 13, Supplement 1, pp. 67–78

Korbin, J E (1991) 'Cross-cultural perspectives and research directions for the 21st century', *Child Abuse and Neglect*, vol. 15, Supplement 1, pp. 67–78

Kotch, J B, Chalmers, D J, Fanslow, J L, Marshall, S & Langley, J D (1993) 'Morbidity and death due to child abuse in New Zealand', *Child Abuse and Neglect*, vol. 17, pp. 233–47

Kreklewetz, C & Piotrowski, C (1998) 'Incest survivor mothers: Protecting the next generation', *Child Abuse and Neglect*, vol. 22, no. 12, pp. 1305–12

Krugman, R (1995) 'Future Directions in preventing child abuse', *Child Abuse and Neglect*, vol. 19, no. 3, pp. 273–9

Kwang-iel Kim & Bokja Ko (1990) 'An incidence survey of battered children in two elementary schools in Seoul', *Child Abuse and Neglect*, vol. 14, no. 2, pp. 273–7

Lamb, M (1994) 'The investigation of child sexual abuse: An interdisciplinary consensus statement', *Journal of Child Sexual Abuse*, vol. 3, no. 4, pp. 93–106

Lamb, M E, Hershkowitz, I, Sternberg, K J, Boat, B & Everson, M D (1996) 'Investigative interviews of alleged sexual abuse victims with and without anatomical dolls', *Child Abuse and Neglect*, vol. 20, no. 12, pp. 1251–60

Lamb, S & Coakley, M (1993) 'Normal childhood sexual play and games – Differentiating play from abuse', *Child Abuse and Neglect*, vol. 17, no. 4, pp. 515–26

Lamb, S & Edgar-Smith, S (1994) 'Aspects of disclosure: Mediators of outcomes of childhood sexual abuse', *Journal of Interpersonal Violence*, vol. 9, no. 3, pp. 307–26

Land, H (1999) 'The changing worlds of work and families', in S Watson & L Doyal (eds), *Engendering Social Policy*, Open University Press: Buckingham, pp. 12–29

Laviola, M (1992) 'Effects of older brother–younger sister incest: A study of the dynamics of 17 cases', *Child Abuse and Neglect*, vol. 16, no. 3, pp. 409–22

*Laws for People: The Report of the Legislative Review* (1991) A Review of Legislation Administered by the Western Australian Department for Community Services, WA Government

Law Reform Commission (New South Wales) (1997) *Research Report 7 – The Aboriginal Child Placement Principle*, Government of New South Wales Publications, www.legalaid.nsw.gov.au/lrc.nsf/pages/RR7TOC (accessed 21 July 2003)

Lawson, C (1993) 'Mother–son sexual abuse: Rare or underreported? A critique of the research', *Child Abuse and Neglect*, vol. 17, no. 2, pp. 261–70

Leahy, T (1992) 'Positively experienced man/boy sex: The discourse of seduction and the social construction of masculinity', *Australian and New Zealand Journal of Sociology*, vol. 28, no. 1, pp. 71–88

Lecercle, J-J. (1990) *The Violence of Language*, Routledge: London

Lee, A C, So, K T, Wong, H L & Lau, S (1998) 'Penetrating pencil injury – An unusual case of child abuse', *Child Abuse and Neglect*, vol. 22, no. 7, pp. 749–52

LegalDay (2003) 'Adoption', *Current Issues in English and International Law*, www.legalday.co.uk/current/adoption.htm (accessed 21 July 2003)

Levesque, R J R (1998) 'Emotional maltreatment in adolescents' everyday lives – Furthering sociolegal reforms and social service provisions', *Behavioral Sciences and the Law*, vol. 16, no. 2, pp. 237–63

Levy, H B, Markovic, J, Kalinowski, M N, Ahart, S & Torres, H (1995) 'Child sexual abuse interviews: The use of anatomic dolls and the reliability of information', *Journal of Interpersonal Violence*, vol. 10, no. 3, pp. 334–53

Lewis, T (2003) 'Arrest after children are left alone', *South China Morning Post* (Hong Kong), 31 January 2003, p. 4

Linstead, S (1993) 'Deconstruction in the study of organizations', in J Hassard & M Parker (eds), *Postmodernism and Organizations*, Sage: London, pp. 49–70

Little, M (1995) 'Child protection or family support? Finding a balance', *Family Matters*, issue 40, pp. 18–21

Look, K M & Look, R M (1997) 'Skin scraping, cupping, and moxybustion that may mimic physical abuse', *Journal of Forensic Sciences*, vol. 42, no. 1, pp. 103–5

Lumby, C (2003) 'Fathers in law', *The Bulletin*, 8 July, 2003, p. 31

Lupton, D (1999a) 'Introduction: risk and sociocultural theory', in D Lupton, (ed.), *Risk and Sociocultural Theory*, Cambridge University Press: Cambridge, pp. 1–11

Lupton, D (1999b) 'Risk and the ontology of pregnant embodiment', in D Lupton (ed.), *Risk and Sociocultural Theory: New Directions and Perspectives*, Cambridge University Press: Cambridge, UK, pp. 59–85

Lytle, C (1994) 'Reaching consensus is a difficult task', *Journal of Child Sexual Abuse*, vol. 3, no. 4, pp. 111–13

MacCallum, M (2002) *Quarterly Essay: Girt by Sea: Australia, The Refugees and the Politics of Fear*, Black Inc.: Melbourne, Australia

MacDonald, K & Tipton, C (1993) 'Using Documents', in N Gilbert (ed.), *Researching Social Life*, Sage: London, pp. 187–200

Magwaza, A S, Killian, B J, Petersen, I & Pillay, Y (1993) 'The effects of chronic violence on preschool children living in South African townships', *Child Abuse and Neglect*, vol. 17, no. 6, pp. 795–804

Mandel, D R, Lehman, D R & Yuille, J C (1994) 'Should this child be removed from home? Hypothesis generation and information seeking as predictors of case decisions', *Child Abuse and Neglect*, vol. 18, no. 12, pp. 1051–62

Manne, R (2001a) 'Woomera', in R Manne, *The Barren Years: John Howard and Australian Political Culture*, The Text Publishing Company: Melbourne, Australia, pp. 136–9

Manne, R (2001b) 'Stolen lives' in R Manne, *The Barren Years: John Howard and Australian Political Culture*, The Text Publishing Company: Melbourne, Australia, pp. 51–62

Manne, R (2001c) 'The return of assimilationism', in R Manne, *The Barren Years: John Howard and Australian Political Culture*, The Text Publishing Company: Melbourne, Australia, pp. 63–5

Manne, R (2001d) 'Regrets and blemishes', in R Manne, *The Barren Years: John Howard and Australian Political Culture*, The Text Publishing Company: Melbourne, Australia, pp. 66–9

Manning, P & Cullum-Swan, B (1994) 'Narrative, content, and semiotic analysis', in N Denzin & Y Lincoln (eds), *Handbook of Qualitative Research*, Sage: Thousand Oaks, California, pp. 463–77, (2nd edition)

Marcus, G (1994) 'What comes (just) after "post"? The case of ethnography', in N Denzin & Y Lincoln (eds), *Handbook of Qualitative Research*, Sage: Thousand Oaks, California, pp. 563–74, (2nd edition)

Mares, P (2001) *Borderline: Australia's treatment of refugees and asylum seekers*, University of New South Wales Press: Sydney, Australia

Margolin, L (1990) 'When vocabularies of motive fail: The example of fatal child abuse', *Qualitative Sociology*, vol. 13, no. 4, pp. 373–85

Margolin, L (1992) 'Deviance on record: Techniques for labeling child abusers in official documents', *Social Problems*, vol. 39, no. 1, pp. 58–70

Margolin, L & Craft, J L (1990) 'Child abuse by adolescent caregivers', *Child Abuse and Neglect*, vol. 14, no. 3, pp. 365–74

Markus, A (2001) *Race: John Howard and the Remaking of Australia*, Allen and Unwin: Sydney

Martin, J A & Elmer, E (1992) 'Battered children grown up: A follow-up study of individuals severely maltreated as children', *Child Abuse and Neglect*, vol. 16, no. 1, pp. 75–88

Mason, J (1994) 'Linking qualitative and quantitative data analysis', in A Bryman & R Burgess (eds), *Analyzing Qualitative Data*, Routledge: London, pp. 89–110

Mass, M (2000) 'On the link between academia and the practice of social work', *Journal for the Theory of Social Behaviour*, vol. 30, no. 1, pp. 99–125

Mathews, R, Dawkins, M, Lambert, D & O'Reilly, P (1995) *New Directions Evaluation Report*, Family and Children's Services, Perth, Western Australia

Matorin, A I & Lynn, S J (1998) 'The development of a measure of correlates of child sexual abuse – The traumatic sexualization survey', *Journal of Traumatic Stress*, vol. 11, no. 2, pp. 261–80

McCarthy, P (2003) 'Home alone on farm', *The Southland Times* (New Zealand), 15 March 2003, p. 6

McCotter, D & Oxnam, H (1981) *Children in Limbo*, Department for Community Welfare, Perth, Western Australia

McCurdy, K & Daro, D (1994) 'Child maltreatment: A national survey of reports and fatalities', *Journal of Interpersonal Violence*, vol. 9, no. 1, pp. 75–94

McDonald, J (2003) 'Children left alone for weeks', *The Sunday Telegraph* (Sydney), 12 January 2003, p. 43

McGee, R A, Wolfe, D A, Yuen, S A, Wilson, S K & Carnochan, J (1995) 'The measurement of maltreatment: A comparison of approaches', *Child Abuse and Neglect*, vol. 19, no. 2, pp. 233–50

McMahon, J, Miles, D, Sceriha, M & Townson, L (1996) 'Women and disability: Difference that makes a difference', in R Thorpe & J Irwin (eds), *Women and Violence: Working for Change*, Hale and Iremonger: Sydney, pp. 32–44

Mejiuni, C O (1991) 'Educating adults against socioculturally induced abuse and neglect of children in Nigeria', *Child Abuse and Neglect*, vol. 15, nos. 1 and 2, pp. 139–46

Mellish, M (2003) 'Baby bonus scheme flawed, says Labor', *Australian Financial Review*, 21 May 2003, p. 4

Mickler, S (1998) *The Myth of Privilege: Aboriginal Status, Media Visions, Public Ideas*, Fremantle Arts Centre Press: Fremantle, Western Australia

Milner, J (1993) 'A disappearing act: The differing career paths of fathers and mothers in child protection investigations', *Critical Social Policy*, vol. 38, pp. 48–68

Milner, J (1994) 'Assessing physical child abuse risk: The child abuse potential inventory', *Clinical Psychology Review*, vol. 14, no. 6, pp. 547–83

Minty, B & Pattinson, G (1994) 'The nature of neglect', *British Journal of Social Work*, vol. 24, pp. 733–47

Mitchell, D (1998) 'Life-course and labour market transitions: Alternatives to the breadwinner welfare state', in M Gatens & A Mackinnon (eds), *Gender and Institutions: Welfare, Work and Citizenship*, Cambridge University Press: Cambridge, UK, pp. 19–37

Moeller, T P, Bachmann, G A & Moeller, J R (1993) 'The combined effects of physical, sexual, and emotional abuse during childhood: Long-term health consequences for women', *Child Abuse and Neglect*, vol. 17, no. 5, pp. 623–40

Moore, N (1996) ' "Me operation": Abortion and class in Australian women's novels, 1920s–1950', *Hecate*, vol. XXII, no. 1, pp. 27–46

Morgan, S (1987) *My Place*, Fremantle Arts Press: Perth, Western Australia

Morison, S & Greene, E (1992) 'Juror and expert knowledge of child sexual abuse', *Child Abuse and Neglect*, vol. 16, no. 4, pp. 595–614

Mulder, M R & Vrij, A (1996) 'Explaining conversation rules to children: An intervention study to facilitate children's accurate responses', *Child Abuse and Neglect*, vol. 20, no. 7, pp. 623–32

Murphy-Berman, V (1994) 'A conceptual framework for thinking about risk assessment and case management in child protective service', *Child Abuse and Neglect*, vol. 18, no. 2, pp. 193–202

Myers, J E B (1993) 'Expert testimony regarding child sexual abuse', *Child Abuse and Neglect*, vol. 17, no. 1, pp. 175–

Nelson, B (1984) *Making an Issue of Child Abuse: Political Agenda Setting for Social Problems*, The University of Chicago Press: Chicago

Ney, P G, Fung, T & Wickett, A R (1994) 'The worst combinations of child abuse and neglect', *Child Abuse and Neglect*, vol. 18, no. 9, pp. 705–14

Nicholls, C (2000) 'Warlpiri graffiti', in J Docker & G Fischer (eds), *Race, Colour and Identity in Australia and New Zealand*, UNSW Press: Sydney, pp. 79–94

Nimkin, K & Kleinman, P K (1997) 'Imaging of child abuse', *Pediatric Clinics of North America*, vol. 44, no. 3, pp. 615ff

O'Hagan, K (1995) 'Emotional and psychological abuse: Problems of definition', *Child Abuse and Neglect*, vol. 19, no. 4, pp. 449–61

Oates, K (1982) 'Child abuse – A community concern', in K Oates (ed.), *Child Abuse: A Major Concern of our Times*, Butterworths: North Ryde, New South Wales, pp. 1–12

Oates, K (1990) 'International Society for Prevention of Child Abuse and Neglect President's message: Establishing priorities', *Child Abuse and Neglect*, vol. 14, no. 1, pp. 1–2

Oates, K & Donnelly, A (1997) 'Influential papers in child abuse', *Child Abuse and Neglect*, vol. 21, no. 3, pp. 319–26

Oberlander, L B (1995) 'Psycholegal issues in child sexual abuse evaluations: A survey of forensic mental health professionals', *Child Abuse and Neglect*, vol. 19, no. 4, pp. 475–90

Ong, B N (1985) 'Understanding child abuse: Ideologies of motherhood', *Women's Studies International Forum*, vol. 8, no. 5, pp. 411–19

Palusci, V J & McHugh, M T (1995) 'Interdisciplinary training in the evaluation of child sexual abuse', *Child Abuse and Neglect*, vol. 19, no. 9, pp. 1031–8

Parra, J M, Huston, R L & Foulds, D M (1997) 'Resident documentation of diagnostic impression in sexual abuse evaluations', *Clinical Pediatrics*, vol. 36, no. 12, pp. 691–4

Parton, N (1979) 'The natural history of child abuse: A study in social problem definition', *British Journal of Social Work*, vol. 9

Parton, N (1985) *The Politics of Child Abuse*, Macmillan: London

Parton, N (1991) *Governing the Family: Child Care, Child Protection and the State*, Macmillan: London

Parton, N (1995) 'Neglect as child protection: The political context and the practical outcomes', *Children and Society*, vol. 9, no. 1, pp. 67–89

Parton, N (1998) 'Risk, advanced liberalism and child welfare: The need to rediscover uncertainty and ambiguity', *British Journal of Social Work*, vol. 28, pp. 5–27

Parton, N (1999) 'Reconfiguring child welfare practices: Risk, advanced liberalism, and the government of freedom', in A S Chambon, A Irving & L Epstein, (eds), *Reading Foucault for Social Work*, Columbia University Press: New York, pp. 101–30

Parton, N & O'Byrne, P (2000) *Constructive Social Work: towards a new practice*, Macmillan: London

Parton, N, Thorpe, D & Wattam, C (1997) *Child Protection: Risk and the Moral Order*, Macmillan: Basingstoke

Patel, N (1995) 'In search of the holy grail', in R Hugman & D Smith (eds), *Ethical Issues in Social Work*, Routledge: London, pp. 16–45

Peile, C & McCouat, M (1997) 'The rise of relativism: The future of theory and knowledge development in social work', *British Journal of Social Work*, vol. 27, pp. 343–60

Pengelly, B (1991) 'A feminist critique of the idea of incest as a product of the dysfunctional family' in P Hetherington (ed.), *Incest and the Community: Australian Perspectives*, University of Western Australia Press: Perth, Western Australia, pp. 184–97

Perez, C M & Widom, C S (1994) 'Childhood victimization and long-term intellectual and academic outcomes', *Child Abuse and Neglect*, vol. 18, no. 8, pp. 617–34

Peters, D K & Range, L M. (1995) 'Childhood sexual abuse and current suicidality in college women and men', *Child Abuse and Neglect*, vol. 19, no. 3, pp. 335–42

Phelan, P (1995) 'Incest and its meaning: The perspectives of fathers and daughters', *Child Abuse and Neglect*, vol. 19, no. 1, pp. 7–24

Phellas, C (2000) 'Cultural and sexual identities in in-depth interviewing', in C Truman, D Mertens & B Humphries (eds), *Research and Inequality*, UCL Press, Taylor and Francis, London, pp. 52–64

Phoenix, A & Woollett, A (1991) 'Motherhood: Social construction, politics and psychology', in A Phoenix, A Woollett & E Lloyd (eds), *Motherhood: Meanings, Practices and Ideologies*, Sage: London, pp. 13–27

Pithouse, A (1987) *Social Work: The Social Organisation of an Invisible Trade*, Avebury: Aldershot

Podell, D M, Kastner, J & Kastner, S (1994) 'Mental retardation and adult women's perceptions of adolescent sexual abuse', *Child Abuse and Neglect*, vol. 18, no. 10, pp. 809–20

Porter, S, Yuille, J C & Bent, A (1995) 'A comparison of the eyewitness accounts of deaf and hearing children', *Child Abuse and Neglect*, vol. 19, no. 1, pp. 51–62

Portwood, S (1998) 'The impact of individuals' characteristics and experiences on their definitions of child maltreatment', *Child Abuse and Neglect*, vol. 22, no. 5, pp. 437–52

Potter, J (1996) *Representing Reality: Discourse, Rhetoric and Social Construction*, Sage: London

Potter, J & Wetherell, M (1987) *Discourse and Social Psychology: Beyond Attitudes and Behaviour*, Sage: London

Prout, A & James, A (1990) 'A new paradigm for the sociology of childhood: provenance, promise and problems', in A James & A Prout (eds), *Constructing and Reconstructing Childhood: Contemporary Issues in the Sociological Study of Childhood*, The Falmer Press: London, pp. 7–34

Qouta, S, Punamaki, R-L. & El Sarraj, E E (1995) 'The impact of the peace treaty on psychological well-being: A follow-up study of Palestinian children', *Child Abuse and Neglect*, vol. 19, no. 10, pp. 1197–1208

Rabinow, P (1984) (ed.) *The Foucault Reader*, Pantheon Books: New York

Ramsland, J (1986) *Children of the Back Lanes: Destitute and Neglected Children in Colonial New South Wales*, New South Wales University Press, Kensington

Realmuto, G M & Wescoe, S (1992) 'Agreement among professionals about a child's sexual abuse status: Interviews with sexually anatomically correct dolls as indicators of abuse', *Child Abuse and Neglect*, vol. 16, no. 5, pp. 719–26

Rector, R (2003) 'The Baucus "WORK" Act of 2002: Repealing welfare reform', *The Heritage Foundation*, www.heritage.org/Research/Welfare/BG1580.cfm (accessed 9 July 2003)

Reidy, T J & Hochstadt, N J (1993) 'Attribution of blame in incest cases: A comparison of mental health professionals', *Child Abuse and Neglect*, vol. 17, no. 3, pp. 371–82

Reiniger, A, Robison, E & McHugh, M (1995) 'Mandated training of professionals: A means for improving reporting of suspected child abuse', *Child Abuse and Neglect*, vol. 19, no. 1, pp. 63–9

Renzetti, C (1992) *Violent Betrayal: Partner Abuse in Lesbian Relationships*, Sage: Newbury Park, California

*Review of Departmental Responses to Child Maltreatment Allegations* (1995), (J Hancock, J Laffer & S Hudd), Department for Community Development, Perth: Western Australia

Reynolds, H (2000) *Why Weren't We Told?*, Penguin, Ringwood, Victoria, Australia (2nd edition)

Richards, L & Richards, T (1994) 'From filing cabinet to computer', in A Bryman & R Burgess (eds), *Analyzing Qualitative Data*, Routledge: London, pp. 146–72

Riessman, C K (1994) 'Subjectivity matters: The positioned investigator', in C K Riessman (ed.), *Qualitative Studies in Social Work Research*, Sage: Newbury Park, California, pp.133–8

Rintoul, S (1993) *The Wailing: A National Black Oral History*, William Heinemann, Australia

Rodriguez, N, Ryan, S W, Rowan, A B & Foy, D W (1996) 'Posttraumatic stress disorder in a clinical sample of adult survivors of childhood sexual abuse', *Child Abuse and Neglect*, vol. 20, no. 10, pp. 943–52

Roesler, T A & Wind, T W (1994) 'Telling the secret: Adult women describe their disclosures of incest', *Journal of Interpersonal Violence*, vol. 9, no. 3, pp. 327–38

Rojek, C, Peacock, G & Collins, S (1988) *Social Work and Received Ideas*, Routledge: London

Rojiani, R H (1994) 'Disparities in the social construction of long-term care', in Riessman, C K (ed.), *Qualitative Studies in Social Work*, Sage: Thousand Oaks, California, pp. 139–52

Rooks, V J, Sisler, C & Burton, B (1998) 'Cervical spine injury in child abuse – Report of two cases', *Pediatric Radiology*, vol. 28, no. 3, pp. 193–5

Rose, N (1989) *Governing the Soul: The Shaping of the Private Self*, Routledge: London

Rose, N (1998) *Inventing Ourselves: Psychology, Power, and Personhood*, Cambridge University Press: Cambridge, UK

Rose, N (1999) *Powers of Freedom: Reframing Political Thought*, Cambridge University Press: Cambridge, UK

Rosen, H (1981) 'How workers use cues to determine child abuse', *Social Work Research and Abstracts*, vol. 17, no. 4, pp. 27–33

Rosenau, P (1992) *Post-modernism and the Social Sciences: Insights, Inroads and Intrusions*, Princeton University Press: Princeton, New Jersey

Roseneil, S & Seymour, J (1999) 'Practising identities: Power and resistance', in S Roseneil & J Seymour (eds), *Practising Identities: Power and Resistance*, Macmillan: UK, pp. 1–10

Rosenfeld, A A (1993) 'Children living through a Desert Storm', *Child Abuse and Neglect*, vol. 17, no. 6, pp. 821–30

Rowan, A B, Foy, D W, Rodriguez, N & Ryan, S (1994) 'Posttraumatic stress disorder in a clinical sample of adults sexually abused as children', *Child Abuse and Neglect*, vol. 18, no. 1, pp. 51–62

Rowley, C D (1970) *The Destruction of Aboriginal Society: Aboriginal Policy and Practice*, Australian National University Press: Canberra

Rowley, C D (1971) *The Remote Aborigines: Aboriginal Policy and Practice*, Australian National University Press: Canberra

Rowley, C D (1972) *Outcasts in White Australia: Aboriginal Policy and Practice*, Penguin: Ringwood, Victoria

Rueschmeyer, D (1983) 'Professional autonomy and the social control of expertise', in R Dingwall & P Lewis (eds), *The Sociology of the Professions: Lawyers, Doctors and Others*, Macmillan: UK, pp. 38–58

Sackett, L (1993) 'A post-modern panopticon: The Royal Commission into Aboriginal Deaths in Custody', *Australian Journal of Social Issues*, August, vol. 28, no. 3, pp. 229–44

Sacks, H (1992) *Lectures on Conversation*, edited by Gail Jefferson, introduction by Emanuel Schegloff, 2 volumes, Oxford: Blackwell

Said, E (1978) *Orientalism*, Pantheon Books: New York

Sainsbury, D (1996) *Gender, Equality and Welfare States*, Cambridge University Press: Cambridge, UK

Sanders, B & Becker-Lausen, E (1995) 'The measurement of psychological maltreatment: Early data on the child abuse and trauma scale', *Child Abuse and Neglect*, vol. 19, no. 3, pp. 315–24

Sanders, R, Colton, M & Roberts, S (1999) 'Child abuse fatalities and cases of extreme concern: Lessons from reviews', *Child Abuse and Neglect*, vol. 23, no. 3, pp. 257–68

Sariola, H & Uutela, A (1994) 'The prevalence of child sexual abuse in Finland', *Child Abuse and Neglect*, vol. 18, no. 10, pp. 827–36

Sarwer, D B & Durlak, J A (1996) 'Childhood sexual abuse as a predictor of adult female sexual dysfunction: A study of couples seeking sex therapy', *Child Abuse and Neglect*, vol. 20, no. 10, pp. 963–72

Sarwer, D B, Crawford, I & Durlak, J A (1997) 'The relationship between childhood sexual abuse and adult male sexual dysfunction', *Child Abuse and Neglect*, vol. 21, no. 7, pp. 649–56

Saunders, E J, Nelson, K & Landsman, M J (1993) 'Racial inequality and child neglect: Findings in a metropolitan area', *Child Welfare*, vol. LXXII, no. 4, pp. 341–54

Saunders, P (2002) *The Ends and Means of Welfare: Coping with Economic and Social Change in Australia*, Cambridge University Press: Cambridge, UK

Saywitz, K & Camparo, L (1998) 'Interviewing child witnesses: A developmental perspective', *Child Abuse and Neglect*, vol. 22, no. 8, pp. 825–43

Schofield, J W (1993) 'Increasing the generalizability of qualitative research', in M Hammersley (ed.), *Social Research: Philosophy, Politics and Practice*, Sage: London, pp. 200–25

Schon, D (1988) 'From technical rationality to reflection-in-action', in J Dowie & A Elstein (eds), *Professional Judgement: A Reader in Clinical Decision Making*, Cambridge University Press: Cambridge, UK, pp. 60–77

Scott, D & Swain, S (2002) *Confronting Cruelty: Historical Perspectives on Child Protection in Australia*, Melbourne University Press: Melbourne

Scott, D (1989) 'Meaning construction and social work practice', *Social Service Review*, vol.63, no. 1, pp. 39–51

Scott, D (1998) 'A qualitative study of social work assessment in cases of alleged child abuse', *British Journal of Social Work*, vol. 28, pp. 73–88

Seaberg, J R (1993) 'Emotional abuse: A study of interobserver reliability', *Social Work Research and Abstracts*, vol. 29, no. 3, pp. 22–9

Segal, U A (1992) 'Child abuse in India: An empirical report on perceptions', *Child Abuse and Neglect*, vol. 16, no. 6, pp. 22–9

Shapira, M & Benbenishty, R (1993) 'Modeling judgements and decisions in cases of alleged child abuse and neglect', *Social Work Research and Abstracts*, June, vol. 29, no. 2, pp. 14–19

Sheppard, M, Newstead, S, Di Caccavo, A, & Ryan, K (2000) 'Reflexivity and the development of process knowledge in social work: A classification and empirical study', *British Journal of Social Work*, vol. 30, pp. 465–8

Siegfried, E, Rasnick-Conley, J, Cook, S, Leonardi, C & Monteleone, J (1998) 'Human papillomavirus screening in pediatric victims of sexual abuse', *Pediatrics*, vol. 101, no. 1, pp. 43–7

Silverman, D (1998) *Harvey Sacks: Social Science and Conversation Analysis*, Oxford University Press: Oxford, UK

Sinal, S H, Lawless, M R, Rainey, D Y, Everett, V D, Runyan, D K, Frothingham, T, Herman-Giddens, M & St Claire, K (1997) 'Clinician agreement on physical findings in child sexual abuse cases', *Archives of Pediatrics and Adolescent Medicine*, vol. 151, no. 5, pp. 497–501

Smart, B (1993) *Postmodernity*, Routledge: London

Smart, C (1996) 'Deconstructing motherhood' in E Bortolaia Silva (ed.), *Good Enough Mothering? Feminist Perspectives of Lone Motherhood*, Routledge: London, pp. 37–57

Smith, D (1974) 'The social construction of documentary reality', *Sociological Inquiry*, vol. 44, pp. 257–68

Smith, D E (1990a) 'K is mentally ill', in D E Smith, *Texts, Facts and Femininity: Exploring the Relations of Ruling*, Routledge: London, pp. 12–52

Smith, D E (1990b) 'Femininity as discourse', in D E Smith, *Texts, Facts and Femininity: Exploring the Relations of Ruling*, Routledge: London, pp. 159–208

Smith, D E (1990c) 'The active text', in D E Smith, *Texts, Facts and Femininity: Exploring the Relations of Ruling*, Routledge: London, pp. 120–58

Smith, D W & Saunders, B E (1995) 'Personality characteristics of father/perpetrators and nonoffending mothers in incest families: Individual and dyadic analyses', *Child Abuse and Neglect*, vol. 19, no. 5, pp. 607–18

Smokowski, P R & Wodarski, J S (1996) 'Effectiveness of child welfare services for poor, neglected children: A review of the empirical evidence', *Research on Social Work Practice*, vol. 6, no. 4, pp. 504–23

SNAICC (Secretariat of National Aboriginal and Islander Child Care) (2002) *SNAICC Briefing Paper – Statistics on Indigenous Family Violence, Child Abuse and Child Neglect*, www.snaicc.asn.au/news/b_p abuse.html (accessed 1 July 2003)

Sobsey, D, Randall, W & Parrila, R K (1997) 'Gender differences in abused children with and without disabilities', *Child Abuse and Neglect*, vol. 21, no. 8, pp. 707–20

Socolar, R R S, Raines, B, Chenmok, M, Runyan, D K, Green, C & Paterno, S (1998) 'Intervention to improve physician documentation and knowledge of child sexual abuse – A randomized controlled trial', *Pediatrics*, vol. 101, no. 5, pp. 817–24

Spratt, T (2001) 'The influence of child protection orientation on child welfare practice', *British Journal of Social Work*, vol. 31, pp. 933–54

Stanley, L (1987) 'Biography as microscope or kaleidoscope? The case of "power" in Hannah Cullwick's relationship with Arthur Munby', *Women's Studies International Forum*, vol. 10, no. 1, pp. 19–31

Stanley, L (1992) *The Auto/biographical I: The Theory and Practice of Feminist Auto/biography*, Manchester University Press: Manchester

Stanley, L & Wise, S (1993) *Breaking Out Again: Feminist Ontology and Epistemology*, Routledge: London, 2nd edition

Stark, E & Flitcraft, A (1988) 'Women and children at risk: A feminist perspective in child abuse', *International Journal of Health Services*, vol. 18, no. 1, pp. 97–118

Stokes, G (1997) 'Citizenship and aboriginality: Two conceptions of identity in Aboriginal political thought', in G Stokes (ed.), *The Politics of Identity in Australia*, Cambridge University Press: UK, pp. 158–71

Straus, M, Hamby, S, Finkelhor, D, Moore, D, & Runyan, D (1998) 'Identification of child maltreatment with the parent–child conflict tactics scales: Development and psychometric data for a national sample of American parents', *Child Abuse and Neglect*, vol. 22, no. 4, pp. 249–70

Sundell, K (1997) 'Child-care personnel's failure to report child maltreatment: Some Swedish evidence', *Child Abuse and Neglect*, vol. 21, no. 1, pp. 93–106

Sweeney, H (2002) 'Danger in leaving kids home alone', *Townsville Bulletin/Townsville Sun*, 18 December 2002, p. 5

Swift, K J (1995) 'An outrage to common decency: Historical perspectives on child neglect', *Child Welfare*, vol. LXXIV, no. 1, pp. 71–91

Tay, F (1976) 'The administration of social service provisions for under-privileged children in Western Australia, 1947–1954' in J Roe (ed.), *Social Policy in Australia – Some Perspectives 190–1975*, Cassell: Stanmore, New South Wales

Taylor, C & White, S (2000) *Practising Reflexivity in Health and Welfare: Making Knowledge*, Open University Press: Buckingham, UK

Taylor, C G, Norman, D K, Murphy, J M, Jellinek, M, Quinn, D, Poitrast, F G, & Goshko, M (1991) 'Diagnosed intellectual and emotional impairment among parents who seriously mistreat their children: Prevalence, type and outcome in a court sample', *Child Abuse and Neglect*, vol. 15, no. 4, pp. 389–402

Taylor, D (1996) 'Citizenship and social power', in D Taylor (ed.), *Critical Social Policy: A Reader*, Sage: London, pp. 156–67

Tharinger, D, Horton, C B & Millea, S (1990) 'Sexual abuse and exploitation of children and adults with mental retardation and other handicaps', *Child Abuse and Neglect*, vol. 14, no. 3, pp. 301–12

*The Wellbeing of the People: The Final Report of the Welfare and Community Services Review in Western Australia* (1984), volume 1, Department for Community Welfare, Perth: Government Printer, Western Australia

Thorpe, D (1994) *Evaluating Child Protection*, Open University Press: Buckingham, UK

Thorpe, D (1995) 'Evaluating child protection programmes', presented to a National Conference, *Rethinking Child Protection: Research Leading the Way*, 11–12 January, Lancaster University, UK

Thorpe, D (1997) 'Policing minority child-rearing practices in Australia: The consistency of "child abuse" ', in N Parton (ed.), *Child Protection and Family Support*, Routledge: London, pp. 59–77

Thorpe, R (1996) 'High expectations, low resources: Mothering, violence and child abuse', in R Thorpe & J Irwin (eds), *Women and Violence: Working for Change*, Hale and Iremonger: Sydney, pp. 109–28

Tite, R (1993) 'How teachers define and respond to child abuse: The distinction between theoretical and reportable cases', *Child Abuse and Neglect*, vol. 17, pp. 591–603

Toohey, P (2003) 'Time to take stock', Features: *The Australian*, Friday, 13 June 2003, p. 11

Truman, C & Humphries, B (1994) 'Re-thinking social research: Research in an unequal world', in B Humphries & C Truman (eds), *Re-thinking Social Research*, Avebury: Aldershot, UK, pp. 1–20

Trute, B, Adkins, E & MacDonald, G (1992) 'Professional attitudes regarding the sexual abuse of children: Comparing police, child welfare and community mental health', *Child Abuse and Neglect*, vol. 16, no. 3, pp. 359–68

Tuchman, G (1994) 'Historical social science: Methodologies, methods, and meanings' in N Denzin & Y Lincoln (eds), *Handbook of Qualitative Research*, Sage: Newbury Park, California, pp. 306–23, 2nd edition

Tuhiwai Smith, L (1999) *Decolonizing Methodologies: Research and Indigenous Peoples*, Zed Books: London/University of Otago Press: New Zealand

Turner, B S (1992) *Regulating Bodies: Essays in Medical Sociology*, Routledge: London

Turner, R (1989) 'Deconstructing the field', in J F Gubrium & D Silverman (eds), *The Politics of Field Research: Sociology Beyond Enlightenment*, Sage: London, pp. 13–29

Tyler, W (1993) 'Postmodernity and the Aboriginal condition: The cultural dilemmas of contemporary policy', *Australian and New Zealand Journal of Sociology*, vol. 29, no. 3, pp. 322–42

Tymchuk, A J (1992) 'Predicting adequacy of parenting by people with mental retardation', *Child Abuse and Neglect*, vol. 16, no. 2, pp. 165–78

Tymchuk, A J & Andron, L (1990) 'Mothers with mental retardation who do or do not abuse or neglect their children', *Child Abuse and Neglect*, vol. 14, no. 3, pp. 313–24

van den Berg, R (1994) *No Options No Choice! The Moore River Experience*, Magabala Books, Aboriginal Corporation: Broome, Western Australia

Van Haeringen, A R, Dadds, M & Armstrong, K L (1998) 'The child abuse lottery – Will the doctor suspect and report – Physician attitudes towards and reporting of suspected child abuse and neglect', *Child Abuse and Neglect*, vol. 22, no. 3, pp. 159–69

van Krieken, R (1991) *Children and the State: Social Control and the Formation of the Australian Welfare State*, Allen and Unwin, North Sydney

van Maanen, J (1988) *Tales of the Field*, University of Chicago Press: Chicago

Varia, R, Abidin, R R & Dass, P (1996) 'Perceptions of abuse: Effects on adult psychological and social adjustment', *Child Abuse and Neglect*, vol. 20, no. 6, pp. 511–26

Verdugo, M A, Bermejo, B G & Fuertes, J (1995) 'The maltreatment of intellectually handicapped children and adolescents', *Child Abuse and Neglect*, vol. 19, no. 2, pp. 205–17

Vernon, M (2001) 'More are required', *Townsville Bulletin/Townsville Sun* (Australia*)*, 11 December 2002, p. 4

Walton, J R, Nuttall, R L & Nuttall, E V (1997) 'The impact of war on the mental health of children: A Salvadoran study', *Child Abuse and Neglect*, vol. 21, no. 8, pp. 737–50

Walton, M (1993) 'Regulation in child protection – Policy failure?', *British Journal of Social Work*, vol. 23, pp. 139–56

Ward, G (1987) *Wandering Girl*, Magabala Books: Broome, Western Australia

Wardinsky, T D (1995) 'Genetic and congenital defect conditions that mimic child abuse', *Journal of Family Practice*, vol. 41, no. 4, pp. 377–83

Warner, J E & Hansen, D J (1994) 'The identification and reporting of physical abuse by physicians: A review and implications for research', *Child Abuse and Neglect*, vol. 18, no. 1, pp. 11–26

Warner-Rogers, J E, Hansen, D J & Spieth, L E (1996) 'The influence of Case and professional variables on identification and reporting of physical abuse: A study with medical students', *Child Abuse and Neglect*, vol. 20, no. 9, pp. 851–66

Weedon, C (1999) *Feminism, Theory and the Politics of Difference*, Blackwell: Oxford

Weick, K (1977) 'The enacted environment', in R L Blankenship (ed.), *Colleagues in Organization: The Social Construction of Professional Work*, John Wiley and Sons: New York, pp. 304–15

Weinstein, D & Weinstein, M A (1992) 'The postmodern discourse of metatheory', in G Ritzer (ed.), *Metatheorizing*, Sage: London, pp. 135–50

Wells, S J, Downing, J & Fluke, J (1990) 'Responding to reports of child abuse and neglect', *Child and Youth Services*, vol. 15, no. 2, pp. 63–72

Western Australian Parliamentary Debates (WAPD) (*Hansard*) (1907) 8 October–20 December, vol. xxxii

Western Australian Parliamentary Debates (WAPD) (*Hansard*) (1927) 28 July–20 October, vol. 76

Western Australian Parliamentary Debates (WAPD) (*Hansard*) (1947) 31 July–23 October, vol. 119

Western Australian Parliamentary Debates (WAPD) (*Hansard*) (1971) 16 November–10 December, vol. 192

Western Australian Parliamentary Debates (WAPD) (*Hansard*) (1972a) 14 March–3 May, vol. 193

Western Australian Parliamentary Debates (WAPD) (*Hansard*) (1972b) 3 May–9 August, vol. 194

Western Australian Parliamentary Debates (WAPD) (*Hansard*) (2002) 'Government Response to the Gordon Inquiry', 3 December 2002, www.parliament.wa.gov.au/hansard/hans35.nsf/0/Hlt515971950Hlt51597195f24f1744374a32548256c9200355e7b?OpenDocument (accessed 30 June 2003)

Wexler, P (1990) 'Citizenship in the semiotic society' in B S Turner (ed.), *Theories of Modernity and Postmodernity*, Sage: London, pp. 164–75

Widom, C S & Ames, M A (1994) 'Criminal consequences of childhood sexual victimization', *Child Abuse and Neglect*, vol. 18, no. 4, pp. 303–18

Williams, R (1982) *A Report on the Child Life Protection Unit and the Development of a Unitary System of Child Protection by Integration with the Field*, Department for Community Welfare, Perth, Western Australia

Windschuttle, K (2002) *The Fabrication of Australian History: vol. 1, Van Diemen's Land 1803–1847*, Macleay Press, New South Wales

Winefield, H R & Bradley, P W (1992) 'Substantiation of reported child abuse or neglect: Predictors and implications', *Child Abuse and Neglect*, vol. 16, no. 5, pp. 661–72

Winefield, H R & Castell-McGregor, S (1987) 'Child sexual abuse cases: Facilitating their detection and reporting by general practitioners', *Australian Journal of Social Issues*, vol. 22, no. 3, pp. 27–37

Wise, S (1985) *Becoming a Feminist Social Worker: Studies in Sexual Politics No 6*, University of Manchester (an edited version of this monograph was reprinted in L Stanley (ed.) (1990) *Feminist Praxis: Research, Theory and Epistemology in Feminist Sociology*, Routledge: London, pp. 236–49)

Wise, S (1991) *Child Abuse: The NSPCC Version*, Manchester University Press: Feminist Praxis: Manchester, UK

Wise, S (1995) 'Feminist ethics in practice', in R Hugman & D Smith (eds), *Ethical Issues in Social Work*, Routledge: London, pp. 104–19

Wissow, L S & Wilson, M E H (1992) 'Use of epidemiological data in the diagnosis of physical child abuse: Variations in response to hypothetical cases', *Child Abuse and Neglect*, vol. 16, no. 1, pp. 45–56

Wolfner, G D & Gelles, R J (1993) 'A profile of violence toward children: A national study', *Child Abuse and Neglect*, vol. 17, pp. 197–212

Wolock, I & Horowitz, B (1984) 'Child maltreatment as a social problem: The neglect of neglect', *American Journal of Orthopsychiatry*, vol. 54, no. 4, pp. 530–43

Wood, B, Orsak, C, Murphy, M & Cross, H J (1996) 'Semistructured child sexual abuse interviews: Interview and child characteristics related to credibility of disclosure', *Child Abuse and Neglect*, vol. 20, no. 1, pp. 81–92

Woodhead, M (1990) 'Psychology and the cultural construction of children's needs', in A James & A Prout (eds), *Constructing and Reconstructing Childhood: Contemporary Issues in the Sociological Study of Childhood*, The Falmer Press: London, pp. 60–77

Wurtele, S K & Miller-Perrin, C (1992) *Preventing Child Sexual Abuse: Sharing the Responsibility*, University of Nebraska Press: Lincoln, Nebraska

Wurtele, S K & Schmitt, A (1992) 'Child care workers' knowledge about reporting suspected child sexual abuse', *Child Abuse and Neglect*, vol. 16, no. 3, pp. 385–90

Yeatman, A (1995) 'Interlocking Oppressions' in B Caine and R Pringle (eds), *Transitions: New Australian Feminisms*, Allen and Unwin, North Sydney, Australia, pp. 42–56.

Young, I M (1990) *Justice and the Politics of Difference*, Princeton New Jersey Press: Princeton, New Jersey

Young, L (1992) 'Sexual abuse and the problem of embodiment', *Child Abuse and Neglect*, vol. 16, no. 1, pp. 89–100

Zellman, G L (1990) 'Report decision-making patterns among mandated child abuse reporters', *Child Abuse and Neglect*, vol. 14, no. 3, pp. 325–36

Zimmerman, D (1974) 'Fact as a practical accomplishment', in R Turner (ed.), *Ethnomethodology*, Penguin: Harmondsworth, UK, pp. 128–43

Zuravin, S, McMillen, C, DePanfilis, D & Risley-Curtis, C (1996) 'The intergenerational cycle of child maltreatment: Continuity and discontinuity', *Journal of Interpersonal Violence*, vol. 11, no. 3, pp. 315–34

# Index

abnormalization 22
*Aboriginal Affairs Planning Authority Act 1972* (WA) 94
Aboriginal and Torres Strait Islander Women's Taskforce on Violence. Report *see* Palm Island
Aboriginal Child Placement Policy 122
Aboriginal children
    protection
        Western Australia
            (1829–1972) 88–91, 91–4
            (1972 on) 95–6, 98–9, 101, 114–15
Aboriginality 81–3, 105, 239–40
    and neglect 244–5
Aborigines, protection, Western Australia 89–91
*Aborigines Act 1897* (WA) 90
*Aborigines Act 1905* (WA) 89, 90, 91
    and removal of children from parents 92–3
*Aborigines Protection Act 1886* (WA) 92
abusers, relationships of children with 168
ACCCA 99
access
    to client files 30
    to professionals 29–30
access (for research) 28–9
accidental injury 183
accountability 2
adolescents, as 'dangerous children' 96
*Adoption of Children Act 1896* (WA) 84
Advisory and Consultative Committee on Child Abuse 99
Alice Mitchell Baby Farm Case (1907) 85
Allston case, constructing maltreatment 135–44, 160
*Archaeology of Knowledge*, (Foucault) 19

Beckford, Jasmine 3, 75
Blake case 196–8
Bourdieu, P. 15, 24–5
    limitations 21
    linguistic communities 8, 11, 20–1
    Theory of Practice 20
*Bringing Them Home* (Human Rights and Equal Opportunity Commission) 80, 89

capital, and symbolic power 20

Carlile, Kimberley 3
cases, selection 31–3
categorisation (rhetorical device) 22, 132–3, 242–3
category entitlement 22
    knowledge 137, 168, 196
    witnesses 142
CCR *see* child concern reports
child
    constructions of identity 51–3, 142, 194–237, 247–50
        policy and practice consequences 53–6
    legal definition 51
    *see also* children
child concern reports 103–4, 113
Child Life Protection Unit (WA) 87–8, 96–7
child maltreatment allegations (CMA) 103–4, 113, 114
    *see also* maltreatment
*Child Protection: Guide to Practice* (Department of Community Services, WA) 100, 108–9, 109–10, 118–19
child protection
    construction of identities 56–9, 245–50
    construction of meanings 56–9, 242–5
    discourse 43–74
        three-part rule 59, 131
    intervention, stages 134, 159–61
    policy
        contexts 108–9
        as discourse 75–105
    practice 71
        as an accomplishment 72–3
        as a technical activity 71–2
    prescribing practice 109–12, 241, 254
        at Suburbia 124–5
        at Urbania 115–16
    social organisation 239–42
*Child Welfare Act 1927* (WA) 85–6
*Child Welfare Act 1947* (WA) 86, 94
children
    as evidence 56, 114, 133, 195, 198–202, 202–3, 212–16, 248
    and assumptions re normal families 231–2
    of normal/abnormal mothering 216–20
    protection *see* child protection

relationships with abusers 168
rights 52
sexuality 53–4
children's rights and liberation perspective
   and constructions of the child 52–3
   state-family relations 48–9
CLPU 87–8, 96–7
CMA *see* child maltreatment, allegations
coercion and consent, sexual abuse 61–2
Colwell, Maria 75
*Community Welfare Act 1972* (WA) 94, 95–6
consensus, and corroboration 23
consent and coercion, sexual abuse 61–2
Constable case 135–44, 160
construction of knowledge, context and 239
constructions of the child *see* child, constructions of identity
context
   and construction of knowledge 239
   and identity 167–70
contrast structures 22, 136, 139, 165, 188, 204–5, 218
corroboration and consensus 23
cultural rules
   at Suburbia 119–20, 125–8
   at Urbania 112–13, 116–18

dangerous individuals 162–3
   identification 164–93
      and context 167–70
      and risk assessment 69
data analysis, research 39–40
data organisation, research 37–8
Davis case 198–202
   and Aboriginal identity 244
de-centred subject 26, 27
defensive practice 119–20, 120–1
Department of Community Services (WA), *Child Protection: Guide to Practice* 100, 108–9, 109–10, 118–19
différance 26, 27, 251, 252
direct responsibility, maltreatment 68
disclosure 157–9
discourse
   analysis 27, 40
   and the body 16–17
   and genealogy 18–19
   and identity 17–18
   orders of 8, 10
      limitations 19–20
   and power/knowledge 16
domestic violence 175
dualism 25

Eakins case

and Aboriginal identity 244
and identity of responsibility 164–70, 193, 245–6
and identity of the child 202–6
*see also* Francis case
emotional abuse 63–4, 187–9
empiricist discourse 23
epistemological issues in research 38–9
*Evaluating Child Protection*, (Thorpe) 103
externalizing devices 23
extrematization (rhetorical device) 148, 208
extreme-cases 22

familialization 46–7
families
   assumptions, and construction of identities 195
   autonomy 46–7
   ethnocentric meanings 231–5
   as focus of child protection practice 44–5
   normal, and welfare families 202–6
   as social institutions 45–7
   and the state 47–9
fathers
   responsibility for maltreatment
      disappears 171–7
      shared with mother 183–6
      strategic dominance 174–7
   *see also* invisible men
foster mothers 216–20
Foucault, Michel 15, 16–19, 24–5
   *Archaeology of Knowledge* 19
   concept of genealogy 10, 18–19
   discourse analysis 27
   limitations 19–20
   orders of discourse 8
   theory of knowledge 19
fractured lens 14–25, 251–61
Francis case
   constructing maltreatment 147–50, 160, 161
   and identity of responsibility 245–6
   and identity of the child 202–6
   *see also* Eakins case

gender
   in constructions of child protection 239–40
   and identities of responsibility 171–89, 246
   and maltreatment 67–8, 69–70
   and victimisation and dangerousness 196–8
gender and generation, politics of 50–1
genealogy
   and discourse 10, 18–19
   and policies 76
   research method 27
Gilman case
   and Aboriginal identity 244

identity of responsibility 171–3, 192, 246
Gordon Report *see Putting the Picture Together*
Gordon, Sue, *Putting the Picture Together* 82
*Guide to Practice* see *Child Protection: Guide to Practice*

Hamilton case, identity of responsibility 187–9
haven in a heartless world 50
*Health Act 1898* (WA), Infant Life Protection clauses 84
Henry, Tyra 3, 75
hierarchy of maltreatment 65–6, 151, 153–4, 154–7, 159
Human Rights and Equal Opportunity Commission, *Bringing Them Home* 80, 89

Ibsen case 114, 118
  and Aboriginal identity 244
  identity of responsibility 174–7, 193, 246–7
identities
  construction 56–9, 245–50
    and assumptions about the family 195
    and context 167–70
    differences, and risk assessment 54
  discourse and 17–18
  of responsibility
    construction 162–93, 245–50
    for maltreatment 66–70
indirect responsibility 68
*Industrial Schools Act 1874* (WA) 91
intellectual disability
  and male disappearing 180–1
  and mothering 126
intergenerational cycle of maltreatment 55–6
intergenerational transmission of abuse 56, 195, 220–6, 227, 248–9
intergenerational transmission of maltreatment 56
International Society for the Prevention of Child Abuse and Neglect 43
intervention, child protection, stages 134, 159–61, 241
interviewing, research method 34–7
intrafamilial relations 49–51
investigation, stage of intervention 137–40, 141–3, 145–6, 148–50, 151–3, 156, 160
invisible men, and responsible mothers 69–70, 171–87, 201, 206, 223
ISPCAN 43

Jones case 118
  constructing maltreatment 151–4, 160, 161

Kelly case 117, 206–12
knowledge
  category entitled 137, 168, 196

construction 239
domains, and risk assessment 58
and power 16
  social work research 26–41
structuring, writing and 253–4
theory of (Foucault) 19
versions 8

language
  and construction of meaning 238–9
  representation of meaning 18
  as strategic device 4, 5, 7
  *see also* rhetorical devices
Lewis case, identity of responsibility 177–80, 193
linguistic communities 8, 11, 20–1, 106–7
  Suburbia 128–9
  Urbania 118–19, 129

maltreatment 5, 9, 13, 240
  and adult identity 55–6
  child maltreatment allegations (CMA) 103–4, 113, 114
  constructing 59–66, 131–61
  defining 42
  hierarchies 151, 159
    partitioning of the body and 133–4, 153–4, 243–4
    and priorities 65–6, 154–5
  identities of responsibility 66–70
  intergenerational cycle 55–6
  intergenerational transmission 56
  meaning 4, 14
  and priorities 243–4
  types 59–65
    hierarchies and priorities 65–6
  *see also* emotional abuse; neglect; physical abuse; risk assessment; sexual abuse
marriage 45
Martini case 118
  constructing maltreatment 144–7, 160, 161
meanings, construction 56–9, 242–5
men, and maltreatment 67–8, 69–70, 177–80
methodology 26–41
Mitchell, Alice 85
Montcalm, Paul 75
Moore River settlement 93
mothering 212–16, 249
  as preferred identity for women 226–8
mothers
  in need of support 190–1
  responsibility, shifting constructions 189–92
  responsibility for maltreatment 171–3, 181–2
    shared with father 183–6
  unprotective 174–80, 198–202

NAPCAN 43
narrative complexity and detail 23
National Association for the Prevention of Child Abuse and Neglect 43
National Referendum on Aboriginal Citizenship 91
National Society for the Prevention of Cruelty to Children 43
*Native Administration Act 1936* (WA) 90–1
*Native Welfare Act 1954* (WA) 89, 94, 95
neglect 206–16
   and Aboriginality 244
   categorisations 64–5
   defined 64
New Directions (Family and Children's Services) 101–4, 108–9, 110–12, 118–19
Nicholson case 116–17, 212–16
normal families, and welfare families 202–6
normalization 22
NSPCC, UK 43

O'Keefe case 121, 125, 126, 192–3
   identity of responsibility 180–2, 246
organisations, sociology of 106–8
outcome, stage of intervention 140, 143, 146–7, 150, 153, 157, 159, 160
over reporting 72, 101

Palm Island 82
parental discipline, and physical abuse 62
parents 46
   gender and responsibility 226–7
Park case 122, 128, 231–5, 237
participant observation 33–4, 38
paternalist perspective
   state-family relations 48
      and haven in a heartless world 50
patriarchal mothering 126, 206, 207, 236
   Davis case 198–202
   Gilman case 171–3
   Hamilton case 187–9
   and identity of responsibility 247
   O'Keefe case 180–2
patriarchy perspective
   state-family relations 48
      and haven in a heartless world 50
physical abuse 62–3, 147–50, 155–6, 199–200
   and parental discipline 62
physical punishment 62
politics of gender and generation 50–1
positioning 2
Potter, J. 15, 24–5
   limitations 23–4
   rhetorical devices 8, 21–3
power/knowledge, and discourse 16
practice consistency 240–1

practice discretion 3
   and situated cultures 7
   *see also* professional discretion
practice regulation 109–12, 241, 254
   at Suburbia 124–5
   at Urbania 115–16
Practice, Theory of 20
private and public patriarchy 49
pro-birth family perspective
   state-family relations 47–8
      and haven in a heartless world 50
professional accountability 2
   *see also* practice discretion; professional discretion
professional discretion 72, 72–3, 238, 250
   *see also* practice discretion; professional accountability; professional roles
professional roles, reconstructing 258–61
professional skills, reconstructing 256–8
psychological abuse 63–4
public and private patriarchy 49
*Putting the Picture Together* (Gordon) 82

Quinn case 121, 125–6, 236
   identity of responsibility 189–92, 193
   and identity of the child 216–20, 246

*R v Alice Mitchell* (1907) 85
race-as-Aboriginality 81–3, 105, 239–40
realism 25
reflexivity 251–2, 253
relativism 252
   and social constructionism 25
reporting/intake
   stage of intervention 135–7, 144–5, 148
   stage of investigation 151–3
representation 26
responsibility, identities, construction 162–93, 245–7
responsible mothers, invisible men 69–70, 171–87, 201, 206
   and sexual abuse 223
rhetorical devices 8, 21–3
   limitations 23–4
Riley case 121, 127
   identity of responsibility 183–6, 193
risk, and social constructionism 255–61
risk assessment 4, 9, 229–31, 236–7
   constructions of the child and 54–6
   knowledge domains and 58
   normal families and welfare families 203–6
   risk society and 57–8
risk management 104, 113–14
risk society 57

sampling 30–3
sexual abuse 59–62, 97–8, 135–47, 151–4, 154–9
   definition 60, 196–8
   diagnosis 60–1
   responsibility of women 67–8
sexuality, children 53–4
sites, selection 30–1
social constructionism 15
   and child protection practice 1–6
   and constructions of the child 51–2
   and relativism 25
   and risk 255–61
   and sexual abuse cases 143–4
   and social organisation of child protection 7–11
social space 47
socioeconomic disadvantage, and problem parenting 3
stages of intervention *see* child protection, intervention, stages
stake and interest 22
*State Children Act 1907* (WA) 85
stolen generations 89
subjectivity 2
Suburbia 119–28
   cultural rules 119–20, 125–8
   culture 29, 33–4
   interpreting organisational policy
      constructing meanings and identities 120–4
      practice regulation 124–5
   as a linguistic community 128–9
symbolic power, and capital 20

Thorpe, David, *Evaluating Child Protection* 103
three–part lists 22, 141, 149, 150, 175, 188, 190, 217, 218, 219
Turner case 121, 125, 127–8, 226–31

under reporting 72, 101

Underwood case 121, 126–7
   constructing maltreatment 154–9, 160, 161
   and identity of the child 221–6
unprotective mothers 174, 177–80, 198–202
Urbania 112–18
   cultural rules 112–13, 116–18
   culture 29, 33
   interpreting organisational policy
      constructing meanings and identities 113–15
      practice regulation 115–16
   as a linguistic community 118–19, 129

Valerio, Daniel 75
vulnerabilities, and risk assessment 54–5

Welfare and Community Services Review (WA) 12, 99–100
welfare families, and normal families 202–6
Western Australia
   Aborigines, policies 89–91
   adolescents, as 'dangerous children' 96
   child protection
      (1972 on) 95–104
      Aboriginal children
         (1829–1972) 88–91, 91–4
         (1972 on) 95–6, 98–9, 101, 114–15
      genealogy 76–83
      legislation, related to British legislation 81, 84
      non-Aboriginal children (1829–1972) 83–8
   Welfare and Community Services Review 99–100
Western Australia. Department of Community Services, *Child Protection: Guide to Practice* 100
women
   and maltreatment 67–8, 69–70
   responsibility for sexual abuse 67–8
writing 26, 40–1
   and structuring knowledge 253–4